An Embodied Reading of the Shepherd of Hermas

Studies in Ancient Religion and Culture

Series Editors:

Philip L. Tite, University of Virginia

Michael Ng, Seattle University

Studies in Ancient Religion and Culture (SARC) is concerned with religious and cultural aspects of the ancient world, with a special emphasis on studies that utilize social scientific methods of analysis. By "ancient world," the series is not limited to Greco-Roman and ancient Near Eastern cultures, though that is the primary regional focus. The underlying presupposition is that the study of religion in antiquity needs to be located within cultural and social analysis, situating religious traditions within the broader cultural and geopolitical dynamics within which those traditions are located.

This series also encourages cross-disciplinary research in the study of the ancient world. Due to the historical development of various academic disciplines, there has arisen a set of largely isolated and competing fields of study of the ancient world. Often this fragmentation in academia results in outdated or caricatured scholarly products when one discipline does use research from another discipline. A key goal of this series is to help facilitate greater cross- and inter-disciplinary work, bringing together those who study ancient history (especially social history), archaeology (of various methods and geographic focuses, as well as theorists in archaeology), ancient philosophy, biblical studies, early patristics/church history, Second Temple and formative Judaism, and Greek and Roman classics, as well as philologists.

Given the focus on the social and cultural context within which religion functions, the series also publishes studies which explore the various social locations in which real people in antiquity practiced or interacted with their religious traditions. Examples include the domestic cult, food production and consumption, temple worship, funerary practices/monuments, development of social networks, military cult, and ancient medicine.

Finally, the series encourages a broader application of theoretical and methodological tools to the study of the ancient world. While the main perspective is social-scientific (understood broadly), specific analyses from the reservoir of critical theory, narrative theories, economic theory, bio-archaeology, gender analysis, anthropology of religion, and cognitive theory are welcome.

An Embodied Reading of the Shepherd of Hermas

The Book of Visions and its Role in Moral Formation

Angela Kim Harkins

SHEFFIELD UK   BRISTOL CT

Published by Equinox Publishing Ltd.

UK: Office 415, The Workstation, 15 Paternoster Row, Sheffield, South Yorkshire S1 2BX

USA: ISD, 70 Enterprise Drive, Bristol, CT 06010

www.equinoxpub.com

First published 2023

© Angela Kim Harkins 2023

All rights reserved. No part of this publication may be reproduced or transmitted in any form or by any means, electronic or mechanical, including photocopying, recording or any information storage or retrieval system, without prior permission in writing from the publishers.

British Library Cataloguing-in-Publication Data

A catalogue record for this book is available from the British Library.

ISBN-13 978 1 80050 327 4 (hardback)
        978 1 80050 328 1 (paperback)
        978 1 80050 329 8 (ePDF)
        978 1 80050 361 8 (ePub)

Library of Congress Cataloging-in-Publication Data

Names: Harkins, Angela Kim, 1973- author.
Title: An embodied reading of the Shepherd of Hermas : the Book of Visions and its role in moral formation / Angela Kim Harkins.
Description: Sheffield, South Yorkshire ; Bristol, CT : Equinox Publishing, 2023. | Series: Studies in ancient religion and culture series | Includes bibliographical references and index. | Summary: "This book uses cognitive literary theory, specifically the approach known as enactive reading, to investigate why a work that was exceedingly popular among elite readers in antiquity has failed to receive the same reception by modern scholars. The study focuses on the first section of The Shepherd known as the Book of Visions, which narrates Hermas's visionary experiences in first-person voice"-- Provided by publisher.
Identifiers: LCCN 2022058393 (print) | LCCN 2022058394 (ebook) | ISBN 9781800503274 (hardback) | ISBN 9781800503281 (paperback) | ISBN 9781800503298 (pdf) | ISBN 9781800503618 (epub)
Subjects: LCSH: Hermas, active 2nd century. Shepherd--Criticism, interpretation, etc. | Christian life--Early works to 1800. | Visions in the Bible. | Cognition in literature. | Psychology and religion.
Classification: LCC BS2900.H5 H37 2023 (print) | LCC BS2900.H5 (ebook) | DDC 229/.94--dc23/eng/20230313
LC record available at https://lccn.loc.gov/2022058393
LC ebook record available at https://lccn.loc.gov/2022058394

Typeset by ISB Typesetting, Sheffield, UK

Contents

	Abbreviations	vii
	Acknowledgements	ix
	Introduction: Seeing the Shepherd of Hermas with New Eyes	1
1.	The Popularity of the Shepherd of Hermas in the Ancient World	29
2.	Taking a Look at Hermas	63
3.	Sticky Thoughts that Make Presence from Absence	100
4.	Experiencing the Journey	131
5.	Immersion in the Narrative World of Apocalyptic Visions	164
	Conclusion	189
	Bibliography	195
	Index of Ancient Texts	216

*For my husband Franklin and to our son Joseph
with all of my love and admiration*

Abbreviations

BETL	Bibliotheca Ephemeridum Theologicarum Lovaniensium
BibInt	*Biblical Interpretation*
BZAW	Beihefte zur Zeitschrift für die alttestamentliche Wissenschaft
CBET	Contributions to Biblical Exegesis and Theology
ConBNT	Coniectanea Neotestamentica
CRINT	Compendia Rerum Iudaicarum ad Novum Testamentum
DSD	*Dead Sea Discoveries*
HTR	*Harvard Theological Review*
HUCA	*Hebrew Union College Annual*
JAJ	*Journal of Ancient Judaism*
JBL	*Journal of Biblical Literature*
JECS	*Journal of Early Christian Studies*
JJS	*Journal of Jewish Studies*
JQR	*Jewish Quarterly Review*
JSJ	*Journal for the Study of Judaism*
JSNT	*Journal for the Study of the New Testament*
JSOT	*Journal for the Study of the Old Testament*
JTS	*Journal of Theological Studies*
MTSR	*Method and Theory in the Study of Religion*
NovT	*Novum Testamentum*
NovTSup	Novum Testamentum Supplement Series
OTP	*Old Testament Pseudepigrapha*, 2 vols. Edited by J. Charlesworth. New York: Doubleday, 1983
RAC	*Reallexikon für Antike und Christentum*. Edited by Theodor Klauser et al. Stuttgart: Hiersemann, 1950.
SBL	Society of Biblical Literature
StPatr	*Studia Patristica*
SUNT	Studien zur Umwelt des Neuen Testaments
ZNW	*Zeitschrift für die neutestamentliche Wissenschaft und die Kunde der älteren Kirche*

Acknowledgments

My interest in and exploration of the cognitive science of religion began in 2010, but my application of its approaches to the visions in the Shepherd of Hermas took final form during a research leave in 2020—a time of pandemic lockdown and tumultuous politics revolving around Black Lives Matter in the United States and around the world. The question of "How do we see?" seemed to take on a new urgency during the writing of this book, as I saw how different people in the United States perceive current events in radically different ways based on their very different embodiments and social contexts.

I completed most of this book while on leave during the fall of 2020. I was supported by a generous Faculty Fellowship at Boston College, for which I am deeply grateful. The chapters in this book benefited from discussions with scholars at various meetings. Discussions of visions and visionary practices were presented to the working group of the Lived Experience of Religion in Eisenach, Germany in 2017, at the annual meeting of the Society of Biblical Literature in 2018, and to the Centro Italiano di Studi Superiori sulle Religioni at their annual meeting on Christian Origins in Bertinoro, Italy in 2018 and 2021. Drafts of Chapter 2 were presented as my presidential address to the New England and Eastern Canada Regional Meeting of the Society of Biblical Literature in March 2021, at the virtual post-graduate research seminar of the Trinity Centre for Biblical Studies at Trinity College in Dublin, Ireland in March 2022, at the virtual seminar for the Institute for Religion and Critical Inquiry at the Australian Catholic University in February 2021, and to the Classics Department at Brandeis University in December 2021. I also presented drafts of Chapter 4 to the Boston Area Patristics Group in January 2019 and at a simultaneous session of the Catholic Biblical Association in July 2021. I am grateful for all of the feedback that I received during those presentations.

As much as we maintain the illusion that a book is the product of our own solitary endeavors, I know that I have been profoundly supported by many friends and colleagues along the way who have engaged with my work and shared my enthusiasm for Hermas and his visions: Luca Arcari, Kelley Coblentz Bautch, Giovanni Bazzana, Jin Young Choi, Jung Choi, John J. Collins, Mary Rose D'Angelo, Frances Flannery, Mary Foskett, Armin Geertz, Bill and Mary Harkins, Amanda Harper Leatherman, Dar

Brooks Hedstrom, Kyoko Horowitz, Jonathan Klawans, Maria Masi, Luther Martin, Janette Ok, Carolyn Osiek, Alan Richardson, Marice Rose, Colleen Shantz, Loren Stuckenbruck, Stellar and Chip Tucker, Rod Werline, Larry Wills, and Archie Wright. I apologize for any whom I have omitted. I am grateful for the amazing support and encouragement I received from all of them during the years marked by the Coronavirus (COVID-19) pandemic. I am deeply grateful to Harry O. Maier. I have learned so much from his life's work on the Shepherd. The present book has been much improved by our many conversations. I wish to thank in a special way Philip L. Tite for accepting this book in his series; and Sarah Lee and Janet Joyce at Equinox Press for their invaluable help. I also thank my research assistants Alexander Klee and Luke Stringfellow for their proofreading assistance. Luke did an amazing job correcting my manuscript. I am forever grateful to him. Special thanks to my dear childhood friend Sheila Boll for her careful help with the footnotes and bibliography.

Finally, I offer my heartfelt gratitude to my family. My husband Franklin has tirelessly supported me throughout this entire process. Our wonderful son Joseph has filled our days and evenings with beautiful music. I could have done nothing without their loving support and encouragement over the years, but especially during my illness during the pandemic. God has been so good to me by giving me this loving family. I have been blessed in countless ways, and my heart is filled to the brim and overflowing with joy.

Angela Kim Harkins
West Roxbury, MA
May 16, 2022

Introduction
Seeing the Shepherd of Hermas with New Eyes

This book is about seeing and visions. More particularly, it is a book about how we see and understand the ancient narrative known as the Book of Visions, the first of three sections of the early Christian work known as the Shepherd of Hermas. As much as it is a book about how we as scholars read and interact with an ancient text reporting visionary experiences, it also speaks to how we visually perceive the world around us and use our experiential knowledge to construct and extend the partial bits of information that we take in through our eyes. This book takes the insights of the cognitive science of seeing and mental imaging, as they have been appropriated by cognitive literary approaches, and applies them to the first part of the Shepherd of Hermas.

The Shepherd of Hermas (70–150 CE) is one of the oldest Christian works from a major urban center.[1] While most of the manuscript evidence of the Shepherd is concentrated in North Africa, it has long-standing association with the city of Rome. It consists of three major sections: Book of Visions, Mandates, and Similitudes. There are five visions that constitute the work known as the Book of Visions, which is largely about an otherwise ordinary man named Hermas. The Book of Visions consists of Hermas's first-person reports of his visionary experiences which take place in various places and over a period of time. The fifth vision is noticeably different in length from the previous ones. The majority of Hermas's visions take place outdoors, except for two nighttime visions, the first of a young man (Vis. 2.4.1 [8.1]) and the second of an elderly woman (Vis. 3.1.2 [9.2]). The fifth vision of the figure called the Shepherd takes place while Hermas is at home, but it is not clearly stated that this takes place at night (Vis. 5.1.1 [25.1]).

---

1. Malcolm Choat and Rachel Yuen-Collingridge, "The Egyptian *Hermas*: The *Shepherd* in Egypt before Constantine," in *Early Christian Manuscripts: Examples of Applied Method and Approach*, ed. Thomas J. Kraus and Tobias Nicklas (Leiden: Brill, 2010), 191–211. For a sense of the diverse literary culture in Egypt see William A. Johnson, *Readers and Reading Culture in the High Roman Empire: A Study of Elite Communities* (Oxford: Oxford University Press, 2010), 179–99.

2   *An Embodied Reading of the Shepherd of Hermas*

This book argues that the Visions function as an immersive narrative that prepares the reader and hearer for the ethical teachings in the sections that follow. The Visions are a series of narratives organized loosely around a foot journey that is told through a character named Hermas. In the Book of Visions, we experience the events from Hermas's perspective, with privileged access to his innermost thoughts and emotions. The fifth vision prepares the reader for the shift that will take place in the following sections known as the Mandates and Similitudes, both of which are presented to readers and hearers as teachings that have been dictated directly to Hermas by the Shepherd (Vis. 5.5 [25.5]).[2]

> 25.5 ὁ δὲ ἀποκριθείς μοι λέγει· Μὴ συνχύννου, ἀλλὰ ἰσχυροποιοῦ ἐν ταῖς ἐντολαῖς μου, αἷς σοι μέλλω ἐντέλλεσθαι. ἀπεστάλην γάρ, φησίν, ἵνα ἃ εἶδες πρότερον πάντα σοι πάλιν δείξω, αὐτὰ τὰ κεφάλαια τὰ ὄντα ὑμῖν σύμφορα. πρῶτον πάντων τὰς ἐντολάς μου γράψον καὶ τὰς παραβολάς· τὰ δὲ ἕτερα καθώς σοι δείξω οὕτως γράψεις· διὰ τοῦτο, φησίν, ἐντέλλομαί σοι πρῶτον γράψαι τὰς ἐντολὰς καὶ παραβολάς, ἵνα ὑπὸ χεῖρα ἀναγινώσκῃς αὐτὰς καὶ δυνηθῇς φυλάξαι αὐτάς.
>
> 25.5 But he said to me, "Do not be confused, but become strong in my commandments, which I am about to give you. For I was sent," he said, "to show you yet again all the things that you saw before, since these are what will chiefly benefit you. First, however, write my commandments and parables; but write the other things just as I show them to you. This is why," he said, "I am commanding you first to write the commandments and parables—that you may read them regularly and so be able to keep them."

Thus, the fifth vision of the Shepherd serves as an important link between the Book of Visions and the ethical material in the twelve Mandates and ten Similitudes. Hermas no longer appears as a named character in the Mandates; instead the Shepherd addresses the reader and hearer in the second-person, as if he were speaking directly to Hermas (=the reader) himself. Each of the three sections transitions the reader into the next, so as to achieve the overall semblance of a single complete work of considerable size.

Our focus is on the Book of Visions and the figure of Hermas. The name Hermas is fairly non-descript; even so, scholars have sought to identify this figure from various ancient references. There are three ancient references that are important when discussing the possibility of a historical Hermas. The first is by Origen who identifies Hermas as the individual named by

---

2. Unless otherwise noted, all translations and texts of the Shepherd are taken from Bart D. Ehrman, *The Apostolic Fathers 2: Epistle of Barnabas, Papias and Quadratus, Epistle to Diognetus, The Shepherd of Hermas*, LCL 25 (Cambridge: Harvard University Press, 2003). Passage references to the Shepherd are coordinated with the traditional format and the new numbering system introduced by Molly Whittaker, *Die Apostolischen Väter. 1 Der Hirt des Hermas*, 2nd ed. (Berlin: Akademie Verlag, 1967).

Paul in Rom. 16.14 in his *Comm. in. Rom* 10.31,[3] although many do not understand this reference to be to the same Hermas of the Shepherd. Eusebius (*Hist. eccl.* 3.3.6) and Jerome (*De vir. ill.* 10) follow Origen on this matter. Carolyn Osiek reasons that this may have been an attempt on Origen's part to date the book as closely as possible to the apostolic period.[4] The second reference is tied to Hermas's second vision of the Lady which concerns a little book (τὸ βιβλίδιον). Here the Lady instructs Hermas to make two copies of the book, one for Clement and the other for Grapte in Vis. 2.4.3 (8.3). This first individual is thought to be Clement of Rome, the putative author of I Clement, which is dated to the late first century, although this too is not certain.[5] More recently, Andrew Gregory has pushed for an even earlier dating of 1 Clement to as early as 70 and as late as 140, similarly dating the Shepherd from 70 to as late as 150.[6] The other figure, Grapte, is presumed to be an otherwise unknown woman. While the name is well-attested in Rome, there is no clear way to identify her from this citation alone. Osiek writes that the name, Grapte, is attested fifty-four occurrences in four centuries among both slave and freedwomen.[7]

The third ancient reference is perhaps the most well-known and appears in lines 73-77 of the Muratorian Fragment, which has been dated anywhere from the second to the fourth century.[8] In this passage, Hermas is identified as the brother of Pope Pius: "Hermas wrote the Shepherd very recently in our days while his brother Pius occupied the episcopal chair of the church of the city of Rome" (*Pastorem vero nuperrime temporibus nostris in urbe Roma Hermas conscripsit sedente cathedra Urbis Romae ecclesiae Pio*

---

3. On the topic of Hermas's relationship to Paul, see Jonathan Soyars, *The Shepherd of Hermas and the Pauline Legacy*, NovTSup 176 (Leiden: Brill, 2019). Soyars book presents a strongly optimistic view of our ability to make such historical and theological connections among the Shepherd and Paul.

4. Carolyn Osiek, *The Shepherd of Hermas*, Hermeneia (Minneapolis: Fortress Press, 1999), 18.

5. Lawrence L. Welborn, "On the Date of First Clement," *Biblical Research* 29 (1984): 35–54. Welborn dates 1 Clement to the 100s or 90s.

6. Andrew Gregory, "Disturbing Trajectories: *1 Clement*, the *Shepherd of Hermas* and the Development of Early Roman Christianity," in *Rome in the Bible and the Early Church*, ed. Peter Oakes (Grand Rapids: Baker Academic, 2002), 142–66. For his dating of 1 Clement, see 149; for his dating of the Shepherd, see 153.

7. Osiek, *The Shepherd of Hermas*, 59 n. 10; also Heikki Solin, *Die griechischen Personennamen in Rom: Ein Namenbuch*, 3 vols. (Berlin: De Gruyter 1982), 1171–73.

8. Albert C. Sundberg, "Canon Muratori: A Fourth–Century List," *HTR* 66 (1973): 1–41. In disagreement with Sundberg is Everett Ferguson, "Canon Muratori: Date and Provenance," *StPatr* 17 (1982): 677–83. So too, Godffrey M. Hahneman, *The Muratorian Fragment and the Development of the Canon* (New York: Oxford University Press, 1992); and Osiek, *The Shepherd of Hermas*, 6 n. 57.

episcopo fratre eius). This reference not only anchors Hermas personally to another known person from the ancient world; it has also been used for the dating of the Muratorian Fragment itself. These three ancient references to the putative author of the Shepherd locate him in the late-first or second century, based on assumptions about the history of the earliest Christian groups.[9]

These scholarly arguments seek to establish the existence of a historical Hermas, but they do not interact with those aspects of the Book of Visions that are of great importance to us and our study. Even if these narratives contain some core of the historical experiences of an actual person named Hermas, it is not possible to extract the historical details from the fictionalized elements. These first-person reports of Hermas's experiences might call to mind the category of autobiography, but they are fiction. Literary critics have long acknowledged how elements of fiction writing and story-telling strongly influence the writing of autobiography. Writing is collaborative and not an activity done by one person. Our study approaches the Book of Visions as a fictionalized account of Hermas and his visionary experiences. It is worth remembering that authors, both then and now, frequently write from different and unusual perspectives and not exclusively from their own point of view. This study uses the descriptions of Hermas and the information given about his embodiment, his emotions, and his interior experiences, and considers how the Book of Visions can be said to contribute to the moral formation of its readers and hearers. The majority of these embodied details about Hermas's kinesthetics and interior experiences are

---

9. See the recent discussion that moves away from understanding these named and unnamed references as early Christian ones, see Ulla Tervahauta, "A Just Man or Just a Man: The Ideal Man in the Visions of Hermas," *Patristica Nordica Annuaria* 35 (2020): 69–97. Tervahauta's new reading of the "Lady" and other named figures from a non-ecclesial framework is a striking departure from studies by Osiek, "The Social Function of Female Imagery in Second Century Prophecy," *Vetera Christianorum* 29 (1992): 55–74; Carolyn Osiek, "The Oral World of Early Christianity in Rome: The Case of Hermas," in *Judaism and Christianity in First-Century Rome*, ed. Karl P. Donfried and Peter Richardson (Grand Rapids: Eerdmans, 1998), 151–72; Mary Rose D'Angelo, "'Knowing How to Preside over His Own Household': Imperial Masculinity and Christian Asceticism in the Pastorals, Hermas, and Luke-Acts," in *New Testament Masculinities*, ed. Stephen D. Moore and Janice Capel Anderson (Atlanta: SBL Press, 2003), 265–95; and more recently, Lora Walsh, "Ecclesia Reconsidered: Two Premodern Encounters with the Feminine Church," *Journal of Feminist Studies in Religion* 33 (2017): 73–91; Lora Walsh, "The Lady as Elder in the *Shepherd of Hermas*," *JECS* 27 (2019): 517–47; Lora Walsh, "Lost in Revision: Gender Symbolism in Vision 3 and Similitude 9 of the Shepherd of Hermas," *HTR* 112 (2019): 467–90.

inconsequential to historical analysis, and thus have not been analyzed fully in the past.

The popularity of the Shepherd as a catechetical text is well documented in the ancient period, especially in the areas of North Africa, a topic that will receive further elaboration in Chapter 1. The enormous appeal of the Shepherd can be demonstrated by its textual remains, which far exceeded that of the Gospels prior to the fifth century. While the sections known as the Mandates and the Similitudes were used for ethical teaching, our study is especially interested in understanding how the Book of Visions contributes to the larger work's overall program of moral formation. This study applies various embodied approaches to Hermas's visions, specifically enactive reading, which understands cognition as an embodied process that dynamically constructs the narrative world.[10] The enactivist understanding of cognition theoretically stands in tension with a classic representational understanding of cognition that assumes the mind is wholly independent from the world. In the revised edition of the foundational work, *The Embodied Mind*, Francisco J. Varela, Evan Thompson, and Eleanor Rosch describe the distinction between enactivism and representationalism in the following way:

> In the enactive program, we explicitly call into question the assumption—prevalent throughout cognitive science—that cognition consists of the representation of a world that is independent of our perceptual and cognitive capacities by a cognitive system that exists independent of the world.[11]

In the case of critical literary theory, both enactivism and representationalism attend to embodied language in narrative by means of cognitive-based approaches, although they differ to the extent to which they understand the body's active role in cognitive processes. Enactivism understands the embodied reader's perceptions and environment to have an active and constitutive role in creation of the narrative world—there is no Hermas apart from the one that is constructed in the reader's and hearer's mind. Enactivism stands in contrast to representationalism which understands that the

---

10. Francisco J. Varela, Evan Thompson, and Eleanor Rosch, *The Embodied Mind: Cognitive Science and Human Experience, Revised Edition* (Cambridge: MIT Press, 1991, 2016), discusses the enactive understanding of cognition as dynamic and constructive. This in contrast to the traditional model of representational understanding of cognition that assumes that the representation of the world in the mind and its perceptual and cognitive capacities exists independently from the world. See the analysis by Pierre Steiner, "Enacting Anti-representationalism. The Scope and the Limits of Enactive Critiques of Representationalism," *Avant* 5 (2014): 43–86; Daniel D. Hutto, Michael D. Kirchhoff, and Erik Myin, "Extensive Enactivism: Why keep it all in?" *Frontiers in Human Neuroscience* 8 (2014): 1–11.

11. Varela, Thompson, and Rosch, *The Embodied Mind*, lxvi.

mind imagines only a replica of a reality that exists completely apart from the reader's imagination. Both enactivism and representationalism rely heavily on the narrative details in the text that speak of embodied experiences, but these details play a different role in the imagination.

Enactive reading is used to understand Hermas's vision of the Lady in Vis. 1 and 2 (Chapter 2), the psychological phenomenon of rumination (Chapter 3) and ecocriticism (Chapter 4) to describe how the Book of Visions might have been read and experienced by ancient readers and hearers as an immersive narrative. These same cognitive approaches also highlight how modern scholars trained to read texts against the grain while searching for exegetical, historical, or theological information fail to notice the very things that made Hermas's narratives entertaining and compelling to ancient readers and hearers. Chapter 5 discusses how these modern habits of academic reading constrain and prevent us from understanding how the Book of Visions could have been experienced as an immersive narrative of a possible world.

The Integrative Approaches Used in this Study

The ideas in this book are deeply influenced by the integrative approaches associated with the cognitive science of religion and the work of Armin Geertz and others who have made a strong case for a biocultural understanding of religion.[12] These approaches push scholars to reintegrate the artificial mind/body dualism that continues to be pervasive in the text-centric disciplines of the humanities. This study uses a variety of emerging approaches and findings from different biocultural studies of cognitive psychology, cognitive literary criticism, and anthropology to reconstruct the flesh-and-blood experience of reading the Shepherd.

While the overall approach of the book is eclectic, cognitive literary theory—as it has been applied to narratives—is especially useful for describing a range of ways embodied reading effects the reader/hearer. Cognitive literary approaches, specifically enactive reading, acknowledges reading as a complex process that engages the sensorimotor areas of the brain, the past life experiences of the reader/hearer and their environment. In the mind, mirror neurons are engaged during processes of mental simulation when we

---

12. Armin W. Geertz, "Global Perspectives on Methodology in the Study of Religion," *MTSR* 12 (2000): 49–73; Armin W. Geertz, "Brain, Body and Culture: A Biocultural Theory of Religion," *MTSR* 22 (2010): 304–21; Armin W. Geertz, "Religious Bodies, Minds and Places. A Cognitive Science of Religion Perspective," in *Spazi e Luoghi Sacri: Espressioni ed Esperienze di Vissuto Religioso*, ed. Laura Carnevale (Santo Spirito [Bari]: Edipuglia, 2017), 35–52.

imagine ourselves doing what we see someone else doing.[13] In addition to these sensorimotor areas of the brain, mirror neurons are also thought to be involved when empathizing emotionally with someone else's experiences. In the case of immersive reading experiences, these areas of the brain also respond when these actions are only mentally visualized from narrative, and not physically perceived with the eyes. Nicole Speer and others conclude:

> [R]eaders dynamically activate specific visual, motor, and conceptual features of activities while reading about analogous changes in activities in the context of a narrative: Regions involved in processing goal-directed human activity, navigating spatial environments, and manipulating objects in the real world increased in activation at points when those specific aspects of the narrated situation were changing. ... These results suggest that readers use perceptual and motor representations in the process of comprehending narrated activity, and that these representations are dynamically updated at points when relevant aspects of the situation are changing.[14]

Speer's study speaks to the different ways the mind may be intensely engaged but which may not include physical activity on the part of the reader or hearer. Elliot Wolfson has spoken similarly about "a psychic province where, paradoxically enough, the somatic tangibility intensifies, even as the coarse materiality is eviscerated and the mental acuity grows more vivid in the muting of the empirical apparatus."[15] These studies suggest that the motionless activity of listening or reading journey narratives, like the first-person reports in the Book of Visions, can be a deeply engaging experience and involve areas of the mind that are responsible for sensorimotor experiences. These studies show that textual representations of kinesthetic experiences, regardless of length, are especially powerful for creating compelling immersive experiences.

Cognitive literary theory refers to a variety of approaches that bring together two largely distinct fields—the empirical sciences and the humanities—and integrate their contrasting discipline-specific perspectives to shed light on the complexity of the human embodied experience of reading.[16]

---

13. Nicole K. Speer, Jeremy R. Reynolds, Khena M. Swallow, and Jeffrey M. Zacks, "Reading Stories Activates Neural Representations of Visual and Motor Experiences," *Psychological Science* 20 (2009): 989–99.

14. Speer et al., "Reading Stories Activates Neural Representations of Visual and Motor Experiences," 996.

15. Elliot R. Wolfson, *A Dream Interpreted within a Dream: Oneiropoiesis and the Prism of Imagination* (New York: Zone Books, 2011), 51.

16. See Alan Richardson, *British Romanticism and the Science of the Mind* (Cambridge: Cambridge University Press, 2001); Lisa Zunshine (ed.), *Introduction to Cognitive Cultural Studies* (Baltimore: Johns Hopkins Press, 2010); Patrick Colm Hogan, *What Literature Teaches Us about Emotion* (Cambridge: Cambridge University Press,

One the one hand, research methods of the empirical sciences seek to identify generalizable patterns in the human experience of reading; and on the other hand, the humanities are closely attuned to the specific "social, political, economic and cultural forces" that give rise to texts and their distinctive literary interpretations.[17] These two contrasting aims are brought together in the integrative field of cognitive literary theory, which acknowledges the complex cognitive processes that are at work when reading. Because cognitive literary approaches rely on studies conducted on a wide range of readers, they offer a useful benchmark for thinking how a non-specialist reader in general might respond to narrative cues. This helps us to see how profoundly our discipline-specific analyses often read against the grain of the

2011); G. Gabrielle Starr, *Feeling Beauty: The Neuroscience of Aesthetic Experience* (Cambridge: MIT Press, 2013); Marco Caracciolo, *The Experientiality of Narrative: An Enactivist Approach* (Berlin: De Gruyter, 2014); Marie-Laure Ryan, *Narrative as Virtual Reality 2: Revisiting Immersion and Interactivity in Literature and Electronic Media* (Baltimore: Johns Hopkins University Press, 2015); Elaine Auyoung, *When Fiction Feels Real: Representation and the Reading Mind* (Oxford: Oxford University Press, 2018); Andrew Elfenbein, *The Gist of Reading* (Stanford: Stanford University Press, 2018). For a discussion of the intersection between the empirical sciences and the humanities, see Geertz, "Global Perspectives on Methodology in the Study of Religion," 49–73; Armin W. Geertz, "Comparing Prayer: On Science, Universals, and the Human Condition," in *Introducing Religion: Essays in Honor of Jonathan Z. Smith*, ed. Willi Braun and Russell T. McCutcheon (London: Equinox, 2008), 113–39; Edward Slingerland, *What Science Offers the Humanities: Integrating Body and Culture* (Cambridge: Cambridge University Press, 2008). Cognitive-based approaches to the study of religion generally include Patrick McNamara, *The Neuroscience of Religious Experience* (Cambridge: Cambridge University Press, 2009); Markus Altena Davidsen, "Fiction-based Religion: Conceptualizing a New Category against History-Based Religion and Fandom," *Culture and Religion* 14 (2013): 378–95. Important too is Varela, Thompson, Rosch, *The Embodied Mind: Cognitive Science and Human Experience. Revised Edition*, which integrates non-western understandings of the body and mind from Buddhism and emerging understandings of the embodied mind; and Niki Kasumi Clements, ed., *Religion: Mental Religion*, Macmillan Interdisciplinary Handbooks (Farmington Hills, MI: Macmillan Reference USA, 2016).

See too the studies that seek to apply these emerging approaches to the study of early Judaism and early Christianity: Colleen Shantz, *Paul in Ecstasy: The Neurobiology of the Apostle's Life and Thought* (Cambridge: Cambridge University Press, 2009); Angela Kim Harkins, *Reading with an "I" to the Heavens: Looking at the Qumran Hodayot through the Lens of Visionary Traditions* (Berlin: De Gruyter, 2012); Risto Uro, *Ritual and Christian Beginnings: A Socio-Cognitive Analysis* (Oxford: Oxford University Press, 2016); István Czachesz, *Cognitive Science & the New Testament: A New Approach to Early Christian Research* (Oxford: Oxford University Press, 2017); Angela Kim Harkins and Harry O. Maier (ed.), *Experiencing the Shepherd of Hermas*, Ekstasis 10 (Berlin: De Gruyter, 2022).

17. Elfenbein, *The Gist of Reading*, 3–4.

narrative and overlook elements that are otherwise crucial for understanding how a story might be compelling and how it might cultivate certain moral dispositions like empathy within readers.

When investigating religion, both past and present, modern scholars rely heavily on texts, investing enormous energy into philological analysis and textual criticism.[18] These are necessary tasks, but, as Armin Geertz points out, the tendency can be to assume that texts were the only voices and conduits for cultural exchange in the ancient world and to forget that there were other non-textualized performative mechanisms—like the body—by which individuals were formed and transformed.[19] We can also add to this discussion the studies that examine the role of the environment in cognitive narrative studies.[20] Scholarly assumptions about texts often impute characteristics about people and families to manuscripts, reflecting sensibilities about lineage and purity that befit the bourgeois class-consciousness of text criticism's origins. This is a point made some time ago by scholars of the 'New Philology', who described the discipline as scholars seeking to establish a text's pure lineage by establishing the paternity or bloodline of a textual tradition from one manuscript generation to the next.[21] While our modern experience of ancient texts is often mediated through bound critical editions, we are better served by imagining how texts were experienced and read by actual people than by understanding the texts themselves as having the characteristics of people. While texts remain important for our analysis, we are also keenly aware of the role of orality/aurality on the experience of the Shepherd, signs of which are present in the text, especially in the Mandates and the Similitudes.[22] Attention to hearing a text being read also provides more undetermined aspects of the experience because the hearer's eyes are not tethered to the page and so the hearer can be stimulated by the space or environment.

---

18. Geertz, "Global Perspectives on Methodology in the Study of Religion," 70–71.
19. Geertz, "Global Perspectives on Methodology in the Study of Religion," 71.
20. For example, Anežka Kuzmičová, "Does It Matter Where You Read? Situating Narrative in Physical Environment," *Communication Theory* 26 (2016): 290–308.
21. Bernard Cerquiglini, *Éloge de la variante: Histoire critique de la philologie* (Paris: Seuil, 1989); Stephen Nichols, "Introduction: Philology in a Manuscript Culture," *Speculum* 65 (1990): 1–10.
22. Osiek, "The Oral World of Early Christianity in Rome: The Case of Hermas," 151–72. For an excellent study of the nuances of oral/aural experiences of John's apocalypse, see Harry O. Maier, *Apocalypse Recalled: The Book of Revelation after Christendom* (Minneapolis: Fortress Press, 2002), 91–122. Also relevant is the way the prolixity of Hermas offers a way of thinking about the formation of its readers. Here see B. Diane Lipsett, "Gender, Volubility, and Transformation in the Shepherd of Hermas," in *Experiencing the Shepherd of Hermas*, ed. Angela Kim Harkins and Harry O. Maier, 57–72.

Increasingly, scholars have sought to expand how we understand the embodied experience of reading texts by introducing integrative biocultural approaches associated more broadly with the study of religion, both past and present.[23] This reorientation to the past seeks to investigate the complexities of individual experiences—complexities that we recognize as a part of life as lived.[24] Attention to the body and embodied experiences of the individual highlights just how cozy scholars have become with assumptions about community/communities in antiquity,[25] as if individuals and groups in the past were like a stick of butter, solid and consistent all the way through. The recent turn to the self recognizes that the individual in antiquity was not predetermined to conform to the large systematic ritual experiences often constructed by modern scholars.[26] We also acknowledge the limitations of studying reading practices in antiquity, and we realize that the cultivation of certain emotional states and predispositions does not predetermine that every reader and hearer would experience the enactive processes and moral formation. This is especially true when we keep in mind how the hearing of texts can be influenced by an individual's immediate environment and lived experiences.

The Cognitive Science of Visual Perception and Embodied Reading

Rather than the popular idea that we see complete scenes with a lot of rich and exact details, like a photograph, cognitive studies show that our visual perception relies on several discrete, focused points of attention that we then extend and complete in our imaginations to give the illusion of a coherent and unified image. In addition to our learned habits of reading, we rely on our experiential knowledge of how the world looks and operates in order to complete the visual image mentally. The Book of Visions often includes discrete details of concrete information about characters and their movements in their literary worlds, simulating how our minds focus in on specific points of visual information. Readers and hearers complete and extend these points

---

23. Geertz, "Brain, Body and Culture: A Biocultural Theory of Religion," 304–21.

24. The shift to the individual and to the phenomenal experiences of the body which has happened steadily in the social sciences during the last 40 years, has emerged more recently in the study of religion through approaches like feminist studies and material studies of religion. These changes in the social sciences in the last thirty years are described well by Robert Desjarlais and C. Jason Throop, "Phenomenological Approaches in Anthropology," *Annual Review of Anthropology* 40 (2011): 87–102.

25. Stanley Stowers, "The Concept of 'Community' and the History of Early Christianity," *MTSR* 23 (2011): 238–56.

26. Jörg Rüpke, "Lived Ancient Religions," *Oxford Research Encyclopedia of Religion* (Oxford: Oxford University Press, 2019), 1–22.

of information based on their knowledge and past life experiences to create a coherent understanding of a narrative world. A key part of enactive reading is an awareness of the cognitive processes by which readers extend their own experiential knowledge about their body's biomechanics and sensory perceptions to the characters and events described in the texts.

According to Marco Caracciolo's description of enactive reading, the reader, first of all, understands him- or herself as distinct from a character in a narrative.[27] The same reader is omniscient by virtue of his or her access to Hermas's interior consciousness, viz., his anguish, experiences of confusion, wonder, and surprise.[28] This information about Hermas's embodied responses to his environment and situation are used to infer other aspects of the narrative world. A reader can become more immersed in the narrative world as he or she reads and accumulates information about the world and how it operates. Caracciolo writes the following:

> Engaging with stories is 'enactive' in the strong sense because it involves imaginatively enacting a non-actual set of situations and events: by coordinating with the sensemaking of the story producers, recipients bring forth a 'world' charged with significance. Narrative is, therefore, one of the means whereby human meaning-making can detach itself from the here and now, exploring possibilities that would be difficult or even impossible to consider in actuality.[29]

Marco Caracciolo goes on to offer that enactive reading is akin to groping through an unknown narrative world relying only on the fragmented details provided by the narrative.[30] When considering enactivist understandings of reading, the reader's past experiences help to fill the gaps that remain from these partial bits of information during the constructive process of imagining a narrative world.

Scholars of the ancient world are already familiar with the many strategies by which ancient authors gave their writings rhetorical power: *ekphrasis*, *enargeia*, and *phantasia*.[31] Our concern is not simply to analyze the rhetorical vividness of the Book of Visions, but to analyze the reading habits

---

27. Marco Caracciolo, "Fictional Consciousnesses: A Reader's Manual," *Style* 46 (2012): 42–65, here 43–9.
28. Caracciolo, "Fictional Consciousnesses," 43–9.
29. Marco Caracciolo, "Narrative, Meaning, Interpretation: An Enactivist Approach," *Phenomenology and the Cognitive Sciences* 11 (2012): 367–84, esp. 373–4.
30. Caracciolo, *The Experientiality of Narrative*, 95–6.
31. As outlined in the ancient handbook the *Progymnasmata*, see Ruth Webb, *Ekphrasis, Imagination and Persuasion in Ancient Rhetorical Theory and Practice* (New York: Ashgate, 2009); Robyn J. Whitaker, *Ekphrasis, Vision, and Persuasion in the Book of Revelation* (Tübingen: Mohr Siebeck, 2015); Michael Wade Martin and Mikeal C. Parsons, *Ancient Rhetoric and the New Testament: The Influence of Elementary Greek Composition* (Baylor University Press, 2018).

of modern scholars whose assessments of the Shepherd's literary style as boring or tedious do not comport with the clear popularity this text enjoyed among ancient readers. Cognitive literary approaches, like enactive reading, can help us to understand why modern scholarly evaluations of this ancient apocalypse known as the Shepherd of Hermas are often in tension with the clear success that this book enjoyed among ancient readers and hearers, who read with different life experiences and different expectations of the text.

Brief literary details about Hermas's extended body in motion within the narrative spaces of the Book of Visions, along with his first-person reports of interior emotional states and experiences, provide the necessary information to enact Hermas's sensorimotor experiences. Not only does this allow readers and hearers to achieve an immersive experience of the narrative, but it also allows them to infer an inner-life and consciousness for Hermas.[32] Reading enactively allows the reader to access Hermas's confusion over his visions, his introspective musings, and his watchful anticipation, thereby allowing for a deeper engagement of the text. Immersion in the narrative world of the Book of Visions also allows for the reader and hearer to cultivate the necessary emotions and predispositions needed for moral formation and heightens their receptivity to the subsequent ethical sections known as the Mandates and the Similitudes. An important way Hermas's visions function in the larger catechetical work is to increase the anticipation of readers and hearers for the fifth vision of the Shepherd that looks forward to the Mandates and to the Similitudes, both of which have a strong moralizing tone.

Cognitive narrative studies highlight that the first-person voice not only lends a dynamic quality to story-telling, but also plays a significant role in enactive reading and immersive experiences, thereby generating a sense of presence from the text.[33] *Proprioception* refers to the awareness of kinesthetic changes in the seer's extended body as it moves through space. It also

---

32. For other studies of ancient characters, see Barbara M. Leung Lai, *Through the 'I'-Window: The Inner Life of Characters in the Hebrew Bible* (Sheffield: Phoenix Press, 2011).

33. Richard J. Gerrig, *Experiencing Narrative Worlds: On the Psychological Activities of Reading* (New Haven: Yale University Press, 1993); Marie-Laure Ryan, "Varieties of Immersion: Spatial, Temporal, Emotional," in *Narrative as Virtual Reality 2*, 85–114; Suzanne Gillmayr-Bucher, "Body Images in the Psalms," *JSOT* 28 (2004): 301–26; Anežka Kuzmičová, "Presence in the Reading of a Literary Narrative," *Semiotica* 189 (2012): 23–48, esp. 24–5; Loren T. Stuckenbruck, "Pseudepigraphy and First Person Discourse in the Dead Sea Documents: From the Aramaic Texts to Writings of the Yaḥad," in *The Dead Sea Scrolls and Contemporary Culture: A Case for Motor Enactment*, ed. Adolfo D. Roitman et al. (Leiden: Brill, 2011), 295-326. For a discussion of the first-person "I" and the actualization of texts through performance theory, see Harkins, *Reading with an "I" to the Heavens*, 69–113.

includes descriptions of the seer's bodily positioning and posture. The Book of Visions also provides abundant details about the seer's awareness of emotion and changes in the skin and viscera, known as *interoception*. These experiences include the sensations that are perceived through our bodies (viz., skin and viscera): "temperature, pain, itch, tickle, sensual touch, muscular and visceral sensations, vasomotor flush, hunger, thirst."[34] They also include emotions of the seer that are displayed in the body. For example, the state of fear can be expressed in the body through various interoceptive experiences: weeping, blanching of the face, goosebumps, nausea, clammy hands, or the trembling of the body. Consideration of proprioception and interoception can broaden and enrich our understanding of embodiment by moving beyond the classic sensorium of the five senses: seeing, hearing, smelling, tasting, and touching. First-person voice and details about the seer's proprioception and interoception are key elements that allow for enactive and immersive experiences of narrated visions. These literary features are regularly present in ancient apocalypses.[35] The following are various ways that ancient apocalypses allow a reader/hearer to access the embodied experiences of the seer: proprioception, interoception, rumination, and enactive perception of the possible narrative world.

The Proprioception of Ancient Apocalyptic Seers

Proprioception includes the awareness of embodied sensations of moving through space that are often reported in apocalypses. For example, in the heavenly journey of Perpetua and Saturus that is recounted at the beginning of Book 4 of the *Martyrdom of Perpetua and Felicity*, the reader is told *exactly how* their bodies ascend to heaven—they are not supine as they go up; rather, their bodies are pitched at a slight angle.[36] Ancient readers may have imagined a cultural form for ascent that is expressed concretely by the artist of the Arco di Portogallo in Rome in a relief of the apotheosis of

---

34. A.D. Craig, "How Do You Feel? Interoception: The Sense of the Physiological Condition of the Body," *Nature Reviews Neuroscience* 3 (2002): 655–6, here 655.

35. For a fuller discussion of the role that proprioception and interoception play in ancient apocalypses see Angela Kim Harkins, "Immersing Oneself in the Narrative World of Second Temple Apocalyptic Visions," in *Reimagining Apocalypticism: Apocalypses, Apocalyptic Literature and the Dead Sea Scrolls*, ed. Lorenzo DiTommaso and Matthew Goff (Atlanta: SBL Press, 2023), 297–327.

36. The newest edition of the *Martyrdom of Perpetua and Felicity* by Thomas J. Heffernan offers the following translation of the text: "But we were moving, not on our backs facing upwards, but as if we were climbing a gentle hill" (XI.3; *Ibamus autem non supine sursum uersi, sed quasi mollem cliuum ascendentes*). See his *The Passion of Perpetua and Felicity* (Oxford: Oxford University Press, 2011).

Sabina, Hadrian's wife. The image depicts Sabina being carried away by the smoke of the funeral pyre and a female angelic being. Proprioception can refer to active or passive sensations of the body moving through space, like a vertical ascent, or the loss of balance and the sensation of falling downward. Proprioception may be either conscious or unconscious. In general, proprioception refers to the embodied self's awareness of movement in and through its surrounding environment.

The Interoception of Ancient Apocalyptic Seers

Interoception refers to an individual's awareness of his or her interior physiological state and is usually mediated through the skin or the viscera. These interoceptive states are evaluative and inflected with a motivational or emotional meaning. Extreme temperatures are disliked and avoided. Also included in these bodily experiences is the awareness of sexual arousal, which may lead an individual to certain actions. Certain negative emotions like fear and disgust have a strong biological basis and are associated with the viscera—these too are considered interoceptive experiences and express an assessment of the environment.[37] In Greek writings, interoceptive experiences are understood through metaphors that connect the body to the emotion. When the emotions are expressed through the body, the physical display functions as a metonym for the emotional state.[38] Douglas Cairns uses the example of φρίκη (φρικάζω, "to shudder"), a figurative way to speak about fear. He writes: "the experiential network in which *phrikè* belongs (in which *phrikê*-type emotions are typified by the lowered body temperature, shivering, and piloerection that are their physical symptoms) encompasses a range of other terms which express complementary aspects of the same imagery."[39] For example, the word φρίκη appears just after Hermas's first vision: "After she had spoken these words, the skies were shut; I was trembling all over

---

37. Anil K. Seth, "Interoceptive Inference, Emotion, and the Embodied Self," *Trends in Cognitive Sciences* 17 (2013): 565–73. Olga Pollatos and Rainer Schandry, "Emotional Processing and Emotional Memory are Modulated by Interoceptive Awareness," *Cognition and Emotion* 22 (2008): 272–87.

38. Douglas Cairns, "Mind, Body, and Metaphor in Ancient Greek Concepts of Emotion," *L'Atelier du Centre de recherches historiques* 16 (2016); http://journals.openedition.org/acrh/7416; and Douglas Cairns, "The Horror and the Pity: *Phrikê* as a Tragic Emotion," *Psychoanalytic Inquiry* 35 (2015): 75–94. David Konstan, *The Emotions of the Ancient Greeks: Studies in Aristotle and Classical Literature* (Toronto: University of Toronto Press, 2001) and Robert A. Kaster, *Emotion, Restraint, and Community in Ancient Rome* (Oxford: Oxford University Press, 2005).

39. Cairns, "Mind, Body, and Metaphor in Ancient Greek Concepts of Emotion," (online).

and upset" (Μετὰ τὸ λαλῆσαι αὐτὴν τὰ ῥήματα ταῦτα ἐκλείσθησαν οἱ οὐρανοί· κἀγὼ ὅλος ἤμην πεφρικὼς καὶ λυπούμενος, Vis. 1.2.1 [2.1]). The interoceptive state expressed by the word φρίκη offers readers an evaluative assessment of the event—in this case, an image of Hermas recoiling with horror.

In the case of the biblical apocalypse, Daniel reports various interoceptive experiences, such as fear, dismay, and trance states. In the midst of retelling the nighttime vision in 7.15, Daniel recounts his interoceptive experiences: "As for me, Daniel, my spirit was troubled within me, and the visions of my head terrified me" (אֶתְכְּרִיַּת רוּחִי אֲנָה דָנִיֵּאל בְּגוֹא נִדְנֶה וְחֶזְוֵי רֵאשִׁי יְבַהֲלֻנַּנִי). Shortly thereafter, readers are given additional interoceptive details of the seer's vasomotor flush in Dan. 7.28: "As for me, Daniel, *my thoughts greatly terrified me*, and *the pallor (of my face) changed*; but I kept the matter in my mind" (אֲנָה דָנִיֵּאל שַׂגִּיא רַעְיוֹנַי יְבַהֲלֻנַּנִי וְזִיוַי יִשְׁתַּנּוֹן עֲלַי וּמִלְּתָא בְּלִבִּי נִטְרֵת). In the Hebrew Bible, idioms for emotions locate them in various internal organs like the heart, liver, belly, or womb.[40]

Texts can be engaged phenomenally through simulative embodied experiences like 'enactive perception,' which Aldo Tagliabue describes in the following way:

> Within this new model, which stresses the role of the body in human cognition and can broadly be defined as 'embodied', some scholars identify a subcategory, the 'enactive perception', according to which perceiving is a way of acting as the world makes itself available to the perceiver through his physical movement and interaction with a given object in a precise environment. In other words, the perception of any object is made possible if one gets close to and moves around it.[41]

In such instances, the reader is guided by the descriptions of the seer's vision and physical locomotion that dominate visionary texts through the use of the first-person voice. Enactive perception indicates that one does not simply perceive a vision with the eyes alone; rather, one sees with the entire body, either by moving closer to inspect the object that is being viewed or by picking up and handling it to get a better look. Visionary texts emphasize visual experiences but are also accompanied by other wide-ranging details about the seer's experiences of physicality and sensory perception within his or her environs—what the seer hears, smells, tastes, touches, and moves

---

40. Mark S. Smith, "The Heart and Innards in Israelite Emotional Expressions: Notes from Anthropology and Psychobiology," *JBL* 117 (1998): 427–36. His opening example is from Lam. 2.11: "My eyes are spent with weeping; *my belly (mei'ay) is in turmoil; my liver (kaved)/bile is poured out on the ground* (נִשְׁפַּךְ לָאָרֶץ כְּבֵדִי) because of the destruction of my people, because infants and babes faint in the streets of the city."

41. Aldo Tagliabue, "An Embodied Reading of Epiphanies in Aelius Aristides' *Sacred Tales*," *Ramus* 45 (2016): 213–30, here 214.

toward, around, or away from. And all these descriptions in first-person voice can greatly facilitate how the scene is experienced in the body.[42] Both enactive reading and enactive perception speak to the ways that first-person referential descriptions of bodily experiences contribute qualities of vividness and solidity to the narrative scene of the Book of Visions.

Rumination as a Way of Making Presence from Absence

Rumination describes a naturally occurring cognitive state in which recurring thoughts intrude in the mind. It is thought to play a role in problem-solving, anticipatory processing, reminiscence. Rumination is also the cognitive process that is engaged when longing for or desiring a loved one who is absent or who has become deceased. Because it is a state in which a person experiences presence from absence, we will discuss the effects of rumination as a way of understanding the visionary experiences that Hermas describes.

Possible Narrative Worlds

The fragmentary details of Hermas's sensorimotor experiences are used to construct a narrative world that is both purely fictional yet imbued with a plausible density and solidity. Enactive reading explains how the partial details about Hermas's embodied experiences and visions could be used by the imagination to create the possibility of the 'realness' of Hermas himself and of his narrative world. This process of immersion into a fictional world, like that of an ancient apocalypse, relies on the imagination and one's "willingness to suspend disbelief" in ways that we might experience in activities

---

42. Tagliabue, "An Embodied Reading of Epiphanies," 214. The visual perception is enhanced by the convergence of other bodily senses in the narrated experience, an important one being that of motion. See also G. Gabrielle Starr, "Multisensory Imagery," *Introduction to Cognitive Cultural Studies*, ed. L. Zunshine (Baltimore: Johns Hopkins University Press, 2010), 275–91 and G. Gabrielle Starr, *Feeling Beauty: The Neuroscience of Aesthetic Experience* (Cambridge: MIT Press, 2015). For a description of the enactive mental imaging of a scene, see the detailed description of breakfast in Hemingway's novel the *Garden of Eden* in which a wide range of sensory imagery achieves the state of experiencing the breakfast (taste, smell, touch, movement) in Kuzmičová, "Does It Matter Where You Read? Situating Narrative in Physical Environment," 223. This kind of phenomenal experience is related to imitative and mirroring processing in the brain; see Elhanan Borenstein and Eytan Ruppin, "The Evolution of Imitation and Mirror Neurons in Adaptive Agents," *Cognitive Systems Research* 6 (2005): 229–42. Marie-Laure Ryan uses the term 'mental simulation' to refer to this phenomenon in immersive reading in which the reader mirrors the emotional experiences or consciousness had by the characters in the text in her, "The Text as World: Theories of Immersion," in *Narrative as Virtual Reality 2*, 78–84.

of make-believe or fantasy.[43] The modern appeal of virtual realities can be seen in a wide range of role-playing video games, the science fiction show known as Star Trek, and the popular fantasy series Harry Potter, all of which have a dedicated group of followers.[44] The compelling quality of these narrative worlds leads to a phenomenon that Markus Altena Davidsen refers to as "fiction-based religion."[45] Recent years have seen an increase in studies that investigate the 'realness' of these modern-day experiences.[46] Research on fiction-based religions analyze how specific activities and texts offer an alternative virtual reality that a participant willingly enters, a phenomenon that can be extended to any writing that would be categorized as narrative, including the Book of Visions.

This book seeks to remind us of the embodied aspects of visual perception. When we read enactively, reading engages not only our entire physical being but also relies on our accumulated experiential knowledge about how the world around us works. Visual perception and imagination cannot be overdetermined and objectified since they are very specific processes that depend on the past experiences and knowledge of the perceiver. Our own seeing happens with the experiential knowledge that comes from our embodiment in a particular environment and from our past experiences, yet we have an obligation to try to imagine how the world might look to someone with a very different body and a different set of life experiences.

Summary of Hermas's Visions

The first book of the early Christian work known as the Shepherd of Hermas has as its protagonist a former slave who reports having a series of visionary

---

43. The quoted phrase is from Samuel Taylor Coleridge, *Biographia Literaria* (London: J. M. Dent, 1975), 169 and appears in Marie-Laure Ryan's discussion of "The Text as World: Theories of Immersion," 61–84, here 75. The same phenomenon undergirds the work of Tanya M. Luhrmann, *Persuasions of the Witch's Craft* (Oxford: Basil Blackwell Ltd., 1989), Tanya M. Luhrmann, *When God Talks Back: Understanding the American Evangelical Relationship with God* (New York: Knopf, 2012); Tanya M. Luhrmann, *How God Becomes Real: Kindling the Presence of Invisible Others* (Princeton: Princeton University Press, 2020).

44. See the extremely stimulating discussion by Rachel Wagner, *GodWired: Religion, Ritual and Virtual Reality* (New York: Routledge, 2012).

45. Davidsen, "Fiction-based Religion: Conceptualising a New Category against History-based Religion and Fandom," 378–95.

46. Perhaps the most notable ones being Luhrmann, *How God Becomes Real*; Greg Anderson, *The Realness of Things Past: Ancient Greece and Ontological History* (Oxford: Oxford University Press, 2018); Dale B. Martin, *Inventing Superstition: From the Hippocratics to the Christians* (Cambridge: Harvard University Press, 2004).

experiences. Hermas has various visions: of different women, of young men, of a tower, and of a spectacular beast (Vis. 4). Many of these visions take place outside while Hermas is journeying by foot (Vis. 1, 2, 3, 4) and at different times of the day and night. Hermas is also visited in a dream vision by a handsome young man while he is sleeping (Vis. 2.4.1 [8.1]). Later, at night a young man appears to Hermas in Vis. 3.10.7–13.4 (18.7–21.4), although it is not clear if this is also a dream vision. Another nighttime vision takes place while Hermas is sitting in bed—this time of a glorious figure of a man called the Shepherd (Vis. 5.1–7 [25.1–7]). While Hermas is assumed to be the recipient of the Shepherd's visit at the beginning of the fifth vision, he is never named in that short section, and he receives no further mention in the later Mandates or the Similitudes.[47] Most of the lengthy visions take place while Hermas is outside walking and ruminating about past events. These are highly mediated and thoroughly edited literary reports that draw upon the emotional contours of foundational narratives and myths.

The Book of Visions combines a journey narrative style with other enactive processes of kinesthetic and spatial knowing. These cognitive approaches speak to how narrative worlds are depicted as being emotionally engaged by literary characters so that flesh-and-blood readers might also access those experiences. The world that readers experience throughout the various episodes of the Book of Visions has qualities of empirical realism; even so, the spaces are not a straightforward description of the world as we know it. Like other narrated worlds, the spaces in the Book of Visions are described as having various counterintuitive and fantastic elements that remind readers that it is not the world as we ordinarily experience it. The Book of Visions recounts sudden bizarre appearances of women (young and old), various men, peculiar conversations, a chair that comes and goes (Vis. 1.2.2 [2.2]; 1.4.1 [4.1]), small books that come and go (Vis. 2.1.3–4 [5.3–4]), an ivory couch and a linen pillow that appear in a field (Vis. 3.1.4 [9.4]), an extraordinary tower (Vis. 3.2.4 ff [10.4 ff]), a strange and monstrous beast (Vis. 4.1.6–10 [22.6–10]), and of course an angel known as the shepherd (Vis. 5.1 ff. [25.1 ff]). These fantastic elements are presented

---

47. According to the argument by Grundeken and Verheyden ("The Spirit Before the Letter: Dreams and Visions as the Legitimization of the *Shepherd of Hermas*: A Study of Vision 5," in *Dreams as Divine Communication in Christianity: From Hermas to Aquinas*, ed. Bart J. Koet, Studies in the History and Anthropology of Religion 3 [Leuven: Peeters, 2012], 23–56), the fifth vision is fictional narrative that serves as a crucial element that ties together the figure of Hermas known from Vis. 1–4 and the material in the Mandates and Similitudes which follows. According to Grundeken and Verheyden, the fifth vision functions to legitimize the revelatory teachings that are contained in the Shepherd (51–52).

to a reader within a vivid narrative style alongside detailed descriptions of Hermas' emotional states and bodily movements.

These counterintuitive elements all work to cultivate the reader's attentiveness to what is happening. Despite their highly constructed elements, literary features of Hermas's first-person narration of his visions can nevertheless give some insight into how ancients might have thought or experienced these scenes enactively. With the help of the integrative approach associated with cognitive literary theory known as enactive reading, this study considers how the process of imagining the visions participates in ethical formation by drawing attention to how the necessary emotions and predispositions are cultivated through the readerly responses to Hermas's visionary experiences.

The Book of Visions is told in such a way that the reader can experientially know what Hermas is experiencing in the story. At the beginning of the third vision, the Lady instructs Hermas to wait in the field for five hours (Vis. 3.1.2 [9.2]). Readers are then told that Hermas does as he is told and "counts down the hours" late at night alone in the field (Vis. 3.1.4 [9.4]). The entire scene leading up to the vision of the Tower is protracted and painstakingly slow-moving—perhaps deliberately trying to recreate for the reader what a five-hour wait in the field was like experientially. The protracted style of the narrative intentionally slows down the narrative pace to allow time for the reader and hearer to emotionally engage the text.[48] Repetition of details may also function to slow down the pace and to allow the reader and hearer multiple chances to practice imagining this scene concretely in their mind.

The first-person narrative style allows a reader to access Hermas's experiences and to infer that he possesses the complexities of an interior consciousness. His experiences are then imagined by the reader who enacts them in the imagination with sensory vividness through enactive processes, a way of describing how the sensorimotor areas of the brain are engaged when we read first-person narratives. For the one who reads or hears the visions, the repetition of the penitential behaviors and emotional responses that Hermas gives, as well as the painstakingly slow pace of some of the visionary scenes all assist in the intensification of attention and afford the mind the time needed to imagine the text with first-hand intensity.

Both the real and fantastic details about the landscape and environment stimulate a reader's ability to experience the narrative as an immersive reality through enactive perception. These experiences that are not strictly

---

48. Readers may be interested in the following study by Marco Caracciolo that was published after I completed the writing of this book on the Shepherd: *Slow Narrative and Nonhuman Materialities* (Lincoln: University of Nebraska Press, 2022).

conceptual; they engage those areas of the brain that govern sensorimotor processes. The reader is given details about Hermas's extended and moving body within his environs lend depth, weightiness, and distance. This scaffolding of perceptible experiences of space helps the landscape go from a two-dimensional literary space to a three-dimensional experiential space. For example, references to the knees (τὰ γόνατα) makes explicit the body's contact with the ground (Vis. 1.1.3 [1.3]; 2.1.2 [5.2]), as Hermas anguishes over the vision he had the previous year (Vis. 2.1.2 [5.2]). He traverses some distance during his walk on the Via Campana (Vis. 4.1.2 [22.2]). He also references periods of elapsed time (five hours in Vis. 3.1.2 [9.2]) or the changing intensity of the sun (Vis. 4.1.6 [22.6]). There is also the peculiar scene in third vision that gives a detailed report of Hermas as he navigates around the ivory couch: Hermas stands, walks, kneels. He makes a move to sit, but then is told to sit on the other side of the couch, which he does (Vis., 3.1.8–9 [9.8–9]). Locomotive details like these appear to have little or no narrative purpose, and it is perhaps scenes like these which led Burnett Hillman Streeter to remark: "Taken in large quantities Hermas is distinctly tedious."[49] Narrative details about space and Hermas' kinesthetic and haptic experiences within those spaces assist in achieving a quality of *solidity* for imagining the scene through Hermas's first-person narration.

The dominant approach used in this book, enactive reading, can help us to understand why the negative reception of the Shepherd by modern scholarly commentators differs so strikingly from the ancient elite readers from the third- and fourth-centuries, who produced copies of the Shepherd with a frequency that rivaled that of the Gospels. This book proposes that ancient readers undertook an immersive reading of Hermas's narrated visionary experiences. Reading immersively was effectively taught in ancient rhetorical handbooks that urged students "to bring the subject matter vividly before the eyes," thereby making what is absent present in the mind.[50] The most helpful details, however, for enactive reading are the mundane descriptions of the body's movements and the emotional states of Hermas—the very details that are often overlooked by modern readers and commentators.

In general, modern scholars do not give much attention to mental visualization because they are deeply formed by modern exegetical, theological,

---

49. Streeter, *The Primitive Church: Studied with Special Reference to the Origins of the Christian Ministry* (The Hewett Lectures; New York: Macmillan, 1929), 210.

50. This is the aim of the rhetorical strategy of *ekphrasis* according to the ancient Greek handbook, *Progymnasmata*, see *Progymnasmata: Greek Textbooks of Prose Composition and Rhetoric*, translated with introduction and notes by George A. Kennedy (Atlanta: SBL Press, 2003) and Webb, *Ekphrasis, Imagination and Persuasion in Ancient Rhetorical Theory and Practice*, 14.

and historical questions that may require reading ancient texts in counterintuitive ways or against the grain. Enactive reading *highlights* the specific ways that an individual's particular embodiment and accumulated life experiences contribute to practices of reading and help to explain why the Shepherd has received such strikingly different receptions by ancient and modern readers who have been trained to read for different purposes. These different purposes for reading produce different experiences and effects of reading. Literary theorist Andrew Elfenbein uses cognitive literary theory to analyze how texts that are read for pleasure are read and processed differently than when they are read for some other purpose like gathering information or analysis.[51] Many important studies from the twentieth century have sought to parse the imagery of the visions in the hope of identifying the historical *realia* behind them, of reconstructing a social history of early Christian life from them,[52] or of understanding the literary genre or form of the Shepherd.[53] The Shepherd was not written for modern scholars and their exegetical, theological, and historical sensibilities. Rather, it was written for ancient readers who read with different aims, including enjoyment. While many modern studies of the Shepherd are concerned with when this text was written or who authored it, here we seek to re-read the Shepherd and imagine how this text was compelling and engaging for an ancient reader. In doing so, we also draw attention to how the Book of Visions sought to shape the moral sensibilities of its ancient reader by cultivating certain emotional responses to what is being described, thereby heightening the reader's receptivity to the Mandates and Similitudes that follow. We are especially concerned to note how features in the Visions reflect experiential patterns that also appear in other apocalyptic

---

51. Elfenbein, *The Gist of Reading*.

52. Examples of these important studies of the social history behind the text are Carolyn Osiek, *The Rich and the Poor in the Shepherd of Hermas: An Exegetical and Social Investigation*, Catholic Biblical Quarterly Monograph Series 15 (Washington, D.C.: Catholic Biblical Association, 1983); Martin Leutzsch, *Die Wahrnehmung sozialer Wirklichkeit im "Hirten des Hermas"*, FRLANT 150 (Göttingen: Vandenhoeck & Ruprecht, 1989); and Harry O. Maier, *The Social Setting of the Ministry as Reflected in the Writings of Hermas, Clement and Ignatius* (Waterloo: Wilfrid Laurier University Press, 1991); Harry O. Maier, "From Material Place to Imagined Space: Emergent Christian Community as Thirdspace in the Shepherd of Hermas," in *Early Christian Communities between Ideal and Reality*, ed. Mark Grundeken and Joseph Verheyden (Tübingen: Mohr Siebeck, 2015), 143–60.

53. David Hellholm, *Das Visionenbuch des Hermas als Apokalypse: Formgeschichtliche und texttheoretische Studien zu einer literarischen Gattung. Vol. 1: Methodologische Vorüberlegungen und makrostruckturelle Textanalyse*, ConBNT 13.1 (Lund: C.W.K. Gleerup, 1980); Carolyn Osiek, "The Genre and Function of the *Shepherd of Hermas*," Semeia 36 (1986): 113–21.

visionary texts and to bring texts and literary references from other early Jewish apocalyptic writings into conversation with the Shepherd.

We cannot fully explain if Hermas's visions stem from actual spiritual experiences, but in the case of a reader's experience of the Book of Visions, the activities of reading and listening offer an opportunity for mental imagery that can be quite intense. Neuroscientist Vittorio Gallese states that

> During the aesthetic experience of fictional worlds, our experience is almost exclusively mediated by a simulative perception of the events, actions and emotions characterizing fictional content. For example, when watching a movie or reading a novel, we not only focus our attention, but our immobility enables us to fully deploy our embodied simulation resources and put them at the service of our immersive relationship with the story.[54]

Immersive experiences can be intense for hearers. Unlike readers whose eyes are tethered to the page, hearers enjoy a freedom of eye movement which could strengthen individual emotional responses and mental imaging. So, in addition to the distinct life experiences that are brought to bear on the narratives that are visually imagined in the mind, a hearer's eyes could wander and see something that might help to intensify the story-telling that is taking place. These also ensure that we cannot overdetermine how an individual might visualize a scene since the experience could be different, even for those present at the same reading.

For scholars who use cognitive literary approaches to study literature, an important effect of reading a narrative is the reader's cultivation of empathy with the characters in the text.[55] This basic insight is applied to how we imagine the enactive reading of Hermas's experiences to contribute to the moral formation of its readers and hearers by cultivating the necessary emotions and predispositions. We seek to explain how the visions and narratives about Hermas are related to the ethical material that follows—namely, the Mandates and the Similitudes—by arguing that the Book of Visions played a strategic role in the overall moral formation of ancient readers of the Shepherd. The Book of Visions succeeds in immersing the reader in Hermas's narrative world and contains paraenetic exhortation throughout it. Our thesis complements and extends the valuable insight of Dan Batovici that our modern conceptualization of visions and laws as literary genres

---

54. Vittorio Gallese, "Mirroring a Liberated Embodied Simulation and Aesthetic Experience," in *Mirror Images: Reflections in Art and Medicine* (Verlag für moderne Kunst, 2017), 27–37, here 35.

55. Merja Polvinen and Howard Sklar, "Mimetic and Synthetic Views of Characters: How Readers Process 'People' in Fiction," *Cogent Arts & Humanities* 6.1 (2019 online), 1687257.

artificially divides the Shepherd.⁵⁶ Apocalyptic and revelatory elements are found not only in the Book of Visions but also throughout the ethical portions of the Shepherd, and similarly, there are many moral exhortations sprinkled throughout the visions. Our investigation seeks to better understand the role that the revelatory experiences in the Book of Visions plays in moral formation.

Summaries of the Chapters

According to Jörg Rüpke, "Hermas' text(s) aim(s) at the practice of fashioning the self."⁵⁷ Our rereading of the Shepherd of Hermas offers a fresh way of imagining how visionary texts participated in the moral formation of their readers. The approach known as enactive reading will be used to examine how the revelatory visions in the Book of Visions can be understood to have contributed to the phenomenon of immersive reading. The reader's immersive experience of the narrative world heightens receptivity to the ethical instruction of the Mandates and Similitudes. With the help of the integrative approaches associated with the cognitive science of religion, we aim to investigate how the process of reading apocalyptic visions like those found in the Book of Visions may have participated in the formation of its ancient readers and hearers.⁵⁸ The question of the self and the construction of identity is especially relevant for the opening Book of Visions, which has a strong moralizing tone, indicating that the work sought to make a lasting impact on its readers. We are especially interested in the ways that late Second Temple Jewish visionary and apocalyptic traditions may have influenced the narrative world that stands behind this ancient text.⁵⁹ This study proposes that the various readerly responses to the visions in the Book of Visions (viz., longing, curiosity, surprise, etc.) can be understood

---

56. Dan Batovici, "Apocalyptic and Metanoia in the *Shepherd of Hermas*," *Apocrypha* 26 (2016): 151–70.

57. Jörg Rüpke, "Two Cities and One Self: Transformations of Jerusalem and Reflexive Individuality in the Shepherd of Hermas," in *Religious Dimensions of the Self in the Second Century CE*, ed. Jörg Rüpke and Greg Woolf (Tübingen: Mohr Siebeck, 2013), 49–65, here 51.

58. Batovici, "Apocalyptic and Metanoia in the *Shepherd of Hermas*," 151–70; Aldo Tagliabue, "Learning from Allegorical Images in the *Book of Visions* of *The Shepherd of Hermas*," *Arethusa* 50 (2017): 221–55.

59. On the use of Second Temple traditions see Graydon F. Snyder (*The Shepherd of Hermas*, The Apostolic Fathers 6 [London: Thomas Nelson & Sons, 1968], 1–12), who compares the Similitudes in the Shepherd to the Parables known from *1 Enoch* (esp. 8–9); R. Joly, *Hermas. Le Pasteur*, ed., trans. R. Joly, Sources Chrétiennes 53 (Paris: Cerf, 1958, 1968), 47.

as strategically cultivating the necessary emotional predispositions for an optimal reading of the ethical material that follows in the Mandates.

Chapter 1, entitled "The Popularity of the Shepherd of Hermas," presents the manuscript evidence for the Shepherd and shows that it was a compelling work for ancient readers, especially for the readers in Oxyrhynchus in the third and fourth centuries. This narrative of a man with a slavish past was a very successful literary work, an achievement that can be measured by the fact that it was produced with a frequency that rivaled or exceeded that of the Gospels. The ancient evidence indicates that the Shepherd was identified by ancient authors as an important catechetical work, but this alone does not account for its widespread popularity. We know that the Shepherd was extremely popular in regions where there was a strong elite literary culture, particularly in third- and fourth-century Oxyrhynchus in Egypt.

This chapter begins by asking generally what the elite literary culture of third- and fourth-century Oxyrhynchus found appealing about the visionary experiences of a former slave. We review all the early manuscript evidence that has survived for the Shepherd, with special attention to the oldest manuscript that preserves the sequence of the Book of Visions and Mandates together in a bookroll format. This is the papyrus manuscript known as P.Oxy. 69.4706, which is dated to the third century. This chapter argues that the physical experience of reading the Shepherd in a bookroll instead of in a codex introduces a new set of questions that scholars of this ancient work have not previously considered. The bookroll apparatus constrains the reader's reading by ensuring that he or she moves through the Visions in a linear way. The format also prevents random access of the later parts of the Mandates and Similitudes, ensuring that the reader moves to those portions of the Shepherd only when he or she is ready to do so.

Chapter 2, "Taking a Look at Hermas," examines references to Hermas's proprioception and interoception in greater detail. This chapter continues to highlight how the modern reception of the Shepherd by scholars stands in contrast to the enormous popularity of the Shepherd among the literary elite in Egypt. Modern commentators routinely note the text's monotony and repetition, with significant disdain for the unheroic character of Hermas. This chapter analyzes the proprioceptive and interoceptive cues in the text to read the Book of Visions enactively and immersively. Painstaking descriptions about Hermas's bodily postures and movement, along with interoceptive details about his physical desire, fear, and anguish are often dismissed as mundane or unimportant by modern scholars who read for analysis and information; yet these are precisely the details needed for enactive reading. Such details are needed to understand Hermas as a compelling character with an interior consciousness. The embodiment of the seer as he moves through the narrative world (proprioception) and the emotional experiences of fear or anguish (interoception) are recognized from our own lived experience and associated strongly with the consciousness of real individuals. The first-person narration that is characteristic of apocalypses allows a reader to imaginatively enact Hermas's proprioceptive and interoceptive cues and greatly assists in a reader's ability to imagine him in a compelling way, as a person with an interior consciousness.

Chapter 3, "Sticky Thoughts that Make Presence from Absence," explores how the cognitive process known as rumination is generated and exploited in the Book of Visions in a way that further grips the readerly imagination. Rumination is the ongoing, involuntary contemplation associated with various cognitive processes: decentering, problem-solving, and the mind's ability to make presence from absence. Arresting narrative scenes, such as the opening image of Hermas helping the beautiful Rhoda as she emerges from bathing in the Tiber River, grab our attention. They also illustrate how texts can generate an experiential frame that allows for the construction and reconstruction of memories of similar affect—in this case sexual desire—either from the reader's own personal experience or remembered from other texts.[60] Here we consider the different ways the Book of Visions uses scenarios and scenes to generate the cognitive state of rumination experientially within the reader. In addition to describing the ways ancient texts sought to place narrative scenes before the eyes of the reader by using rhetorical strategies like *ekphrasis* and *enargeia*, this chapter proposes that the cognitive processes associated with rumination can shed light on two elements of Hermas's visions: (1) the excessive desire that Hermas has for

---

60. Barsalou et al., "Embodiment in Religious Knowledge," *Journal of Cognition and Culture* 5 (2005): 14–57, considers how cognitive processes work to create mundane knowledge about objects and experiences and applies these processes to the construction of religious imagining. Barsalou uses multiple theories about the representation of knowledge that consider the physical embodiment of the individual. These include simulation theories, embodied theories, and situated theories of knowledge. While Barsalou integrates all three in his model, the most relevant for our study is simulation theory in which egocentric visualizing and imagining of experiences could take place with some degree of automaticity. In the studies discussed by Barsalou, reading a text that mentions an object can stimulate areas in the brain that simulate the appropriate visualizing and phenomenal handling of that object or stimulate other bodily states, including appropriate emotional responses; Barsalou et al., "Embodiment in Religious Knowledge," 27, 28; see also Pascal Boyer, "What Are Memories For? Functions of Recall in Cognition and Culture," *Memory in Mind and Culture*, ed. P. Boyer and J. V. Wertsch (Cambridge: Cambridge University Press, 2009), 3–28. For the integration of personal experiences in the actualization of first-person prayer texts, see Harkins, *Reading with an "I" to the Heavens*.

the bathing Rhoda, and (2) the regret and longing that Hermas experiences through his recurring acts of compunction. While often connected to grief, rumination is a way of speaking about the cognitive processes associated with problem-solving and pining for romantic love. Rumination includes the cognitive processes that are associated with different varieties of recurrent thinking, 'sticky thoughts' that persist and create palpable experiences of presence for the reader.

Chapter 3 explores how the arresting scene of the bathing Rhoda that opens the Book of Visions can be said to generate 'sticky thoughts' that stay with Hermas and create the opportunity for him to be confronted by his excessive desire in the form of the heavenly Lady. This provides a model whereby readers can examine and ponder their own innermost thoughts, perhaps especially necessary for evaluating those thoughts that were not acted upon. Hermas's recurring weeping and remorse-filled actions throughout the Book of Visions resemble those of early Jewish apocalypticists whose practices can be said to have contributed to the ruminative states that led to the experiencing of visions, in which presence is made from absence.

Chapter 4, "Experiencing the Journey," uses the cognitive literary approach associated with wayfinding and foot travel. How do porous narrative worlds, such as those found in ancient apocalypses like the Book of Visions, take on the quality of 'realness'—what we might describe as the solidity of space? Narrative spaces serve as more than just a literary backdrop for events and activities that take place in the foreground. Here we propose that the otherwise mundane details about Hermas's walk in the field and his nighttime waiting just prior to his vision of the Tower provide important proprioceptive and interoceptive cues that can be read enactively. These drawn-out details are often dismissed by modern scholars as being repetitive and prolix, but they effectively slow down the pace of reading and experientially simulate the passing of time in the field for the reader. When read enactively, these literary details allow the reader to experience Hermas's fear and anticipation, thereby preparing him or her for the important vision of the Tower that follows. This chapter argues that the modern critical readings of the Book of Visions underappreciate the kinds of literary cues of proprioception and interoception that are necessary for enactive reading. These details were used by readers to achieve an immersive experience of the narrative, one that predisposed the reader to experience the preparatory emotions of longing, surprise, or anticipation that can heighten receptivity to subsequent ethical portions of the Shepherd.

Chapter 4 is divided into two sections. The first discusses how cognitive literary theory's understandings of spatiality and journeying can be understood strategically to heighten a reader's watchfulness for what will happen in the narrative. Hermas's nighttime journey and waiting in the field function purposefully to prepare the reader for the vision of the Tower in Vision 3. This strategic framing is found in other apocalypses and has not been appreciated by modern scholars who rush to interpret the Tower vision. The second part of the chapter applies cognitive literary theory's understanding of narrative worlds and spaces, including approaches known as eco-criticism and wayfinding, and applies them to Hermas's fourth vision of the beast. This chapter argues that reading the Book of Visions in a bookroll format allows for the accumulation of affect and anticipation within the reader as he or she moves from this portion of the Shepherd into the later sections of ethical instruction.

While overwhelming evidence points to the widespread popularity of the Shepherd and its fame as a catechetical work, the majority of modern scholarship on the Shepherd has been driven by discipline-specific questions that seek exegetical, theological, and historical information. Since the focus of our study is on the first book of the Shepherd of Hermas known as the Book of Visions, Chapter 5 turns to examine how the Shepherd has been understood within the broad scholarship of ancient 'apocalypse'. In contrast to the Shepherd's generally positive reception in the ancient world, modern scholars have received the work with ambivalence. This chapter examines how the literary form of visions, or what modern scholars call the apocalypse genre, contributed to the Shepherd's popularity among ancient readers. We argue that the analytical framework for categorizing the world disclosed by revelatory literature as 'thisworld' or 'otherworld' is peculiar to the modern academy and limits how we might understand a text like the Book of Visions. Historical-critical understandings of the apocalyptic seer that focus solely on historical existence fail to appreciate what made Hermas a character who was vivid and appealing to ancient readers of diverse backgrounds and historical periods.

This chapter begins with the modern form-critical understanding of 'apocalypse' and raises questions about the strong conceptual divide established between 'thisworldly' and 'otherworldly' experiences. In contrast to the stark divide between the spaces and experiences that perpetuates an analytical bifurcation of reality, our discussion presumes that the worldview found in ancient apocalypses is porous and 'spirit-infused'.[61] As a 'possible world', ancient apocalypses understand 'thisworld' and the 'otherworld' to be experientially fluid, intertwined, and overlapping. Apocalypses provide

---

61. 'Spirit-infused' is the term used by Paul Christopher Johnson in his introduction to *Spirited Things: The World of 'Possession' in Afro-Atlantic Religions* (Chicago: University of Chicago Press, 2014), 3.

readers with access to the kinds of embodied experiences that allow them to infer the presence of an interior consciousness and to gather information about the possible world of the seer to offer readers and hearers a vivid immersive experience. Ancient texts like P.Oxy. 1.5 preserve possible traces of one possible experiential effect of enactive reading: a later reader/hearer whose immersion in the narrative world may have given them access to further information.

The book concludes by returning to the opening discussion of the bookroll as a format that limits and constrains the reader's experience of the narrative. The Book of Visions cultivate emotional predispositions for introspection and self-examination that accumulate as Hermas's interior consciousness becomes disclosed more and more to the reader/hearer. Watchfulness increases as the reader/hearer imagines Hermas along his foot journey through the narrative world of the Book of Visions. These effects of enactive reading contribute to the moral formation of the reader by drawing the reader immersively into Hermas's narrative world and cultivating the emotional states that generate the necessary emotions and predispositions for reading the subsequent sections known as the Mandates and the Similitudes, namely a watchfulness, curiosity, and a heightened state of anticipation.

Chapter One

The Popularity of the Shepherd of Hermas in the Ancient World

The ancient work known as the Shepherd of Hermas stands out among the oldest Christian works from a major urban center.[1] It consists of five visions, twelve mandates, and ten similitudes, all of which amount to a lengthy and complex text that is surely the result of a long process of growth.[2] This chapter presents the manuscript evidence for the Shepherd and considers how the physical experience of reading the Book of Visions can be said to contribute to the moral formation of readers of the third and fourth century, the time period for which there is ample evidence for the production and copying of the Shepherd in North Africa. As this chapter shows, there is early dating for the copying of the Visions in a bookroll, a format that strategically directs how a text would have been experienced by flesh-and-blood readers.[3] Unlike a codex, the bookroll naturally constrains the pace of reading and prevents

---

1. For a presentation of the traditional arguments for dating the Shepherd, see Maier, *The Social Setting of the Ministry as Reflected in the Writings of Hermas, Clement and Ignatius*, 55–86; A. Gregory, "Disturbing Trajectories: *1 Clement*, the *Shepherd of Hermas* and the Development of Early Roman Christianity," 150–3.

2. The three sections of the Shepherd of Hermas differ markedly in vocabulary and tone; see Grundeken and Verheyden, "The Spirit Before the Letter," 23–56. Some scholars have concluded from these literary features that the work is the product of multiple authors. For this view, see Stanislas Giet, *Hermas et les pasteurs. Les trois auteurs du Pasteur d'Hermas* (Paris: Presses universitaires de France, 1963); W. Coleborne, "The Shepherd of Hermas: A Case for Multiple Authorship and Some Implications," *StPatr* 10 (1970): 65–70. The majority of scholars take the position that the Shepherd is the product of a single author with complex layers of redaction, Anton Hilhorst, "Hermas," *RAC* 14 (1988): 682–701; Maier, *The Social Setting of the Ministry as Reflected in the Writings of Hermas, Clement and Ignatius*, 56; Philippe Henne, O.P., *L'unité du Pasteur d'Hermas*, Cahiers de la Revue Biblique (Paris: Gabalda, 1992); Osiek, *The Shepherd of Hermas*, 13–15; Jörg Rüpke, "Apokalyptische Salzberge: Zum sozialen Ort und zur literarischen Strategie des 'Hirten des Hermas'," *Archiv für Religionsgeschichte* 1 (1999): 148–60; Ehrman, *Apostolic Fathers*, vol. 2 (Ehrman, LCL 25), 166.

3. Important studies on the topic of the formats used for this text are: Choat and Yuen–Collingridge, "The Egyptian *Hermas*: The *Shepherd* in Egypt before Constantine," in *Early Christian Manuscripts: Examples of Applied Method and Approach*, ed. Thomas J. Kraus and Tobias Nicklas, Texts and Editions for New Testament Study 5 (Leiden: Brill, 2010), 191–212; Thomas A. Wayment, *The Text of the New Testament Apocrypha (100–400 CE)* (London: Bloomsbury, 2013), 81–169, with select images of the mss on 286–390.

one from advancing too quickly to topics for which a reader may be unprepared. In this way, reading from a scroll can be said to replicate the effects of the journeying by foot, which structures the Book of Visions.

The second part of this chapter establishes why a work that centers on the visionary experiences of an ordinary man with a servile past would have been appealing and engaging to the readers in third and fourth century Egypt, where there is an abundance of evidence of the work's popularity. Here, our focus is on the question, what are the literary qualities that made this catechetical text so popular for this ancient North African population? Malcolm Choat's and Rachel Yuen-Collingridge's recent discussion of the manuscript evidence for the Shepherd highlights its enormous success as a popular teaching text.[4] Didymus the Blind refers to the work as ὁ βίβλος τῆς κατηχήσεως τῇ Ποιμένι, and Eusebius identifies it as an "indispensable" text for those who need "elementary instruction."[5]

The early dating of the text has implicated this work in several arguments about the early social history of Christianity, with many scholars taking the view that Hermas was a historical figure.[6] Even so, a text's historicity does not account for its popularity among ancient readers. The material evidence that will be reviewed in this chapter shows that the Shepherd was a popular catechetical work, particularly in North Africa from the second to the fourth centuries CE, a region for which there is evidence of a Jewish presence.[7] This chapter establishes some reasons for why the literary features of the Book of Visions would have been appealing, especially for its third and fourth century Egyptian audience.

Moving through the Manuscripts of the Shepherd

Our examination focuses on the first of three sections of the Shepherd, known as the Book of Visions. These visions are thought to constitute the

---

4. Choat and Yuen-Collingridge, "The Egyptian *Hermas*," 201–4.
5. Choat and Yuen-Collingridge, "The Egyptian *Hermas*," 201–204, give the relevant passage from Eusebius, *Hist. eccl.* 3.3 as "Others, however, have judged it indispensable, especially to those in need of elementary instruction (ὑφ' ἑτέρων δὲ ἀναγκαιότατον οἷς μάλιστα δεῖ στοιχειώσεος εἰσαγωγικῆς, κέκριται)," trans. G.A. Williamson, revised by A. Louth (Harmondworth: Penguin Books, 1989), 66.
6. Studies of the social history behind the text: Leutzsch, *Die Wahrnehmung sozialer Wirklichkeit im "Hirten des Hermas"*; Osiek, "The Social Function of Female Imagery in Second Century Prophecy," 55–74 Carolyn Osiek, "The Oral World of Early Christianity in Rome: The Case of Hermas," 151–72; Maier, *The Social Setting of the Ministry as Reflected in the Writings of Hermas, Clement and Ignatius*, 1–28.
7. The commentary by Snyder (*The Shepherd of Hermas*) is especially attentive to the parallels and references to Jewish writings in the Shepherd.

oldest portion of the work.⁸ According to the numbering system introduced by Molly Whittaker in 1956, now standard in most scholarly editions of the Shepherd, the three sections of the work correspond to the following chapter divisions: 1.1–25.7 (Book of Visions), 26.1–49.5 (Mandates), and 51.1–114.4 (Similitudes).⁹ Whittaker's numbering also allows one to see readily that the Visions and the Mandates together are approximately equal in length to the Similitudes. The disadvantage of Whitaker's system is that it conceals which of the major sections any given passage is in (viz., Vis., Mand., or Sim.). It also unfortunately projects an illusory model of the final form of the Shepherd by presuming that the form of the work as we encounter it today was also its form in antiquity. In other words, Whittaker's numbering system gives a false impression of the stability of ancient texts.

The manuscript evidence indicates the Shepherd's popularity. It is one of the best attested Christian texts from antiquity. The work's popularity arguably exceeded that of the writings that would later become the canonical Gospels. For example, nearly twenty manuscripts of the Shepherd have been identified prior to the year 400 CE, with as many as eleven papyrus copies from Egypt in the years prior to Constantine.¹⁰ By contrast, we have only a single copy of the Gospel of Mark and six of Luke from the period up to the time of Constantine.¹¹ Many early Christians regarded the Shepherd as authoritative and cited it in their own writings, but its scriptural status was controversial. Eusebius tells us that the Shepherd was used in

---

8. Osiek, *The Shepherd of Hermas*, 10.
9. Whittaker, *Die Apostolischen Väter. 1 Der Hirt des Hermas*.
10. Wayment (*The Text of the New Testament Apocrypha [100–400 CE]*, 81–169) discusses the content and physical features of eighteen manuscripts while Choat and Yuen-Collingridge discuss the eleven manuscripts that have been dated prior to Constantine and the manuscripts of the Shepherd in Egypt after the time of Constantine (Table 3), "The Egyptian *Hermas*," 191–212, esp. Table I on 194–5, and Table 3 on 203–4; also Giovanni B. Bazzana, "'You Will Write Two Booklets and Send One to Clement and One to Grapte': Formal Features, Circulation, and Social Function of Ancient Apocalyptic Literature," in *Scribal Practices and Social Structures among Jesus Adherents: Essays in Honour of John S. Kloppenborg*, ed. William Arnal, BETL 285 (Leuven: Peeters, 2016), 43–70, esp. 52–9. See the most recent work by Paolo Cecconi, "1200 Years of Materialities and Editions of a Forbidden Text," in *Antike Texte und ihre Materialität: Ancient Texts and Their Materiality: Presence, Media Semantics, and Literary Reflection in Daily Life. Alltägliche Präsenz mediale Semantik, literarische Reflexion*, ed. Cornelia Ritter-Schmalz and Raphael Schwitter, Materiale Textkulturen 27 (Berlin: De Gruyter, 2019), 309–30.
11. Choat and Yuen-Collingridge, "The Egyptian *Hermas*," 196; they also note the fourteen copies of Matthew and seventeen copies of John from this time period. See Dan Batovici, "A New Hermas Papyrus Fragment in Paris," 20–36.

a popular manner (δεδημοσιευμένον).[12] According to the Muratorian Fragment, this popular catechetical work may be read but not in public worship.[13] The far-reaching influence of the Shepherd during the first few centuries CE is attested in part by the many languages in which it was copied: Latin, Ethiopic, Coptic, Middle Persian, and Georgian.[14] As many as twenty-eight Latin manuscripts of the Shepherd extend into the medieval period.[15]

An important early witness to the Shepherd has been preserved in the fourth century pandect known as Codex Sinaiticus. This is the oldest Greek manuscript of the entire Christian Scriptures, discovered in 1844 at St. Catherine's Monastery on the Sinai Peninsula.[16] Dated paleographically to the fourth century, this codex ends with the Shepherd as its final book. It is preceded by the books of the Septuagint, the early Christian books that would later become known as the New Testament, and the Epistle of Barnabas.[17] The manuscript clearly preserves the Book of Visions and the first portion of the Mandates, stopping at Mand. 4.3.1 (31.1), the precise place where the possibility of post-baptismal repentance is discussed.[18] According to Dan Batovici, fragments of two leaves of Codex Sinaiticus that contain text from

12. Eusebius, *Hist. eccl.* 3.3; Choat and Yuen-Collingridge, "The Egyptian *Hermas*," 201–202. Notice that Williamsons's translation, cited by Choat and Yuen-Collingridge, references "public worship" but (δεδημοσιευμένον) is not necessarily a statement about liturgical use.

13. The relevant section of the Muratorian Fragment is translated by Bruce Metzger: "But Hermas wrote the Shepherd very recently, in our times, in the city of Rome, while bishop Pius, his brother, was occupying the [episcopal] chair of the church of the city of Rome. And therefore it ought indeed to be read; but it cannot be read publicly to the people in the church either among the prophets, whose number is complete, or among the apostles, for it is after [their] time," see the discussion in Dan Batovici, "The *Shepherd of Hermas* in Recent Scholarship on the Canon: A Review Article," *ASE* 34 (2017): 89–105, here 98.

14. Batovici, "The *Shepherd of Hermas* in Recent Scholarship on the Canon," 91.

15. I am grateful to Dan Batovici for sharing an advance manuscript of his forthcoming study of the texts of the Shepherd. Readers are urged to consult D. Batovici, *The Shepherd of Hermas in Late Antiquity* (Piscataway, NJ: Gorgias Press, forthcoming); also his earlier discussions of the later Greek manuscripts of the *Shepherd*, e.g., Papyrus Pragensis 1 + Papyrus Weill I 96 (4th/5th c.) see Dan Batovici, "A New Hermas Papyrus Fragment in Paris," in *Archiv für Papyrusforschung* 62 (2016): 20–36. Also helpful is Cecconi, "1200 Years of Materialities and Editions of a Forbidden Text," 320–3; Christian Tornau and Paolo Cecconi, ed., *The Shepherd of Hermas in Latin: Critical Edition of the Oldest Translation Vulgata* (Berlin: De Gruyter, 2014), 10–19.

16. David C. Parker, *Codex Sinaiticus: The Story of the World's Oldest Bible* (London: British Library, 2010).

17. Batovici, "Textual Revisions of the *Shepherd of Hermas* in Codex Sinaiticus," 443, esp. 469–70.

18. Mand. 4.3.2 (31.2) begins by affirming the view found in Heb. 6.4–6 which

Similitudes 6, 7, and 9 were identified in 1975 but omitted from many critical discussions of the Codex, and thus of the Shepherd, that are widely available today.[19] Apart from the important witness of the fourth century Codex Sinaiticus, none of the oldest manuscripts of the Shepherd (dating from 100 to 400 CE) contain all three sections (Visions, Mandates, Similitudes), and few have more than one section. As Table 1 shows, most of the early copies of the Shepherd are in a codex format. This likely points to the practice of copying individual sections of the work from smaller booklets. The large size of the work may have precluded its easy transmission in a single bookroll. Issues of practical handling would have made papyrus bookrolls particularly inadequate for the preservation of large texts like the Shepherd.[20]

The Book of Visions is attested in the following manuscripts: P.Bodmer 38 (codex); P.Oxy. 69.4705 (bookroll); P.Oxy. 69.4706 (bookroll). Of these, only P.Oxy. 69.4706 has the distinction of preserving more than one section of the Shepherd. Here, as in Codex Sinaiticus, the Book of Visions and the Mandates are clearly preserved together. Table 1 provides the manuscript evidence for the various sections of the Shepherd up to 400 CE in chronological order.[21]

---

presumes that one is expected not to sin after having been baptized; it continues, however, to discusses the possibility of post-baptismal repentance for those who have lapsed.

19. Dan Batovici, "Textual Revisions of the *Shepherd of Hermas* in Codex Sinaiticus," *ZAC* 18 (2014): 443–70, here 444. He discusses the manuscript fragments and the layers of corrections to these passages of the Shepherd that were discovered in 1975. Among the modern editions that omit discussion of these fragments: Ulrich H. J. Körtner and Martin Leutzsch (eds.), *Papiasfragmente: Hirt des Hermas*, Schriften des Urchristentums 3 (Darmstadt: Wissenschaftliche Buchgesellschaft, 1998), 105–510; *Apostolic Fathers*, vol. 2 (Ehrman, LCL 25); Michael W. Holmes, *The Apostolic Fathers: Greek Texts and English Translations*, 3rd ed. (Grand Rapids: Baker Academic, 2007), 442–685.

20. Menahem Haran, "Book-Scrolls at the Beginning of the Second Temple Period: The Transition from Papyrus to Skins," *HUCA* 54 (1983): 111–22. Elsewhere, Haran argues that the move to vellum assisted in copying large scrolls, but even so there were limits to the size of the scroll based on what would permit efficient handling; Menahem Haran, "The Size of Books in the Bible and the Division of the Pentateuch and the Deuteronomistic Work," *Tarbiz* 53 (1984): 329–52 (in Hebrew).

21. Table 1 is based on the data in Wayment, *The Text of the New Testament Apocrypha (100–400 CE)*; Choat and Yuen-Collingridge, "The Egyptian *Hermas*," and Bazzana, "'You Will Write Two Booklets and Send One to Clement and One to Grapte'," 52–59; Paolo Cecconi, "1200 Years of Materialities and Editions of a Forbidden Text," 314–22, although we have not included the manuscripts of quotations from the Shepherd, e.g., P.Oxy. 5; P.Oxy. 404; P.Mich. 6427.

Table 1. *Manuscript Evidence for the Shepherd up to 400 CE*

Manuscript Name and Provenance	Date, Format	Book of Visions	Mandates	Similitudes
P.Mich. 2/2 130	II c., bookroll		Mand. 2, 3	
P.Oxy. 50.3528	II/III c., codex			Sim. 9
P.Oxy. 69.4706, 27 frgs.	II/III c. bookroll	Vis. 3, 4	Mand. 2, 4, 5, 6, 7, 8, 9, 10	
P.Oxy. 69.4705	III c. reused bookroll	Vis. 1		
P.Oxy. 69.4707	III c. codex			Sim. 6 (end), 6 (beginning)
P. Mich. 2/2 129 (inv. 917) (Theadelphia/ Bata-el-Hatit)	III c., codex			Sim. 2, 3, 4, 5, 6, 7, 8, 9
P.Oxy. 15.1828	III c., codex (vellum)			Sim. 6 (recto and continued on the verso)
P.Oxy. 50.3527	III c., codex			Sim. 8
P.Iand 1 4 (Hermopolis)*	III/IV c., codex		Mand. 11, 12	
P.Berl. 5513/ BKT 6.2.1 (Fayyum)	III c. bookroll			Sim. 2, 4
P.Oxy. 3.404/ Bodleian Ms	III/IV c. codex			Sim. 10
Codex Sinaiticus	IV c. codex, parchment	Vis. 1, 2, 3, 4, 5	Mand. 1, 2, 3, 4	Sim. 7, 8, 9
P.Oxy. 50.3526 *same codex as P.Oxy. 9.1172	IV c., codex		Mand. 5–6 on P.Oxy. 50.3526	Sim. 2 on P.Oxy. 9.1172
P.Oxy. 15.1783/ ms gen 1026/22	IV c., mini-codex		Mand. 9	
P.Oxy. 9.1172/ British Library 2067; *same codex as P.Oxy. 50.3526	IV c., codex			Sim. 1
P.Berl. 13272 (Hermopolis)	IV c., codex			Sim. 5
P.Oxy. 13.1599/ British Library Pap 2467	IV c., codex			Sim. 8
P. Bodmer 38 (Dishna)	IV/V c., codex	Vis. 1, 2, 3		
P.Hamburg 24/ P.Iand. inv.45 (Egypt)	IV/V c., codex			Sim. 4, 5

1. *The Popularity of the Shepherd of Hermas in the Ancient World*   35

Most of the early manuscripts for the Shepherd is fragmentary and overwhelmingly preserves smaller passages in codex format. Most also come from Egypt, whose arid climate allowed the preservation of these texts.[22] According to the data in Table 1, the most abundant literary type from these centuries are the twelve copies of the Similitudes, all of which were preserved in a codex format except for one bookroll from Fayyum known as P.Berl. 5513/BKT. Because the larger literary context of these manuscripts is lost and only small parts of the Similitudes have survived, it is difficult to say if each manuscript can be said to represent the entire corpus of ten parables.[23] The Mandates are the next best attested section of the Shepherd, with four manuscripts and two additional manuscripts that show the Mandates sequenced after the Book of Visions, P.Oxy. 69.4706, and Codex Sinaiticus.

The section known as the Book of Visions is by far the rarest literary section of the Shepherd, with only two copies (P.Oxy. 69.4705; P.Bodmer 38) in addition to P.Oxy. 69.4706 and Codex Sinaiticus. The collection of the three visions found in P.Bodmer 38 has been reconstructed at the front of a codex that also contained a collection of other visions and poems copied in a different hand.[24] There is enough space to allow for the reconstruction of the fourth vision in this codex which has been dated to the late fourth, early fifth century.[25] The two early copies of the Book of Visions are copied on scrolls dated to the late second or early third centuries (P.Oxy. 69.4706 and P.Oxy. 69.4705). The writing of the first vision (Vis. 1.1.8–9 [1.8–9]) in P.Oxy. 69.4705 is found on the recto of a scroll whose verso is dated to the second century. Because it is a reused scroll, P.Oxy. 69.4705 is considered to be a copy for private use.[26]

---

22. Choat and Yuen-Collingridge, "The Egyptian *Hermas*," 193–94.

23. For example, P.Oxy. 50.3528; P.Oxy. 69.4707; P.Oxy. 15.1828; P.Oxy. 50.3527; P.Berl. 5513/BKT 6.2.1; P.Oxy. 3.404; P.Oxy. 9.1172; P.Berl. 13272; P. Oxy. 13.1599; P. Hamburg 24/ P.Iand. 45.

24. Antonio Carlini, with the collaboration of Luigi Giacconi, *Papyrus Bodmer XXXVIII. Erma: Il Pastore (Ia–IIIa visione). Edito con introduzione e commentario critico. Appendice: Nouvelle description du Codex des Visions par Rodolphe Kasser, avec la collaboration de Guglielmo Cavallo et Joseph van Haelst*, Fondation Martin Bodmer Cologny-Genève (Munich: Saur, 1991). The other contents of the codex are the *Vision of Dorotheus* (P. Bodmer 29) and other poems associated with biblical figures that were published separately by André Hurst and Jean Rudhardt, *Papyri Bodmer XXX–XXXVII. "Codex des Visions" Poèmes divers. Edités avec une introduction générale des traductions et des notes* (Munich: Saur, 1999).

25. The appendix found in Carlini's critical edition *Papyrus Bodmer XXXVIII*, prepared by Rodolphe Kasser, reverses an earlier ordering of the contents which had placed the visions of Dorotheus first and the visions of Hermas at the end of the codex. P.Bodmer 38 clearly began with Hermas's visions, with some space for the fourth vision.

26. Cecconi, "1200 Years of Materialities and Editions of a Forbidden Text,"

The manuscript known as P.Oxy. 69.4706 consists of 27 fragments and gives evidence of the early sequencing of the Book of Visions prior to the Mandates in a single bookroll.[27] This Greek papyrus is copied in a semi-cursive hand and contains fragments of the third and fourth vision (Vis. 3.4.3 [12.3], 3.6.6 [14.6], 3.9.7 [17.7], 3.13.4–4.1.1 [21.4–22.1], 4.1.7–9 [22.7–9]) and fragments of several Mandates (Mand. 2.4–5 [27.4–5], 4.1.1.7–9 [29.7–9], 4.3–4 [31–32], 5.1.6–7 [33.6–7], 6.1.3–5 [35.3–5], 7.5 [37.5], 8.6 [38.6], 9.7–8 [39.7–8], 10.1.1 [40.1]); we can be reasonably certain that this scroll contained a significant portion of both literary sections.[28] The other important manuscript of the Book of Visions is P.Bodmer 38, which is dated to the second half of the fourth to the beginning of the fifth century.[29] The Bodmer Papyrus 38 codex contains significant sections of the first three visions of the Book of Visions, possibly the fourth vision as well. The fourth-century Codex Sinaiticus also preserves portions from both the Book of Visions and the Mandates (Vis. 1.1.1–Mand. 4.3.6 [1.1–31.6]), in addition to some fragments from the Similitudes.[30]

Another sizable manuscript that is often referenced in discussions of the Visions is the Michigan Papyrus 129 (P.Mich. 129).[31] The thirty-one codex leaves of P.Mich. 129 are early, dating to the third century. Based on manuscripts that section the Shepherd into smaller units, several scholars are persuaded that a collection of four visions was transmitted independently as

319; Bazzana ("'You Will Write Two Booklets and Send One to Clement and One to Grapte',") writes that this manuscript was "written on the back of a reemployed roll … a clear indicator of the 'private' nature of this papyrus" (55). Bazzana goes on to note that this script is fuller and reflects punctuation and other editorial markings that indicate literary engagement with the text. Campbell Bonner, "A New Fragment of the Shepherd of Hermas (Michigan Papyrus 44–H)," *HTR* 20 (1927): 105–116.

27. Bazzana, "'You Will Write Two Booklets and Send One to Clement and One to Grapte'," 52; Choat and Yuen-Collingridge, "The Egyptian *Hermas*," 191–212.

28. M. Depauw and T. Gheldof, "Trismegistos. An Interdisciplinary Platform for Ancient World Texts and Related Information," in *Theory and Practice of Digital Libraries—TPDL 2013 Selected Workshops*, ed. L Bolikowski, V. Casarosa, P. Goodale, N. Houssos, P. Manghi, J. Schirrwagen, *Communications in Computer and Information Science* 416 (Cham: Springer, 2014), 40–52.

29. For the *editio princeps*, see A. Carlini, L. Giaccone, R. Kasser, G. Cavallo, and J. van Haelst, *Erma; edito con introduzione e commentario critic da Antonio Carlini, Papyrus Bodmer 38* (Cologny-Genève, 1991).

30. Batovici, "Textual Revisions of the *Shepherd of Hermas* in Codex Sinaiticus," 443; see too Paolo Cecconi, "The Codex Sinaiticus and Hermas: The Ways of a Crossed Textual Transmission," *ZAC* 22 (2018): 278–95.

31. Bazzana, "'You Will Write Two Booklets and Send One to Clement and One to Grapte'," 55.

an 'apocalypse' and that a collection of the fifth vision and Mandates circulated as a 'catechetical work'. According to Giovanni Bazzana:

> Hermas's work circulated—besides its full threefold form—in two other "editions", one more "catechetical" (comprising only Visions 5 to the end, as in PMich 129) and one more "apocalyptic" (comprising Visions 1–4, as in the fourth-century PBodmer 38, the so-called "codex of visions"), one could have an additional piece of explanation for the varied forms of transmission of the *Shepherd*.[32]

A hypothetical text of the fifth vision and the Mandates had been reconstructed by Campbell Bonner at the beginning of the codex known as P.Mich. 129, largely based on the pagination found in the codex.[33] Several scholars have embraced the possibility that this is an example of a "catechetical" edition or format of the text.[34] Some of the appeal of this proposal comes from a perception of the different literary styles found throughout the various sections of the Shepherd—features that have led some scholars to propose that the different sections of the work were composed by multiple authors.[35] The codex known as P.Mich. 129 is thought to offer concrete

---

32. Bazzana, "'You Will Write Two Booklets and Send One to Clement and One to Grapte'," 58–9.
33. Campbell Bonner, *A Papyrus Codex of the Shepherd of Hermas (Similitudes 2–9) with a Fragment of the Mandates*, University of Michigan Studies Humanistic Series 22 (Ann Arbor: University of Michigan, 1934), 8–11; Cecconi writes that "it probably contained the whole *Revelation of the Shepherd*," by which he means all of the material from the fifth vision onward, Cecconi, "1200 Years of Materialities and Editions of Forbidden Text," 318.
34. Bazzana ("'You Will Write Two Booklets and Send One to Clement and One to Grapte'," 58 n. 76) refers to the discussion in A. Carlini, "I nuovi papyri di Ossirinco e il testo del Pastore di Erma," in *Studi offerti ad Alessandro Perutelli*, ed. P. Arduini (Rome: Aracne, 2008), 207–216; and the "cautious support" given by Choat and Yuen-Collingridge, "The Egyptian *Hermas*," 201. Other scholars who have proceeded from Bonner's understanding of P.Mich 129 include: Joly, *Hermas. Le Pasteur*, 15; Snyder, *The Shepherd of Hermas*, 4; A. Carlini, "La tradizione testuale del Pastore di Erma e I nuovi papyri," in *Le strade del testo*, ed. G. Cavallo (Lecce: Adriatica Editrice, 1987), 23–43, esp. 32–4; J. J. Ayán Calvo, *Hermas: El Pastor*, Fuentes Patrísticas 6 (Madrid: Ciudad Nueva, 1995), 23–24; Osiek, *The Shepherd of Hermas*, 3; Leutzsch, *Die Wahrnehmung sozialer Wirklichkeit im "Hirten des Hermas"*, 123; Henne, *L'Unité du Pasteur d'Hermas: Tradition et redaction* (Paris: Gabalda, 1992). See the important critique of this view by Dan Batovici, "Two Notes on the Papyri of the *Shepherd of Hermas*," *Archiv für Papyrusforschung* 62 (2016): 384–95; Dan Batovici, *The Shepherd of Hermas in Late Antiquity*, 135.
35. The view of multiple authorship is a minority view that was put forward by Giet, *Hermas et les pasteurs. Les trois auteurs du Pasteur d'Hermas*; Coleborne, "The Shepherd of Hermas: A Case for Multiple Authorship and Some Implications," 65–70; L.W. Barnard, "The Shepherd of Hermas in Recent Study," *Heythrop Journal* 9 (1968):

support for the popular scholarly view that the first four visions of the Book of Visions had a compositional history that was independent from the fifth vision, which appears to serve as a transition and introduction to the Mandates and the Similitudes.[36] Most recently, Paolo Cecconi has argued that there were "two different originally autonomous works," which he calls the *Revelation of the Church*, a work that contained the first four visions, and the *Revelation of the Shepherd*, which contained the remainder of the work.[37] It is important to note that, even though P.Mich. 129 has been reconstructed to support these literary observations, no material evidence has survived which supports this hypothesis that a smaller collection of only the fifth vision circulated with the Mandates.[38] The reconstruction of P.Mich. 129 as a smaller work beginning with the fifth vision overdetermines the text of the Shepherd based on what we know of later editions and manipulates the text based on a cut-and-paste model familiar from modern word processing.[39] The process of hand-copying differs considerably from the printing-press reproduction of a text; many variants and revisions were introduced into manuscript copies at the time of copying, resulting in a high degree of textual pluriformity.[40] The transmission process for the individual sections of the Shepherd may have resulted in variants that create the effect of multiple

29–36, esp. 31–2. Barnard alters Giet's proposal of three authors to two authors (1) Vis. 1–4 and (2) Vis. 5 to the end (32–33).

36. For example, Stanislas Giet (*Hermas et les pasteurs*) proposed that the fifth vision, Mandates, and the material through Sim. 8 and 10 (except for Sim. 9) were authored by an anonymous hand. Barnard critiques Giet's distinctions as being motivated by later doctrinal concerns, "The Shepherd of Hermas in Recent Study," 32.

37. Cecconi, "1200 Years of Materialities and Editions of a Forbidden Text," 310.

38. See Batovici on P.Mich. 129 in "Two Notes on the Papyri of the Shepherd of Hermas," 384–95; Batovici, *The Shepherd in Late Antiquity*, 135.

39. A similar overdetermination of ancient manuscripts based on our modern assumptions of the stability of the literary text also is true for the ancient Dead Sea Scrolls and the reconstruction of the Qumran Hodayot, a.k.a., the Thanksgiving Hymns from Caves 1 and 4. See the discussion of the implausibility of the reconstruction of 4Q428 in Angela Kim Harkins, "Another Look at the Cave 1 Hodayot: Was CH I Materially Part of the Scroll 1QHodayot^a? *DSD* 25 (2018): 185–216.

40. George Brooke's comments on the copying and transmission process of the Hebrew Bible also highlight models that pertain to this discussion of the Shepherd ("The Qumran Scrolls and the Demise of the Distinction between Higher and Lower Criticism," in *New Directions in Qumran Studies: Proceedings of the Bristol Colloquium on the Dead Sea Scrolls, 8–10 September 2003*, ed. J. G. Campbell, W. J. Lyons, and L. K. Pietersen [London: T & T Clark International, 2005], 26–42). Brooke writes: "From a canonical perspective it is tempting to view scribes solely as copyists, as was largely the case in relation to the Hebrew Bible from late antiquity onwards. However, in the Second Temple period, scribes were also creative participants in the transmission process and their activity needs analysis in ways which take into account its complete

authorship. Because the pagination upon which the reconstruction depends was not written in the hand of the copyist, it is extremely difficult to know the original literary context of codex P.Mich. 129.[41] The manuscript itself contains only a few Similitudes and reflects a sectioning of the text that was common and which we might expect from a copying process—one that was not unlike the *pecia* method used for copying texts in the medieval universities.

A significant amount of the manuscript evidence for the Shepherd has been identified among the findings at Oxyrhynchus in what was used as a rubbish heap. The manuscripts found there were discarded. We might imagine these codices of the Shepherd in a strictly functional way, existing primarily for the sake of mass producing the text. The Shepherd of Hermas is a long work, far exceeding the length of any single book that later became a part of the NT. The proliferation of the codex copies of the various sections of the Shepherd during the fourth century reflect the work's enormous popularity. The codex facilitated the task of copying by enabling the work to be divided into manageable units like the Book of Visions, the Mandates, and the Similitudes, which could be borrowed and copied more efficiently and more easily than a bookroll. It seems likely that practical considerations such as the size of the Shepherd led to its being copied in codex format during the third century. Over time these papyrus codices became unusable from handling, and they were gathered and discarded alongside other ephemeral writings like correspondences. The many codices of the Shepherd point to the rapid reproduction of the work, especially during the third and fourth centuries, but their presence in a rubbish heap indicates that their usefulness had been exhausted.[42] In this way, the Oxyrhynchus findings may be compared to a modern-day recycling station for discarded newspapers. Many of these recycled newspapers may indicate the popularity of a particular newspaper for a certain region, but we cannot conclude on the basis of such a finding that newsprint is the only medium or even the primary format in which the people of that area accessed the news. The codex format can facilitate scribal production and so serve a practical purpose that

---

character. The analytical approaches of the so called 'higher critics' are required for this undertaking" (41).

41. Choat and Yuen-Collingridge, "The Egyptian *Hermas*," 208.

42. That the Oxyrhynchus Papyri were discarded because they were no longer usable is a theory put forward by Don C. Barker, "Codex, Rolls, and Libraries in Oxyrhynchus," *Tyndale Bulletin* 57 (2006): 131–48, here 140 n. 33; see too AnneMarie Luijendijk ("Sacred Scriptures as Trash: Biblical Papyri from Oxyrhynchus," *Vigiliae Christianae* 64 [2010]: 217–43), where she offers her hypothesis that there was a desacralization ritual of tearing up manuscripts that were no longer needed before disposal (249).

can be exhausted; but it may not necessarily have been the format of the finished composition. Early editions of the Shepherd in the bookroll format from the early second and third century serve no practical role in the copying process but such format successfully achieves the other desirable readerly effect of constraining the pace of reading.

The oldest manuscripts of the Book of Visions testify to a diversity of formats for this text. Ancient witnesses, like P.Oxy. 69.4706 and the fourth century pandect known as Codex Sinaiticus, clearly connect the Book of Visions with the Mandates in a material way. It is clear that the Shepherd was copied in both codices and bookrolls.[43] While scholars hold the view that the Shepherd as we know it today is the product of a lengthy literary development, P.Oxy. 69.4706 provides early evidence that the Book of Visions was copied on a bookroll along with the section known as the Mandates. Given the length of the entire Shepherd text, it is reasonable to imagine that the text was divided strategically into smaller booklets at literary seams for practical reasons, in order to ease the copying process. The oldest copy of both the Visions and the Mandates, P.Oxy. 69.4706, is preserved in a bookroll. The text known as P.Oxy. 69.4705 (Vis. 1) and P.Berl. 5513/ BKT (Sim. 2, 4) are also bookrolls. The two Oxyrhynchus copies of the Shepherd were made on bookrolls that had been used previously and had been discarded in the rubbish heap. Nevertheless, that these early copies of the Shepherd were made on bookrolls did not serve the practical purpose of copying; in fact, scrolls often needed to be disassembled for copying. No practical advantage would have been gained by copying the Shepherd on a bookroll; the bookroll simply was the traditional format for literary works.

Although a rare format for ancient copies of the Shepherd, the bookroll was "an icon of elitism" and a mark of prestigious writing.[44] The number of bookrolls of non-Christian texts has been cataloged: approximately 1009 of the 1218 manuscripts of classical Greek literary texts, amounting to roughly 83%, were copied on bookrolls during the third century.[45] By contrast, of

---

43. Dieter Lührmann makes the point that none of the books that later became part of the New Testament survived in the bookroll format. Dieter Lührmann, *Die Apokryph gewordenen Evangelien: Studien zu neuen Texten und zu neuen Fragen,* NovTSup 112 (Leiden: Brill, 2004).

44. Johnson, *Readers and Reading Culture,* 26.

45. AnneMarie Luijendijk, "Reading the *Gospel of Thomas* in the Third Century: Three Oxyrhynchus Papyri and Origen's Homilies," in *Reading New Testament Papyri in Context/ Lire les papyrus du Nouveau Testament dans leur contexte,* ed. Claire Clivaz and Jean Zumstein, in collaboration with Jenny Read-Heimerdinger and Julie Paik, BETL 242 (Leuven: Peeters, 2011), 241–67, here 248. These data have also been discussed by Harry Gamble, who has argued well that in the specific case of the Pauline corpus, the letters were well-suited to the codex format, which allowed them to

182 third-century Christian texts, 40 (or 22%) were copied on bookrolls and 142 (78%) were copied in codices.[46] A bookroll often did not preserve the details that would assist in the reading and pronunciation of the text (e.g., accents, breathing marks), thus the proper proclamation of the text depended on the competency of a skilled lector.[47] Scholars often focus on how the formatting of a text might shed light on its canonicity or whether it was used publicly or privately,[48] but one important aspect of the experience of using a bookroll that we wish to highlight is how the reader must move through the text in a linear way, from beginning to end. A reader of a scroll is not able to randomly locate specific places in the text easily because a bookroll has no pagination. The manuscript evidence for the Shepherd shows that there was an early practice of copying the Book of Visions and the Mandates in a bookroll format. Because there are no early copies of the Shepherd that contain the Book of Visions, Mandates, and the Similitudes—all three together—this study will not engage the Similitudes.

---

be randomly accessed; see Harry Y. Gamble, *Books and Readers in the Early Church: A History of Early Christian Texts* (New Haven: Yale University, 1995), 42–81, esp. 63–6. According to Gamble's thesis, the rise in Paul's authority eventually contributed to the elevation of the codex format from an ephemeral status to a legitimate one (62–3, 80–81).

46. Luijendijk, "Reading the *Gospel of Thomas* in the Third Century," 248.
47. Johnson, *Readers and Reading Culture*, 25.
48. Martin K. Heide, "Assessing the Stability of the Transmitted Texts of the New Testament and the *Shepherd of Hermas*," in *The Reliability of the New Testament: Bart D. Ehrman & Daniel B. Wallace in Dialogue*, ed. R.B. Stewart (Minneapolis: Fortress Press, 2011), 125–208. Heide writes, "A further point worth mentioning is that the earliest manuscripts of the *Shepherd of Hermas* from the second century (P. Michigan 130; P. Oxy 4706) were written on scrolls and not bound in the codex form as is the case with the earliest known New Testament manuscripts. Theological discourses and excerpts were also written on scrolls; the Codex style, however, was the prevalent technique of writing among canonically relevant manuscripts" (147–8). Unfortunately, it is not possible to evaluate Heide's proposal because we cannot determine that there was a systematic and conscious decision throughout the ancient world to reserve the codex format only for highly regarded works important to Christianity, such that a particular format could be taken as a marker of canonicity during the third century. It is important to note the recent publication by Geoffrey Smith, "The Willoughby Papyrus: A New Fragment of John 1:49–2:1 (P134) and an Unidentified Christian Text," *JBL* 137 (2018): 935–58, which argues that John was copied on a bookroll dated to the third or fourth century.

Luijendijk ("Reading the *Gospel of Thomas* in the Third Century") offers an excellent consideration of the different formats for the Christian texts at Oxyrhynchus. Her discussion of the impact that the format of a text exerts on how it was used focuses on whether a text was used privately or publicly and does not consider the effects of reading that are discussed here, 267.

We propose that the early sequencing of the Book of Visions and the Mandates in P.Oxy. 69.4706 is best understood as intentional and strategic.[49] Carolyn Osiek has described the Mandates as a series of twelve teachings that are structured in a progressive way.[50] She writes that the first teaching is concerned with "the foundational virtues of faith, simplicity, fear of the Lord, and restraint," and continues to discuss the "elementary virtues: simplicity, love of truth, chastity, and courageous endurance" through to the fifth mandate.[51] The second half of the Mandates deals with the more complex topic of discernment of spirits, with the final three Mandates (Mand. 9–12) understood as an even deeper discussion of this spiritual discipline.[52] With this general structure in mind, a scroll like P.Mich. 2/2 130 (containing Mand. 2, 3) ensures that a reader would not rush ahead or anticipate teachings for which they have not been sufficiently prepared. We might also describe Hermas himself to be constrained in the Book of Visions. Here in Vis. 3.2.1–2 [10.1–2], Hermas is not permitted to sit on the right side of the bench, even though he desires to, because of his "many shortcomings":

> 10.1 Τί, φημί, ὑπήνεγκαν; Ἄκουε, φησίν· μάστιγας, φυλακάς, θλίψεις μεγάλας, σταυρούς, θηρία εἵνεκεν τοῦ ὀνόματος· διὰ τοῦτο ἐκείνων ἐστὶν τὰ δεξιὰ μέρη τοῦ ἁγιάσματος, καὶ ὃς ἐὰν πάθῃ διὰ τὸ ὄνομα· τῶν δὲ λοιπῶν τὰ ἀριστερὰ μέρη ἐστίν. ἀλλὰ ἀμφοτέρων, καὶ τῶν ἐκ δεξιῶν καὶ τῶν ἐξ ἀριστερῶν καθημένων, τὰ αὐτὰ δῶρα καὶ αἱ αὐταὶ ἐπαγγελίαι· μόνον ἐκεῖνοι ἐκ δεξιῶν κάθηνται καὶ ἔχουσιν δόξαν τινά. 2 σὺ δὲ κατεπιθυμεῖς εἰ καθίσαι ἐκ δεξιῶν μετ᾿ αὐτῶν, ἀλλὰ τὰ ὑστερήματά σου πολλά· καθαρισθήσῃ δὲ ἀπὸ τῶν ὑστερημάτων σου· καὶ πάντες δὲ οἱ μὴ διψυχοῦντες καθαρισθήσονται ἀπὸ πάντων τῶν ἁμαρτημάτων εἰς ταύτην τὴν ἡμέραν.

> 10.1 "What have they endured?" I asked. "Listen," she said: "floggings, imprisonments, great tribulations, crucifixions, and wild beasts—for the sake of the Name. For this reason, the right side of Holiness belongs to them, and to anyone who suffers on account of the name. And the left side is for the others. The same gifts and promises belong to both—those seated on the right and those on the left. But they alone sit on the right and have a certain glory. 2 You want to sit on the right side with them, but you have many shortcomings. But you will be cleansed of your shortcomings. And all those who are not of two minds will be cleansed from all the sins they have committed up to this day."

---

49. We can assume that the section known as the Similitudes were also part of this early edition, although evidence for texts from this section have not survived in P.Oxy. 69.4706.
50. Osiek, *The Shepherd of Hermas*, 103.
51. Osiek, *The Shepherd of Hermas*, 103.
52. Osiek, *The Shepherd of Hermas*, 103.

This passage signals Hermas's strong desire but emphasize his lack of readiness. Thus, Hermas's restrained eagerness fits well with the way a bookroll naturally holds back a reader from reading passages for which they have been unprepared. A scroll apparatus not only imposes the sequence and order for reading a text; the manner of writing found therein often demands a skilled lector who must read carefully without rushing through the text.[53]

The material evidence indicates that the Shepherd was regarded as a popular catechetical work, particularly in North Africa. Awareness of a text's pedagogical function for late antique readers does not tell us what made it successful. What made this text engaging? Why did ancient readers find Hermas's narrative appealing? Our modern scholarly preoccupation with literary genres may obscure this question since modern readers may assess an ancient catechetical text based on its content and the degree to which it conforms or not to later standards of theological teaching, thereby overlooking the literary features that made the text effective and appealing to a wide audience. The catechetical genre may also lead to the false assumption that moral teachings are consolidated in specific sections of the Shepherd—the Mandates and Similitudes and not in the Book of Visions. On this point, it is important to consider how the categorical distinctions between visions and paraenetic material is blurred in the case of the Shepherd, a crucial point made well by Dan Batovici.[54] Paraenetic material appears throughout the Book of Visions, which alternates ethical exhortations with apocalyptic revelations (e.g., the paraenesis at Vis. 3.9.1–10 [17.1–10]).[55] The surprising or unexpected nature of the visions also strategically prepares readers and hearers for the moral exhortations that Hermas receives and accumulates the emotions that ready the reader for the subsequent section known as the Mandates. The visions cultivate states of surprise, wonder, regret, and amusement that heighten receptivity to what will happen next by increasing anticipation and watchfulness. These readerly responses to Hermas's visions replicate the lived experiencing of journeying by foot in which the sojourner would be met by surprising encounters along the way. The narrative structure cultivates a disposition of anticipation, thereby heightening readers' and hearers' receptivity to the ethical exhortations found within the Book of Visions and later in the Mandates.

---

53. The early bookroll known as P.Mich. 130 preserves sections of Mand. 2 and 3. The format of the bookroll fits with the progressive literary structuring of the Mandates, although we do not know the larger literary context since it has not survived.

54. Dan Batovici, "Apocalyptic and Metanoia in the *Shepherd of Hermas*," *Apocrypha* 26 (2015): 151–70.

55. See the discussion of the alternating paraenetic structure throughout the Book of Visions in Osiek, *The Rich and the Poor in the Shepherd of Hermas*, 41–56.

The Popularity of a Former Slave in an Ancient Reading Society

While we can easily imagine its appeal to a popular audience, why was a narrative about a former slave so appealing to a group of *literati* like the one at Oxyrhynchus? The practice of borrowing and copying texts among the *literati* in Egypt is well documented by various letters that record these transactions, especially for Oxyrhynchus, which is where most manuscripts of the Shepherd have been found. For example, the second century letter known as P.Oxy. 2192 describes various postscripts exchanged by people collaborating to make multiple copies of works like Hypsicrates's *Men who Appear in Comedies* and Thersagorus's *Myths of Tragedy*.[56] William Johnson has noted that texts like P.Oxy. 2192 provide evidence for a deep and broad literary culture of book copying, sharing, and enjoyment.[57]

Andrew Gregory argues for an early dating of the Shepherd and places it in the orbit of 70–140 CE, making it a close contemporary of 1 Clement. The early dating and wide dissemination of the Shepherd offer us access to a period when canonical boundaries were elastic and provide a glimpse of popular piety in a major urban center, Rome.[58] This early dating for the Shepherd has invited many scholarly studies that seek to reconstruct the doctrines, canon, and social world of the earliest Christian groups.[59] Several details in the Shepherd suggest a familiarity with the geography and the cultural practices characteristic of Roman life.[60] Hermas sees Rhoda bathing in the Tiber River (Vis. 1.1.1–2 [1.1–2]), a major waterway which runs through central Italy and the city of Rome. The scene also indirectly evokes the Roman Empire through the trope of a beautiful woman bathing out in open waters, a scene that evokes Hesiod's myth of the goddess Venus and her birth from the severed genitals of Uranus (*Theogony*, §173). Another geographical reference to Italy appears at the beginning of the fourth vision: "I was going into the country on the Via Campana. This is just over a mile off the public

---

56. Johnson, *Readers and Reading Culture*, 180–2.
57. Johnson, *Readers and Reading Culture*, 185.
58. Gregory, "Disturbing Trajectories: *1 Clement*, the *Shepherd of Hermas* and the Development of Early Roman Christianity," 142–66.
59. For example, Osiek, "The Oral World of Early Christianity in Rome: The Case of Hermas," Maier, *The Social Setting of the Ministry as Reflected in the Writings of Hermas, Clement and Ignaatius*, Soyars, *The Shepherd of Hermas and the Pauline Legacy*; Jonathan Lookadoo, *The Shepherd of Hermas: A Literary, Historical, and Theological Handbook* (London: T & T Clark, 2021), 167–85.
60. Mark R. C. Grundeken, "The Shepherd of Hermas and the Roman Empire," in *People Under Power: Early Jewish and Christian Responses to the Roman Empire*, ed. Michael Labahn and Outi Lehtipuu (Amsterdam: Amsterdam University Press, 2018), 187–204; Kirsopp Lake, "The Shepherd of Hermas and Christian Life in Rome in the Second Century, *HTR* 4 (1911): 25–46.

road; the place is easily reached" (ὑπῆγον εἰς ἀγρὸν τῇ ὁδῷ τῇ Καμπανῇ. ἀπὸ τῆς ὁδοῦ τῆς δημοσίας ἐστὶν ὡσεὶ στάδια δέκα· ῥαδίως δὲ ὁδεύεται ὁ τόπος, Vis. 4.1.1 [22.1]). So too, the Roman agricultural method of using elm trees to train grape vines is described in the parable in Sim. 2.1–4 [51.1–4], which is then used to describe the proper relationship between the rich and the poor (Sim. 2.5–10 [51.5–10]). Andrew Gregory makes the point that texts like the Shepherd "shed light on 'Roman Christianity', in that they are shaped by the Roman cultural world in which they were written, but they do so primarily in a way that might be appropriate for any urban setting from Rome to the eastern boundaries of the empire rather than in a way that is necessarily distinctive to and characteristic of the city of Rome itself."[61] The references to Roman geography are general and speak to characteristic features of Roman culture. Specific place references are used throughout the Book of Visions, but the geographic references are ultimately inconsequential since the journey segments are not contiguous.

While there are clear references to Rome throughout the Shepherd, we do not know exactly how popular this text was among Romans in Rome or in the region known as Italy today. Carolyn Osiek identifies only one fresco in the Catacomb of San Gennaro in Naples, Italy, that has been conclusively identified as an image from the Shepherd, in which women are bringing stones to build the tower (Sim. 9.2–3).[62] We can, however, be certain that the text was very popular in North Africa based on the abundant manuscript evidence for the Shepherd in Egypt, especially at Oxyrhynchus, which is located along "Joseph's Canal" near the Nile River.[63] While Africa's arid climate can account for the chance survival of these manuscripts, a number of early Christian authors from North Africa also confirm the Shepherd's popularity in that region.[64] The early dating of the Shepherd has led to scholarly studies interested in the development of doctrine.[65] Tertullian, in Carthage,

---

61. Gregory, "Disturbing Trajectories," 143–44.

62. Osiek, *The Shepherd of Hermas*, 7. There are very few images from the early centuries. This is a phenomenon that may be a result of Judaism's general prohibition of images. Some think that the absence of visual images among adherents to Christianity was an effort to distinguish themselves from the larger Greek and Roman religions where iconography was present everywhere. On this topic, see Harry O. Maier, "Vision, Visualisation, and Politics in the Apostle Paul," *MTSR* 27 (2015): 312–32, esp. 313.

63. Brent Nongbri, *God's Library: The Archaeology of the Earliest Christian Manuscripts* (New Haven: Yale University Press, 2018), 217.

64. The Shepherd was also known and highly regarded by the second century Irenaeus of Lyon, who considered the text scriptural.

65. On the Shepherd's importance for the historical understanding of development of Christology, see Bogdan G. Bucur, "The Son of God and the Angelomorphic Holy Spirit: A Rereading of the Shepherd's Christology." *ZNW* 98 (2007): 120–42. Significant

makes reference to the Shepherd three times, speaking strongly against its teaching that there is a second repentance.[66] The Shepherd was also familiar to other North African authors. Clement of Alexandria appears to have freely used the work and makes clear that he considered it to be inspired revelation.[67] Origen and his student Didymus the Blind, both in Alexandria, make reference to the Shepherd.[68] Malcolm Choat and Rachel Yuen-Collingridge have observed that the work had a strong presence in Egypt prior to Constantine, a region that enjoyed a vibrant literary culture at that time.[69]

According to the opening to the Book of Visions, the figure of Hermas was a former slave (Vis. 1.1.1 [1.1]).[70] Hermas is a man who has left his slavish past, but he has retained certain servile traits like extreme deference and cowardliness. The Shepherd was popular in North Africa. Why? Perhaps the Shepherd's many references to Roman life and the Umbrian countryside made the work especially appealing among North African readers who longed sentimentally or nostalgically for these faraway cooler and more temperate places.[71] The literary framework of a journey-by-foot is a

---

attention is often given to the Shepherd's teaching on repentance; see Martin Dibelius, *Der Hirt des Hermas*, Die Apostolischen Väter 4 (Tübingen: Mohr Siebeck, 1923), 423; and the more recent discussions by Moshe Blidstein, *Purity, Community, and Ritual in Early Christian Literature* (Oxford: Oxford University Press, 2017), 120 and by Lookadoo, *The Shepherd of Hermas: A Literary, Historical, and Theological Handbook*, 167–85.

66. It is said that there is a possibility for repentance after adultery, in Mand. 4.1.7–8 (29.7–8). The possibility of a second repentance was a controversial topic that was strongly opposed by Tertullian, who associated the Shepherd with adulterers; see *Or.* 16; and *Pud.* 10 and 20; see Osiek, *The Shepherd of Hermas*, 4–5.

67. Dan Batovici, "Hermas in Clement of Alexandria," *StPatr* 66 (2013): 41–51, writes that "the authority Hermas enjoys with Clement of Alexandria seems to lay on different ground—its apocalyptic character, which Clement considers to be genuine" (51). Osiek, *The Shepherd of Hermas*, 5.

68. Edmon L. Gallagher, "Origen on the Shepherd of Hermas," *Early Christianity* 10 (2019): 201–15.

69. Choat and Yuen-Collingridge, "The Egyptian *Hermas*," 191–211; also Johnson, *Readers and Reading Culture*, 179–92.

70. On the topic of slavery and early Christian groups, see Dale B. Martin, *Slavery as Salvation: The Metaphor of Slavery in Pauline Christianity* (New Haven: Yale University Press, 1990); P. Garnsey, *Ideas of Slavery from Aristotle to Augustine* (Cambridge: Cambridge University Press, 1996); Jennifer Glancy, "Slaves and Slavery in the Matthean Parables," *JBL* 119 (2000): 67–90; J. Albert Harrill, *Slaves in the New Testament: Literary, Social, and Moral Dimensions* (Minneapolis: Fortress, 2006); also Marianna Bjelland Kartzow, *The Slave Metaphor and Gendered Enslavement in Early Christian Discourse: Double Trouble Embodied* Routledge Studies in the Early Christian World (New York: Routledge, 2018).

71. Luijendijk ("Sacred Scriptures as Trash," 217–54) notes that the climate of Oxyrhynchus is exceedingly arid with little rainfall (224).

powerful literary form, especially for readers and hearers in a cosmopolitan setting like North Africa, who themselves—both slave and free—may have migrated over long distances. Nancy Easterlin speaks about the effects of such narrated journeys:

> Many forms of writing—travel literature, the picaresque, the bildungsroman, the long poem—involve journeys. Whether these journeys define the basic narrative frame or are incorporated into another, larger, structure, travel in these works is rarely incidental but instead central to the overall purpose and meaning of the work. This coheres with the basic phenomenology and epistemology of wayfinders, since movement and travel presuppose engagement with new environments and thus always entail expanded knowledge.[72]

Hermas's journeys are not continuous, and his destinations are not always clearly articulated. The experience of journeying by foot can cultivate the disposition of watchfulness or wayfinding that one might experience as one enters an unfamiliar landscape. Perhaps we can imagine a reader seeing the Umbrian countryside for the first time, along with the visions as they are told through Hermas's eyes.[73]

The pattern of sequencing a journey narrative full of wondrous events (Book of Visions) prior to a block of ethical material (Mandates) also resembles the literary configuration of the wonders that happened during the wilderness journey prior to the revelation of the law at Sinai. Like Hermas's journeys, the wilderness wanderings specify the scenery and signposts that were seen along the way, but they do not provide the kinds of details necessary for an exact reconstruction of the route taken. The exact location of Sinai, of course, is unknown and, more importantly, unnecessary for the narrative to achieve the effect of inculcating watchfulness. The foundational story of migration from Egypt to Canaan is mediated through various formats, in songs and other performative media. In support of the popularity of wilderness traditions in North Africa, the manuscript known as P.Oxy. 8.1079 (also known as P.Oxy. 8.1075) contains a copy of the end of the Greek Exodus on one side and the beginning of Rev. 1.4–7 on the other. While the larger literary context for joining these two has not survived, Brent Nongbri has proposed that the apocalypse has not been copied on a repurposed bookroll, but that these two writings were associated

---

72. Nancy Easterlin, "Cognitive Ecocriticism: Human Wayfinding, Sociality, and Literary Interpretation," in *Introduction to Cognitive Cultural Studies*, ed. Lisa Zunshine (Baltimore: Johns Hopkins University Press, 2010), 257–74, here 266–7. Steven Mithen, "The Evolution of Imagination: An Archaeological Perspective," *SubStance* 30 (2001): 28–54, here 50.

73. This aspect of the Book of Visions will be discussed further in Chapter 4.

deliberately in a codex, thus illustrating that the story of the Exodus was linked with visions and apocalypses.[74]

The geographical location of Oxyrhynchus, approximately 180 kilometers south of Cairo, was the home of a vibrant Jewish community. Other material remains found there suggest that there was a strong Jewish presence at Oxyrhynchus. According to Aryeh Kasher,

> [T]the Hebrew papyri from Oxyrhynchus inform us of local communal institutions: the *rashē ha-knesseth* (the heads of the synagogue), *ziqnē ha-knesseth* (the elders of the synagogue) and *prostatin* (προστάται in Greek, namely the superintendents or simply the leaders).[75]

Among the texts that Kasher cites is the deed of sale of a property dated to 133 CE (recorded in P.Oxy. 100=CPJud. III, 454) which references Jewish property "in the Cretan Quarter and in the Jewish [Street]." It is possible to get a good sense of the vibrant Jewish community at Oxyrhynchus during the first and early second centuries from the texts discussed by Kasher and Epp. This population was severely impacted by the response to the revolt in 115–117 CE and greatly diminished. According to Eldon Jay Epp, "no evidence of Jews or Jewish presence or activity is extant from Oxyrhynchus, with one or two possible exceptions: the family of a certain Onias and some Hebrew soldiers."[76] Some of the difficulty of identifying Jews based on names alone from the time of the revolt onward is due to the complications

---

74. Brent Nongbri, "Losing a Curious Christian Scroll but Gaining a Curious Christian Codex: An Oxyrhynchus Papyrus of Exodus and Revelation," *NovT* 55 (2013): 77–88. It is not clear why these texts were associated with one another in a codex, but there are other instances of heterogeneous codices from this period. The manuscript of the Book of Visions known as P.Bodmer 38 was also in a codex with other visions and miscellaneous poems and writings; see André Hurst and Jean Rudhardt, *Papyri Bodmer XXX–XXXVII "Codex des Visions" Poèmes divers*; See too, Bazzana's discussion of Nongbri's work on this manuscript in " 'You Will Write Two Booklets and Send One to Clement and One to Grapte," 48–9.

75. Aryeh Kasher, "The Jewish Community of Oxyrhynchus in the Roman Period," *JJS* 32 (1981): 151–7, esp. 153–7; also A.E. Cowley, "Notes on Hebrew Papyrus Fragments from Oxyrhynchus," *Journal of Egyptian Archaeology* 2 (1915): 209–213. On the presence of Jews in North Africa generally, see Franklin T. Harkins, "Nuancing Augustine's Hermeneutical Jew: Allegory and Actual Jews in the Bishop's Sermons," *JSJ* 36 (2005): 41–64.

76. E. J. Epp, "The Jews and the Jewish Community in Oxyrhynchus: Socio-Religious Context for the New Testament Papyri," in *New Testament Manuscripts: Their Texts and Their World*, ed. T. J. Kraus and T. Nicklas (Leiden: Brill, 2006), 13–52, here 27, also 28–30. Epp describes Kasher as overstating the evidence; he gives the following assessment of Kasher's discussion of P.Oxy. 355 as "whether or not this is somewhat overdrawn, it is clear that there was an organized and recognized Jewish community in Oxyrhynchus around 85 CE" (25).

1. *The Popularity of the Shepherd of Hermas in the Ancient World*   49

that arise with the increase in Christian use of biblical names.[77] In the following comments, AnneMarie Luijendijk gives the impression that there were no Jews from Oxyrhynchus from the early second century to the late third century:

> Furthermore, following the devastation of Jewish communities in Egypt after the Jewish Revolt in 115–117 C.E., evidence for Jews at Oxyrhynchus surfaces only from the end of the third century, when the synagogue, that is, the community, paid for the manumission of a female slave and her children (*P. Oxy*. IX 1205, dated April 14, 291 C.E.).[78]

Nevertheless, the text about the manumission of the Jewish slave woman and her children suggests that the synagogue was "well-organized, well-connected, and apparently affluent" by the late third century.[79] While there is clear evidence for at least one Jew, Onias, and a soldier at Oxyrhynchus during the second and third centuries, it seems more likely that a small remnant of Jews survived at Oxyrhynchus during the second and third century, who did not have the practice of using Jewish names. It is possible that Jews were not totally extinguished from Egypt.[80] It is, of course, true that there are few documentary remains of actual Jews from Oxyrhynchus, but it is also the case that the original excavators, Bernard Grenfell and Arthur Hunt, had no concern to identify or preserve the material remains of past Jewish communities. They were intent on recovering the origins of the Christian presence in Egypt.[81] The plentiful manuscript discoveries at Oxyrhynchus

---

77. Epp, "The Jews and the Jewish Community in Oxyrhynchus," 17–23.

78. Luijendijk, "Reading the *Gospel of Thomas* in the Third Century," 264; also R. Scholl, " 'Freilassung unter Freunden' im römischen Ägypten," in *Fünfzig Jahre Forschungen zur antiken Sklaverei an der Mainzer Akademie 1950–2000. Miscellanea zum Jubiläum*, ed. H. Bellen and H. Heinen, Forschungen zur antiken Sklaverei 35 (Mainz: Akademie der Wissenschaften und der Literatur, 2001), 159–69; Epp, "The Jews and the Jewish Community in Oxyrhynchus," 34–7.

79. Epp, "The Jews and the Jewish Community in Oxyrhynchus," 34–7, quote from 48.

80. Kasher, "The Jewish Community of Oxyrhynchus in the Roman Period," 151–7; also Cowley, "Notes on Hebrew Papyrus Fragments from Oxyrhynchus," 209–13; Cowley dates these papyri to 400 CE.

81. See Nongbri (*God's Library*, 216–46) for further discussion of the overwhelmingly Christian sensibilities of the archaeologists of late antique Egypt. See also Darlene Brooks Hedstrom, *The Monastic Landscape of Late Antique Egypt: An Archaeological Reconstruction* (Cambridge: Cambridge University Press, 2017) for an excellent account of how particularly modern western understandings of Christianity strongly biased early archaeologists of ancient monastic sites (7–39) who viewed the Egyptian Christian monks with "eyes of pity" (12–13) or with imperialist and ethnocentric eyes (14–19). The excavations of Oxyrhynchus (1896–1907) were led by scholars who earnestly sought early Christian texts, not Jewish ones (21–2).

include texts that show evidence of Jewish scribal practices. While lived Judaism in antiquity was diverse, our modern systems of identifying texts as Christian or Jewish is complicated and often inadequate.[82] In an Egyptian cosmopolitan setting, we can expect some familiarity and knowledge of early Jewish apocalypses and pseudepigrapha. A vibrant social community revolving around books is especially demonstrable in the case of North Africa, the locale which has produced much of the textual evidence for the Shepherd from the second to fourth centuries.[83]

References to Jewish literature and traditions appear in the Visions in the form of a citation to the lost or imaginary *Book of Eldad and Modat* (Ἐγγὺς Κύριος τοῖς ἐπιστρεφομένοις, ὡς γέγραπται ἐν τῷ Ἐλδὰδ καὶ Μωδάτ, τοῖς προφητεύσασιν ἐν τῇ ἐρήμῳ τῷ λαῷ, Vis. 2.3.4 [7.4]) which appears in the second vision. Eldad and Medad are two characters named in the wilderness stories in Numbers 11. In that tale, Joshua criticizes the pair for prophesying outside the camp, but Moses later vindicates them by declaring that it would be good if all of Israel would prophesy. The reference to this lost

---

82. Nongbri, *God's Library*, 229; there Nongbri describes one manuscript, P.Oxy. 7.1007, a leaf of a Greek copy of Genesis: "The word ϴΕΟC is contracted in the usual way (ΘC), but the divine name, generally translated as ΚΥΡΙΟC and contracted as K̄C in Christian manuscripts, is instead replaced by a double paleo-Hebrew letter yod" (229). Interestingly, Nongbri does not cite Kasher, "The Jewish Community of Oxyrhynchus in the Roman Period" or Cowley, "Notes on Hebrew Papyrus Fragments from Oxyrhynchus," in his bibliography. Some of the discussion on the difficulties in reconstructing Jewish or Christian identification of the people based on the material culture have to do with the various debates about how to understand Judaism in antiquity and the inadequacies of our modern categories in describing more complex phenomena like identity. For some examples of these discussions, see Jonathan Z. Smith, "Fences and Neighbors: Some Contours of Early Judaism," in *Imagining Religion: From Babylon to Jonestown* (Chicago: University of Chicago Press, 1982), 1–18; Daniel Boyarin, *Judaism: The Genealogy of a Modern Notion* (New Brunswick: Rutgers University Press, 2019), Daniel Boyarin, *Border Lines: The Partition of Judaeo-Christianity* (Philadelphia: University of Pennsylvania Press, 2004); Daniel Boyarin, "Semantic Differences or 'Judaism'/ 'Christianity'," in Adam H. Becker and Annette Yoshiko Reed, (ed.), *The Ways that Never Parted: Jews and Christians in Late Antiquity and the Early Middle Ages* (Tübingen: Mohr Siebeck, 2003), 65–85; Steve Mason, "Jews, Judeans, Judaizing, Judaism. Problems of Categorization in Ancient History," *Journal for the Study of Judaism* 38 (2007): 457–512; Seth Schwartz, "How Many Judaisms Were There? A Critique of Neusner and Smith on Definition and Mason and Boyarin on Categorization," *JAJ* 2 (2011): 208–38; Daniel Stökl Ben Ezra, "De l'arbre à la forêt: Quelques pensées quantitatives sur les papyrus littéraires juifs et chrétiens de l'Égypte ancienne," in *Reading New Testament Papyri in Context: Lire les Papyrus du Nouveau Testament dans leur contexte*, ed. Claire Clivaz and Jean Zumstein, in collaboration with Jenny Read-Heimerdinger and Julie Paik, BETL 242 (Leuven: Peeters, 2011), 169–88.

83. Choat and Yuen-Collingridge, "The Egyptian *Hermas*," 191–211.

book speaks to some extent to Hermas's own experience of the spirit. Hermas's identity as a former slave aligns him with the Hebrews wandering in the wilderness who were recently enslaved in Egypt. Hermas's slave past also places him outside the social camp of elite *literati*. Readers of early Jewish apocalypses will recognize Hermas's behavior in the tower vision (Vis. 3.2.5-9 [10.5-9]). He asks the Lady about the meaning of "the parables of the tower" (τὰς παραβολὰς τοῦ πύργου, Vis. 3.3.1-2 [11.1-2]) and boldly expresses his desire to know so that he can then "proclaim it to his brothers [and sisters]" (τοῖς ἀδελφοῖς ἀναγγείλω). Like other ancient seers such as Daniel (7.16), Hermas inquires persistently after the meanings of the visions he has experienced.

> 11.1 Δείξασά μοι ταῦτα ἤθελεν ἀποτρέχειν. λέγω αὐτῇ· Κυρία, τί μοι ὄφελος ταῦτα ἑωρακότι καὶ μὴ γινώσκοντι τί ἐστιν τὰ πράγματα; ἀποκριθεῖσά μοι λέγει· Πανοῦργος εἶ ἄνθρωπε, θέλων γινώσκειν τὰ περὶ τὸν πύργον. Ναί, φημί, κυρία, ἵνα τοῖς ἀδελφοῖς ἀναγγείλω, καὶ [ἱλαρώτεροι γένωνται, καὶ ταῦτα] ἀκούσαντες γινώσκωσιν τὸν Κύριον ἐν πολλῇ δόξῃ. 2 ἡ δὲ ἔφη· Ἀκούσονται μὲν πολλοί· ἀκούσαντες δέ τινες ἐξ αὐτῶν χαρήσονται, τινὲς δὲ κλαύσονται· ἀλλὰ καὶ οὗτοι, ἐὰν ἀκούσωσιν καὶ μετανοήσωσιν, καὶ αὐτοὶ χαρήσονται. ἄκουε οὖν τὰς παραβολὰς τοῦ πύργου· ἀποκαλύψω γάρ σοι πάντα. καὶ μηκέτι μοι κόπους πάρεχε περὶ ἀποκαλύψεως· αἱ γὰρ ἀποκαλύψεις αὗται τέλος ἔχουσιν· πεπληρωμέναι γάρ εἰσιν. ἀλλ᾽ οὐ παύσῃ αἰτούμενος ἀποκαλύψεις· ἀναιδὴς γὰρ εἶ. 3 ὁ μὲν πύργος ὃν βλέπεις οἰκοδομούμενον ἐγώ εἰμι, ἡ Ἐκκλησία, ἡ ὀφθεῖσά σοι καὶ νῦν καὶ τὸ πρότερον· ὃ ἂν οὖν θελήσῃς ἐπερώτα περὶ τοῦ πύργου, καὶ ἀποκαλύψω σοι, ἵνα χαρῇς μετὰ τῶν ἁγίων.

> 11.1 When she had shown me these things, she wanted to hurry away. I said to her, "Lady, what good is it for me to see these things if I do not know what they mean?" She answered and said to me, "You, fellow, are a crafty one, wanting to know about the tower." "Yes, Lady," I said, "I want to announce it to the brothers that they can become more cheerful; for when they hear these things they will know the Lord in great glory." 2 She said, "Many will indeed hear; and some of those who hear will rejoice, but some will weep. But even these latter, if they hear and repent, will rejoice as well. Hear therefore the parables of the tower. For I will reveal everything to you. Then trouble me no further about the revelation. For these revelations are completed and fulfilled. But you will not stop asking about [*or: for*] revelations, because you are shameless. 3 The tower, which you see being built, is I, the church, who has appeared to you both now and previously. And so, ask whatever you wish about the tower and I will reveal it to you, that you may rejoice with the saints.

While these literary features are not exclusive to ancient Jewish writings, they are attested by them. This passage also illustrates how ethical material is not only consolidated in the Mandates but also interspersed throughout the Book of Visions. These moral exhortations accompany each vision, often pertaining to specific teachings that Hermas must take back to his community.

We can consider other reasons why a text like the Shepherd would be attractive to the *literati* in North Africa. The first reason is that Hermas is a figure who seems to have internalized the kind of servile qualities that social elites might hope to find in their own slaves—Hermas is scrupulous and eagerly desires to be obedient to the task that is repeatedly given to him, namely, to disseminate the revelation to God's chosen ones (Vis. 2.2.3 [6.3]; 3.3.1–2 [11.1–2]; 4.2.5 [23.5]). For example, in the fourth vision, the lady in bridal attire urges Hermas to be virtuous as she instructs him to take the revelation and proclaim it to those whom she calls "the elect of the Lord" (τοῖς ἐκλεκτοῖς τοῦ Κυρίου):

> ὕπαγε οὖν καὶ ἐξήγησαι τοῖς ἐκλεκτοῖς τοῦ Κυρίου τὰ μεγαλεῖα αὐτοῦ, καὶ εἰπὲ αὐτοῖς ὅτι τὸ θηρίον τοῦτο τύπος ἐστὶν θλίψεως τῆς μελλούσης τῆς μεγάλης· ἐὰν οὖν προετοιμάσησθε καὶ μετανοήσητε ἐξ ὅλης καρδίας ὑμῶν πρὸς τὸν Κύριον, δυνήσεσθε ἐκφυγεῖν αὐτήν, ἐὰν ἡ καρδία ὑμῶν γένηται καθαρὰ καὶ ἄμωμος, καὶ τὰς λοιπὰς τῆς ζωῆς ἡμέρας ὑμῶν δουλεύσητε τῷ Κυρίῳ ἀμέμπτως. ἐπιρίψατε τὰς μερίμνας ὑμῶν ἐπὶ τὸν Κύριον, καὶ αὐτὸς κατορθώσει αὐτάς.

> And so, go and explain the great acts of the Lord to his chosen ones, and tell them that this wild beast is a foreshadowing of the great affliction that is coming. If then all of you prepare and repent before the Lord from your whole heart, you will be able to escape it—if your heart becomes clean and blameless and you serve the Lord blamelessly the rest of your days. (Vis. 4.2.5 [23.5])

The visions regularly place Hermas in the subordinate role of one who receives commands, like a slave, and as such, he is eager to do what is expected. The model of the ancient slave as it is understood in the character of Hermas is highly idealized and exaggerated, and therefore would have had wide appeal as an entertaining story among social elites and slaves of every standing. The manuscript evidence for the Shepherd reflects a range of copy hands and social contexts for the story's reception.

One task that Hermas is expected to execute requires some literacy on his part. In the second vision, Hermas admits to his lack of proficiency in reading: "I took it (the book) and going away to another part of the field, where I copied the whole thing, letter by letter, for I could not distinguish between the syllables. And then, when I completed the letters of the book, it was suddenly seized out of my hand; but I did not see by whom" (ἔλαβον ἐγώ, καὶ εἴς τινα τόπον τοῦ ἀγροῦ ἀναχωρήσας μετεγραψάμην πάντα πρὸς γράμμα· οὐχ ηὕρισκον γὰρ τὰς συλλαβάς. τελέσαντος οὖν τὰ γράμματα τοῦ βιβλιδίου ἐξαίφνης ἡρπάγη μου ἐκ τῆς χειρὸς τὸ βιβλίδιον· ὑπὸ τίνος δὲ οὐκ εἶδον, Vis. 2.2.4 [6.4]). Here we learn that Hermas was a slave who had benefited from a minimal education and who was at least semi-literate.[84] We know from the

---

84. Soyars, *The Shepherd of Hermas and the Pauline Legacy*, 32–42.

1. *The Popularity of the Shepherd of Hermas in the Ancient World* 53

writings that have survived from the ancient world that there were many different types of slaves, ranging from managerial slaves who held prestigious roles to household slaves and menial labor slaves.⁸⁵ In the Roman period, some managerial or household slaves may have had access to education and travel, and in some instances, they were able eventually to leave their slave station.⁸⁶ At the same time, the literary trope of the upwardly mobile slave was a common theme for various popular genres of writing, including satires.⁸⁷ Dale Martin summarizes one such fictional story from Petronius's Latin novel called *Satyricon*, which describes a household slave who managed to improve his life and become a success:

> Later in the supper, after Trimalchio is quite drunk, he proudly tells his story himself. He admits unabashedly his servile origins. In his eyes, his low beginnings only emphasize the virtues, sound sense (*corcillum*), and business acumen ("Buy well and sell well!") by which he rose to wealth. He came from Asia as a slave boy. For fourteen years he was his master's sexual pet and entertained his mistress as well. He gained power in the household-by the will of the gods, naturally. He pursued business, overcame hardships, inherited his owner's wealth, and became a powerful and immensely wealthy man in his own right: a first century rags-to-riches success story and all thanks to a well-connected and well-used slavery. Or, as Trimalchio says, "Who was a frog is now a king!" (*Qui fuit rana, nunc est rex*, 77). The statement is a fitting end for a scene begun with a wall painting of Trimalchio on the slave block.⁸⁸

Martin explains that Petronius's novel speaks to social elites who see the literary trope of the upwardly mobile slave as worthy of ridicule. While the Book of Visions does not present Hermas in a scornful way, it does offer occasional scenes at which a reader or hearer of any social class might chuckle at Hermas's expense. For instance, in the third vision, a nighttime vision in the field (cited previously), Hermas is depicted as striving for a seat on the right side of the ivory couch. He is quickly told that he is unworthy of this position at the moment, but that he may possibly attain to it in the future if he continues in his simplicity (ἀλλὰ ὡς ἐμμένεις τῇ ἁπλότητί σου, Vis. 3.1.9 [9.9]). A reader who performs this scene can easily introduce comedic elements that can cut some of the mounting tension of Hermas's nighttime encounter with the Lady in the field.

---

85. Glancy, "Slaves and Slavery in the Matthean Parables," 67–90.
86. Martin, *Slavery as Salvation*, 30–42, here 31–2, and Thomas E. J. Wiedemann, *Greek and Roman Slavery* (Baltimore: Johns Hopkins University Press, 1981), 13.
87. Martin, *Slavery as Salvation*, 35.
88. Martin, *Slavery as Salvation*, 36–7.

Portraits of slaves in antiquity emphasized how deeply slavery was embodied in the flesh and seared into one's identity—it was not something that could be easily left behind. According to J. Albert Harrill:

> Greeks in general defined the slave, like the animal, in terms of its body alone. A common word in Greek for "slave" was simply "body" (*sōma*); other ancient terms included "boy" (Greek *pais*; Latin *puer*), "rogue" (that is someone who needs a whipping: *mastigia*; *verbero*), "garbage" (*katharma*) and "Man-footed creature" (*andrapodon*), the last term derived from a common word for cattle (*tetrapodon*). The somatic vocabulary reflects a cultural habit that tended to define the slave by its (my use of neuter is pointed) outer corporality alone—a mere "body."[89]

Indeed, the language for slavery conveyed the extent to which belonging to this group was experienced deeply in the body. Jennifer Glancy notes that the slave's body was marked by corporal punishment, which left tortured wounds that also scarred the slave's inner being.[90] Slavery was associated with various traits that ancient Greeks and Romans imagined as externally encoded in the body's posture and comportment and as seared into one's character.[91]

The figure of Hermas may be understood from within this literary trope of a minimally educated managerial slave who has somehow become more than just a slave, but is unable to fully escape his servile past. In the opening to the Book of Visions, we read: "The one who reared me sold me to a certain woman named Rhoda in Rome. After many years, I was reacquainted with her and I began to love her as a sister" (Ὁ θρέψας με πέπρακέν με Ῥόδῃ τινὶ εἰς Ῥώμην. μετὰ πολλὰ ἔτη ταύτην ἀνεγνωρισάμην καὶ ἠρξάμην αὐτὴν ἀγαπᾶν ὡς ἀδελφήν, Vis. 1.1.1 [1.1]).[92] Hermas's reference to Rhoda as "a sister" (ὡς ἀδελφήν) is often taken to mean that years later both had become

---

89. J. Albert Harrill, *Slaves in the New Testament*, 20.

90. Glancy, "Slaves and Slavery in the Matthean Parables," 83–90.

91. Harrill, *Slaves in the New Testament*, 37–44. Harrill writes, "Physiognomics, the pseudoscience of reading an individual's body to detect character, status, or destiny, influenced Greek and Roman constructions of the female, the barbarian, the beast, and the slave as fixed character types" (37). Harrill identifies passages from Aristotle, *Politics* 1.2 (1254b25-35), that speak to this cultural assumption of biological determinism which assumed that the body's weak form could even predetermine servile character traits.

92. Based on a rereading of P.Bodmer 38, Emanuele Castelli offers an alternative interpretation of this passage; Rhoda is not a slave owner but was a slave who had been sold in Rome. According to Castelli, the two are reunited in this scene. See the discussion later in Chapter 2. Emanuele Castelli, "Gli esordi alternativi del *Pastore* di Erma," *Adamantius* 26 (2020): 551–75; Emanuele Castelli, "Dati storici e aspetti romanzeschi nelle prime due Visioni del *Pastore* di Erma. Una riconsiderazione del problema alla luce di nuove scoperte testuali," *Augustinianum* 60 (2020): 321–40, Emanuele Castelli,

Christian. According to this reasoning, Hermas no longer related to Rhoda as an enslaved man to a free woman, but as a brother to a sister in Christ. Hermas's first vision is of a heavenly figure. He says: "I saw the woman I had desired" (καὶ βλέπω τὴν γυναῖκα ἐκείνην ἣν ἐπεθύμησα, Vis. 1.1.4 [1.4]). While the opening scene is recounted as Hermas recalling his encounter with a certain woman named Rhoda, Hermas actually addresses her in the vision as 'Lady' (Κυρία). Even though Hermas refers to Rhoda by name, protocol demands that a slave would address his female slave owner by the title, 'Lady'. This use of the impersonal address, 'Lady', creates some ambiguity over the identity of the interlocutor in the first and second visions. While the word 'Lady' (Κυρία) is used here as a translation, other alternatives like 'Madam' or 'Mistress' are inadequate at expressing the social relationship of a slave to a female slave owner. Hermas addresses Rhoda appropriately as a slave would address his female slave owner, and thus he addresses all the women whom he encounters throughout the Book of Visions. In so doing, even if Hermas is a freed slave, he persists in using the protocols that frame his relationships as subordination; like a slave, Hermas dutifully addresses all the women in his visions as 'Lady' (Κυρία) —the same word used for a female slave master. Marianne Kartzow discusses how Hermas's narrative is one of transformation, tracing his development from "an effeminate male slave of a woman" to being "a male slave of God."[93]

We do not know if Hermas was sold by Rhoda to another master or if he was manumitted. The text simply does not say, although the majority of scholars have inferred this based on certain details in the text, many of which are ambiguous.[94] For example, Hermas's freedom of movement in the Umbrian countryside (e.g., Vis. 1.1.3 [1.3]; 2.1.1 [5.1]; and 4.1.1 [22.1]) is often taken as evidence of his free status, but it does not preclude the possibility that he was a managerial slave sent out on a mission.[95] While the text does mention Hermas's wife and family (e.g., Vis. 2.2.2–3 [6.2–3]), this alone does not prove that he was manumitted, since some slaves were known to have families in the Roman Empire.[96] The idea that Hermas was

"Il I capitolo del *Pastore* di Erma alla luce delle recenti acquisizioni sul P. Bodmer XXXVIII e sulla *Vulgata*," *Vetera Christianorum* 57 (2020): 65–84.

93. Kartzow, *The Slave Metaphor and Gendered Enslavement in Early Christian Discourse,* 107–11.

94. For an excellent summary of these arguments, see Osiek, *Rich and Poor in the Shepherd of Hermas*, 130–32.

95. Osiek, *Rich and Poor in the Shepherd of Hermas*, 131.

96. Henrik Mouritsen, "The Families of Roman Slaves and Freedmen," in *A Companion to Families in the Greek and Roman Worlds*, ed. Beryl Rawson (Oxford: Blackwell, 2011), 129–44.

manumitted and had gained some material advantages as a freedman does, however, align with the many paraenetic sections that urge wealthy slaves and former slaves to behave more ethically toward the poor. It may also be the case that these passages are intended for wealthy hearers of the text. Hermas had already become a Christian prior to his encounter with Rhoda, which begins the Book of Visions. Even so, the narrative includes many stories of him struggling to escape his servile past and negotiating his identity in the face of new and changing circumstances. For example, even though Hermas has been told that the angel Thegri (Θεγρί)[97] has shut the mouth of the beast rendering him harmless (Vis. 4.2.4 [23.4], Hermas still fearfully looks back at the beast when he is startled by a noise (Vis. 4.3.7 [24.7]). One might imagine both slaves and social elites in Egypt being amused by this image of Hermas whose servile subjectivity is exposed by his cowardly fear. These examples of Hermas's inability to escape his servile past serve to reassure those who are privileged that their social location is secure. Perhaps most importantly, Hermas offers an interesting example of the complexities of intersectional identity. He is an ambiguous hybrid figure whose social standing is unclear. At times Hermas's adventures are narrated in a humorous fashion, depicting him as he navigates his surprising encounters with uncertainty and an abundance of caution. These humorous elements to Hermas's character make him less threatening to the social order.

Among the tasks that Hermas is repeatedly given is to proclaim the revelations to his group and to copy texts. This is a scenario that we can readily imagine in ancient Egypt, for which we have evidence for an extensive culture of book copying, sharing, and enjoyment. William Johnson writes:

> We have found evidence, for example, of a *culture of sharing* whereby leading elites were expected to share with their *comites* not only utilitarian items such as used clothing, but also resources centered around texts. These

---

97. J. Rendel Harris, "On the Angelology of Hermas," in *Hermas in Arcadia, and Other Essays* (Cambridge: The University Press, 1896), 21–5. Harris proposed reading the angel's name Θεγρί as a corruption of Σεγρί (Segri), caused by a confusion of the θ and σ in the uncial script. This would allow for a clear pun on the Aramaic word which appears in Dan. 6.23, "he shut (סְגַר) the mouth of the lion." Harris's suggestion is later cited enthusiastically by J. Armitage Robinson [*Barnabas, Hermas and the Didache* (London: SPCK, 1920], 31) who writes: "Dr Rendel Harris has shown from a comparison of Dan. vi. 22, to which allusion is here made, that the angel's name must be Segri (the Shutter)." Also cited by Snyder, *The Shepherd of Hermas*, 58 in his notes to Vis. 4.2.4 (23.4). While this suggestion is an attractive option to some readers, there is no evidence to support that Σεγρί was attested in any of the surviving manuscripts of the Book of Visions. It also assumes that the more difficult and obscure reading (Θεγρί) is secondary. While it is possible that the more difficult reading of Θεγρί is secondary, most textual critics, as a rule, would prefer the more difficult reading as original.

1. *The Popularity of the Shepherd of Hermas in the Ancient World* 57

> included the space for recitations: a variety of social contexts at *domus* and *villa* (walkways, gardens, baths, dining rooms, sitting rooms) suitable for various types of readings and text-centered discussions; participants for the readings, including both *docti* of rank and an entourage of the intellectually curious of all stripes. Leading men also made the books themselves available, by maintaining both a library and the staff necessary to assess, acquire, and copy the books, and they provided trained *lectores* who presented certain books in certain situations (e.g., comedy at dinner) as entertainment for the group. The more influential the man, the larger was the group of *amici* and the greater the demand on resources.[98]

While Johnson speaks of the *vir magnus* and the literary culture of elite males in the Graeco-Roman society throughout his work, it is known that women were also participants in the vibrant book culture which held early Jewish writings and pseudepigrapha in high esteem.[99] Among the massive cache of papyri from Oxyrhynchus is a private letter which shows that women were also actively engaged in book sharing and enjoyment.[100] This brief letter (P.Oxy. 4365) records the lending and borrowing of 'Ezra', perhaps referring to the pseudepigrapha and visions associated with this figure, and a work known as 'little Genesis', presumably the Book of Jubilees, a late Second Temple rewriting of Genesis and portions of Exodus. The pseudepigraphic work known as *4 Ezra* shares some similarities with the character of Hermas insofar as they both engage in anguished dialogue with angelic interlocutors. The letter known as P.Oxy. 4365 is dated to the early fourth century and demonstrates the lasting hold that these early Jewish apocalypses and pseudepigrapha had on late antique readers.[101] These elite women writers and readers who are attested by P.Oxy. 4365 and P.Oxy. 1467 may also have found appealing the vision of the Lady instructing Hermas to make two copies of the little book:

> 5.3 μετὰ δὲ τὸ ἐγερθῆναί με ἀπὸ τῆς προσευχῆς βλέπω ἀπέναντί μου τὴν πρεσβυτέραν ἣν καὶ πέρυσιν ἑωράκειν, περιπατοῦσαν καὶ ἀναγινώσκουσαν βιβλαρίδιον. καὶ λέγει μοι· Δύνῃ ταῦτα τοῖς ἐκλεκτοῖς τοῦ Θεοῦ ἀναγγεῖλαι; λέγω αὐτῇ· Κυρία, τοσαῦτα μνημονεῦσαι οὐ δύναμαι· δὸς δέ μοι τὸ βιβλίδιον, ἵνα μεταγράψωμαι αὐτό. Λάβε, φησίν, καὶ ἀποδώσεις μοι. 4 ἔλαβον ἐγώ, καὶ εἴς τινα τόπον τοῦ ἀγροῦ ἀναχωρήσας μετεγραψάμην πάντα πρὸς γράμμα· οὐχ

---

98. Johnson, *Readers and Reading Culture*, 202.
99. Nongbri, *God's Library*, 228–40.
100. Eldon Jay Epp, "The Oxyrhynchus New Testament Papyri: 'Not Without Honor Except in their Hometown'?" *JBL* 123 (2004): 5–55.
101. Epp, "The Oxyrhynchus New Testament Papyri," 17–18, esp. 17 n. 44, 45. Choat and Yuen-Collingridge, "The Egyptian *Hermas*," 191–211. Kim Haines-Eitzen, also discusses various evidence for elite ancient woman writers and readers (e.g., P.Oxy. 1467, P.Oxy. 4365) in *The Gendered Palimpsest: Women, Writing, and Representation in Early Christianity* (Oxford: Oxford University Press, 2012), 20–52.

ηὕρισκον γὰρ τὰς συλλαβάς. τελέσαντος οὖν τὰ γράμματα τοῦ βιβλιδίου ἐξαίφνης ἡρπάγη μου ἐκ τῆς χειρὸς τὸ βιβλίδιον· ὑπὸ τίνος δὲ οὐκ εἶδον.

> 5.3 When I arose from prayer I saw across from me the elderly woman I had seen the year before, walking and reading a little book. And she said to me, "Can you announce these things to the ones chosen by God?" I said to her, "Lady, I cannot remember so many things. Give me the book to make a copy." "Take it," she said, "and then return it to me." 4 I took it and went away to another part of the field, where I copied the whole thing, letter by letter, for I could not distinguish between the syllables. And then, when I completed the letters of the book, it was suddenly seized from my hand; but I did not see by whom.

Even though Hermas is literate, he cannot read well (Vis. 2.2.3–4 [6.3–4]), thus confirming that he would be unable to alter the things he is copying.[102] Hermas's limited education also ensures that he is not a true competitor for the social capital enjoyed by the elite literati, even though he is someone who has enough competence to function instrumentally in their book culture. Copying and literary revision can happen during the same process. They are not always sequenced stages in a manuscript's transmission. The narrative suggests that Hermas was a slave, possibly manumitted, with some social standing, but who lacks intellectual sophistication. These elements suggest that he can be entrusted with the task of copying texts without tampering with them. Even if Hermas were manumitted, his servile subjectivity and limited education would have ensured that he would not disrupt the social structure. Since Hermas is depicted as a former low-status male, he would have been non-threatening—even amusing to social elites and slaves alike. His limited literacy would have supported the social order that ultimately served the status quo.

Conclusion

The ancient manuscript evidence for the Shepherd demonstrates its popularity during the early centuries as a catechetical work. Bart Ehrman writes:

> The *Shepherd* of Hermas was one of the most popular books of early Christianity. Judging from the manuscript remains, it was copied and read more widely in the second and third centuries than any other noncanonical book, even more than many of the books that later came to be included in the New Testament.[103]

---

102. Perhaps this is not unlike the rationale that the elders who hear Peter's speech in Acts 3 and 4 conclude about Peter's authority, since he is an uneducated commoner (Acts 4.13).

103. "Introduction," *Apostolic Fathers*, vol. 2 (Ehrman, LCL 25), 162.

1. *The Popularity of the Shepherd of Hermas in the Ancient World* 59

Even though the book functioned to instruct those who were new to Christianity, this alone does not account for its popularity and appeal, especially at Oxyrhynchus, which enjoyed a vibrant literary culture. Our discussion has focused on the early bookroll known as P.Oxy. 69.4706. Because an ancient reader of P.Oxy. 69.4706 would have to move through the bookroll in a linear way, we have proposed that it is worthwhile trying to imagine how this experience might also have contributed to the moral formation of its readers and hearers. The pattern of sequencing the Book of Visions prior to the twelve Mandates resembles other well-established foundational patterns from Judaism which depict the revelation of the law within vivid and dramatic journey narratives that include religious and spiritual wonders. The crossing of the sea, manna, quails, water from a rock, and theophany in Exod. 14–17, 19 are fantastic wonders that are vividly recounted just prior to the giving of the law at Sinai which takes place in Exod. 20–24. The physical activity of reading the Book of Visions in a bookroll reminds us that readerly responses (e.g., affect, wonder, surprise, puzzlement) would have accumulated as the reader moves through the book.[104]

Relevant aspects of cognitive literary criticism can assist in conceptualizing how the human mind experiences the physical environments described in visionary texts, especially when those scenes are read in sequence as a bookroll would require. Spatial details figure prominently in each of these visionary encounters and serve to generate a phenomenal experience of embodiment and encounter. For example, Chapter 4 discusses how the painstakingly tedious narrative of Hermas's nighttime wanderings in the field at the beginning of Vision 3 functions to prepare the reader for the vision of the tower. These narrations about Hermas's journeys simulate processes like 'wayfinding' in which the mind might imagine moving through a new terrain with vividness. The one who travels by foot keeps a watchful eye on landmarks and other changes in the environment to retrace his or her steps and return home. The watchful disposition associated with wayfinding is exaggerated even more when narratives describe wonderous or surprising events that happen along the way. The bookroll format allows for the deliberate sequencing of these readerly responses: surprise, confusion, amusement, and most importantly, anticipation throughout Hermas's journey narrative in the Book of Visions. Immersive reading of the Book of Visions can be said to participate in the overall task of moral formation by cultivating the necessary predispositions of attentiveness and watchfulness,

---

104. Further discussion of the accumulation of affect in the case of Vision 3 will be discussed in Chapter 4.

which increase receptivity to the ethical teachings that Hermas receives from his chance encounters.

Despite the early dating of the Shepherd, it contains no appeal to apostolic authority and virtually no references to texts that would later become canonical. It is also the case that the Book of Visions makes inconsistent references to external named figures and texts. The second vision mentions a figure named Maximus and the unknown *Book of Eldad and Modat* (Vis. 2.3.4 [7.4]), in addition to referencing a certain Clement and Grapte. The fourth vision alludes to two scriptural passages: Dan. 6.22 (Dan. LXX 6.23) appears in Vis. 4.2.4 (23.4), and Ps. 55.22a (Ps. LXX 54.23a) in Vis. 4.2.5 (23.5). Mark Grundeken and Joseph Verheyden do well to argue that the Book of Visions relies principally on the visionary experiences themselves as the guarantee of the revelations and paraenesis found within them.[105] Hermas is expected to proclaim these revelations and paraenetic material to others.

In closing, while the Shepherd was well-known as a text used for catechetical instruction, this alone does not tell us what ancient readers found appealing or enjoyable about the work. We have proposed that various aspects of the Book of Visions would have appealed to the *literati* in North Africa, at a place like Oxyrhynchus which enjoyed a wide range of literary genres and which was comprised by a diverse literate population that included an established Jewish presence during the period in which the Shepherd was being copied and transmitted. The narrative presentation of Hermas is widely appealing as an endearingly earnest figure who struggles to escape his servile past, but who does not threaten the status quo.

Throughout the secondary literature on the Shepherd of Hermas, there has been a consistently strong line of scholars who have argued that the narratives about Hermas's visions are a kind of historical autobiography written by a semi-literate former slave who strives to move up the social hierarchy.[106] Scholars who have an optimistic view of our ability to recover historical information are motivated by a search for discipline-specific information

---

105. Grundeken and Verheyden, "The Spirit Before the Letter," 23–56, esp. 51. On the topic of visions, Hermas is depicted as frequently engaging in self-diminishing practices of weeping, collapsing on his knees, and confessing his sins; practices that are closely associated with various Jewish apocalypticists. These visionary practices will be discussed further in Chapter 3.

106. Åke von Ström, *Der Hirt des Hermas. Allegorie oder Wirklichkeit?* (Uppsala: Wretmans, 1936), 3–7; Osiek, "The Oral World of Early Christianity in Rome: The Case of Hermas," 152–5.

1. The Popularity of the Shepherd of Hermas in the Ancient World 61

about the social history or theology of early Christ followers.[107] This is true for the most recent study of the Shepherd by Jonathan E. Soyars who understands Hermas as an early witness to Paul:

> Nevertheless, I argue that Hermas could have come to know Pauline letters at Rome meaningfully and deeply, even if that knowledge was not necessarily developed through the technology of reading a book and voicing its words himself. One way that Hermas might have encountered Pauline letters is indeed by reading them. He could have done so either with his own voice or through an intermediary.[108]

The investigations that argue optimistically for the historicity of Hermas as an author of the work known as the Shepherd aim to investigate the development and transmission of Christian theology—more specifically, in the case of Soyars, the teachings of Paul. They do not fully account for why the Shepherd was appealing to ancient readers, specifically the group of *literati* at Oxyrhynchus during the early centuries—historicity alone does not explain the popular reception of a catechetical text. While Hermas's experiences as a recently freed slave may reflect some historical kernel of the actual social mobility of slaves in the Roman Empire, it remains an identifiable and entertaining literary trope for a wide audience.

The search for origins which drives the field of biblical studies is the same one that fuels the strong desire to find a historical Hermas and, at the same time, the putative author of the stories in the work that we know today as the Book of Visions. Nevertheless, the figure of Hermas as he is known from the Shepherd has been thoroughly fictionalized and fashioned into a literary character, one who is non-threatening and entertaining to the readers at Oxyrhynchus where the Shepherd was copied and disseminated with some frequency prior to 400 CE. Unlike other studies that have sought to read the Shepherd in search of details about the historical, social, or theological world of early Christ followers, I analyze the Book of Visions first and foremost as an appealing narrative that had been enthusiastically received by North African readers. The appeal of the Book of Visions to ancient readers has not been examined in modern studies of the Shepherd, which often prioritizes discipline-specific questions about authorship, social history, and theology.

The number of manuscripts of the Shepherd that have survived from the ancient period at Oxyrhynchus far exceeds the number of Gospel

---

107. Osiek, "The Oral World of Early Christianity in Rome: The Case of Hermas," 152.
108. Soyars, *The Shepherd of Hermas and the Pauline Legacy*, 103.

manuscripts for that region. Remarkably, despite the success that the Shepherd enjoyed among ancient readers, modern scholars have not received it to the same degree. Why this is the case is a topic that will be taken up in the next chapter.

Chapter Two
Taking a Look at Hermas

The Book of Visions of the Shepherd of Hermas preserves lengthy first-person narrations of visionary experiences of a protagonist, Hermas, who is often distraught and stricken with anxiety. Many modern commentators point out how unappealing the character of Hermas is to them. For example, in the forward to his commentary on the Shepherd, Norbert Brox comments on how peculiar the work is to modern readers, who find its protracted narratives about visions and parenesis to be exceedingly repetitive and monotonous:

> Der "Hirt" des Hermas ist ein merkwürdiges Buch… Dem heutigen Leser geht es anders mit diesem Buch. Was die Alten fasziniert hat, wirkt auf ihn wie eine Abfolge von Banalitäten. Zumal der große Handlungsrahmen, die visionäre Welt des Hermas, deren Fülle an stupenden Gestalten und Abläufen in ihren Bann ziehen will, mutet als triviale Fiktion an. Die Erzählungen und Deutungen der Visionen und ihrer Botschaft von der rettenden Buße sind weithin langatmig, die ausgetretenen Paränesen monoton. Hermas hat eine unendliche Vorliebe für Wiederholungen.[1]

Brox writes: "What had fascinated ancient readers strikes [the modern] one as a series of banalities" ("Was die Alten fasziniert hat, wirkt auf ihn wie eine Abfolge von Banalitäten").[2]

Brox is not alone in his negative assessment of the literary form and content of the Shepherd. His description does not differ much from Theodor Zahn who, nearly 125 years earlier, spoke of Hermas's writing style as "a tireless monotony from beginning to end" ("von Anfang bis zum Ende von einer ermüdenden Monotonie").[3] Both Brox and Zahn give full-throated criticism of Hermas's literary style and illustrate what might be a typical response to the work in the modern period.

---

1. Norbert Brox, *Der Hirt des Hermas*, Ergänzungsreihe zum Kritisch-exegetischen Kommentar über das Neue Testament Band 7 (Göttingen: Vandenhoeck & Ruprecht, 1991), 5.
2. Brox, *Der Hirt des Hermas*, 5.
3. Theodor Zahn, *Der Hirt des Hermas* (Gotha: Friedrich Andreas Perthes, 1868), 486.

This chapter investigates the question of why the Shepherd was so popular and engaging to ancient readers but not to modern ones.[4] The negative assessments of the literary style of the Shepherd may reflect the rejection of highly structured and predictable writing and the preference for originality and individualism guided by the sensibilities of Romanticism. Great authors were assumed to impart their works with original creative style, in much the same way that DNA is passed along from parent to child. The classic image is one of the stormy Lord Byron, a figure who was notorious for living life to excess and for the dramatic quality of his literary works.[5] According to the eighteenth century critic Edward Young, a text's originality and creativity reflected the strong personal qualities of its author as a creative genius whose artistic skill is uncultivated by the study of forms or other models, but the product of pure inspiration.[6] Meyer H. Abrams writes, "German thought was much more receptive than English to Young's suggestions that a great work of literature grows out of the impenetrable depths of the mind of genius."[7] Abrams writes that Young was well received in Germany, "a country where youthful writers were chafing at the long subjection of the native literary tradition to foreign models and rules."[8] Very

---

4. This is the question posed at the start by Choat and Yuen-Collingridge, "The Egyptian *Hermas*," 191. One of the conclusions of their excellent study is that the Shepherd was an important catechetical text—even so, this alone does not explain why it was popular or engaging to ancient readers.

5. The identification of certain anonymous texts as the writings of the Teacher of Righteousness at Qumran based on perceptions of their lively and dramatic writing style, also reflects the powerful hold that Romantic ideas of authorship have over the imaginations of modern scholars. Gert Jeremias (*Der Lehrer der Gerechtigkeit*, SUNT 2 [Göttingen: Vandenhoeck & Ruprecht, 1963]) remarked that there was a qualitative difference between the "lebendigen Sprache" found in the Teacher Hymns and the rest of the scroll, which he characterized as "erstarrte Wendungen und monotone Widerholungen" (171). See Angela Kim Harkins, "Who is the Teacher of the Teacher Hymns? Re-examining the Teacher Hymns Hypothesis Fifty Years Later," in *A Teacher for All Generations: Essays in Honor of James C. VanderKam*, Vol. 1, ed. Eric F. Mason et al. (Leiden: Brill, 2012), 1: 449–67, here 455.

6. D. W. Odell, "The Argument of Young's 'Conjectures on Original Composition'," *Studies in Philology* 78 (1981): 87–106, 89.

7. Meyer H. Abrams, *The Mirror and the Lamp: Romantic Theory and the Critical Tradition* (Oxford: Oxford University Press, 1953), 202. In this passage, Abrams references Edward Young, the author of *Conjectures on Original Composition* (London: A. Millar, 1759), who emphasized the idea of the natural born genius and who also imported many metaphors from the plant world to express his understanding of the ideal organic (uncultivated) artistic genius (198–9). See also the discussion of Young by Odell, "The Argument of Young's 'Conjectures on Original Composition'," 87–106.

8. Abrams, *The Mirror and the Lamp*, 202. Abrams goes on to say that Young's

few modern readers, however, would recognize Hermas, the putative author of the Shepherd, as a genius.

Romanticism's rejection of the Enlightenment's literary formalism holds a powerful influence over readers today who continue to be shaped by Romanticism and its resurgence as Neo-Romanticism in the early to mid-twentieth century in Germany and later in England.[9] The Shepherd makes frequent mention of Hermas in a state of distress and collapsing on his knees in prayer. While introspective descriptions of Hermas should resonate with modern readers today who prize individual experiences and desire to be emotionally engaged by texts, they do not. Perhaps it is because these interior descriptions are repeated so frequently, they become formulaic and lose any suggestion of spontaneity. It is also the case that the emotional states of grief-stricken anguish that are highlighted in the Book of Visions are precisely the ones that many seek to avoid today.

Modern scholars largely agree in their dislike of Hermas. Burnett H. Streeter describes Hermas's undesirable character traits by calling him the "White Rabbit":

> Hermas is the "White Rabbit" of the Apostolic Fathers. That is why we can be certain that he wrote in his own name. Pseudonymous writers always adopt the style and title of some great and impressive figure of the past; the Hermas described in this book is singularly unheroic—a timid, fussy, kindly incompetent, middle-aged freedman, delightfully naïve, just a little vain of his prophetic gift, and with a wife and children decidedly out of hand.[10]

Streeter's reference to a "White Rabbit" points back to a literary character from the works of Lewis Carroll whom he described in a footnote as "'elderly,' 'timid,' 'feeble,' and 'nervously shilly-shallying'."[11] Interestingly Streeter reasons that the first-person narrative must be autobiographical, since if it were the work of another, one would hardly choose to highlight such deplorable "singularly unheroic" personality traits for the protagonist. Streeter understood the first-person voice of the Book of Visions as a marker of autobiographical writing. He published his thoughts

---

theory was much more compatible with the psychology of Leibniz popular in Germany at the time and less compatible with English empiricism.

9. Dennis F. Mahoney (ed), *The Literature of German Romanticism* (Rochester, NY: Camden House, 2004). According to Richardson (*British Romanticism and the Science of the Mind*, 1), Romanticism of the late eighteenth and early nineteenth centuries along with the neo-Romanticism of the mid-twentieth century were both movements that emphasized individuality and the emotions, and interestingly accompanied by the emergence and the re-emergence of scientific interest in the cognitive processes.

10. Streeter, *The Primitive Church*, 203.

11. Streeter, *The Primitive Church*, 203.

approximately a generation before literary critics like Georges Gusdorf argued that autobiography was not a truth-telling genre, since the same literary features used in the writing of autobiographies are found regularly in the writing of narrative fiction.[12] Twentieth century discussions of autobiography since Gusdorf have wrestled with how the diverse forms understood under the umbrella term, "autobiography" should be analyzed. Philippe Lejeune defines autobiography as a "retrospective prose narrative written by a real person concerning his own existence, where the focus is his individual life, in particular the story of his personality."[13] He continues to say that within such a writing, "the *author*, the *narrator* and the *protagonist* must be identical."[14]

The activity of writing, however much modern scholars insist on it being a solitary activity, was profoundly social and collaborative—particularly in the ancient period, as we saw in the previous chapter. William Johnson makes the point well, that our persistent image of premodern writing as a solitary activity is not supported by the material evidence, which points instead to a dynamic and collaborative literary culture.[15] While there are disputes over single or multiple authors for the Shepherd as a whole, we take the view that writing, even when assumed to have been done by a single author, was a collaborative practice. The questions of single or multiple authorship do not interfere with our examination of the literary effect that the persona of Hermas produces in the Book of Visions and the Mandates, which is that of a single individual. Ironically, early Jewish apocalypses written in the name of a foundational figure of Enoch, Moses, or Ezra are preemptively assumed to be wholly literary fabrications.[16] In the

---

12. Georges Gusdorf writes ("Conditions and Limits of Autobiography," in *Autobiography: Essays Theoretical and Critical*, trans. James Olney [Princeton: Princeton University Press, 1980], 28–48, here 45; originally published as, "Conditions et limites de l'autobiographie," in *Formen der Selbstdarstellung: Analekten zu einer Geschichte des literarischen Selbstportraits*, ed. Gunther Reichenkron and Erich Hasse [Berlin: Duncker & Humblot, 1956], 105–24) "Autobiography is not a simple repetition of the past as it was, for recollection brings us not the past itself but only the presence in spirit of a world forever gone," 38. See also James Olney, "Autobiography and the Cultural Moment," in that volume, *Autobiography*, 3–27, which provides an excellent survey of the modern history of the critical discussion of the genre of autobiography to the 1980s.

13. Philippe Lejeune, "The Autobiographical Pact," in *On Autobiography*, trans. Katherine Leary (Minneapolis: University of Minnesota Press, 1989), 3–30, here 4; first published in French in 1975. Also, the discussion by Maria DiBattista and Emily O. Wittman, "Introduction," in *The Cambridge Companion to Autobiography* (Cambridge: Cambridge University Press, 2014), 1–20, here 3.

14. Lejeune, "The Autobiographical Pact," 5.

15. Johnson, *Readers and Reading Culture*, 179–99.

16. Certain scholars have resisted the view that early Jewish apocalypses were purely

case of Hermas, it is usually the opposite—that is to say, scholars assume him to be a historical figure and take his experiences of revelation to be, in some degree, a form of truth-telling. It seems unlikely that the name is used pseudonymously, since there is no celebrated figure of Hermas, of the magnitude enjoyed by the figures of Moses, Enoch, or Ezra during the Second Temple period. Even though Hermas is not a pseudonym, it does not follow that the Shepherd is a reliable historical record of a living person. It is not possible to know if the protagonist of the Book of Visions is a historical person from the past. We take the view that Hermas's experiences are completely fictionalized, but that they are described to speak in a compelling way to actual lived experiences.[17]

Let us return now to Burnett Streeter's comments about the Shepherd being an autobiographical work since no one would willingly create a persona of a figure who is so decidedly 'unheroic'. Streeter concludes that the author of the Shepherd was a historical person named Hermas, based on the common assumption that autobiography is a truth-telling genre. Streeter supposes that the author of the Book of Visions and the character of Hermas were one and the same.[18] While autobiography is a powerful way to access an individual's life experiences, it is heavily constructed and not a reality TV show.[19] Autobiography strategically uses various literary devices that are associated with the writing of fiction. Given what we can see of the density and pervasiveness of the literary culture in the Roman

---

fantasy writings, and have held the view that early Jewish apocalypses were generated from some kind of spiritual or religious experience had by an anonymous author; see Alan F. Segal, "Religious Experience and the Construction of the Transcendent Self," in *Paradise Now: Essays on Early Jewish and Christian Mysticism*, ed. April D. DeConick (Atlanta: Scholars, 2006), 27–40; Moshe Idel, "Mystical Techniques," in *Essential Papers on Kabbalah*, ed. Lawrence Fine (New York: New York University Press, 1995), 438–94; Daniel Merkur, "The Visionary Practices of Jewish Apocalyptists," *The Psychoanalytical Study of Society* 14 (1989): 119–48; Michael E. Stone, "A Reconsideration of Apocalyptic Visions," *HTR* 96 (2003): 167–80 and Michael E. Stone, "Apocalyptic—Vision or Hallucination?" *Milla Wa Milla* 14 (1974): 47–56, reprinted in *Selected Studies in Pseudepigrapha and Apocrypha with Special Reference to the Armenian Tradition* (Leiden: Brill, 1991), 419–28; Harkins, *Reading with an "I" to the Heavens*.

17. Chapter 3 discusses how descriptions of Hermas's interoceptive experiences contribute to generating the phenomenon of rumination and enactivism.

18. The point has already been made by scholars of the "New Philology" that scholars typically treat texts as if they were living people, seeking to establish their blood lines by establishing the paternity of a textual tradition from one manuscript generation to the next; Cerquiglini, *Éloge de la variante: Histoire critique de la philologie*; Nichols, "Introduction: Philology in a Manuscript Culture," 1–10.

19. To be sure, reality TV gives a heavily edited media perspective and not a simple report of events as they happened.

Empire, especially in North Africa where the Shepherd enjoyed a particularly wide following, we should not overdetermine ancient authors as only writing from their own personal experiences. Instead, it seems far more likely that skilled authors would want to depict characters, events, and narrative worlds that are unusual or different from their own.

We do well not to project the characteristics and traits described in texts onto the ancient authors, but rather to imagine how texts were received and experienced by readers—what kind of affective response was had by the way a text was written? What kind of sensory perceptions influenced how a text was experienced when it was read or heard? How did the physical apparatus of a scroll or a codex influence how a text might be experienced?[20] In this chapter, the approach known as enactive reading will be applied to the opening scene of the Book of Visions. Enactive reading can be understood as one of many different types of cognitive literary approaches which are heuristically informed by the cognitive science of visual perception. Like the critical literary theorists who use enactive reading, I use what is known about the cognitive science of visual perception "critically and pragmatically," always with the specific purpose of gaining greater insight into how the narratives known as ancient apocalypses were imagined in the minds of readers and hearers.[21] Ancient readers were free, of course, to interpret narratives in multiple ways, including ways that may not have been intended by the authors of those texts.[22] In the case of the Shepherd, modern attitudes toward this work have been overdetermined by the discipline-specific questions that seek to reconstruct the history of theological doctrines or the social history of the early Church. Instead, our approach asks what made the Book of Visions appealing or engaging, such that it could be useful as a catechetical work, which is how it was widely known.

Enactive reading expands how the imagined experiences of ancient and modern readers are understood by introducing integrative biocultural understandings of the embodied mind within a larger cultural context.[23] In so

---

20. See the thesis of Harkins (*Reading with an "I" to the Heavens*) that the apparatus of the scroll should inform how we imagine a collection of emotionally arousing first-person narrative prayers to have been experienced by an ancient reader.

21. Lisa Zunshine, "Introduction to Cognitive Literary Studies," in *The Oxford Handbook of Cognitive Literary Studies* (Oxford: Oxford University Press, 2015), 1–9, 2.

22. It is always the case that readers are free to interpret against the grain of the narrative.

23. Geertz, "Religious Bodies, Minds and Places. A Cognitive Science of Religion Perspective," 35–52; Geertz, "Brain, Body and Culture: A Biocultural Theory of Religion," 304–21. Also relevant is Geertz, "Global Perspectives on Methodology in the Study of Religion," 49–73. See also the important studies of narratives and fictional worlds on readers' imaginations by Markus Altena Davidsen, "Fiction-based Religion:

doing, the approach helps to overcome the persistent mind-body dualism that often pervades text based scholarship of the ancient world. The reader's experiential knowledge is key to understanding how enactive reading can lead to immersive experiences of the narrative world of the text. It may also help explain why a work that was so compelling and popular in the ancient world does not generate the same enthusiasm in modern academic readers who have a different conceptualization of the world and of the individual's place within it.

Making Images Vividly Present in the Mind

Ancient rhetorical strategies were concerned to create palpable experiences of mental images. According to the ancient Greek handbook known as the *Progymnasmata*, *ekphrasis* is defined as "speech that brings the subject matter vividly before the eyes."[24] Modern discussions of ancient *ekphrasis* often remark that it is a "literary description of a work of visual art" and offer Hesiod's description of Achilles's shield as the classic example, but the ancient understanding was much broader than this.[25] James A. Francis writes, "the paradox, of course, is that while scenes in Homer are often cited by the *Progymnasmata* and other rhetorical treatises as examples of *ekphrasis* in antiquity, the shield is not. It becomes the prime illustration of *ekphrasis* only with the narrowing of the definition in the renaissance and modern period."[26] The emphasis in the ancient handbooks is on the overall *effects* of

---

Conceptualising a New Category against History-Based Religion and Fandom," 378–95; Markus Altena Davidsen and Bastiaan van Rijn, "Studying Religions as Narrative Cultures: Angel Experience Narratives in the Netherlands and Some Ideas for a Narrative Research Program for the Study of Religion," in *Narrative Cultures and the Aesthetics of Religion*, ed. Dirk Johannsen, Anja Kirsch, and Jens Kreinath (Leiden: Brill, 2020), 91–122.

24. Webb, *Ekphrasis, Imagination and Persuasion in Ancient Rhetorical Theory and Practice*, 14; Whitaker, *Ekphrasis, Vision, and Persuasion in the Book of Revelation*. For the study of ancient rhetorical forms and early Christian writings, see the recent discussion of *ekphrasis* by Martin and Parsons, *Ancient Rhetoric and the New Testament: The Influence of Elementary Greek Composition*, 109–140.

25. This critique of the narrow modern understanding of ancient *ekphrasis* as pertaining only to works of art made by James A. Francis, "Metal Maidens, Achilles' Shield, and Pandora: The Beginnings of 'Ekphrasis'," *American Journal of Philology* 130 (2009): 1–23, here 1.

26. Francis, "Metal Maidens, Achilles' Shield, and Pandora," 8 n. 22. As James A. Francis notes well, ancient rhetoricians often pointed to scenes from Homer's writings as examples of *ekphrasis*—except for Achilles's Shield (*Illiad*, 18.468–608). Francis also discusses the example of Hesiod's account of the making of the statue, Pandora, in his *Theogany*. Her stunning visual beauty as an object that has been fashioned or built

rhetorical speech, thus reminding readers "not to approach texts as distanced artefacts with a purely critical eye, but to engage with them imaginatively, to think themselves into the scenes and to feel as if they were present."[27] Quintilian's handbook discusses the effects of *enargeia*, which bears some resemblance to what the *Progymnasmata* calls *ekphrasis*, as making present that which is absent—"laying out the subject before the eyes" (*sub oculos subiectio*).[28] The term *enargeia* is one that emerges in philosophical circles, and also came to have a much wider and broader use in the mimetic arts of poetry and the visual arts. These strategies rely on culturally specific ways of seeing, also known as 'visuality,' which is distinguished from the act of sight.[29] The rhetorical techniques discussed thus far are also present in a broad swath of literary forms, such as classical letter writing or formal orations.[30] Harry O. Maier discusses the experiential aspects of these rhetorical strategies with special attention to the emotions aroused by these techniques for visual imaging: "For Plato and Aristotle, as well as the Stoics, vivid speech through the evocative power of imagery and its role in prompting the memory awakens sense perception associated with the image, as well as a host of emotions that accompany it."[31] Rhetorical strategies like *ekphrasis* and *enargeia* aim to generate 'vivid mental pictures' or *phantasia*, which then compel or move

moves ambivalently between an *object d'art* and a living woman. Such a transformation is emblematic of the effect that textual descriptions can have on the person who hears them. See too, Graham Zanker, *Modes of Viewing in Hellenistic Poetry and Art* (Wisconsin: University of Wisconsin Press, 2003), 7.

27. Webb, *Ekphrasis, Imagination and Persuasion in Ancient Rhetorical Theory and Practice*, 19.

28. Quintilian (*Inst.* 9.2.30.) is citing Cicero, *De or.* 3.202. According to Webb (*Ekphrasis, Imagination and Persuasion in Ancient Rhetorical Theory and Practice*, 74–90), Quintilian's understands what is described in the *Progymnasmata* as *enargeia* (74).

29. These culturally specific ways of visually perceiving are brought to bear on the literary descriptions and representational arts in Zanker, *Modes of Viewing in Hellenistic Poetry and Art*. The audience for Zanker's work is both those who work with literary texts that rely on the reader's and hearer's imaginative construction of the person or thing that is described and those who study the *objects d'art* that can be examined physically from various perspectives. See the helpful critique that Zanker's work overdetermines ancient visuality by giving the impression that there was great uniformity and convergence in perspectives, a point made well by Jane M. F. Heath, "Ezekiel Tragicus and Hellenistic Visuality: The Phoenix at Elim," *JTS* (n.s.) 57 (2006): 23–41, here 32.

30. Readers are directed to the studies of the visual imagery and rhetorical effects found in the Pauline corpus, see Jane M. F. Heath, "Absent Presences of Paul and Christ: *Enargeia* in 1 Thessalonians 1–3," *JSNT* 32 (2009): 3–38; and Jane M. F. Heath, *Paul's Visual Piety: The Metamorphosis of the Beholder* (Oxford: Oxford University Press, 2013); Maier, "Vision, Visualisation, and Politics in the Apostle Paul," 312–32.

31. Maier, "Vision, Visualisation, and Politics in the Apostle Paul," 321.

the reader and hearer to the topic at hand.[32] In fact, the mental representation is not so much a distanced viewing but an immersive one in which the individual may even become a participant in the scene.[33] Recently, Jonas Grethlein and Luuk Huitink compare enactive reading with the ancient techniques for *enargeia* in their discussion of Homer, and conclude that they are not incompatible analytical approaches.[34] Classical rhetorical strategies like *enargeia* and *phantasia* place importance on brief narrative descriptions of the body engaged in kinesthetic experiences as necessary for constructing vivid visual immersive experiences; thus they rely on similar kinds of narrative details that are crucial for enactive reading.[35]

Classical strategies for making compelling and immersive mental images from narrative are similar to modern enactive ways of reading, but the culturally specific role that the particular life experiences of an individual in the process of imagining narrated experiences is especially highlighted in the cognitive literary approach of enactive reading. Enactive approaches are more useful for investigating our primary research question: why has the Shepherd not been received by modern scholars with the same enthusiasm it enjoyed in the ancient world? Critical literary theorists note that reading includes aspects of automaticity and trained ways of seeing.[36] The particular way of reading associated with modern scholarship is often to read against the grain of a text or to search for specific types of information. Simple kinesthetic details or accounts of embodied perception are often not the focus of modern scholars who endeavor to reconstruct a social history from the narrative details in the Shepherd. Deeply learned scholarly habits of reading and cultural expectations of modern scholars are the life experiences that

---

32. Quintillian, *The Orator's Education*, trans. Donald A. Russell, 5 Vols. LCL (Cambridge: Harvard University Press, 2001), 3.59–61; *Progymnasmata: Greek Textbooks of Prose Composition and Rhetoric*, trans. Kennedy; and the discussion by Maier, "Vision, Visualisation, and Politics in the Apostle Paul," 321.

33. Ruth Webb, "Sight and Insight: Theorizing Vision, Emotion and Imagination in Ancient Rhetoric," in *Sight and the Ancient Senses*, ed. M. Squire (London: Routledge, 2016), 205–19, here 213.

34. Jonas Grethlein and Luuk Huitink, "Homer's Vividness: An Enactive Approach," *Journal of Hellenic Studies* 137 (2017): 67–91. For an important earlier study that applies cognitive science approaches to classical texts, see Jocelyn Penny Small, *Wax Tablets of the Mind: Cognitive Studies of Memory and Literacy in Classical Antiquity* (London: Routledge, 1997).

35. Grethlein and Huitink, "Homer's Vividness," 87.

36. For some of these distinctions between automatic and learned ways of reading, see Elfenbein, *The Gist of Reading*, who applies the insights of cognitive psychology to draw theoretical distinctions between reading for pleasure and enjoyment and the trained reading done by scholars for literary analysis.

are used to extend and complete the fragmentary details found in the Book of Visions. Applying enactive reading approaches can help us to understand why the Shepherd has been received less enthusiastically by modern readers.

Seeing through the Eyes of Fictional Characters

Do readers engage with a literary character differently based on whether they understand that character to be historical or purely fictional?[37] The content of the Shepherd, viz., Hermas's visions and their interpretations, aims to captivate the interest of its reader, but it fails with many modern readers who have regarded it as "trivial fiction" based on its implausibility.[38] Most modern readers have found Hermas to act in an unseemly manner and the writing style of the Shepherd to be repetitive and disjointed. It is also the case that the details about Hermas's history as a former slave, as told in the opening scene of the Book of Visions, stand in tension with texts like the Muratorian Fragment which describes him as the brother of Pius.[39]

The rereading of the Book of Visions that this study offers is not concerned with any specific ancient person's experiences—such experiences simply cannot be recovered. Instead, enactive reading will be used to analyze the embodied experiences of the reader and the immersive processes of mental imaging from narrative. These participatory and immersive ways of reading offer a potentially rich way to conceptualize how a text like the Book of Visions cultivated the predispositions needed for moral formation. We argue that the literary style of the Book of Visions offers a compelling immersive narrative and that this has been overlooked by modern scholars whose training and interest in the Shepherd is first and foremost grounded in history. Modern scholars largely agree upon the early dating of the Shepherd. The dating of the Shepherd is during a time when the Christian canon was still open. Most scholars who read the Shepherd have been trained to read for history and to look for information and inferences about the social

---

37. This is the research question that drives the authors, Polvinen and Sklar, "Mimetic and Synthetic Views of Characters," 1–16, which we will discuss later in this chapter.

38. For example, Brox, *Der Hirt des Hermas*, 5; Dibelius, *Der Hirt des Hermas*, 503; and Joly, *Hermas. Le Pasteur*, 17–21 also understood the biographical details about Hermas to be largely fictional and based on other literary traditions and writings. Martin Leutzsch points out that calling into question the historicity of Hermas has implications for how we understand the social details about Roman Christianity from this time, Leutzsch, *Die Wahrnehmung sozialer Wirklichkeit im "Hirten des Hermas"*, 23.

39. This tension is noted by Joly, *Hermas. Le Pasteur*, 17; also discussed by Martin Leutzsch, *Die Wahrnehmung sozialer Wirklichkeit im "Hirten des Hermas"*, 24.

world of the author in the hopes of recovering a picture of what the early Christian church was like during this period. Modern scholars have underappreciated the literary style of the Book of Visions, which makes repeated references to Hermas's quotidian activities, viz., walking, sitting, kneeling, and standing (i.e., his proprioception) and his interior—frequently anguished—thoughts and emotions (interoception). These first-person reports are concrete details of embodiment—the very things that modern commentators assess as repetitive, 'monotonous', or 'banal'—are, in fact, crucial literary devices for giving depth to characters and density to narrative worlds. These are the kind of literary details that make possible the immersive experience that we associate with reading for enjoyment.

The lasting power and enormous popularity of the work suggests its great success should be understood in terms of readerly engagement, rather than its facticity.[40] Even though it presents itself as an autobiography written in first-person voice, some modern scholars take the view that the Book of Visions is a fictionalized narrative, and so do we.[41] Here we recognize its similarity to apocalypses and other fiction writing in which the reader enjoys the privileged position of omniscience, knowing every excruciating detail of the seer's thoughts as he experiences his visions. Even so, Hermas's visions are assumed to be relatable to lived experiences that would

---

40. The ability to immerse oneself in a narrative does not depend upon the text being historically factual. According to Cain Todd ("Fictional Immersion: Attending Emotionally to Fiction," *Journal of Value Inquiry* [2012]: 449–65), humans have the natural capacity to suspend disbelief, even when the content is known to be fictional. See the work on narrative cultures in contemporary contexts by Davidsen, "Fiction-based Religion: Conceptualising a New Category against History-Based Religion and Fandom," 378–95; Markus Altena Davidsen and Bastiaan van Rijn, "Studying Religions as Narrative Cultures," 91–122; Sarah Iles Johnston, "How Myths and Other Stories Help to Create and Sustain Beliefs," in *Narrating Religion*, Macmillan Interdisciplinary Handbooks (Farmington Hills, MI: Macmillan, 2017), 141–56; Sarah Iles Johnston, *The Story of Myth* (Cambridge: Harvard University Press, 2018). Most recently, see Luhrmann, *How God Becomes Real*, 27; Rachel Wagner, "A Sense of Presence: Mediating an American Apocalypse," *Religions* 12 (2021): 1–11; Angela Kim Harkins, *Experiencing Presence in the Second Temple Period: Revised and Updated Essays*, CBET 111 (Leuven: Peeters, 2022). For a discussion of the way Second Temple texts also seek to create a literary (fictional) world of an idealized culture of total commitment, see A. K. Harkins, "The Pro-Social Role of Grief in Ezra's Penitential Prayer," *BibInt* 24 (2016): 466–91.

41. The implausibility of the historicity of the opening scene of Hermas's encounter with Rhoda is discussed later in this chapter. We do not take the position that Hermas was an actual historical person because we do not think that it is possible to prove that Hermas existed historically. Even so, this overly optimistic view of historical methods is a common perspective and one that is found in the most recent study of the Shepherd, see Soyars, *The Shepherd of Hermas and the Pauline Legacy*, 40–4.

ring true for ancient readers as real experiences. Ancient readers like Tertullian and others certainly perceived Hermas with the quality of 'realness'.[42] While the work itself is only loosely tethered to a figure from antiquity, a reader's ability to imagine with vividness the scenes described through the eyes of Hermas relies on certain literary strategies employed in the text that we will examine through the cognitive literary approach known as enactive reading.

Biocultural Models of Visual Perception

The most recent theorizing about the body from cognitive science argues that human perception is not based on "abstract, propositional representations,"[43] but rather is shaped comprehensively by the interaction of the body and the mind, which together work to construct meaning from fragmentary sensory experiences. According to J. Kevin O'Regan,

> The new view of seeing suggests that there is no 'internal replica' of the outside world where all aspects of the scene are simultaneously 'projected' for us to 'see all at once.' On the contrary, seeing is constituted by the fact of using the tools provided by our visual system to extract and cognitively 'manipulate' parts of the scene. This makes an important prediction: we will only effectively see those parts of a scene that we are actively engaged in 'manipulating.' Furthermore, the parts that are seen will be seen in the light of the particular type of manipulation we are exercising, with the knowledge and mental background which that involves. Everything else in the scene will not actually be seen. This surprising claim has received impressive confirmation from recent research.[44]

Visual perception is constructed in the mind by extending what we know of the world experientially to complete the fragments of images that have grabbed our attention. This new conceptualization of seeing accounts for everyday phenomena like 'inattentional blindness', which happens when we do not see something in the space that we are looking right at, simply because our attention was not focused on it.[45] The popular conception of

---

42. Osiek, *The Shepherd of Hermas*, 4–5.
43. Karin Kukkonen and Marco Caracciolo, "What is the 'Second Generation?'" *Style* 48 (2014): 261–74, here 261.
44. J. Kevin O'Regan, "The Illusion of Seeing Everything," in *Why Red Doesn't Sound Like a Bell: Understanding the Feel of Consciousness* (Oxford: Oxford University Press, 2011), 50–61, here 50.
45. O'Regan ("The Illusion of Seeing Everything," 52) describes the well-known experiment in which a viewer is asked to watch a brief video of six people passing two different basketballs and instructed to count how many passes are made by only the three players wearing white, not black, t-shirts. According to O'Regan, it is typical for a third to half of the viewers to not notice that a person in a gorilla costume has slowly walked

seeing as a 'snapshot' suggests that when we see, we see everything simultaneously and take in information all at once. Our actual experience of seeing, however, takes place in a piecemeal fashion by focusing our attention on specific points that are then extended and constructed into a coherent representation in our mind. Merja Polvinen describes this phenomenon in the following way:

> The snapshot conception underlies for example Ernst Mach's famous 1886 drawing of the visual field, but it was overturned by twentieth-century research showing how visual perception, instead of registering a full picture of the space in view all at once, actually consists of fragmentary information gained from sequential focusing on various details through the eyes' saccadic movements. In addition, our visual accuracy is hounded by actual physical blind spots, change blindness or inattentional blindness (such as the case of the invisible gorilla), and visual experiences of things we do not strictly speaking see (such as the Kanizsa triangle). As a result, the seamless, detailed visual field has been deemed an illusion—in the sense of it being a representation produced in our brains on the basis of the fragments provided by our eyes.[46]

If we look at a busy urban scene, our minds are trained to extend and expand the fragmentary details of a yellow taxi or a black Honda Civic such that we can achieve a sense of its real presence, even though the majority of its body is visually obscured by the traffic around it.[47] O'Regan writes that "What we see is strongly determined by our expectations and prior knowledge."[48] When we imagine how seeing takes place in the mind, it is far more constructive and reconstructive than we might ordinarily think.

This theoretical understanding of how the experience of seeing is constructed from partial experiences can be applied to how readers can come to perceive a narrative world through the brief details of a character's own visions and embodied experiences. Specific descriptions of sensory experiences can be enacted by a reader who extends and completes these details in their imagination based on their own embodied experiential knowledge of the world and their assumptions about how that world works. This process allows the reader to construct a more complex representation of the narrative world in their mind and to have different observations or insights about

---

onto the court, pounded his chest and walked off. A video of the selective attention demonstration may be found on http://www.theinvisiblegorilla.com.

46. Merja Polvinen, "Enactive Perception and Fictional Worlds," in *The Cognitive Humanities: Embodied Mind in Literature and Culture*, ed. Jean Peter Garratt (London: Palgrave, 2016), 19–34, esp. 27–30, quote from 27.

47. Kevin J. O'Regan and Alva Noë, "A Sensorimotor Account of Vision and Visual Consciousness," *Behavioral and Brain Sciences* 24 (2001): 939–1031.

48. O'Regan, "The Illusion of Seeing Everything," 52.

the narrative world, a process that might lead readers to fresh exegetical insights. Elaine Auyoung writes,

> According to cognitive theories of the embodied mind, features of our empirical experiences become encoded in memory as multimodal 'traces' of the original experiences themselves, and these experiential traces can subsequently be retrieved and combined to form new mental representations. After words become linked to these traces through repeated association (as when young children are repeatedly prompted to say the name of an object aloud), they can serve as cues that activate experiential traces in the minds of readers and listeners.[49]

When language about a character's sensory experiences is enacted by a reader, the activity of reading can come to have the capacity to be immersive. Enactive reading and enactive perceiving are ways of speaking phenomenally about our ability to gain access to the sensory perceptions of a fictional character. The fragmentary first-person reports of the things that grab the visual attention of a literary character can serve as prompts for readers to fill out and complete in their minds, based, of course, on what they experientially know already about the lived world. This mental representation of a visual image or scene is one that has been constructed from various visual points—its coherence and unity is largely illusory.[50] Cognitive literary theorists like Anežka Kuzmičová and Marco Caracciolo argue that the phenomenon of immersive reading, that is, achieving an experience of presence in a narrative world, relies on first-person narration that divulges partial details about a character's proprioceptive and interoceptive experiences.[51] These embodied details about Hermas's proprioception and

---

49. Auyoung, *When Fiction Feels Real*, 12; Rolf A. Zwaan and Carol J. Madden, "Embodied Sentence Comprehension," in *Grounding Cognition: The Role of Perception and Action in Memory, Language, and Thinking*, ed. Diane Pecher and Rolf A. Zwaan (Cambridge: Cambridge University Press, 2005), 224–45. Notice that Auyoung does not employ an enactive approach, nevertheless, the attention that is placed on literary details of embodiment are common to both enactivism and representationalism.

50. Anežka Kuzmičová, "Literary Narrative and Mental Imagery: A View from Embodied Cognition," *Style* 48 (2014): 275–93 at 275–6; and Anežka Kuzmičová, "Presence in the Reading of Literary Narrative: A Case for Motor Enactment," *Semiotica* 189 (2012): 23–48; Nicole K. Speer et al., "Reading Stories Activates Neural Representations of Visual and Motor Experiences," 289–99.

51. Kuzmičová, "Presence in the Reading of Literary Narrative," and Marco Caracciolo, "Ungrounding Fictional Worlds: An Enactivist Perspective on the 'Worldlikeness' of Fiction," in *Possible Worlds Theory and Contemporary Narratology*, ed. Alice Bell and Marie-Laure Ryan (Lincoln: University of Nebraska Press, 2019), 113–31; Marco Caracciolo, "Fictional Consciousnesses," 42–65. See also the work of classicists Grethlein and Huitink, "Homer's Vividness: An Enactive Approach," 72–3; and Aldo Tagliabue, "Experiencing the Church in the *Book of Visions* of the *Shepherd of Hermas*," in

interoception allow a reader to read the Book of Visions enactively, from the seer's experience. According to enactive reading, the reader uses his or her own lived experience of the world to fill in the gaps created by the fragmentary accounts of Hermas's experiences. The first-person voice can intensify how a reader experiences a text because it allows for the performative enactment of a text. Texts that use the first-person voice can connect a character's interior experiences with our own experiences of the real people whom we encounter—individuals whom we naturally know to possess consciousness, interior emotional experiences, and an extended body. Nevertheless, the experience of reading first-person narratives like the Book of Visions far exceeds our day to day encounters with real people because we do not have access to their innermost thoughts and feelings. In this sense, the reader understands the narrative world through the 'I' of the text which enscripts emotions, desires, and experiences of characters within the reader,[52] thereby granting a privileged glimpse of how the world looks through the eyes of another. This ability to see through the perspective of another is what allows narrative to cultivate empathy and other dispositions within the reader. Marco Caracciolo writes that concrete descriptions about a character's bodily and emotional experiences allow for the following: "Readers can enact a fictional consciousness, they can perform it on the basis of textual cues."[53] According to Caracciolo a character's consciousness does not exist apart from its enactment by a reader. In other words, the process of actualizing a character's consciousness is one that is actively generated in the imagination of the reader—fictional consciousness is not passively received by a reader.[54] When readers are able to imagine a character's fully extended physical body interacting in a narrative world, with the complexities of an inner self-consciousness, they heighten their own experience of deeply empathizing with the figure in the text.[55] Literary characters and the things that constitute their inner-consciousness, namely their desires, emo-

---

Experience, Narrative, and Criticism in Ancient Greece: Under the Spell of Stories, ed. Jonas Grethlein, Luuk Huitink, and Aldo Tagliabue (New York: Oxford University Press, 2020), 104–24.

52. Harkins, *Reading with an "I" to the Heavens*, 69–113. The first-person voice allows a reader to read and to perform the enscripted emotions that can assist in cultivating desired predispositions.

53. Caracciolo, "Fictional Consciousnesses," 43.

54. Caracciolo, "Fictional Consciousnesses," 43–5. Caracciolo does well to insist that fictional consciousness is enacted and not just passively received from the narrative. This contrast is like the following discussion which contrasts understandings of the eye as actively seeing or passively receiving visual data.

55. Caracciolo, "Fictional Consciousnesses," 43; Jenefer Robinson, *Deeper than Reason: Emotion and Its Role in Literature, Music, and Art* (Oxford: Clarendon Press,

tions, and embodied experiences, are not simply received passively by readers but rather constructed in the imaginations of readers. There is no Hermas apart from the one who is enacted by the reader and constructed in his or her imagination.

The Sociocultural Context of Seeing: Past and Present

Today our tendency is to understand seeing as an activity of the eyes alone. If we have trouble seeing, we immediately visit an eye specialist, known as an opthamologist or an optometrist, who localizes and treats our vision problem by closely examining the organs that we call our eyes. In truth, though, sight is integrated with other embodied experiences and closely connected to kinesthetic and other sensory perceptions. Louise Lawrence's work adds much needed nuance to how sightedness and blindness are imagined today in the modern West, drawing attention to how sighted people tend to overdetermine the experience of blindness as a massive undifferentiated experience of total darkness, which it is often not.[56] Georgina Kleege writes that the idea of blindness is culturally constructed, "The definition has more to do with the ability to read print or drive a car than with the ability to perceive colour, light, motion or form. If I lived in a different culture or a different age, no one would define me as blind."[57] Thus, similar to the way literacy is profoundly embedded in social contexts and not a solitary experience, understandings of sensory perception are also closely tied to sociocultural contexts and measured by what is valued in a particular society. An impairment of vision would naturally require the sensory perception of touch in the form of groping or seeing with the hands, which practice might be culturally disdained and so suppressed by a modern sighted community today.[58] Among the many salutary aspects of Lawrence's cross-cultural discussion is her point that how we understand the sensorium is sociocultural—seeing is closely integrated with other sensory perceptions (e.g., touch, hearing) and tied to the movement of the body.

2007); David S. Miall, "Emotions and the Structuring of Narrative Responses," *Poetics Today* 32 (2011): 323–48.

56. Louise J. Lawrence, *Sense and Stigma in the Gospels: Depictions of Sensory-Disabled Characters* (Oxford: Oxford University Press, 2013), 31–56, esp. 47–8. For a stimulating discussion of a disability studies approach to the Hebrew Bible, but without the same degree of engagement with cross-cultural anthropology, see Saul M. Olyan, *Disability in the Hebrew Bible: Interpreting Mental and Physical Differences* (Cambridge: Cambridge University Press, 2008).

57. Georgina Kleege, *Sight Unseen* (New Haven: Yale University Press, 1999), 14; and the discussion of her work in Lawrence, *Sense and Stigma in the Gospels*, 48.

58. Lawrence, *Sense and Stigma in the Gospels*, 45.

Among elite intellectuals in the classical world, the phenomenon of seeing depended upon one's commitment to various Greek and Roman philosophical schools.[59] According to Aristotle, "sight is the most highly developed perceptive sense" (*On the Soul*, 3.3, 429a), and it is preferred over all the other senses (*Metaphysics*, 980a). In contrast, Plato's Theory of Forms reserved the highest esteem for those truths that were completely immaterial and invisible, thus expressing doubts about the certainty and reliability of visual perception (*Republic*, Book 10). While the modern world may understand the eye passively as taking in information, the ancient mind culturally understood the eye to actively emit rays that reached out to touch the object of sight.[60] This is because seeing depended on an unobstructed sight line, much like how the sense of touch relies on our hand's ability to access that which we seek to apprehend in an unobstructed way. The activity of seeing and touching were understood to be closely connected in the ancient world. The eye's agency was understood to be active and potent in further ways, like in the pan-Mediterranean phenomenon of the "evil eye." A well-placed look could do real harm and is likened to a "poisoned missile" by Plutarch (*Moralia*, 681e–f).[61] The image from the classical world is clearly one of an active, not passive, oracular organ, one that was closely connected to haptic or tactile sense perception.

The kinesthetic and haptic dimension to seeing is largely suppressed or unnoticed among sighted people in the modern West and does not factor into how the eyes are routinely imagined as passively taking in visual data. While our modern popular imagination tends to segregate and isolate the body and its sensory functions in an artificial way by conceptualizing the sensorium as one of five distinct separate sensory experiences, cognitive science research understands visual perception to be significantly more dynamic and constructive.[62] In the case of ancient narrative descriptions of spaces and landscapes, a reader is totally dependent on the partial details of characters and landscapes that have never been experienced first-hand. It is this experience of reading that Catherine Emmott and Marco Caracciolo

---

59. The discussion of seeing in Aristotle and Plato relies on the discussion found in Michael Squire, "Introductory Reflections: Making Sense of Ancient Sight," in *Sight and the Ancient Senses*, ed. Michael Squire (New York: Routledge, 2016), 1–35, here 12–17.

60. Squire, "Introductory Reflections," 16–17.

61. Squire, "Introductory Reflections," 26–8.

62. According to Yael Avrahami's study of sensory perception in the Hebrew Bible (*The Senses of Scripture: Sensory Experience in the Hebrew Bible* [New York: T&T Clark, 2012]), the visual and the kinesthetic are conflated perceptions—together, both express the idea of understanding gained by empirical investigation.

compare to the image of a blind person who taps out the world with a cane.[63] Emmott writes that the reader is like a blind person who "receives only intermittent signals of the presence of the characters from the text and must therefore monitor the fictional context mentally."[64] Mental imaging of a narrative, especially a narrative world that has never been seen, like those described in apocalypses, cannot be easily constructed by a modern reader and so relies even more on the details that are provided in the text. These literary studies follow upon the cognitive science research that underscores how our mental imaging of a scene is highly constructed, blending our own lived experiences with narrative details about spaces. Emmott and Caracciolo argue that the experience of reading is much like groping one's way through a story, touching and encountering only those things that the author has deemed important to know through partial details. While sighted individuals do not typically imagine their experience of the world through haptic terms, this way of describing our readerly experience of gradually coming to know a narrative world, like the one that Hermas describes, can be an especially useful way for us to imagine his experiences of the landscape and the beings whom he encounters along the way. Readers of apocalypses do not always see or understand what is being experienced by the seer because the experience that is taking place can be dramatically different from our own modern experiences.

A reader's sensory perception is heightened by the concrete descriptions of the speaker's bodily movement toward the object being viewed. Seeing is assisted by the body's ability to pick up and inspect an object to view it more closely. Thus, descriptions of how an individual engages his/her environment naturally involve kinesthesia. Even if natural variation in sensory experiences which can be expected over any given population is allowed, embodied engagement of a text is generally recognized to involve the sensory and motor faculties of the brain. Enactive reading refers to the cognitive processes by which texts can be experienced with the perceptions of sensorimotor movement.[65] According to Gabrielle G. Starr, seeing and movement are closely connected in how we process mental images, but also

---

63. Catherine Emmott, *Narrative Comprehension: A Discourse Perspective* (Oxford: Clarendon Press, 1997), 118; Caracciolo, *The Experientiality of Narrative*, 93–109.

64. Emmott, *Narrative Comprehension*, 118; Caracciolo, *The Experientiality of Narrative*, 95.

65. Kuzmičová, "Presence in the Reading of Literary Narrative, 23–48; Anežka Kuzmičová, "Mental Imagery," 275–93; Starr, "Multisensory Imagery," 279–91; Ellen J. Esrock, *The Reader's Eye: Visual Imaging as Reader Response* (Baltimore: Johns Hopkins University, 1994).

in our lived experiences.⁶⁶ They are especially connected when we imagine ourselves moving or doing something. Starr writes:

> Motor imagery is, I believe, a better paradigmatic case for imagery than is visual imagery: the mind's body is more encompassing than the mind's eye. Indeed, if multisensory imagery is the norm rather than the exception across sensory modes, this is nowhere clearer than in imagery of motion. Generally people imagine motion along with sight—the experience of moving one's body is, for sighted persons, both visual and kinetic. Of note, however, when we imagine other people moving, we usually, and preferentially, employ visual images: imagine, for example, your mother walking across a room. On the other hand, when we imagine ourselves moving—clapping our hands, reaching for the stars, sticking out our tongues—we may use visual images, but unlike in the case of an imagined other, we also imagine the sensations of movement for ourselves—what it would be like *if we actually were to do what we are thinking*. Instead of using solely or primarily parts of the brain that correspond to vision and imagined vision, we use areas normally employed in planning our own movements.⁶⁷ (italics original)

When we read texts about figures and imagine ourselves in the role of that character, we engage areas of our brain that not only process visual images but also sensorimotor areas. References to the body and its experiences can give strong cues for how readers might respond as they imagine themselves in a similar scenario, especially to a text presented in the first-person voice.⁶⁸ Movement through space is a natural way in which the embodied mind can imagine the act of seeing, thus apprehending the environment through the senses. Aldo Tagliabue refers to this mimetic process as a text's ability to simulate cognitive aspects of embodied perceptions: "enactive perception, according to which perceiving is a way of acting as the world makes itself available to the perceiver through his physical movement and interaction with a given object in a precise environment."⁶⁹

Spatial details in apocalypses and writings that report visionary experiences are important ways by which these first-person narratives construct a perceptible narrative world in which readers can immerse themselves. The cognitive processing areas of a reader's mind are engaged by narrative descriptions of the seer's embodied experiences.⁷⁰

---

66. Starr, *Feeling Beauty: The Neuroscience of Aesthetic Experience*, 82.
67. Starr, *Feeling Beauty: The Neuroscience of Aesthetic Experience*, 82.
68. Gillmayr-Bucher, "Body Images in the Psalms," 325.
69. Tagliabue, "An Embodied Reading of Epiphanies," 214.
70. Kuzmičová, "Literary Narrative and Mental Imagery," 275–6.

Seeing through the Eyes of Hermas

Among the various models for understanding character representation in fictional works is the mimetic model, in which the character is thought to possess the complexity of living individuals.[71] This verisimilitude is contrasted with the structuralist approach, which analyzes the character primarily as a literary artifact and understands him or her primarily in terms of their functional role as a protagonist, antagonist, or supporting character.[72] Descriptions of the narrative world found in the Book of Visions range from brief glimpses to full-blown descriptions like that of the tower in Vision 3. These partial images are sufficient to allow readers and hearers to gain a sense of the narrative world and to infer an interior life for Hermas, the one who inhabits it.

Let us look at the scene of Hermas assisting the beautiful—and naked—Rhoda from the Tiber River. This opening to the Book of Visions offers a tantalizing brief image that is then filled out in the imagination. The scene, a beautiful woman bathing, reuses a common trope known from early Jewish and Roman writings.[73] The Book of Visions introduces Hermas as he retells the story of his chance encounter with Rhoda:

> 1.1 (Ὅρασις ά 1.1) Ὁ θρέψας με πέπρακέν με Ῥόδῃ τινὶ εἰς Ῥώμην. μετὰ πολλὰ ἔτη ταύτην ἀνεγνωρισάμην καὶ ἠρξάμην αὐτὴν ἀγαπᾶν ὡς ἀδελφήν. 2 μετὰ χρόνον τινὰ λουομένην εἰς τὸν ποταμὸν τὸν Τίβεριν εἶδον, καὶ ἐπέδωκα αὐτῇ τὴν χεῖρα καὶ ἐξήγαγον αὐτὴν ἐκ τοῦ ποταμοῦ. ταύτης οὖν ἰδὼν τὸ κάλλος διελογιζόμην ἐν τῇ καρδίᾳ μου λέγων· Μακάριος ἤμην εἰ τοιαύτην γυναῖκα εἶχον καὶ τῷ κάλλει καὶ τῷ τρόπῳ. μόνον τοῦτο ἐβουλευσάμην, ἕτερον δὲ οὐδέν.
>
> 1.1 The one who raised me sold me to a certain woman named Rhoda, in Rome. After many years, I regained her acquaintance and began to love her as a sister. 2 When some time had passed, I saw her bathing in the Tiber River; and I gave her my hand to help her out of the river. When I observed her beauty I began reasoning in my heart, "I would be fortunate to have a wife of such beauty and character." This is all I had in mind, nothing else.

---

71. Polvinen and Sklar, "Mimetic and Synthetic Views of Characters," 6–7. Polvinen and Sklar have collaborated to combine empirical studies of readerly responses to the main character in *Flowers for Algernon* with theoretical models of reading.

72. Polvinen and Sklar, "Mimetic and Synthetic Views of Characters," 7.

73. The following parallels from the ancient literature are often cited: (Ps-)Plutarch, *Love Stories*, 1.771 E in the *Mor.*; Longus, *Daphn.*, 1.32; *Anthologia Palatina* (5.209), the story of Actaeon and Artemis, as told by Callimachus, *Hymn.* 5.107–66, Ovid, *Metam.* 3.138–252, David and Bathsheba (2 Sam. 11), and the story of Susanna and the Elders from the deuterocanon; see Antonius Hilhorst, "Erotic Elements in the Shepherd of Hermas," in *Groningen Colloquia on the Novel IX*, ed. H. Hofmann and M. Zimmerman (Groningen: Egbert Forsten, 1998), 195; Leutzsch, *Die Wahrnehmung sozialer Wirklichkeit im "Hirten des Hermas"*, 20–49, esp. 31–41.

Rhoda is a woman who is assumed to be his former slave master. Thus the scene is not only voyeuristic, it includes the additional complication of Hermas's subordinate status to the woman whom he desired, a topic that Marianne Bjelland Kartzow has discussed in detail.[74] However, based on a rereading of the Bodmer Papyrus, Emanuele Castelli has argued recently that Rhoda was not a slave master, but rather a slave, one who had been sold in Rome herself.[75] In such a context, this opening scene can be understood as describing the moment when she and Hermas are reacquainted with each other after some time.

The scene takes place at the Tiber River, one of the major waterways of Rome. The story of Hermas and Rhoda is an arresting scene that reuses a stock image from early Jewish and Roman writings: watching a beautiful woman as she bathes. The story and the excessive desire (ἐπιθυμία) that it generates within Hermas will be discussed in more detail in Chapter 3. Here, we wish to discuss the striking image of the beautiful woman, Rhoda. The author of the Book of Visions has chosen to describe her beauty indirectly, in a brief and very condensed way, far more fleeting than other descriptions like that of the Tower in Vision 3 or the curious beast in Vision 4. Hermas later has a vision of a woman in the heavens, who confronts him about his desire (ἐπιθυμία). It is widely held that the woman in the vision is Rhoda, because of the identification of her as "the woman I had desired," (τὴν γυναῖκα ἐκείνην ἣν ἐπεθύμησα, Vis. 1.1.4 [1.4]) but I would suggest that the exchange with the heavenly Lady is ambiguous. The vision is never called Rhoda, but only as "Lady." This is true too for the other visions of women Church that take place later. Hermas's use of the title befits his slavish subjectivity well.

Hermas's excessive desire (ἐπιθυμία) in the form of sexual arousal is an example of his body's interoceptive experience, which he attempts to conceal from the heavenly Lady. While he denies it in line 2, his penitential act of kneeling to confess his sins just prior to his vision in line 3 suggests otherwise. As he sputters his defense, vigorously denying any lascivious thoughts, Hermas says, "Have I not always thought of you as a goddess?" (οὐ πάντοτέ σε ὡς θεὰν ἡγησάμην, Vis. 1.1.7 [1.7]).

1.4 προσευχομένου δέ μου ἠνοίγη ὁ οὐρανός, καὶ βλέπω τὴν γυναῖκα ἐκείνην ἣν ἐπεθύμησα ἀσπαζομένην με ἐκ τοῦ οὐρανοῦ, λέγουσαν· Ἑρμᾶ, χαῖρε.

---

74. Kartzow, *The Slave Metaphor and Gendered Enslavement in Early Christian Discourse*.

75. Emanuele Castelli, "Gli esordi alternativi del *Pastore* di Erma," Emanuele Castelli, "Dati storici e aspetti romanzeschi nelle prime due Visioni del *Pastore* di Erma," and Emanuele Castelli, "Il I capitol de *Pastore* di Erma alla luce delle recenti acquisizioni sul P. Bodmer XXXVIII e sulla *Vulgata*."

5 βλέψας δὲ εἰς αὐτὴν λέγω αὐτῇ· Κυρία, τί σὺ ὧδε ποιεῖς; ἡ δὲ ἀπεκρίθη μοι· Ἀνελήμφθην ἵνα σου τὰς ἁμαρτίας ἐλέγξω πρὸς τὸν Κύριον. 6 λέγω αὐτῇ· Νῦν σύ μου ἔλεγχος εἶ; Οὔ, φησίν, ἀλλὰ ἄκουσον τὰ ῥήματα ἅ σοι μέλλω λέγειν. ὁ Θεὸς ὁ ἐν τοῖς οὐρανοῖς κατοικῶν καὶ κτίσας ἐκ τοῦ μὴ ὄντος τὰ ὄντα, καὶ πληθύνας καὶ αὐξήσας ἕνεκεν τῆς ἁγίας ἐκκλησίας αὐτοῦ, ὀργίζεταί σοι ὅτι ἥμαρτες εἰς ἐμέ. 7 ἀποκριθεὶς αὐτῇ λέγω· Εἰς σὲ ἥμαρτον; ποίῳ τρόπῳ; ἢ πότε σοι αἰσχρὸν ῥῆμα ἐλάλησα; οὐ πάντοτέ σε ὡς θεὰν ἡγησάμην; οὐ πάντοτέ σε ἐνετράπην ὡς ἀδελφήν; τί μου καταψεύδῃ, ὦ γύναι, τὰ πονηρὰ ταῦτα καὶ ἀκάθαρτα;

1.4 While I was praying the sky opened up and I saw the woman I had desired, addressing me from heaven: "Hermas, greetings!" I looked at her and said, "Lady, what are you doing here?" 5 She replied to me, "I have been taken up to accuse you of your sins before the Lord." 6 I said to her, "So now are you accusing me?" "No," she said, "but listen to what I have to say to you. The God who dwells in heaven and who, for the sake of his holy church, created, increased, and multiplied that which exists out of that which does not exist, is angry at you for sinning against me." 7 I answered her, "Have I sinned against you? In what way? When did I speak an inappropriate word to you? Have I not always thought of you as a goddess? Have I not always respected you as a sister? Why do you make such evil and foul accusations against me, O woman?"

In the next line, the Lady goes on to say knowingly that "an evil desire" (ἡ ἐπιθυμία τῆς πονηρίας) arose in Hermas's heart (1.1.8 [1.8]).

Hermas's reply to the heavenly Lady is defensive. He insists that he regarded her "as a goddess" (ὡς θεάν, Vis. 1.1.7 [1.7]). Antonius Hilhorst describes this as a polytheistic element.[76] Here, however, we might imagine that ancient readers associated the image of the beautiful bathing Rhoda with the goddess Venus. Depictions of her bathing are commonplace and linked closely to ancient Rome, the setting of the encounter. The heavenly Lady, "the woman whom I had desired" (τὴν γυναῖκα ἐκείνην ἣν ἐπεθύμησα, Vis. 1.1.4 [1.4]) is also like the goddess Venus who somehow knows what is deep within Hermas's heart. Here we might add that Rhoda was not bathing in a Roman bathhouse but bathing out in the open in a natural waterway. This too fits well Hesiod's story about the birth of Venus, who emerges from Uranus's severed genitals that had been tossed into the sea.[77]

As readers, we do not receive complete visual descriptions, but rather fragmentary narrative details about characters, their bodies, and their encounters with its space as we 'grope' our way through the narrative world. Ancient and modern readers have interpreted the opening scene of Rhoda bathing in the Tiber River very differently based on their lived experiences and cultural assumptions. Here, modern commentators often interpret the scene from

---

76. Antonius Hilhorst, "Erotic Elements in the Shepherd of Hermas," 193–204.
77. Hesiod, *Theogony*, §173.

an ethnocentric vantagepoint when they remark on the presumed Christian identity of Rhoda, who is related to Hermas as a 'sister'. The praise of her moral character (Vis. 1.1.1–2 [1.1–2]) is understood by modern readers as a stark contradiction to the fact that she is bathing out in the open and allowing a man, who is not her husband, to assist her from the waters. Martin Leutzsch writes:

> Ein weiterer Widerspruch besteht Dibelius und Joly zufolge zwischen Rhodes von Hermas attestierter moralischer Höhe und ihrem faktischen Verhalten: Eine sittsame Frau bade nicht im Tiber und lasse sich nicht von einem Mann aus dem Wasser helfen.[78]

In his commentary on this scene, Graydon Snyder gestures to the implausibility of the scene when he writes, "that a Roman matron would have been bathing openly in the Tiber is incredible."[79] So too, Antonius Hilhorst writes, "there is a historical improbability in a Lady bathing in public."[80] He goes on to say, "Every respectable villa or mansion was equipped with its own baths…. So there was no need for a well-to-do lady to use a river."[81] These modern scholars read the scene and extended what they know from their own life experiences of their social class and their expectations of modern Christianity to their understanding of the past.

In contrast, this picturesque scene of a bathing woman can be placed alongside the other references in the Shepherd that evoke the temperate and soothing images associated with Rome and the Umbrian countryside discussed briefly in the first chapter. Images of a woman bathing easily conjure mental images associated with Rome, including the infamous bathhouses of Rome, which was the setting for amorous relations, even for Christians.[82] Of course the detail that Hermas was Rhoda's former slave may also generate arousing mental images since Roman law permitted male and female slaves to be used sexually by both their male and female owners.[83] Here we

---

78. Leutzsch, *Die Wahrnehmung sozialer Wirklichkeit im "Hirten des Hermas"*, 29.
79. Snyder, *The Shepherd of Hermas*, 28.
80. Hilhorst, "Erotic Elements in the Shepherd of Hermas," 196.
81. Hilhorst, "Erotic Elements in the Shepherd of Hermas," 196 n. 8.
82. For example, Ovid, *Ars amatoria* 3.639-40; Juvenal, *Satire* 6.419–25; Clement, *Paed.* III, 32–3; Cyprian, *De habitu virginum*, 19; Tertullian, *Apol.* 42.2; Tertullian, *Spect.* 8.9; Tertullian, *Paen.* 11.3; see the discussion of these texts by Roy Bowen Ward, "Women in Roman Baths," *HTR* 85 (1992): 125–47, esp. 142–7.
83. Jennifer Glancy, "The Sexual Use of Slaves: A Response to Kyle Harper on Jewish and Christian *Porneia*," *JBL* 134 (2015): 215–29. Glancy is right to criticize Harper's discussion as imposing too strict an understanding of Jewish laws concerning the sexual use of slaves. Greek and Roman law permitted men to use their slaves sexually, and contra Harper, Jewish law permitted the same and did not understand such acts as *porneia* (216–17). Glancy discusses K. Harper's views in his article, "*Porneia*: The

note that the narrative does not describe any sexual contact taking place between Hermas and Rhoda. The text speaks in multiple ways of Hermas's desire (ἡ ἐπιθυμία), thus focusing the attention of readers and hearers on the voyeuristic aspects of the scene and not on a specific act that consummates the desire.

We see from the above examples that a modern male reader imagines the opening scene through an ethnocentric looking-glass. They extend the fragmentary details of the narrative, using their own life experiences of what middle-class Christian women in a modern society would reasonably do. What might an ancient reader visualize as they read the opening scene of Rhoda bathing in the Tiber River? The narrative lends itself to the visuality of the Roman Empire of the bathing goddess Venus who was closely connected with the city of Rome. Ancient first-century authors make note of the prominent beauty of her statues for the benefit of those who have not journeyed to the city themselves. According to Pliny, "there is a Venus of his at Rome, a work of extraordinary beauty, in the buildings of Octavia" (*Nat.* 36.5). Pliny preserves many stories about Greek artists and sculptures, and describes the Greek Praxiteles sculpting the Aphrodite of Knidos, the model on which many of the Roman Venus statues are based.[84] Ovid, of course, gives an even more elaborate discussion of Pygmalion's sexual desire for

---

Making of a Christian Sexual Norm," *JBL* 131 (2012): 363–83; K. Harper, *Slavery in the Late Roman World AD 275–425* (Cambridge: Cambridge University Press, 2011); K. Harper, *From Shame to Sin: The Christian Transformation of Sexual Morality in Late Antiquity* (Cambridge: Harvard University Press, 2013). Other studies of the sexual use of slaves include: Catherine Hezser, *Jewish Slavery in Antiquity* (New York: Oxford University Press, 2005); David P. Wright, " 'She Shall Not Go Free as Male Slaves Do': Developing Views about Slavery and Gender in the Laws of the Hebrew Bible," in *Beyond Slavery: Overcoming Its Religious and Sexual Legacies*, ed. Bernadette J. Brooten with Jacqueline L. Hazelton, Black Religion/ Womanist Thought/ Social Justice (New York: Palgrave Macmillan, 2010), 125–42; Joseph A. Marchal, "The Usefulness of an Onesimus: The Sexual Use of Slaves and Paul's Letter," *JBL* (2011): 749–70, esp. 753 where Marchal describes the exchange between the male slave Gastron and "the female master who has already used him sexually" (753). Keith Bradley (*Slavery and Society at Rome*, Key Themes in Ancient History [Cambridge: Cambridge University Press, 1994]) writes, "it is taken without question that slaves can and do become objects of sexual gratification for both the men and women who own them. It is one of the prerogatives of ownership and the servile response is scarcely worth considering" (28).

84. On the enormous popularity of statues of the bathing Venus in the ancient period, see Andrew Stewart, "A Tale of Seven Nudes: The Capitoline and Medici Aphrodites, Four Nymphs at Elean Herakleia, and an Aphrodite at Megalopis," *Antichthon* 44 (2010); 12–32; Brunilde Sismondo Ridgway, *Hellenistic Sculpture II: The Style of c. 200–100 BC* (Madison, WI: University of Wisconsin Press, 2008), 13; Christine Mitchell Havelock, *The Aphrodite of Knidos and Her Successors: A Historical Review of the Female Nude in Greek Art* (Ann Arbor: University of Michigan Press, 1995).

the statue of the goddess in his *Metamorphoses*—a memorable tale that Clement of Alexandria summarizes in his *Protrepticus* 4.57.3.[85] Angelos Chaniotis describes how such statues were culturally infused with emotions and agency, and known for the way they generated excessive desire in their viewers.[86]

There were many different depictions of Rome's bathing goddess. The Capitoline Venus, dated to the second century CE, measures over six feet tall.[87] Her body positioning expresses her vulnerability, a pose known as the *Venus Pudica*, with one arm covering her breasts and her other covering her groin area.[88] Christine Mitchell Havelock comments on the strategic effect of the modest pose (*Venus Pudica*) in arousing and not suppressing desire:

> [The arms] do not suppress the body; they hardly even touch it. And they never truly conceal the breasts. Whether curved toward the pubic area or the breasts, the arms retrace and echo, without apology, the soft swelling of the young female body. Rather than shielding or hiding their nudity, their gestures are intended to emphasize it.[89]

Other popular depictions depict Venus crouching as she bathes or washes her hair, a pose known as *Venus Anadyomene*. These statues were well-known for their arousing beauty. On account of her close association with Rome, cities throughout the empire prominently positioned statues of Venus in public places, both to imitate Rome and to serve as reminders of their military subjugation to the city.[90] The beautiful statue known as the "Venus of Cyrene" is an example of Roman imperial rule and influence in North

---

85. Patricia Salzman-Mitchell, "A Whole Out of Pieces: Pygmalion's Statue in Ovid's *Metamorphoses*," *Arethusa* 41 (2008): 291–311.

86. Angelos Chaniotis, "The Life of Statues: Emotion and Agency," in *Emotions in the Classical World: Methods, Approaches, and Directions*, ed. Douglas Cairns and Damien Nelis (Stuttgart: Franz Steiner Verlag, 2017), 143–58, esp. 153–54. Chaniotis refers to this phenomenon as "agalmatophilia" (153); see also A. Corso, "Ancient Greek Sculptors as Magicians," *Quaderni Ticinesi. Numismatica e Antichità Classiche* 28 (1999): 97–111; G. L. Hersey, *Falling in Love with Statues: Artificial Humans from Pygmalion to the Present* (Chicago: University of Chicago Press, 2009); D. T. Steiner, *Images in the Mind: Statues in Archaic Greek Literature and Thought* (Princeton: Princeton University Press, 2001).

87. Capitoline Venus is approximately 1.93 m tall. It is modeled on the Greek Praxiteles's statue of the Knidian Aphrodite.

88. Other popular sculptures of the goddess in Rome during this period include the Esquiline Venus which is dated to Rome's early Imperial Period.

89. Havelock, *The Aphrodite of Knidos and Her Successors*," 79.

90. See the discussion of the 2008 excavation of a Venus Pudica statue by Marina Ončevska Todorovska, "The Statue of Venus Pudica from Skupi," *Folia archaeologica Balkanica* 11 (2011): 347–58.

Africa.[91] While not much statuary survived in North Africa, depictions of Venus bathing in natural settings is a common theme in the mosaics found throughout the bathhouses in North Africa at Sétif, Tébessa, Thina, and Sidi Ghrib.[92] While the beauty of Venus testified to her role as a fertility goddess, her cult evolved into a symbol of Roman military power. For example, the "Venus of Cyrene" is tied to Sulla's victory over Carthage in the second century BCE and emblematic of Rome's military dominance over North Africa.[93] The recent discovery of a *Venus Pudica* in Skupi in 2008, in northern Macedonia, testifies to the ubiquitous presence of these statues as a marker of Imperial Roman rule and the 'citational' ease with which they can be positioned throughout the empire. Marina Ončevska Todorovska writes, "Sculptures in provincial baths demonstrate the influential role of sculptures in urbanization and the Romanization of their land."[94]

When our minds cognitively process visual descriptions like the one that appears at the start of the Book of Visions, we extend and fill in these brief and incomplete details based on our prior memories or life experiences. Hermas's interoceptive response to seeing Rhoda bathing can be easily understood and enacted by ancient readers who are free to supply their own life experiences of seeing images of the goddess Venus, popularly depicted in the act of bathing. These statues and depictions of the goddess

---

91. Also relevant are the events surrounding the repatriation or return of the Venus of Cyrene statue, that had been taken by Italy in 1911, and the decision to return it to Libya in 2008; see Alessandro Chechi, "The Return of Cultural Objects Removed in Times of Colonial Domination and International Law: The Case of the Venus of Cyrene," *Italian Yearbook of International Law* 18 (2008): 159–81; Gilbert Bagnani, "Hellenistic Sculpture from Cyrene," *The Journal of Hellenic Studies* 41 (1921): 232–46; and Ernest A. Gardner, "The Aphrodite from Cyrene," *The Journal of Hellenic Studies* 40 (1920): 203–205.

92. Katherine M. D. Dunbabin, "Baiarum Grata Voluptas: Pleasures and Dangers of the Baths," *Papers of the British School at Rome* 57 (1989): 6–46, here 23.

93. Bagnani, "Hellenistic Sculpture from Cyrene," 232–46. James B. Rives, "Venus Genetrix Outside Rome," *Phoenix* 48 (1994): 294–306; and James B. Rives, *Religion and Authority in Roman Carthage from Augustus to Constantine* (Oxford: Clarendon Press, 1995), does well to argue against a model of a comprehensive and unified Roman religion throughout the empire. Instead, in places like the Roman colony in north Africa, the religious cult was determined locally and preserved its ties to local deities. Our point about the "Venus of Cyrene" is simply that it is a visible symbol of Roman military presence, and not a claim about the uniformity of colonies participating in the Roman Venus cult throughout the empire.

94. Ončevska Todorovska, "The Statue of Venus Pudica from Skupi," 357. The Venus statue recently excavated in Skupi in northern Macedonia is dated to the second century CE. She is crafted in the tradition of the naked Aphrodite of Cnidus by Praxiteles, reflecting the precise technical skill of the Roman Imperial Period (355).

were emblematic of Rome and proliferated throughout the empire, reminding those who saw them of Roman military dominance.

What is striking about the terse opening scene of the Book of Visions is the haptic detail that makes the scene titillating—Hermas extends his hand to assist Rhoda out of the water. Here, just as we naturally move closer to get a better look at something, Hermas also moves closer to the naked Rhoda and touches her as he helps her out of the water. Readers can enactively imagine their own hand reaching out to touch Rhoda. Where exactly he touched Rhoda, we do not know—perhaps she took his extended hand, or perhaps he firmly held her elbow to support her as she stepped from the water. If readers imagine Rhoda in the form of the beautiful Capitoline Venus (*Venus Pudica*), with her arms modestly covering her body, Rhoda would further expose herself by extending her hand to Hermas. Because we are not told, the reader's imagination is unfettered and could entertain countless other possibilities. The scene with Hermas and Rhoda illustrates well how the work of imagining narrative worlds is like mentally 'groping' through a space. Like one who is visually impaired, a reader can only 'see' the details that are given by the author, which is likened to that which is 'felt' with the hand or the body. When one steps onto a threshold, it is not necessary to run one's hand over every inch of the lintel of a doorframe to know that you have reached a passageway—so too, the text is not explicit about what exactly Hermas sees or how precisely he assisted Rhoda as she emerged from the bath. In fact, these undetermined aspects of the scene allow it to be even more voyeuristic and erotic to readers who must both remain at a distance watching the scene and who must also place themselves in the scene, imagining concretely what it might be like to touch Rhoda's wet flesh. Readers, of course, supply their own lived memories of ordinary bathing and the feel of skin, wet and scrubbed clean at a bath, but they can also easily access the many seductive images of the goddess bathing. This process of extending and imagining the scene in a voyeuristic direction fits the narrative, which goes to great lengths to reveal Hermas's interoceptive experience of arousal through his exchange with the heavenly Lady. Images of a woman bathing, in the form of the specific goddess Venus, were predictable and commonplace throughout the Roman Empire and well documented in ancient writings. These images could easily fill out the arresting scene that opens the Book of Visions, especially among readers who are elite *literati*, like those at Oxyrhynchus, the place where many copies of the Shepherd were found.

Cognitive literary approaches use mimetic theorization of characters, according to which readers extend their own experiential knowledge of their bodies and sensory perceptions to the characters in the text, thus allowing the characters to achieve a vibrancy and the quality of lived experience. Elaine Auyoung describes this process of embodied reading in the following way:

A number of critics whose approaches are otherwise quite distinct have proposed that the act of reading fiction functions as exercise, practice, or training for actual life. Yet if novelists depend on the store of experiential traces that readers have acquired from their own everyday lives, literary experience seems less like practice for real life than like one of the payoffs of our quotidian labor. It is in ordinary lived experience, in which we routinely find ourselves stepping on slippery pieces of ice, fussing with loose buttons, stumbling over our own words, and freeing a hook that has snagged on something else, that we equip ourselves with the sensorimotor knowledge that automatically comes to mind when we read.[95]

The concreteness with which characters are depicted in specific everyday situations helps readers to achieve this mimetic effect. In the example of Rhoda emerging from the waters of the Tiber, readers from the city of Oxyrhynchus, where copies of the Shepherd were especially numerous, might also associate their own lived experiences of seeing bathers in the river Nile or the Joseph canal. These fragmentary descriptions of Hermas in motion or interacting with his environment and his experience of arousal at seeing Rhoda bathing are sufficient cues for readers to complete and enact on their own based on their lived experience and voyeuristic tendencies. Even though the description of Rhoda is extremely condensed, it can become vivid and real for ancient readers who, more readily than modern readers, call to mind Rome's ubiquitous Venus statuary or their own memories of the rivers and waterways in Egypt. Concrete details strategically enliven a narrative, by making it compelling and memorable. While modern scholars imagine Hermas helping Rhoda from her bath with disbelief, describing it as "incredible" or implausible,[96] ancient readers would have had a host of mental images at hand to fill out this condensed reference to Rhoda bathing. An enactive approach highlights how the reader/hearer participates in co-constructing the sensory perceptions of the scene. This level of active participation on the part of the reader and hearer refocuses our attention on

---

95. Auyoung, *When Fiction Feels Real*, 34. In this quoted passage, Auyoung's focus is not to contrast a representational understanding of reading with an enactive approach to narrative, the latter which understands the reader as having a more active participatory approach to reading. Instead, Auyoung's work brings together several different embodied approaches, some of which are in tension with each other, to think more about the experience of reading of nineteenth century literature. Ultimately, Auyoung holds a representational view of cognition in which readers construct a "free-standing model" (5) of a narrative world that feels real but which is transient and not real. This differs from enactivism, which emphasizes the embodied sensorimotor aspects of cognition and the active co-construction of the narrative world and sensory perceptions of it within the reader.

96. Leutzsch, *Die Wahrnehmung sozialer Wirklichkeit im "Hirten des Hermas"*, 29; Snyder, *The Shepherd of Hermas*, 28.

how the narrative can engage a reader's own experiences, thus allowing the text to serve in a larger program of individual moral formation and examination of conscience.

Other descriptions of the narrative world in the Book of Visions are discrete isolated referential details that are imprecise and frustratingly fragmentary. Ironically, these partial details simulate our lived experience of seeing, which does not happen in large complete saturated images all at once. We see by looking with focused attention on specific points of interest, which are then used to construct a more complete visual image of a scene by filling in gaps based on our lived experiences. In the case of the first vision, the reader is told that it takes place while Hermas is walking, but the description is vague about where exactly he has traversed.

> 1.3 μετὰ χρόνον τινὰ πορευομένου μου εἰς κώμας καὶ δοξάζοντος τὰς κτίσεις τοῦ θεοῦ, ὡς μεγάλαι καὶ ἐκπρεπεῖς καὶ δυναταί εἰσιν, περιπατῶν ἀφύπνωσα. καὶ πνεῦμά με ἔλαβεν καὶ ἀπήνεγκέν με δι᾽ ἀνοδίας τινός, δι᾽ ἧς ἄνθρωπος οὐκ ἐδύνατο ὁδεῦσαι· ἦν δὲ ὁ τόπος κρημνώδης καὶ ἀπερρηγὼς ἀπὸ τῶν ὑδάτων. διαβὰς οὖν τὸν ποταμὸν ἐκεῖνον ἦλθον εἰς τὰ ὁμαλά, καὶ τιθῶ τὰ γόνατα καὶ ἠρξάμην προσεύχεσθαι τῷ κυρίῳ καὶ ἐξομολογεῖσθαί μου τὰς ἁμαρτίας. 4 προσευχομένου δέ μου ἠνοίγη ὁ οὐρανός, καὶ βλέπω τὴν γυναῖκα ἐκείνην ἣν ἐπεθύμησα ἀσπαζομένην με ἐκ τοῦ οὐρανοῦ, λέγουσαν· Ἑρμᾶ, χαῖρε. 5 βλέψας δὲ εἰς αὐτὴν λέγω αὐτῇ· Κυρία, τί σὺ ὧδε ποιεῖς;

> 1.3 When some time had passed, I was traveling to the countryside, glorifying the creations of God and thinking how great, remarkable, and powerful they are. On the way I fell asleep and a spirit took me and carried me through a certain deserted place that was impassable, for the place was steep and split up by the courses of water. When I crossed the river I came to level ground and bowed my knees; and I began praying to the Lord and confessing my sins. 4 While I was praying the sky opened and I saw the woman I had desired, addressing me from the heaven: "Hermas, greetings!" 5 I looked at her and said, "Lady, what are you doing here?" (Vis. 1.1.3–5a [1.3–5a])

The description of the narrative world is impressionistic and vague. While there are some spatiotemporal details, such as "when some time had passed," (μετὰ χρόνον τινὰ), the narrative does not specify an exact time or place (Vis. 1.1.3 [1.3]). Hermas walks while contemplating God's creation and suddenly enters a dissociative state ("while walking about, I fell asleep," περιπατῶν ἀφύπνωσα, Vis. 1.1.3 [1.3]). He is transported to another place by a spirit ("a spirit took me and carried me through a certain deserted place that was impassable," καὶ πνεῦμά με ἔλαβεν καὶ ἀπήνεγκέν με δι᾽ ἀνοδίας τινός, Vis. 1.1.3 [1.3]). Dramatic changes in the landscape are reported: Hermas is carried up a steep incline and across a terrain cut with deep fissures. After being lifted over rushing rivers, Hermas kneels down and prays. The text also says that Hermas "confessed his sins," suggesting that his thoughts of Rhoda were not as chaste as he had previously insisted (Vis. 1.1.2 [1.2]).

The reader mentally constructs the solidity of the space where this vision takes place by using these references to Hermas's proprioception, viz. his movement through the space and his bodily contact with the environment. These proprioceptive and interoceptive experiences help the reader gain a sense of Hermas's movement into a new narrative space. The vision began with Hermas joyfully contemplating God's creation, but his being transported has left a strong emotional impression on him, which he immediately expresses through his kneeling and desire to confess his sins. While Hermas's description of the new landscape is brief and incomplete, it may be extended and completed when the seer's own movements in those spaces are vividly enacted by the reader's imagination. A reader can imagine Hermas's knees pressing into the soft ground near the river (Vis. 1.1.3 [1.3]), thus gaining a greater sense of the space where the vision is taking place. The riverbank, where Hermas is confronted by the heavenly Lady whom he desired, resembles the space where Hermas had seen Rhoda bathing in the Tiber River. It is a setting that fittingly evokes the episode that begins the Book of Visions. The details allow the reader to vicariously access those spaces as they arise and to imagine their own further exploration of the narrative world.

The woman whom Hermas meets in this opening vision is "the woman whom I had desired" (τὴν γυναῖκα ἐκείνην ἣν ἐπεθύμησα, Vis. 1.1.4 [1.4]) and clearly identified at the start as Rhoda, the woman whom Hermas saw emerging from the Tiber River. We have suggested that the reference to a woman bathing and his comparison of her as a 'goddess' (Vis. 1.1.7 [1.7]) would lead readers to visualize the famous statues of Venus, which were closely associated with Rome and commented on by ancient authors like Pliny, Ovid, and Clement of Alexandria. Because this specific visionary encounter with the heavenly Lady will be discussed in greater detail in the following chapter as an example of rumination, I will not say more about it here. Like the incomplete and vague references to the environment, Hermas immediately goes into his second visionary encounter with a woman after he is struck with anguish and compunction (Vis. 1.2.1–2 [2.1–2]). The vision of the woman elder (γυνὴ πρεσβῦτις), also called 'Lady', must be constructed by the reader through the multiple fragmentary references to her physical body. The Lady achieves solidity from the way her physical embodiment is described, part by part, and from her physical positioning in relation to other characters. Hermas describes her appearance in the following way:

> ταῦτά μου συμβουλευομένου καὶ διακρίνοντος ἐν τῇ καρδίᾳ μου βλέπω κατέναντί μου καθέδραν λευκὴν ἐξ ἐρίων χιονίνων γεγονυῖαν μεγάλην· καὶ ἦλθεν γυνὴ πρεσβῦτις ἐν ἱματισμῷ λαμπροτάτῳ, ἔχουσα βιβλίον εἰς τὰς χεῖρας, καὶ

2. Taking a Look at Hermas 93

ἐκάθισεν μόνη, καὶ ἀσπάζεταί με· Ἑρμᾶ, χαῖρε. κἀγὼ λυπούμενος καὶ κλαίων εἶπον· Κυρία, χαῖρε.

> While I was mulling these things over in my heart and trying to reach a decision, I saw across from me a large white chair, made of wool, white as snow. And an elderly woman came, dressed in radiant clothes and holding a book in her hands. She sat down, alone, and addressed me, "Greetings, Hermas." And I said, still upset and weeping, "Greetings Lady." (Vis. 1.2.2. [2.2])

First, Hermas sees a great white chair and then a woman elder in splendid clothing. She is described as holding a little book in her hands. The body of the Lady takes on a sense of solidity as she moves, first by sitting in the white chair and then by the detail that she is holding a little book in her hands. After her exchange with Hermas, the narrative gives further details about the Lady's bodily movements: "When she finished reading and *rose* from her chair, four young men came and took away the chair and went away toward the east. Then she called me over and touched my breast" (Ὅτε οὖν ἐτέλεσεν ἀναγινώσκουσα καὶ ἠγέρθη ἀπὸ τῆς καθέδρας, ἦλθαν τέσσαρες νεανίαι καὶ ἦραν τὴν καθέδραν καὶ ἀπῆλθον πρὸς τὴν ἀνατολήν. 2 προσκαλεῖταί δέ με καὶ ἥψατο τοῦ στήθους μου, Vis. 1.4.1–2 [4.1–2]). After her parting words with Hermas, "two other men appeared and took her by the arms and went away toward the east, where the chair had also was. She went away cheerfully;" (δύο τινὲς ἄνδρες ἐφάνησαν καὶ ἦραν αὐτὴν τῶν ἀγκώνων καὶ ἀπῆλθαν, ὅπου καὶ ἡ καθέδρα, πρὸς τὴν ἀνατολήν. ἱλαρὰ δὲ ἀπῆλθεν, Vis. 1.4.3 [4.3]).

Although these references to the Lady's physical embodiment are fragmentary, they are notable for their concreteness. For example, while the Lady's body is not visible to Hermas on account of her long robes, the reader can easily construct an imagine of her *legs* in motion—bending and straightening as she sits down on and stands up from the white chair. These kinesthetic details contribute to the reader's perception of the chair's solidity as well. The Lady appears with a little book in her *hands* (τὰς χεῖρας, Vis. 1.2.2 [2.2]), one of which the reader is invited to visualize as it reaches out to touch Hermas's chest (Vis. 1.4.2 [4.2]). This tantalizingly brief reference is completed by a reader who must supply the additional details needed to imagine the physical interaction concretely, either as a firm reassuring press of her hand or as a gentle brushing of her fingertips above Hermas's heart. The Lady is also taken by her *arms* and physically led away at the conclusion of the vision by certain unidentified men (Vis. 1.4.1 [4.1]). All of the brief descriptions of the Lady's extended body parts as they are in motion are occasional and incomplete, yet they allow for the enactive reading of the scene. These partial references to the Lady's extended enrobed body—her *hands* holding a book and reaching out to touch Hermas, her *legs* as she sits in or stands up from the chair, and her *arms*—are all fragmentary aspects of her physicality (proprioception), but sufficient for the reader to complete imaginatively to achieve the solidity of her bodily presence as it interacts with objects and with Hermas himself. In the first vision, these mundane references to the Lady's limbs and their movements are extremely effective for making her—as she is seen through the eyes of Hermas—gain solidity.

In the case of the encounter with the Lady in first vision, we are given an extraordinary amount of privileged information about Hermas's interoceptive experiences, far more than we would have if Hermas were an actual person whom we encountered in the flesh. For example, we read of Hermas's emotional and interior state just prior to his vision of the Lady—he was "trembling and grieved" (εφρικὼς καὶ λυπούμενος, Vis. 1.2.1 [2.1]) and "grieved and weeping" (λυπούμενος καὶ κλαίων, Vis. 1.2.2 [2.2]). We are also told that he meets the "woman elder," the Lady while he was in anguish over his earlier exchange with the "Lady whom I had desired" (Vis. 1.1.4 [1.4]). Throughout the Book of Visions, Hermas's emotional state (interoception) and his responses to what is happening convey the complexity of his interior consciousness. As readers, we know to associate this fictive consciousness with real individuals. Even though we are never truly able to access another person's interior thoughts in real life, we recognize them from our own consciousness. Our ability to see other characters vicariously through the eyes of Hermas and *to see into the interior of Hermas himself* are precisely the features that we recognize from fiction writing and not from our encounters with flesh-and-blood individuals, whose innermost thoughts are inaccessible to us. It is here that we can appreciate that the Book of Visions may be regarded by both ancient and moderns as a fictional work and not dependent upon any historical Hermas for its compelling vividness. While the features of Hermas's personality and the character's strong insecurities have led some to conclude that the Shepherd is an autobiographical work in which the author has divulged his anguished personal experiences, we do well to avoid overdetermining the work in this way. Authors then and now frequently choose to write in detail about experiences and characters that are very different from their own lived experiences.

The approach of enactive reading that has been outlined in this chapter shares the desire to make textual images vivid with these classical rhetorical techniques. In both instances, the reader and hearer are expected to make the connection between what is being described with their own concrete experience of the world as it is known to them. Harry Maier writes:

> For these theoreticians vivid speech awakens emotions associated with the visualizations of things, situations, and actions the orator occasions. Critical in this task, then, is that the orator not stray too widely from lived experience. By staying within the bounds of what can reasonably be supposed the

audience has also experienced or knows, the rhetor can rely upon listeners to furnish details to the visual experience even if they are not detailed by the orator.[97]

In the case of Hermas's report of his excessive desire for the bathing woman, we can imagine that ancient readers might call to mind the visual depictions of the bathing goddess Venus that would have been commonplace throughout the Roman Empire. Without overdetermining how ancient visuality would have occurred, the suggestion that readers and hearers would have recalled concrete images of the goddess and other women also finds support in the text of Hermas's first Vision which refers to the Lady, not as Rhoda, but as a "goddess" (ὡς θεὰν) and also as a "sister" (ὡς ἀδελφήν) (Vis. 1.1.7 [1.7]).[98] Modern scholars like Martin Leutzsch, Graydon Snyder, and Antonius Hilhorst fail to appreciate how the cultural visuality of the Roman Empire would have invited ancient readers and hearers to make the move from Hermas's visionary report to the voyeuristic representations of the goddess that were plentiful in the Roman Empire. Even so, these scholars illustrate well how modern readers naturally extend their own culturally specific expectations to Hermas's visions in a way that greatly restricts how we see the power of the text to invite readers and hearers to conduct a personal examination of their own excessive desires.

Conclusion

The Shepherd of Hermas was extremely popular during the early centuries and continued to be read well into the Middle Ages. Its ability to deeply engage readers of the past invites modern scholars to reread it with this question: why was it so compelling to ancient readers but not to modern ones? While we know it was widely read as an important catechetical work, this

---

97. Maier, "Vision, Visualisation, and Politics in the Apostle Paul," 321.
98. See Angela Kim Harkins, "Entering the Narrative World of Hermas's Visions," in *Experiencing the Shepherd of Hermas*, ed. Angela Kim Harkins and Harry O. Maier, 125, n. 21. Hilhorst discusses that possibility that some mss attempted to smooth out the divine language here by reading 'aunt' (θείαν) instead of 'goddess' (θεαν); see Hilhorst, "Erotic Elements in the Shepherd of Hermas," 200 n. 21, where he references the discussion found in A. Hilgenfeld's review of O. Gerhardt and A. Harnack, *Shepherd*, in *Zeitschrift für wissenschaftliche Theologie* 21 (1878): 123–33. Hilgenfeld writes, "Aber das θεὰν ist offenbar zu berichtigen in θείαν, Tante, wozu das folgende ἀδελφὴν gut stimmt" (126). While it is possible that the reference to 'Aunt' may be understood as a term of endearment; the more difficult reading of 'goddess' is likely the original reading. Dibelius writes that this reference to 'goddess', along with other erotic elements in the opening scene, is influenced by Greek literary sources that depict encounters between goddesses and humans; Dibelius, *Der Hirt des Hermas*, 429–30.

alone does not tell us what made the Shepherd appealing or compelling to ancient readers. Enactive reading is a fruitful way of imagining how texts like the Shepherd functioned to form and transform ancient readers and hearers. It (enactive reading) does this by first immersing them into the narrative world of the text and then leading them into a process of self-examination, a necessary step for the work of moral formation.

This study of the Shepherd relies on the cognitive process of constructing mental imagery from narrative details—what cognitive literary theorists refer to as enactive reading. In other words, the fragmentary details of the seer's visual perception and locomotion found throughout visionary texts can be understood to assist a reader in constructing a complete image of the narrative world. This visualization is not overdetermined by the text but constructed from many different kind of details from a reader's lived experience or knowledge. One does not simply perceive a vision with the eyes, but just as in lived experience, one sees by moving closer to inspect the object that is being viewed. Visual apprehension comes from a total experience of the body's perceptions, including those of other senses, such as sound, touch, smell, taste, and movement toward, around, or away from.[99] Details that not only encompass proprioceptive but also interoceptive awareness of experiences in the skin or viscera, like temperature, tickle, or sexual arousal, can make characters seem even more real. Both enactive reading and enactive perception speak to the ways that referential descriptions of bodily experiences within a literary context can be accessed with varying degrees of vividness by a reader's or hearer's cognitive processes in ways that imitate the lived experiences of the body.

Attention to the embodied mind also reminds us that hearing and reading engage cognitive processes in complex ways to generate experiences of spatial perception that compare in intensity with first-hand bodily experiences. Hermas addresses his hearers directly, suggesting that this text was read aloud (e.g., "What I saw, brothers [sic] was this," Vis. 3.1.1 [9.1]; and "What I saw, brothers [sic], twenty days after the previous vision occurred," Vis. 4.1.1 [22.1]). The earliest manuscript of this book has markings for oral reading, thus requiring that we also expand our focus beyond the activity of reading to the experience of listening—perhaps similar to the reading of the little books referenced in Vis. 2.4.3 (8.3):

---

99. Tagliabue, "An Embodied Reading of Epiphanies," 214. The visual perception is enhanced by the convergence of other bodily senses in the narrated experience, an important one being that of motion. Kuzmičová, "Does it Matter Where you Read? Situating Narrative in Physical Environment," 223.

8.3 γράψεις οὖν δύο βιβλαρίδια καὶ πέμψεις ἓν Κλήμεντι καὶ ἓν Γραπτῇ. πέμψει οὖν Κλήμης εἰς τὰς ἔξω πόλεις, ἐκείνῳ γὰρ ἐπιτέτραπται. Γραπτὴ δὲ νουθετήσει τὰς χήρας καὶ τοὺς ὀρφανούς. σὺ δὲ ἀναγνώσῃ εἰς ταύτην τὴν πόλιν μετὰ τῶν πρεσβυτέρων τῶν προϊσταμένων τῆς ἐκκλησίας.

> 8.3 And so, you will write two little books, sending one to Clement and the other to Grapte. Clement will send his to the foreign cities, for that is his commission. But Grapte will admonish the widows and orphans. And you will read yours in this city, with the presbyters who lead the church.

Here it is worth remembering that the bodies of readers and hearers do not need to be in motion for the vivid perception of space or movement to take place, as we know from our contemporary experiences of the virtual worlds accessed through video gaming, viewing art, or reading narratives. On this point, the work of cognitive science theorist Vittorio Gallese suggests that the physical body's immobilization while reading or hearing a text may allow for the greater intensification of the imagined body's active participation in a textualized scene. According to his hypothesis, immobility actually "liberates new simulative energies ... Our being still simultaneously enables us to fully deploy our simulative resources at the service of the immersive relationship with the fictional world, thus generating an even greater feeling of body. Being forced to inaction, we are more open to feelings and emotions."[100]

Integrative approaches that consider the embodied experience of the individual engaged in practices that are not strictly ceremonial, such as the enactive reading and perception of catechetical texts like the Shepherd, offer a way to conceptualize how traditions moved from region to region, from the past to the future, between individuals and groups in larger social networks.[101] The performative practice of enactive reading may well have been an effective means by which texts participated in wider social mechanisms for the formation of identity. In other words, narratives that are instrumental in shaping and forming the self are effective because their literary style is persuasive in drawing the reader and hearer in—not because they are 'historical'.[102] Readers have the natural capacity to suspend disbelief, even

---

100. Vittorio Gallese, "Mirroring, a Liberated Embodied Simulation and Aesthetic Experience," 27–37.

101. Esther Eidinow, "Networks and Narratives: A Model for Ancient Greek Religion," *Krenos* 24 (2011): 9–38.

102. Johnston, "How Myths and Other Stories Help to Create and Sustain Beliefs," 141–56; relevant too are the studies of how fiction can achieve a quality of solidity and realism, Elaine Scarry, *Dreaming by the Book* (Princeton: Princeton University Press, 1999); and studies of the compelling quality of narrative worlds, see the prior references in the discussion found in the introduction to this monograph. Also, Harkins, "The Pro-Social Role of Grief in Ezra's Penitential Prayer," 490–91 where Ezra's prayer in

when the content is known to be fictional.[103] The Shepherd is only loosely tethered to a named historical figure from antiquity. Because these visions and experiences are mediated through a literary framework, we have taken the view that it is a fictional narrative. Even so, the vividness of his visions and his introspective musings allow ancient readers to access Hermas's proprioceptive and interoceptive experiences, thus gaining a sense of Hermas's interior consciousness and making his character appear more real and true to life. Consideration of embodied experiences of texts, both enactive reading and enactive perception, help us as modern readers to appreciate why an apocalypse like the Shepherd was so popular in antiquity and effective for moral formation.

Hermas's proprioception and interoception are conveyed to the reader through Hermas's dramatic fearful responses to the visions and also his sexual arousal and desire for Rhoda. Readers can glimpse Hermas's interiority through his introspective examination of his moral state and his expression of compunction which is displayed in his body through his posture (kneeling), tears, and anguished thoughts. Questions about the facticity of the events that are described are quickly overshadowed by the vividness of the imagery, the concreteness with which the action is described, and the ruminative and multisensory experience of enactive reading. Hermas's behaviors resemble the self-diminishing practices frequently found in other Second Temple texts that describe visionary experiences (viz., weeping, praying, confessing sins, kneeling). They are performative behaviors that generate emotional states that could have been enacted by ancient readers and hearers of the text. The Book of Visions contains many mundane references to Hermas and other figures standing, sitting, and doing other quotidian activities that seem to have little consequence in the larger narrative. For example, as we will see in Chapter 4, the lengthy description of Hermas's nighttime activity of walking, standing, sitting here or there, in the field just prior to the vision of the Tower (Vis. 3.1.1–2.4 [9.1–10.4]) appears to be tedious and monotonous, but such details can be appreciated anew when considered from the approach of enactive reading. The details of the seer's proprioceptive and interoceptive experiences that modern readers find repetitive or mundane are the very details that are used in enactive

---

Ezra 9 and the description of its reception in Ezra 10 effected the recommitment of readers to the ideals of the second commonwealth; Auyoung, *When Fiction Feels Real*.

103. Lisa Zunshine refers to this imaginative ability to suspend disbelief as "coexistence thinking." Lisa Zunshine, "Why Reasonable Children Don't Think that Nutcracker is Alive or that the Mouse King is Real," in *Romanticism and Consciousness*, ed. Richard C. Sha and Joel Faflak (Edinburgh: Edinburgh University Press, 2021).

reading to slow down the pace and to make the narrative world solid, dense, and three-dimensional.

The vivid sensory language used to describe Hermas's experiences resembles the reports ascribed to other worthy seers like Enoch, Ezra, and Daniel. These will be discussed in Chapter 5. The proprioceptive and interoceptive experiences of these seers are detailed enough for a reader to enact their interior and emotional states, thus expressing traits that readers associate with the consciousness of living individuals. This integrative approach to understanding reading offers a potentially rich way to conceptualize how reading deeply engaged readers and hearers by cultivating responses and predispositions.[104] The cumulative reading of the Book of Visions works to build the recurring affective experiences needed to heighten receptivity to the paraenetic material, both that found throughout the Book of Visions and in the later sections known as the Mandates and Similitudes. Hermas's experiences, like those of ancient Jewish apocalyptic seers, draw readers and hearers into the narrative world and convey a quality of presence. The lasting power of apocalypses has little to do with their 'historicity' and more to do with the narrative's ability to create a vivid and compelling experience for the reader through kinesthetic imagery and first-person reports of emotion and sensory perceptions.

---

104. Ari Mermelstein, "Constructing Fear and Pride in the Book of Daniel: The Profile of a Second Temple Emotional Community," *JSJ* 46 (2015): 449–83, esp. 450. The emotional effect of reading Daniel is described well by Mermelstein, who uses a social-constructivist understanding of emotion to consider how emotions are used in the formation of common values and beliefs. See more recently Mermelstein's stimulating book, *Power and Emotion in Ancient Judaism: Community and Identity in Formation* (Cambridge: Cambridge University Press, 2021).

Chapter Three
Sticky Thoughts that Make Presence from Absence

Concrete descriptive language about Hermas's proprioception and interoception allow for the possibility of an enactive reading of the Book of Visions. We wish to argue that the Book of Visions offers yet another way of creating vivid experiences, by inviting the effects of rumination to take hold in the imaginations of the reader and hearer. Readers are presented with Hermas's own reports of his rumination over the encounter at the Tiber River in Vis. 1.1.2–3 (1.2–3). Hermas's ruminative state and penitential prayer practices precede his visionary experience of the heavenly Lady in Vis. 1.1.4 (1.4). Rumination is a kind of recurring thinking that naturally makes presence from absence, as the mind unintentionally and persistently returns to a particular idea or thought.[1] According to psychologists Leonard Martin and Abraham Tesser, it is possible to describe rumination generally as "a class of conscious thoughts that revolve around a common instrumental theme and that recur in the absence of immediate environmental demands requiring the thoughts."[2] These are described inclusively as "several varieties of recurrent thinking, including making sense, problem-solving, reminiscence, and anticipation."[3]

The previous chapter discussed how the opening scene of the Book of Visions invites the reader and hearer to extend and complete the partial images provided by the narrative into a voyeuristic contemplation of other objects of desire. For the ancient reader, ancient representations of the goddess Venus were commonplace in the Roman Empire and could easily become part of the visualization of the scene. In the opening scenario of unrequited romantic love, Hermas obsessively contemplates the image of Rhoda bathing in the Tiber River—'sticky thoughts' of her that linger and occasion his deep introspection in Vis. 1.1.1–1.2.2 (1.1–2.2) (cf. Mand. 12.1 [44.1]). This chapter uses Sara Ahmed's theorizing about 'sticky emotions'

---

1. Leonard L. Martin and Abraham Tesser, "Some Ruminative Thoughts," in *Advances in Social Cognition*, ed. R. S. Wyer, Jr., Ruminative Thoughts 9 (Mahwah: Lawrence Erlbaum Associates, Inc., 1996), 1–47, here 6–7.
2. Martin and Tesser, "Some Ruminative Thoughts," 7.
3. Martin and Tesser, "Clarifying Our Thoughts," in *Advances in Social Cognition*, ed. R. S. Wyer, Jr., 189–208, here 192.

to present the reader's engagement as the 'sticky thoughts' of inappropriate desire (ἐπιθυμία) that are introduced by the narrative. These thoughts generate rumination in the readers and hearers, shaped by images from their own personal thoughts of excessive desire.[4] The mental state of rumination can also be cultivated through the enactive reading of the various mourning practices that Hermas routinely engages in throughout the Book of Visions. As the previous chapter made clear, Hermas is presented to us and to ancient readers as a fictional character, given the narrative form of the Book of Visions and our ability to access his innermost thoughts and emotional states. Even so, Hermas's ruminative states depict situations that resemble the lived experiences that would have been familiar to readers and hearers in the ancient world. The occasion for Hermas's rumination, seeing a beautiful bathing woman, is a common literary trope that easily calls to mind other well-known ancient narratives or personal experiences that may be in the memories of readers or hearers.

Sticky Thoughts of Rumination

The title of this chapter, "Sticky Thoughts that Make Presence from Absence," draws on Sara Ahmed's work which theorizes how material objects can carry and transmit emotions, functioning as what Bruno Latour calls, 'actants'.[5] According to Ahmed, "affect is what sticks, or what sustains or preserves the connection between ideas, values, and objects."[6] In her theorizing, 'sticky' material objects can move an individual from the 'outside-in'—a model we expand to include ideas, memories, and other ruminative remembrances.[7] The lived experience of rumination can be easily recognized in the experience of romantic love and in the experience

---

4. For a stimulating discussion of affect theory, particular Sara Ahmed, and the Similitudes, see Maier, "The Affect and Happy Objects of the Shepherd of Hermas," 73–97.

5. Sara Ahmed, *The Cultural Politics of Emotion*, 2d ed. (Edinburgh: Edinburgh University Press, 2014). See Bruno Latour, *Reassembling the Social: An Introduction to Actor-Network-Theory* (Oxford: Oxford University Press, 2005), 63–86; also Seigworth and Gregg, "An Inventory of Shimmers," in *The Affect Theory Reader*, ed. Gregory J. Seigworth and Melissa Gregg (Durham, NC: Duke University Press, 2010), 1–28, esp. 6.

6. Sara Ahmed, "Happy Objects," in *The Affect Theory Reader*, ed. Melissa Gregg and Gregory J. Seigworth, 29–51, here, 29.

7. See the application of Ahmed's theorizing to the effect that the ritual remembrances of Second Temple prayers have on Paul, as seen in 2 Cor.; Angela Kim Harkins, "Sticky Emotions from Second Temple Prayers: A Study of Paul's Grief in 2 Corinthians," in *Experiencing Presence in the Second Temple Period*, 159–83.

of bereavement occasioned by death and loss, two experiences that are not necessarily separated in real life.

This chapter presents two literary contexts for the cognitive process known as rumination. The first is Hermas's sexual desire for Rhoda in the arresting opening scene at the Tiber River—a scenario that provides the occasion for individualized introspective self-examination. The second context is that of the mourning practices that Hermas routinely engages in as a sign of his compunction throughout the Book of Visions. Such scenes depicting Hermas's mourning practices may be read enactively and contribute to a reader's rumination on forbidden thoughts. Both scenarios can occasion the intrusive experience of rumination that affects an individual from the 'outside-in'. Both these common occasions for rumination are familiar situations in the Book of Visions. In the first instance, we see Hermas overcome with infatuation or romantic love, expressing a deep longing for someone who is either absent or who does not return his love. In the second, Hermas experiences the grief that is cultivated from various mourning practices. Mourning practices continue the relational bonds and longing for the one who is now deceased.

In describing Hermas's interior states of rumination, the narrative invites readers to associate memories enactively from their own lived experiences. This contributes to readerly perceptions of Hermas as a figure with a real consciousness and thus as a plausible model for introspective self-examination. Rumination is a way of speaking inclusively about the intrusive recurrent thinking involved in various cognitive processes that continue bonds, such as romantic love and grieving losses. While these cognitive processes have been described generally thus far, the intensity with which they are experienced depend on an individual's capacity for absorption.[8]

The Book of Visions makes Hermas's ruminative experiences accessible to readers with experiential vividness, what we might call an experience of making presence from absence. This experiential effect is a strategic and overlooked aim of the Book of Visions that contributes to the Shepherd's effectiveness as a text for the moral formation of its readers. Presence is understood as a cognitive state in which a reader gains awareness of being

---

8. Thomas J. Coleman III, James E. Bartlett, Jenny M. Holcombe, Andrew Atkinson, Sally B. Swanson, Christopher F. Silver, Ralph W. Hood, "Absorption, Mentalizing, and Mysticism: Sensing the Presence of the Divine," *Journal for the Cognitive Science of Religion* (2019): 63–84. There, the authors write that absorption includes various psychological states such as "imaginative involvement, hyper-focus, full-commitment of attentional resources, situations seeming overly real, and an altered sense of self" (66).

in a particular narrative world or in a specific space.⁹ The narrative style of the Book of Visions allows the reader to access the interior thoughts and musings of Hermas's consciousness, thereby enriching the vividness of the narrated experiences and making Hermas more real. Hermas's emotional responses can also be understood as enscripting the emotional responses that the reader may be intended to have to the various paraenetic passages in the Book of Visions, such as Hermas's response to the Lady's reproach of Hermas's innermost desires (Vis. 1.1.4–9 [1.4–9]) and scenes that display Hermas's regret and compunction (e.g., Vis. 1.2.1–2 [2.1–2]). These passages allow the visions to generate a quality of experiential vividness. This effect of the Shepherd to generate immersive experiences in readers is a way to consider its effectiveness as a text used for moral formation; having entered the narrative world of the text, readers could then imagine the various ethical scenarios that arise in the Book of Visions and in the Mandates as relating to their lived experiences.

The recurring intrusive thoughts associated with rumination participate in the continuing bonds created and maintained in instances of love and longing when the beloved is either absent (or not reciprocating their love) or deceased. According to John Archer and Helen Fisher, these two states of romantic infatuation and bereavement are related:

> Infatuated men and women also become emotionally and physically dependent on the relationship. Many change their habits and priorities, even their appearance, to win the beloved. Most feel powerful empathy for their amour; in fact, many report they would die for their beloved. Lovers are strongly motivated to win the beloved. A striking property of romantic love is intrusive thinking, in which the lover thinks obsessively about the beloved. This is also a feature of grief, although in this case intrusive thoughts are typically associated with distress because they bring the loss to the person's attention.[10]

Both romantic love and bereavement continue bonds with the beloved who is absent. Rumination can, at times, result in moments of remarkable vividness that possess the quality of presence.[11] In the case of grieving the death

---

9. Kuzmičová, "Presence in the Reading of Literary Narrative," 23–48; Marie-Laure Ryan, "The Text as World: Theories of Immersion," 61–84.

10. John Archer and Helen Fisher, "Bereavement and Reactions to Romantic Rejection: A Psychobiological Perspective," in *Handbook of Bereavement Research and Practice: Advances in Theory and Intervention*, ed. Margaret S. Stroebe, Robert O. Hansson, Henk Schut, and Wolfgang Stroebe (Washington, D.C.: American Psychological Association, 2008), 349–72.

11. The natural effects of mourning and rumination are applied to visionary experiences in Angela Kim Harkins, "Ritual Mourning in Daniel's Interpretation of Jeremiah's Prophecy," *The Journal of Cognitive Historiography* 2.1 (2015): 14–33; and Angela Kim Harkins, "The Function of Prayers of Ritual Mourning in the Second Temple Period,"

of a loved one, the bereft may experience unexpected moments of presence or a sense of continuing bonds: "Grief includes depressed mood, yearning, loneliness, searching for the deceased, the sense of the deceased being present, and the sense of being in ongoing communication with that person."[12] In studies of the phenomenology of grief, the bereft experiences an ambiguous awareness of the deceased's presence.[13] Thomas Fuchs writes, "The bereaved continue to feel, perceive and behave as if their loved ones were still alive, although they know intellectually that they are dead in reality."[14] The suggestion is that there is a deep imprint in the physical remembering of the other that takes place in the body. These intrusive thoughts are repetitive and not triggered by the environment but happen unconsciously to continue bonds with the one who has died.

The Book of Visions describes Hermas's interoceptive awareness of his sexual desire and his overwhelming anxiety and self-doubt. These episodes are familiar to both ancient and modern readers. Our first discussion concerns rumination's role in the opening scene of the Book of Visions. Hermas's brief encounter with Rhoda at the Tiber River allows us to glimpse Hermas's innermost thoughts, thus giving his character the quality of interior consciousness and realism. Then we will discuss how the practices and emotions that Hermas repeatedly displays throughout the Book of Visions may be connected to the visionary practices of ancient apocalyptic seers. In both instances, the sticky thoughts of romantic infatuation and of anguished grief are depicted as leading to an awareness of another's presence, which is described materially as visionary experiences. These experiences are familiar ways that our cognitive processes of rumination allow for the possibility of experiencing the presence of someone who is otherwise not physically present.

---

in *Functions of Psalms and Prayers in the Late Second Temple Period. Conference proceedings for the Copenhagen Meeting*, ed. Mika S. Pajunen and Jeremy Penner, BZAW 486 (Berlin: De Gruyter, 2017), 80–101. To be sure, the state of rumination is one that is achieved during experiences of mourning or during ritually induced experiences of mourning, but it is also the case that rumination is an effect of other cognitive states, as a response to unfamiliar or strange circumstances, or decentering.

12. K. Goodkin et al., "Physiological Effects of Bereavement and Bereavement Support Group Interventions," in *Handbook of Bereavement Research*, ed. M. S. Stroebe et al. (Washington, D.C.: American Psychological Association, 2001), 671–703.

13. Thomas Fuchs, "Presence in Absence. The Ambiguous Phenomenology of Grief," *Phenomenology and the Cognitive Sciences* 17 (2018): 43–63. Fuchs describes this experience of presence and absence as a memory of the deep intercorporeality shared between two partners (45–46).

14. Fuchs, "Presence in Absence," 52.

3. *Sticky Thoughts that Make Presence from Absence* 105

The Book of Visions also begins with an arresting scene—what we might describe as a sticky situation. It is a scene that is told and retold in various tales from Jewish and Christian scriptures as well as classical literature: a man spies on a beautiful but unattainable woman as she bathes.[15] David gazes upon Bathsheba, the beautiful wife of Uriah as she bathes, according to 2 Sam. 11.2. Similarly, the lascivious elders peer at the beautiful and vulnerable Susanna as she washes in her private garden, according to the addition to Daniel known as the story of Susanna and the Elders. The image of a man viewing a bathing woman is a sticky scene because the intrusive, recurring thoughts of what is seen continue to be contemplated, inciting desire in the viewer.

The literary trope of a man spying on a bathing woman is one that early Jewish writings take up and expand in detail, often to impugn the viewer. The scene is attached to the story of the incest between Reuben and Bilhah, his father's concubine—an event that is mentioned but not described in any detail in Gen. 35.22; 49.4; 1 Chron. 5.1. In later expansions of this story, Reuben's lust is ignited when he sees his father's concubine bathing. While the story of Reuben spying on Bilhah as she bathes is nowhere found in the Hebrew Bible, it becomes securely attached to Jacob's son in various Second Temple texts like the *Book of Jubilees* 33.15 and the *T. Reu.* 3.11–15. The passage from the *Testament of Reuben* reads as follows:

> 3.11 εἰ μὴ γὰρ εἶδον ἐγὼ Βάλλαν λουομένην ἐν σκεπεινῷ τόπῳ, οὐκ ἂν ἐνέπιπτον εἰς τὴν ἀνομίαν τὴν μεγάλην. 12 συλλαβοῦσα γὰρ ἡ διάνοιά μου τὴν γυναικείαν γύμνωσιν, οὐκ εἴασέ με ὑπνῶσαι, ἕως οὗ ἔπραξα τὸ βδέλυγμα. 13 ἀπόντος γὰρ Ἰακὼβ τοῦ πατρός μου πρὸς Ἰσαὰκ τὸν πατέρα αὐτοῦ, ὄντων ἡμῶν ἐν Γαδὲρ πλησίον Ἐφραθὰ οἴκου Βηθλεέμ, ἦν ἡ Βάλλα μεθυσθεῖσα καὶ ἦν κοιμωμένη ἀκάλυπτος ἐν τῷ κοιτῶνι αὐτῆς. 14 εἰσελθὼν οὖν ἐγὼ καὶ θεασάμενος τὴν γύμνωσιν αὐτῆς ἔπραξα τὴν ἀσέβειαν, μὴ ἀσθανθείσ[ης] αὐτῆς, καί, καταλιπὼν αὐτὴν κοιμωμένην, ἐξῆλθον. 15 καὶ εὐθέως ἄγγελος τοῦ θεοῦ ἀπεκάλυψεν τῷ πατρί μου περὶ τῆς ἀσεβείας μου· καὶ ἐλθὼν ἐπένθησεν ἐπ᾽ ἐμοί, μηκέτι αὐτῆς ἁψάμενος.

> For if I had not seen Bilhah bathing in a sheltered place, I would not have fallen into this great lawless act. For so absorbed were my senses by her naked femininity that I was not able to sleep until I had performed this revolting act. While our father, Jacob, had gone off to visit his father, Isaac, and

---

15. Carolyn Osiek writes that "Leutzsch (31–39) counts nine scenes of mortal men surprising goddesses at their bath, eighteen references to the ritual washing of goddess statues or pictures, nine erotic scenes connected with bathing, three biblical or intertestamental: Ruben and Bilha (T. Rub. 3.11–15), David and Bathsheba (2 Sam. 11:2), and Susanna," see "The Oral World of Early Christianity in Rome," 153 n. 8. Martin Leutzsch, *Die Wahrnehmung sozialer Wirklichkeit im "Hirten des Hermas"*, 31–39. Not included in this list is the *Book of Jubilees*.

we were at Gader near Ephratha in Bethlehem, Bilhah became drunk and was sound asleep, naked in her bedchamber. So when I came in and saw her nakedness, I performed the impious deed without her being aware of it. Leaving her sleeping soundly, I went out. And immediately a messenger from God revealed it to my father. He came and made lamentation over me, and never again touched her" (3.11–15).[16]

This particular retelling of the literary trope, which includes Reuben and Bilhah, bears the closest resemblance to the opening scene of Hermas and Rhoda. That the man is somehow subordinated to the women whom he desires, either by virtue of a familial relationship (in the incestuous case of Reuben and Bilhah) or as a slave to his owner (as in the case of Hermas and Rhoda), is a detail that underscores the impropriety and scandal of the event, and so makes the scene more titillating. Reuben and Hermas share other features as well: both narratives describe how each man's crime is concealed from the woman he desires, but divinely revealed by a heavenly agent. In the case of Bilhah, she remains fast asleep and unaware of Reuben's act. So too, Rhoda is unaware of Hermas's desire—or at least we are not told that she is aware of it. Hermas emphatically denies any illicit thoughts (Vis. 1.1.2 [1.2]) but acknowledges his desire for her when he sees the vision of the heavenly Lady and recognizes Rhoda: "I saw the woman whom I had desired" (βλέπω τὴν γυναῖκα ἐκείνην ἣν ἐπεθύμησα ἀ, Vis. 1.1.4 [1.4]). Bilhah is unable to accuse Reuben since she was unconscious when he violated her, but Reuben's incest is revealed to him and to his father, Jacob, by an "angel of God" (ἄγγελος τοῦ θεοῦ, T. Reu. 3:15). So too, Hermas's inner desire is laid bare by a heavenly informant, the Lady.

While the expansions in the *Book of Jubilees* and the *Testament of Reuben* are often compared to one another, they offer different understandings of the two parties involved.[17] *Jubilees* goes to great lengths to exculpate Bilhah, who cries out loudly as a raped woman is supposed to do according to the laws of Deuteronomy (22.24, 27). In this retelling, Bilhah responds to the violation in a manner similar to Tamar when she is raped by her half-brother Amnon in 2 Sam. 13.12 (cf. *Jub.* 33.4). In the case of Bilhah, she discloses the rape to Jacob; he would not otherwise know of the offense since she was

16. Kee (trans.) *OTP* 1: 783. *T. Reu.* (2d c. BCE) resembles the account preserved in *Jub.* 33.2–9 but has significant differences. Both are dated to approximately the same period. The Greek text of *T. Reu* is taken from The Greek Pseudepigrapha, Accordance.

17. Avigdor Shinan and Yair Zakovitch, *The Story of Reuben and Bilhah* (Jerusalem: Magnes Press, 1983, Hebr.); James Kugel, "Reuben's Sin with Bilhah in the *Testament of Reuben*," in *Pomegranates and Golden Bells: Studies in Biblical, Jewish, and Near Eastern Ritual Law, and Literature in Honor of Jacob Milgrom*, ed. D.P. Wright et al. (Winona Lake: Eisenbrauns, 1995), 525–54; Ishay Rosen-Zvi, "Bilhah the Temptress: *The Testament of Reuben* and 'the Birth of Sexuality'," *JQR* 96 (2006): 65–94.

not a virgin. This differs from the case of Tamar, whose virginal state also made disclosure of the rape obligatory. *Jubilees* roundly presents Bilhah as acting with propriety and, like the *Testament of Reuben*, lays blame squarely on Reuben as the aggressor.

The *Testament of Reuben* is the pseudepigraphic tale that bears the strongest resemblance to the opening scene in the Shepherd. Both texts are confessional narratives in the first-person voice with moralizing aims. They also share a clear moralizing tone admonishing the incestuous act and altogether condemning the man's excessive sexual desire (ἐπιθυμία). According to the *Testament of Reuben*, the responsibility for moral behavior lies with the man. Bilhah is presented in a completely passive way; she is incapacitated from drinking and sleeping in bed totally naked. According to Kugel, her drunkenness allows the *Testament of Reuben* to present her as totally innocent of the incestuous act.[18] Reuben comes to her bedroom when she is asleep and alone. These details are unique to the *Testament of Reuben* and dramatically increase Reuben's responsibility, expressing the view that the burden of morality falls on the man. The pseudepigraphic retelling aligns with a conceptualization of a 'gender economy,' which Ishay Rosen-Zvi describes as entailing the male as the desirer and the female as a completely passive temptress.[19] The instructive lesson gained from the Testament's retelling of Reuben and Bilhah is one that is shared with the Shepherd of Hermas, namely that there is a dynamic interior struggle that takes place within the moral agent. According to the Shepherd, the offense is the immoderate desire (ἐπιθυμία) that arises within Hermas (Vis. 1.1.8 [1.8]). So too, the crime in the *Testament of Reuben* is desire (ἐπιθυμία, *T. Reu.* 1.10), a sin that is born from "the spirit of seeing" (2.4; cf. 4.9), specifically seeing what should not be seen. It is precisely this desire (ἐπιθυμία), rooted in the act of seeing, that is recounted later in the *Testament of Reuben* when it describes the Watchers, a class of angels who had looked at human women, saw their beauty ("goodness"), and were thus overcome by a desire (ἐπιθυμία) to possess them (*T. Reu.* 5.5–6; 6.4; also Gen. 6.2).

> 5.5 φεύγετε οὖν τὴν πορνείαν, τέκνα μου, καὶ προστάσσετε ταῖς γυναιξὶν ὑμῶν καὶ ταῖς θυγατράσιν ἵνα μὴ κοσμῶνται τὰς κεφαλὰς καὶ τὰς ὄψεις αὐτῶν, ὅτι πᾶσα γυνὴ δολιευομένη ἐν τούτοις εἰς κόλασιν τοῦ αἰῶνος τετήρηται. 6 οὕτως γὰρ ἔθελξαν τοὺς ἐγρηγόρους πρὸ τοῦ κατακλυσμοῦ· κἀκεῖνοι συνεχῶς ὁρῶντες αὐτὰς ἐγένοντο ἐν ἐπιθυμίᾳ ἀλλήλων, καὶ συνέλαβον τῇ διανοίᾳ τὴν πρᾶξιν,

---

18. According to Kugel, ("Reuben's Sin with Bilhah in the *Testament of Reuben*,") the retellings seek to protect Bilhah's reputation as the mother of two of Israel's tribes by making her totally passive and unaware during the entire rape. It is clear that she did nothing to encourage Reuben (534–5).

19. Rosen-Zvi, "Bilhah the Temptress," 73–74.

καὶ μετεσχηματίζοντο εἰς ἀνθρώπους, καὶ ἐν τῇ συνουσίᾳ τῶν ἀνδρῶν αὐτῶν συνεφαίνοντο αὐταῖς·

> 5 Flee, therefore, fornication, my children, and command your wives and your daughters that they not adorn their heads and faces, because every woman who acts treacherously in these [charms] will be set aside for an eternal punishment. 6 For thus they charmed the Watchers who were before the flood, those [Watchers] *who were looking at them continually*. They lusted for them [the women], and they conceived of the deed in the mind. They changed themselves into the shape of men and they appeared to them [the women] while they were having sexual intercourse with their husbands.

According to the reasoning of the *Testament of Reuben*, it is the act of seeing that generates the sexual desire (ἐπιθυμία) in the mind, which in turn leads to the physical deed (ἀκεῖνοι συνεχῶς ὁρῶντες αὐτὰς ἐγένοντο ἐν ἐπιθυμίᾳ ἀλλήλων, 5.6). James Kugel notes that the phrase, "seeing continually" (συνεχῶς ὁρῶντες, 5.6) in this passage refers to the rumination that happens in the mind: "it was this continuous contemplation that ultimately led to lust."[20] In the case of the fallen angels story, the consequence of this desire (ἐπιθυμία) is the sexual union that takes place between the angels and the human women, an act that results in the ill-fated birth of giants, primordial beings who bring violence and destruction on the earth.

According to Kugel, the activity that generates excessive sexual desire (ἐπιθυμία) is 'seeing continuously', in other words, seeing the image that lingers in the mind long after the event of seeing has passed. Similarly, according to the author of the *Testament of Reuben*, the recurring thoughts—what we might call the 'sticky thoughts'—of Bilhah's beauty give rise to Reuben's persistent desire for her, which in turn leads to the incestuous rape. In many instances where this literary trope appears in Second Temple pseudepigrapha, the act of seeing a beautiful, unattainable woman bathing is one that generates excessive sexual desire in the one who gazes. These narrative scenes describe events in which elite men—the firstborn son of Jacob (Reuben), the king of Israel (David), two judges (the unnamed elders) who spy on Susanna—act or scheme to act on their illicit desires. In all these instances, the narrative exposes how the voyeur succumbs to his desire. As these stories highlight the tragic demise of an otherwise virtuous figure who succumbs to lust, they occasionally provide the opportunity for a subordinate male to demonstrate his extraordinary virtue. Sometimes this is a status-enhancing opportunity, as in the case of Daniel, who becomes celebrated even more; or Uriah the Hittite (Bathsheba's husband), who, even though a foreigner, proves himself to be more loyal to David than David

---

20. Kugel, "Reuben's Sin with Bilhah in the *Testament of Reuben*," 548.

was to him. In the case of the story of Bilhah and Reuben, Jacob is also elevated even more by choosing to abstain from Bilhah from that moment on (*T. Reu.* 3.15).

Seeing with the mind's eye—or 'seeing continuously' as the *Testament of Reuben* puts it—is a way of speaking about the sticky recurrent thoughts that intrude and linger long after the moment of physical seeing has passed. This describes well the events at the beginning of the Book of Visions. After seeing Rhoda emerge from her bath, Hermas was still thinking of her while walking into the countryside some time later (μετὰ χρόνον τινὰ πορευομένου μου εἰς κώμας, Vis. 1.1.3 [1.3]). This detail suggests that Hermas had been ruminating about the event for quite a while.

The arresting scene with which the Book of Visions opens could have been easily filled out by ancient readers for whom images of the bathing goddess, Venus, were commonplace, or salacious images from a variety of popular stories. Calling such images to mind may also have made readers aware of their own interoceptive responses to such images. As discussed in the previous chapter, sexual desire was enflamed by images of the beautiful goddess bathing. Here, images of the beautiful statue of the goddess can be understood according to Sara Ahmed's theory of non-persons that become 'sticky' with emotion, capable of affecting emotions like desire from the 'outside-in'.[21] While we think of statues as inanimate objects, ancient authors imagined them to have agency, affecting responses and emotions in their viewers. Ovid made the arousing effect of beautiful statues well-known through his story of the mythical king Pygmalion, who experienced excessive desire for his statue. According to Angelos Chaniotis, stories like the one about Pygmalion, which describe him "losing control, of being driven to irrationality through love," do not attribute the cause of the emotion of desire to the sculptor, Praxiteles, or to the patrons who commissioned the statue, but to the statue itself.[22] Interestingly, Chaniotis notes that these tales are not placed in a treatise about statues, but in one that concerns the heart and emotions.[23] The statue itself is a sticky object that affects the emotional state of continual contemplation of desire in the viewer. The resulting exchange between Hermas and the heavenly Lady, the woman whom he desired, is an arresting scene that lays bare a man's innermost desires for all to see. The scenario immediately brings to mind other tales that describe

---

21. Ahmed, *The Cultural Politics of Emotion*, 8–10. See especially Maier, "The Affects and Sticky Objects of the *Shepherd of Hermas*," 73–97. Other significant studies of objects and affect include Jane Bennett, *Vibrant Matter: A Political Ecology of Things* (Durham: Duke University Press, 2010).
22. Chaniotis, "The Life of Statues: Emotion and Agency," 154.
23. Chaniotis, "The Life of Statues: Emotion and Agency," 154.

all too familiar scenarios in which seeing and desiring lead inevitably to other grave consequences. In the case of Reuben, the desire generated by his continually seeing Bilhah's beauty in his mind results in his illicit rape of Bilhah, doubly scandalous because it is incestuous.

Hermas's desire is far more complicated than these literary examples of Reuben and Bilhah or the Watchers and human women because Hermas's lust (ἐπιθυμία) is not acted upon; thus it appears to have no grave consequences. Because it is wholly interior, it can be concealed from others, making Hermas appear more virtuous than he is. The arresting scene becomes the occasion for the author to lead Hermas—and the reader—through an examination of conscience. This is what makes the Shepherd an effective catechetical work. The passage begins by revealing Hermas's admiration of Rhoda's beauty, even entertaining chaste fantasies of what it would be like to be married to someone like her. Hermas's own insistence that "this is all I had in mind, nothing else" (Vis. 1.1.2 [1.2]), suggests that he is hiding something from himself or that he is not fully unaware of his innermost desires. Hermas reveals that the thought of Rhoda bathing has become akin to a 'sticky thought' that remains in his mind, which he then sees continuously. Hermas ruminates about her long after the actual encounter—a sign of his excessive desire (ἐπιθυμία). Ironically, although the sticky thought is of the naked Rhoda, it is Hermas's inner thoughts that becomes exposed to readers and hearers. The interoceptive awareness that Hermas gradually comes to acknowledge is the fruit of a process from his encounter with a heavenly Lady, one who is never identified as Rhoda, but only as "the woman whom I had desired" (τὴν γυναῖκα ἐκείνην ἣν ἐπεθύμησα, Vis. 1.1.4 [1.4]). This ambiguity allows readers and hearers to enact 'sticky thoughts' of desire from their own past, by personalizing the face and voice of the heavenly Lady with memories of their own lived experiences. Hermas's emotional experiences of the confrontation by the heavenly Lady can be understood as enscripting audience responses to the events in the Book of Visions. Hermas's emotional acts of compunction, expressed through the various mourning practices and confession of sin, build the audience's pathos and empathy for the figure of Hermas and offer the opportunity for their own examination of conscience.[24]

The above discussion describes how stock scenarios like watching a woman bathing can generate affective responses of excessive desire in readers. In the case of the opening scene of the Book of Visions, the stock image can be vividly imagined with several different depictions of the goddess

---

24. Quintilian, 6.2.7–12, 20–36. This enscripting of readerly emotions is very much like the phenomenon that Harry Maier describes as an effect of the emotions of John of Patmos, *Apocalypse Recalled*, 57–8.

3. Sticky Thoughts that Make Presence from Absence 111

bathing that were commonplace in the Roman Empire, making readers aware of their own interoceptive responses of desire to those images of a woman bathing. The consideration of the embodied cognitive processes involved in moving from text to experience can illuminate why compositional techniques for visionary texts reuse established literary images and scenarios known from older narratives. Early Jewish and Christian apocalypses regularly redeploy stock images for their new compositions and these malleable scenes become sites of 'sticky' remembrances for other tales, thereby intensifying the act of remembering. This process can also be described from a theoretical literary perspective as a representational model of reading. Literary theorist Elaine Auyoung describes recent psychological understandings of the reading process in her study of the phenomenology of reading, and notes that the representational model of reading known as the 'situation model' makes the most lasting impressing on readers' memories.[25]

> [T]he situation model consists of a mental representation not of the linguistic features of the text itself but rather of the state of affairs being described. Here the words of the text cue readers to draw upon their existing background knowledge, such as what kind of object a rolling pin is or what it means to pinch something, to construct a mental representation of the manual operations that Mrs. Garth performs on her dough.[26]

Here Auyoung is speaking about George Eliot's description of Mrs. Garth, as she works the pastry dough with her rolling pin. The particular literary patterns of a story can be instrumental in connecting with readers' actual lived experiences or with similar literary descriptions. Auyoung continues:

> While readers typically do not retain in long-term memory the exact words of the surface code or the propositional content of the textbase, they can often recall the situation model even after they have finished reading. Here we might think of how readily readers can recall the gist of a story despite being unable to remember it word for word. Because the structure of the situation model corresponds to that of the physical world instead of to the linguistic structure of the text, it helps us account for an aspect of literary experience that readers and critics have struggled to pin down.[27]

Salacious stories like seeing a beautiful woman bathing provide entertaining and erotic narratives found throughout Jewish, Christian, and Roman

---

25. Auyoung, *When Fiction Feels Real*, 4–5. Notice that the author espouses a representational understanding of cognition, not an enactive one in which the reader herself actively constructs the character Mrs. Garth. Nevertheless, the illustration is helpful in conceptualizing the importance of concrete kinesthetic details and how the framing of such scenes takes place in the imagination.
26. Auyoung, *When Fiction Feels Real*, 5.
27. Auyoung, *When Fiction Feels Real*, 5.

writings that use the scenario to impugn or valorize the one who gazes. This literary trope can generate a lasting impression on the reader, both by what it describes and by what it leaves unsaid. Using enactive reading practices, readers can easily fill in the details that are missing from the story by extending the scene with their own recollections of similar experiences or by recalling other familiar narratives. The narrative is stripped of details describing how exactly Rhoda appears; instead, it is reduced to a stock literary trope for excessive desire, and readers then supply the details that are lacking.

Previously we discussed the Shepherd's renown as a catechetical text. With this in mind, the opening scene between Hermas and Rhoda illustrates a scenario that precisely speaks to that which ordinary readers may wonder about the Christian life. How exactly does a Christian exercise continence and restrain his sexual desires when confronted with the challenging temptation of seeing a beautiful woman as she emerges from bathing or even the many depictions of the bathing goddess prominently displayed throughout the Roman Empire? Even though Hermas does not act on his desire, readers and hearers can easily fill in the narrative with their past experiences or with stories of how such familiar scenes play out in other writings like the popular story of Ovid's *Metamorphoses*. More importantly, the arresting scene allows readers to immediately engage the story and respond emotionally. The opening scene generates the necessary pathos for the Book of Visions. Without overdetermining readerly responses, readers are offered the enscripted emotions of Hermas, who does not act on his desire (ἐπιθυμία) but who expresses compunction. They can enact his situation and undergo their own examination of conscience. Readers may also respond with surprise, curiosity, or skepticism. While a range of emotional responses is possible, the arresting scene helps to propel the reader even more into the Book of Visions.

Enactive reading and the mental imaging that results are part of a generative process whereby a sensory representation is produced in a malleable way within the individual mind, a process that is guided by the scripted emotions and cues in the narrative. Even though a positive identification of the historical Hermas has been frustrated by the absence of information, the protagonist of the Book of Visions is described with complex personality traits that give his character vividness and attribute to him the characteristics of life as lived. He expresses insecurity and worry, agonizes over his state of sinfulness (e.g., Vis. 1.2.1 [2.1]), and openly displays emotions of regret in the form of weeping (e.g., Vis. 1.2.2 [2.2]).

Emotional memories are long-lasting and can be rather accurate, calling to mind similar scenes from both personal experience or similarly related scenarios from the literary imagination.[28] The arresting scene at the riverbank that opens the Book of Visions effectively provides an experiential, emotional frame for the reader to re-experience in the act of remembering. Such an experiential frame could then be updated or changed as readers merge or blend details from their own memories, thus allowing for a deeper intensification of the experience.[29] It is in the emotional remembering of these scriptural and pseudepigraphic narratives—or the mimetic process, if you will—that individual experiencing takes place; this is when the egocentric recollection of personal memories could take place in the situational model of reading and remembering.

Let us recall our discussion in the previous chapter of Hermas relating his encounter with Rhoda, his former slave master, and his insistence on his chaste thoughts concerning the event (Vis. 1.1.1–2 [1.1–2]). Hermas has a vision of a heavenly Lady who confronts him about his desire (ἐπιθυμία), which he had preemptively denied ever having (Vis. 1.1.2 [1.2], cf. 1.1.7 [1.7]). In the following scene, the ambiguous heavenly Lady begins to disclose to Hermas his innermost thoughts, which had been concealed from readers up to this point:

> 1.8 γελάσασά μοι λέγει· Ἐπὶ τὴν καρδίαν σου ἀνέβη ἡ ἐπιθυμία τῆς πονηρίας. ἢ οὐ δοκεῖ σοι ἀνδρὶ δικαίῳ πονηρὸν πρᾶγμα εἶναι ἐὰν ἀναβῇ αὐτοῦ ἐπὶ τὴν καρδίαν ἡ πονηρὰ ἐπιθυμία; ἁμαρτία γέ ἐστιν, καὶ μεγάλη, φησίν. ὁ γὰρ δίκαιος ἀνὴρ δίκαια βουλεύεται. ἐν τῷ οὖν δίκαια βουλεύεσθαι αὐτὸν κατορθοῦται ἡ δόξα αὐτοῦ ἐν τοῖς οὐρανοῖς καὶ εὐκατάλλακτον ἔχει τὸν Κύριον ἐν παντὶ πράγματι αὐτοῦ. οἱ δὲ πονηρὰ βουλευόμενοι ἐν ταῖς καρδίαις αὐτῶν θάνατον καὶ αἰχμαλωτισμὸν ἑαυτοῖς ἐπισπῶνται, μάλιστα οἱ τὸν αἰῶνα τοῦτον περιποιούμενοι καὶ γαυριῶντες ἐν τῷ πλούτῳ αὐτῶν καὶ μὴ ἀντεχόμενοι τῶν ἀγαθῶν τῶν μελλόντων. 9 μεταμελήσονται αἱ ψυχαὶ αὐτῶν, οἵτινες οὐκ ἔχουσιν ἐλπίδα, ἀλλὰ ἑαυτοὺς ἀπεγνώκασιν καὶ τὴν ζωὴν αὐτῶν. ἀλλὰ σὺ προσεύχου πρὸς τὸν Θεόν, καὶ ἰάσεται τὰ ἁμαρτήματά σου καὶ ὅλου τοῦ οἴκου σου καὶ πάντων τῶν ἁγίων.

> 1.8 But she laughed and said to me, "The desire for evil did rise up in your heart. Or do you not think that it is evil for an evil desire to arise in the heart of an upright man? Indeed," she said, "it is a great sin. For the upright man intends to do what is right. And so, when he intends to do what is right his reputation is firmly established in heaven and he finds that the Lord looks favorably on everything he does. But those who intend in their hearts to do evil bring death and captivity on themselves—especially those who are invested in this age, who rejoice in their wealth and do not cling to the good things yet to come. 9 Those who have no hope but have already abandoned themselves and their lives will regret it. But pray to God, and he will heal your sins, along with those of your entire household and all of the saints."

---

28. Boyer, "What Are Memories For? Functions of Recall in Cognition and Culture," 3–28.
29. Barsalou et al., "Embodiment in Religious Knowledge," 14–57.

This second exchange reveals how Hermas's interior state becomes exposed and subject to scrutiny by a moral standard external to him in the form of an embodied figure who appears unexpectedly from elsewhere—the figure of the Lady. Like an actual encounter, the heavenly Lady confronts Hermas with his sin of inordinate desire in a conversation that, like an encounter with a flesh-and-blood person, both challenges and surprises him. If we allow that the episode provides a dynamic experiential frame, the hearers of this story would also remember details about what happens to the person who inappropriately sees the bathing woman from other writings like the *Testament of Reuben*, or stories that detail the desire ignited in the one who gazes on the statue of the bathing goddess by Ovid. According to these tales, seeing continually leads to excessive desire that then moves the viewer to act on his desire. That an individual might spontaneously remember a similar episodic event from another tale, and its lamentable consequences, may be among the undetermined aspects of the process of enactive reading.

This discussion of the cognitive processes of enactive reading and enactive perception has focused on the importance of the style and imagery of the opening visions in the Shepherd of Hermas. The text scripts responses and cultivates certain 'readerly' predispositions such as longing and desire, regret and compunction. By inhabiting the role of Hermas, an ancient reader might achieve a vivid experiential state. The cultivation of the self through these enactive reading practices involves imaginative egocentric cognitive processes that participate in the construction of ethical constraints on behavior. The visionary encounter of the Lady is perceived as a real encounter with a moral standard external to the self, one in which the self is intruded upon or 'acted upon' in ways that generate unexpected discomfort and unease in our protagonist Hermas. Hermas's visionary encounters possess the complexities of lived experience by allowing readers to access his interoceptive awareness of sexual desire. The vision of the heavenly Lady exerts an external force on Hermas that leads him through an examination of conscience. Such experiences model for ancient readers and hearers how to conduct an interior self-examination. As a catechetical text, it reveals the challenges of avoiding excessive desire (ἐπιθυμία) in daily thoughts.

Rumination: The Sticky Thoughts of Grief

The Book of Visions preserves protracted first-person narrations of visionary experiences of a protagonist who is oftentimes distraught and stricken with anxiety. Why were the very emotional states that many seek to avoid today—desolation, worry, mourning—so prominently displayed in an ancient text that was widely used for moral formation? The ritualized experience of grief can bring about a state of rumination and longing by which the mind naturally makes presence from absence. Practices associated with mourning were used for various social mechanisms besides the grieving of the deceased. The repetition of the self-diminishing practices of weeping, praying, confessing sins, and kneeling highlights the highly ritualized and performative dimension of grief in the ancient world. For example, public displays of grief, what we refer to as 'mourning', were used throughout the Roman Empire within various social contexts, including judicial proceedings.[30] These practices functioned strategically and not simply as an expression of personalized anguish over someone's death.[31] The repetitive elements in the Shepherd of Hermas speak to ruminative practices and suggest that these experiences were familiar and recognizable to the ancient reader as well. The ritual enactment of funerary practices and the performance of prayers that enact petitioning and the confession of sins can cultivate experiences of self-diminishment that effectively optimize the naturally occurring state of rumination and heighten receptivity to an experience of presence. Funerary practices and self-diminishing prayers were frequently associated with covenant remaking experiences, perhaps because they simulate the experience of liminality that would naturally occur otherwise in the experience of encounter with the deity.[32]

Prior to his dramatic encounter with the Lady in the first Vision, Hermas crosses the river, kneel, pray, and confess his sins (Vis. 1.1.3 [1.3]). After his distressing exchange with this woman, Hermas, in a state of grief-filled agitation, begins to worry about the sins of desire (ἐπιθυμία) that have been revealed to him (Vis. 1.2.1–2 [2.1–2]). He encounters the second woman,

30. Christopher Degelmann, "Symbolic Mourning," in *Lived Religion in the Ancient Mediterranean World: Approaching Religious Transformations from Archaeology, History and Classics*, ed. Valentino Gasparini, Maik Patzelt, Rubina Raja, Anna-Katharina Rieger, Jörg Rüpke, Emiliano Urciuoli (Berlin: De Gruyter, 2020), 447–67. In the Roman republic, close relations were permitted to display public signs of mourning to arouse compassion in the courtroom and in the streets outside of the courthouse (448). These practices that Degelmann calls "symbolic mourning" took place among social elites and were used to sway popular opinion, especially during times of election. The practice relied on literary traditions and lived experiences that were mutually reinforcing (452).

31. Gary Anderson, *A Time to Mourn, a Time to Dance: The Expression of Grief and Joy in Israelite Religion* (University Park, PA: Pennsylvania State University Press, 1991); Saul Olyan, *Biblical Mourning: Ritual and Social Dimensions* (Oxford: Oxford University Press, 2004); A. K. Harkins, "The Function of Prayers of Ritual Mourning in the Second Temple Period," 80–101; A. K. Harkins, "The Pro-Social Role of Grief in Ezra's Penitential Prayer," 466–91; A. K. Harkins, "Ritual Mourning in Daniel's Interpretation of Jeremiah's Prophecy," 14–33; Degelmann, "Symbolic Mourning," 447–68.

32. Angela Kim Harkins, "The Emotional Re-Experiencing of the Hortatory Narratives Found in the Admonition of the Damascus Document," *DSD* 22 (2015): 285–307.

seated in a white chair, while he is in a weeping state of grief and distress. In this second vision, the Lady instructs him to copy a book. Prior to this second encounter, Hermas is engaged in similar behaviors: walking alone, thinking about the previous year's vision, kneeling, praying, and contemplating God's greatness and his own sinful state (Vis. 2.1.1–2 [5.1–2], cf. Vis. 3.1.4–5 [9.4–5]). In the second vision, Hermas copies the book, but we also read that he is said to ruminate over the contents of the writing while fasting and praying for fifteen days (Vis. 2.2.1 [6.1]). In the third vision, there are multiple encounters with the Lady. The third vision begins with Hermas fasting for a long time and praying a great deal (Vis. 3.2.2 [10.2]). His encounters with the Lady happen at night, which could suggest either that he was sleep deprived or that the vision resembled a dream experience.[33]

Ancient apocalypses often depict seers who take on various practices associated with mourning, viz., fasting, weeping, sitting in ashes, shaving the head and beard, lying prostrate, and wearing disheveled, unkempt clothing. From the perspective of neuroscience, Patrick McNamara refers to such practices as 'decentering' practices, which can generate different cognitive states that "put the individual into a receptive and integrative mode."[34] Funerary practices that

---

33. The second vision begins as a revelation that comes to Hermas in his sleep. He is asked the identity of the old Lady who has appeared to him, and he identifies her (incorrectly) as the Sybil. Both female figures are said to be of old age, sitting, holding a book, and identified as revealing knowledge. The Sibyl was probably well known in Rome during this time; Osiek, *The Shepherd of Hermas*, 58 n. 2, 3.

34. McNamara, *The Neuroscience of Religious Experience*, 1–43, 44–58, quote from 5. McNamara's discussion offers limited usefulness as a general heuristic model. While appealing to our modern way of thinking, it is ultimately anachronistic and problematic for understanding antiquity, because his idea of an 'executive self' idealizes agency and autonomy (41). While this model is potentially useful for understanding modern western minds, it projects an ethnocentrism when thinking about the past. It also has limited applications for thinking about the self and subjectivity in non-western cultures. The modern privileging of the 'agentic self' has a long genealogy that Giovanni Bazzana traces back to the early modern period. Using the work of Paul Christopher Johnson ("An Atlantic Genealogy of 'Spirit Possession'." *Comparative Studies in Society and History* 53 [2011]: 393–425), Bazzana writes: "the use of 'possession' in the ethnographic writing on the history of religions begins in earnest with the modern European 'encounter' with 'possession' among the peoples of West Africa. Associating 'possession' with Africans enabled early modern European explorers and ethnographers to cast the peoples they encountered as defined by their inferior self, diminished by their lack of control, autonomy, and individual rationality. Thus, in the writing of European intellectuals as influential as Locke and Hobbes, the discourse of 'possession' did become a strong underpinning for trajectories that did eventually lead to the ideological justification of racism, colonial domination, and—given the dire implications of understanding 'possession' as the surrendering of 'ownership' of one's own body and self—enslavement"; Bazzana, *Having the Spirit of Christ: Spirit Possession and Exorcism in the*

cultivate states of liminality routinely appear alongside Second Temple narrative prayers that emphasize self-diminishment (e.g., confession of sin, penitential prayers).[35] Daniel Merkur called these behaviors the visionary practices of Jewish apocalypticists.[36] Ritual mourning can be understood as a decentering practice that can bring on the naturally occurring state of rumination, which makes presence from absence.[37] In those scenarios, Merkur explains that "the seers rehearsed what they knew in order to encourage their psychic states to manifest further and unknown matters on the same topics."[38] Michael Stone has observed that "the widespread mention of prayer, solitude, fasting and penitence" often precede visionary experiences.[39] The seers also engaged in exaggerated mourning, which was the crucial psychological element of their technique for inducing an alternate psychic state.[40] Similar visionary practices are commonly used in apocalypses like *4 Ezra* and *2 Baruch*.[41] Together with first-person prayers of petition and confession of sins, these ritual mourning practices can generate liminality and decentering that can heighten an individual's receptivity to experience grief and rumination. Among other things, rumination refers to cognitive processes that can lead to the experiencing of presence from absence, as well as the processes involved in problem-solving and transformation.[42]

Early Christ Groups (New Haven: Yale University Press, 2020), 16–17. According to this model, practitioners of African and Afro-Atlantic religions who engaged in spirit possession were generally considered as not being in full possession of their 'self'. This 17th century view has a long reach and also appears as recently as the 1960s, in Godfrey Leinhardt's work, *Divinity and Experience: The Religion of the Dinka* (Oxford: Clarendon Press, 1961), where he concludes that the Dinka people from the South Sudan had no 'self'. Such social scientific evaluations claim to have the air of objectivity, but when they are situated amid cross-cultural studies and post-colonialism, they can be seen as "provincializing the premise of the autonomous modern individual"; see Paul Christopher Johnson, "Introduction: Spirits and Things in the Making of the Afro-Atlantic World," in *Spirited Things: The Work of "Possession" in the Afro-Atlantic World* (Chicago: University of Chicago, 2014), 1–20, here 6.

35. Harkins, "Ritual Mourning in Daniel's Interpretation of Jeremiah's Prophecy," 14–33.
36. Merkur, "The Visionary Practices of Jewish Apocalypticists," 119–48.
37. Harkins, "The Function of Prayers of Ritual Mourning in the Second Temple Period," 80–101.
38. Merkur, "The Visionary Practices of Jewish Apocalypticists," 141.
39. Michael E. Stone, "Apocalyptic Literature," in *Jewish Writings of the Second Temple Period*, ed. M.E. Stone (Assen and Philadelphia: van Gorcum and Fortress Press, 1984), 430.
40. Merkur, "The Visionary Practices of Jewish Apocalypticists," 125.
41. Merkur, "The Visionary Practices of Jewish Apocalypticists."
42. McNamara, *The Neuroscience of Religious Experience*. Also, Martin and Tesser, "Clarifying our Thoughts," 189–208.

Second Temple apocalypses use the interoceptive experiences and emotional responses of the seer to the events that are seen to draw readers immersively into the text. Second Temple apocalypses (e.g., Dan. 9; *4 Ezra* 8.19–36) construct vivid images that are emotionally engaging and enscript emotions of longing and desire through the first-person voice. Particularly after the exile, foundational narratives were retold first and foremost to inculcate a common memory of a shared past, but also to enscript the emotional responses of the seer for readers. The use of bizarre or counterintuitive elements in the narrative world of the apocalypse cultivate the experience of surprise or curiosity, which may also lead the reader to anticipate or to heighten watchfulness for what might happen next.

Grief: Past and Present

Important shifts have taken place in bereavement studies since Sigmund Freud's early and highly influential study, "Mourning and Melancholia," first published in 1917.[43] There Freud articulated what would later become the widely held understanding that well-functioning mourning is a process in which the bereft becomes detached from the deceased loved one, a process known as 'decathexis'.[44] Freud's model has persisted in western understandings of mourning and has gained a foothold in the popular imagination. In contrast, new understandings of mourning based on comparative cultural studies have departed significantly from Freud's views by noting the significant role that mourning and rumination have in the experience of *continuing bonds*. In this model, mourning is understood as a process of cognitive restructuring that reimagines the relationship of the bereft to the deceased. It is this more recent development in bereavement studies that influences our present discussion.[45]

---

43. Sigmund Freud "Mourning and Melancholia," *The Standard Edition of the Complete Psychological Works of Sigmund Freud*, vol. 14, ed. and trans. James Strachey (London: Hogarth Press, 1957, repr. 1917), 237–59. The term 'grief work' is also used to describe Freud's understanding of the bereft's process of detachment from the beloved. Freud's work was uncritically continued by Erich Lindemann ("Symptomatology and Management of Acute Grief," in *Beyond Grief: Studies in Crisis Intervention*, ed. Erich Lindemann and Elizabeth Lindemann [New York: Aronson, 1979], 59–77), who made unresolved grief into a pathology and made Freud's view into a mainstream idea. For this history of Freud's work and his legacy in grief studies, see Dennis Klass and Edith Maria Steffen, "Introduction: Continuing Bonds—20 Years On," in *Continuing Bonds in Bereavement: New Directions for Research and Practice*, ed. D. Klass and E. M. Steffen (New York: Routledge, 2018), 1–14, esp. 2–4.

44. Freud "Mourning and Melancholia," 244–5.

45. For further discussion of this departure from early twentieth-century views

We can assume that the early readers of the Shepherd shared the cultural sensibilities that were widely practiced in the ancient world by ancient Jews, Romans, and Greeks. In the Book of Visions, Hermas regularly engages in practices and prayers that are associated cross-culturally with grief: he weeps, trembles with fear, offers anguished statements of regret over past failings, engages in lengthy periods of fasting, positions his body in lowly postures by collapsing on his knees, and verbalizes his worries and anxieties. Anthropological studies highlight how funerary practices were powerfully used for multiple occasions, far exceeding the lamentation of the dead.[46] Weeping, tearing the hair and clothes, wearing ashes, lamentation, and lowering the body on the ground or collapsing are part of a larger constellation of practices that are primarily identified as ritual expressions of grief but that were used for a relatively wide range of purposes: as part of a ritual of petitioning/penitential prayer, or to mourn general political calamity, or to grieve the loss of or the compromise of individual states of purity or holiness.[47] While the rituals and practices surrounding mourning can come to function in diverse ways, Saul Olyan rightly notes that all of these diverse purposes are predicated on the paradigmatic experience of mourning the dead, which is highly performative and strongly regulated in every culture, even modern ones.[48] Funerary practices and the social expression of grief (viz., mourning) is manifest in diverse ways across time and cultures, including in the Second Temple period. The rumination or continuous thinking and longing for the deceased is a way in which presence can be felt and experienced. Scholars have noted how mourning practices are associated with the rituals and narratives of covenant remaking during the

---

associated with Freud, see George Hagman, "Beyond Decathexis: Toward a New Psychoanalytic Understanding and Treatment of Mourning," in *Meaning Reconstruction & the Experience of Loss*, ed. Robert A. Neimeyer (Washington, D.C.: American Psychological Association, 2000), 13–31; and Margaret S. Stroebe, Robert O. Hansson, Henk Schut, and Wolfgang Stroebe, "Bereavement Research: Contemporary Perspectives," in *Handbook of Bereavement Research and Practice: Advances in Theory and Intervention*, ed. M. Stroebe, R. O. Hansson, H. Schut, and W. Stroebe (Washington, D.C.: American Psychological Association, 2008), 3–25; Mary Frances O'Connor, *The Grieving Brain: The Surprising Science of How We Learn from Love and Loss* (New York: HarperOne, 2022).

46. Anderson, *A Time to Mourn, a Time to Dance*; Olyan, *Biblical Mourning: Ritual and Social Dimensions*.

47. For example, skin disease is the example that Olyan discusses, but we might also include instances of rape such as Tamar's response to her rape by her half-brother Amnon.

48. Olyan, *Biblical Mourning: Ritual and Social Dimensions*, 62–96.

Second Temple period.⁴⁹ These express the Deuteronomic longing for God after the exile. These are also attached to visionary or transformative experiences (e.g., Dan. 9–10; *4 Ezra*). Therefore, we can expect that ritual displays of grief had significant complexity as we consider how loss was expressed and displayed in distinct ways by Second Temple groups and in the Greek and Roman worlds.

According to David Konstan, ancient Greeks understood grief (λύπη) within a socially-embedded context, and not as a private interior state, as it is commonly conceptualized in the modern period.⁵⁰ It differed, however, from the other *pathe* whose experiences were restricted according to social standing, gender, or class insofar as λύπη was something that affected everyone, regardless of their social standing. For example, to experience indignation, one had to possess dignity at the start. The broader experiencing of λύπη, unrestricted by social class or gender, can account to some degree for why the meaning of λύπη could range from 'grief' or, more inclusively, as 'pain'. Mourning still remains performative and regulated by social norms to some extent in the modern world, in which grieving is controlled and regulated by laws that restrict who is legally able to take time from work to mourn a loved one.⁵¹ Kenneth Doka writes:

> Every society has norms that frame grieving. These norms include not only expected behaviors but also feeling, thinking, and spiritual rules. These grieving rules govern what losses one grieves, how one grieves them, who legitimately can grieve the loss, and how and to whom others respond with sympathy and support. These norms exist not only as folkways, or informally expected behaviors, but also as laws, meaning that these norms may carry sanctions. For example, these norms are evidenced in company policies that extend bereavement leave to certain individuals as well as regulations and laws that define what family member or other person has control of the deceased's body or funeral rituals.⁵²

Doka goes on to say that such legally prescribed rules and norms do not adequately reflect how we as individuals are connected to larger networks in which relationships with non-family members can be significant and

---

49. E. Lipinski, *La liturgie penitentielle dans la bible* (Paris: Cerf, 1969).
50. David Konstan, *The Emotions of the Ancient Greeks*, 244–61.
51. On the topic of unacknowledged experiences of grief and loss in society, such as the death of an ex-spouse, see Kenneth J. Doka, "Disenfranchised Grief in Historical and Cultural Perspective," in *Handbook of Bereavement Research and Practice: Advances in Theory and Intervention*, ed. Margaret S. Stroebe et al. (Washington DC: American Psychological Association, 2008), 223–40. There Doka's opening discussion concerns a recently divorced woman who was not legally permitted to grieve the death of her ex-husband. The situation applies equally well to same-sex partners and third-cousins.
52. Doka, "Disenfranchised Grief," 225.

intense, arousing strong experiences of grief. In the case of ancient contexts, such intersubjectivity would include relationships between individuals and spiritual beings or supernatural beings.[53]

The ancient world had strong expectations for how grief should be expressed as mourning. Norms and regulations around bereavement do not prevent individuals from experiencing grief in the ways that are natural for them, but laws do give us a way of assessing how grief is understood within a particular cultural context. As we might expect, real flesh-and-blood individuals should not be overdetermined to experience grief in any specific way. This point has been well-made by Nicola Denzey Lewis, who notes that there was not such a sharp gender division of the roles that men and women held in actual funerary rituals and practices.[54] In the case of Roman rituals, we cannot assume that there was an exclusive divide according to gender for various funerary practices, but we can speak of gendered expectations that were especially attuned to the appropriateness of a given behavior in light of an individual's social class. Seneca writes to Lucilius about various moral topics in the *Epistulae morales* during the early second half of the first century in Rome. In Letter 99, Seneca makes the point that the expectations that high-status men should withhold their tears when they are bereft of a loved one is unreasonable. He writes:

> Now, at this time, am I advising you to be hard-hearted, desiring you to keep your countenance unmoved at the very funeral ceremony, and not allowing even your soul to feel the pinch of pain? By no means! … Tears fall, no matter how we try to check them, and by being shed they ease the soul. What, then, shall we do? Let us allow them to fall, but let us not command them do so; let us weep according as emotion floods our eyes, but not as much as mere imitation shall demand. … Let us, indeed, add nothing to natural grief, nor augment it by following the example of others. (*Epist.* 99)

For Seneca and others it is unseemly for a man to grieve without restraint. If tears are there, they should flow naturally and not for the sake of performance. They should neither be forced to flow nor lead to overwrought emotional displays.

---

53. Esther Eidinow, "Oracular Consultation, Fate, and the Concept of the Individual," in *Divination in the Ancient World: Religious Options and the Individual*, ed. Veit Rosenberger, Potsdamer altertumswissenschaftliche Beiträge 46 (Stuttgart: Franz Steiner Verlag, 2013), 21–39.

54. Nicola Denzey Lewis describes such stark scholarly divisions between male and female roles in funerary practices as a "feminist fantasy," in her review of Kathleen E. Corley, *Maranatha: Women's Funerary Rituals and Christian Origins* (Minneapolis: Fortress, 2010) published in *CBQ* 74 (2012): 594–96, here 596. This point is a valuable one for those who seek to recover the possible on-the-ground experiences of grief within a specifically ancient Roman context.

We have already noted that Hermas routinely engages behaviors in the Visions that would have been culturally coded to ancient readers as generally unseemly behaviors for a freed-man. While it is true that both flesh-and-blood men and women were capable of performing funerary rituals in Rome, there remained a strong social expectation of general restraint for men, an expectation that was likely heightened in accord with the man's social standing. On this point, it is worth noting that Hermas is a freed slave according to the opening of the Book of Visions, yet he is said to be regularly weeping and overwrought emotionally by the experiences that he has. Such behaviors were associated with slavish men or lower-class men. Diane Lipsett's recent study argues well that Hermas's garrulousness signals a lack of self-restraint and thus serves as another marker of his lack of masculinity.[55] For example, in the Visions, Hermas is described as being grieved or in a state of sorrow several times.[56] Thus, we might hear the sharp words of the Lady to him in the first vision, "Act like a man, Hermas!" (Ἀνδρίζου Ἑρμᾶ, Vis. 1.4.3 [4.3]) to be speaking to the culturally inappropriateness of Hermas's behaviors in light of this gender and social-class distinction.[57] In Brittany Wilson's study of *Unmanly Men*, she writes that ancient '*man*dates' for manliness idealized power and self-control.[58] Hermas's overwrought behaviors, excessive speech, and emotional displays would have been extremely distasteful to Roman elites and associated with lower-class, servile men.[59] Their preservation in the text as behaviors that Hermas, a freed slave, is regularly engaging in suggests that these practices were retained despite the strong cultural disdain for them. These mourning behaviors suggest that

---

55. Lipsett, "Gender, Volubility, and Transformation in the Shepherd of Hermas," 57–62.

56. Some form of the verb λυπέω or noun λύπη is used to describe Hermas's interior state in Vis. 1.2.1 [2.1]; 1.2.2 [2.2]; 3.1.9 [9.9]; 3.11.3 [19.3]; 3.13.2 [21.2]; 4.3.4 [24.4]; 5.1.4 [25.4].

57. Steve Young, "Being a Man: The Pursuit of Manliness in *The Shepherd of Hermas*," *JECS* 2 (1994): 237–55. Young's study observes that the female figures in the visions embody manliness for Hermas, thus taking the view that conceptualizations of gender were underdetermined. See also Maud W. Gleason, "The Semiotics of Gender: Physiognomy and Self-Fashioning in the Second Century CE," in *Before Sexuality: The Construction of Erotic Experience in the Ancient Greek World*, ed. David M. Halperin, John J. Winkler and Froma I. Zeitlin (Princeton: Princeton University Press, 1990), 389–415, here 391. Lipsett, "Gender, Volubility, and Transformation in the Shepherd of Hermas," 57–72.

58. Brittany E. Wilson, *Unmanly Men: Refigurations of Masculinity in Luke-Acts* (New York: Oxford University Press, 2015), 58–75.

59. See Lipsett, "Gender, Volubility, and Transformation in the Shepherd of Hermas," 57–72. Her thesis is that Hermas's prolixity shows his lack of self-restraint, but his repetitive and reiterative speech also point to an alternative means for his transformation.

these decentering practices were recognized to be efficacious at deploying or heightening other naturally occurring cognitive processes. Galen makes the point that grief is peculiar in that it can launch and intensify other cognitive and emotional states, such as desire for revenge or morose melancholy.[60] In the case of the Shepherd, such culturally embarrassing practices and emotional displays may have been retained since they were experientially useful for generating the preconditions that allow even deeper contemplation and visionary experiences to occur. Mourning practices could be understood to be strategies for decentering that cultivate the necessary experience of liminality,[61] which is a precondition for religious experiences. These practices heighten receptivity, without, of course, predetermining that such experiences will happen.

Visions: Experiencing Presence from Absence

Michael E. Stone, Moshe Idel, and others have already demanded that we should recognize some aspect of the lived experience of religion as underlying visionary texts.[62] For these scholars, texts that describe visionary experiences should be considered as more than just creative fictionalized writings that serve some specific agenda: these texts can be understood to reflect some aspect of lived experience of religion. It was thought that visions had their cognitive basis in dream experiences.[63] Visions resembled certain types of revelatory dream experiences in which angels disclosed otherworldly secrets to seers or transported them on massive journeys through never-before-seen landscapes.[64] The view that visionary literature is strictly

---

60. Daniel King, "Galen and Grief: The Construction of Grief in Galen's Clinical Work," in *Unveiling Emotions, Vol. II*, ed. Angelos Chaniotis (Stuttgart: Franz Steiner Verlag, 2012), 251–72.

61. McNamara, *The Neuroscience of Religious Experience*, 44–58.

62. Stone, "Apocalyptic—Vision or Hallucination?" 428; Stone, "A Reconsideration of Apocalyptic Visions," 167–80, here 180; Stone, *Ancient Judaism: New Visions and Views* (Grand Rapids: Eerdmans, 2011), 90–121. See also Elliot R. Wolfson, *Through a Speculum that Shines: Visions and Imagination in Medieval Jewish Mysticism* (Princeton: Princeton University Press, 1994), 124; and Moshe Idel, "Mystical Techniques," and Daniel Merkur, 'The Visionary Practices of Jewish Apocalypticists," All of these studies were influential on my own work, *Reading with an "I" to the Heavens*, 25–9.

63. F.C. Burkitt, *Jewish and Christian Apocalypses* (London: Oxford University Press, 1914); John J. Collins, *The Apocalyptic Vision of the Book of Daniel* (Missoula: Scholars Press, 1977), 83.

64. Otherworldly divine secrets were disclosed by angels to seers through apocalyptic dreams and visions. Oftentimes the subject of these revelations were astronomical phenomena, various details about heavenly beings (the names of angels and their functions) and revelations about the nature of God and the nature of otherworldly landscapes,

literary is a long-standing scholarly assumption. While they are highly stylized and heavily redacted writings, visionary reports also can be studied as the product of various complex neurological processes.[65]

Such an understanding of visionary practices of rumination and contemplation on a particular scriptural passage seems to describe well what we see in Daniel 9. In this scene, the prophet's rumination on Jeremiah's prophecies is generative and followed by a vision in which a revelation from the Angel Gabriel expands what that scriptural verse says. We might say that such a process could be recognized in the opening scene of the first vision, in which Hermas is obsessing about Rhoda's unclad body at the shore of the Tiber. In that first vision, Hermas is enraptured and carried away by the Spirit where he encounters "that woman whom I had desired"— namely Rhoda. The vision of the heavenly woman then confronts Hermas with the charge of the evil desire that has taken root in his heart (ἐπιθυμία; Vis. 1.1.8). This scene is not unlike the one in Daniel 9, where the prophet/seer, in a state of fasting and prayer, prays and ruminates on the invisible God's 'face', 'ear', 'eyes', and 'hand', thereby rhetorically constructing in his imagination the presence of a being with a physical human-like body, complete with extended limbs. The seer's ruminative contemplation on Jeremiah's prophecies thus could be said to lead to the generative experience of a vision of the angel Gabriel, who, of course, becomes present to him in a human-like body.[66] So too the 'sticky thoughts' of Hermas's hidden desire for Rhoda could be generative in a similar way, leading to his heavenly vision of the lady whom he desired. That a heavenly figure confronts him about his inner desires is also an indication that his longings for her occupied his psychic state.

In her study of contemporary Muslim dreams and visions, anthropologist Amira Mittermaier writes:

> Whether stories of dreams and visions are real, projected, or made up is the wrong question to ask. The dreams themselves—that is, the experiences that preceded the narratives—cannot meaningfully be made the subject of an anthropological investigation, and they even elude the dreamers' own narration. Although it can make a fundamental difference whether people believe that particular stories refer to something real according to their own

---

both heaven and hell; Merkur, "The Visionary Practices of Jewish Apocalypticists," 120; Christopher Rowland, *The Open Heaven: A Study of Apocalyptic in Judaism and Early Christianity* (New York: Crossroad, 1982).

65. In Daniel Merkur's analysis of visionary experiences, he proposed that this phenomenon be considered as a product of various cognitive processes that resemble bipolar disorder; see "The Visionary Practices of Jewish Apocalypticists," 133–4.

66. Harkins, "Ritual Mourning in Daniel's Interpretation of Jeremiah's Prophecy."

3. *Sticky Thoughts that Make Presence from Absence* 125

standards, I hold that the anthropologist is not the ultimate arbiter of the 'real,' and that the way this category is commonly used tends to erase other forms of relevance."[67]

Like the dreams of the individuals whom Mittermaier is interviewing in her ethnographies, ancient visionary experiences cannot gainfully be made the subject of examination. Nevertheless, the emotional and physical experiences of dreams and visions that are divulged or reported could still be said to retain elements of religious experience as lived, thus disclosing relevant aspects of the general phenomenon of visionary experiences. We might add that the verisimilitude of Hermas's reports would have been compelling for ancient flesh-and-blood readers and hearers who would be willing to suspend disbelief and see the vividness of the visions as real reports. As Dan Batovici notes well, the authority of the Shepherd in the works of Clement of Alexandria was not based on any apostolic authority, as was true of his esteem for other works like the Epistle of Barnabas; rather it was based on his assessment that Hermas had truly experienced these visions. Batovici writes, "the authority Hermas enjoys with Clement of Alexandria seems to lay on different grounds—its apocalyptic character, which Clement considers to be genuine."[68]

We cannot say that there was a historical Hermas, or whether he ever existed. We have taken the position that Hermas is a highly fictionalized character. We can, however, affirm that Hermas's visionary experiences resemble patterns of thoughts and practices that are common among early Jewish apocalyptic visionary texts; namely, that a vision or experience of presence follows a series of decentering practices. In the case of Hermas, rumination is generated by various recurring thoughts and specific ritual practices of weeping, confessing sins, and the physical lowering of the body. Ritually induced cognitive states can be achieved that resemble ongoing rumination or uncontrolled obsessive thinking about something that is not there. Such cognitive states can then lead to the heightened sense of presence, in the same way, perhaps, as obsessive worrying or rumination can make that concern take up more and more space in your mind, leading to the feeling that the concern is looming larger and evermore present. We know that such experiences, even if we consider them to be only imagined, can have serious this-worldly effects on the individual who has them. So, whether Hermas's visions—or anyone else's—are 'real' or 'imagined' we

---

67. Amira Mittermaier, *Dreams that Matter: Egyptian Landscapes of the Imagination* (Berkeley: University of California Press, 2011) 27–8; Tanya Luhrmann, *When God Talks Back*.

68. Dan Batovici, "Hermas in Clement of Alexandria," 51.

cannot know, but we can be certain that the experiences of worry, anxiety, and fear, which are the effects of the visions, are real. His visions, whether they are real or not, generate a response within him. While visionary experiences are not verifiable, their effects are measurable and have consequences in this world.

Moral Decision-Making

The general cognitive process that allows for the vivid perception of someone who is not there is one of the natural effects of rumination and a cognitive process that is employed in moral decision-making. The cognitive processes that make presence from absence are used in episodic memory making and in the creation of vivid images. According to Pascal Boyer, the mind's capacious ability to generate compelling mental images has a strong adaptive value.[69] This is especially so in the case of what psychologists call 'false memories' or 'source confusion', in which an individual might misremember him- or herself egocentrically in a vivid way while reconstructing a memory that is rich with sensory-perceptual details.[70] While we tend to imagine memory making and recall with the metaphor of a photograph, there is an adaptive advantage to the source confusion that frequently happens in memory construction and reconstruction. These cognitive processes for (false) memory reconstruction are the same areas of the brain that are used when imagining the 'future contingencies' that influence moral decision-making.[71] According to Pascal Boyer, the imagination's ability to generate vivid egocentric sensory experiences, in the case of the source confusion that arises during episodic memory reconstruction, is the same

---

69. Boyer, "What are Memories For? Functions of Recall in Cognition and Culture," 3–28.

70. Karen J. Mitchell and Marcia K. Johnson, "Source Monitoring 15 Years Later: What Have We Learned from fMRI about the Neural Mechanisms of Source Memory," *Psychological Bulletin* 135 (2009): 638–77, esp. 654. Linda A. Henkel, N. Franklin, and M. K. Johnson. "Cross–modal Confusions between Perceived and Imagined Events," *Journal of Experimental Psychology: Learning, Memory, & Cognition* 26 (2000): 321–35; "On a given trail, an event was experienced from one of four sources (visual perception, auditory perception, visual imagery, or auditory imagery) and over the course of the trials, some events were experienced from two different sources. Some were, for example, visually imagined and at some other point were actually heard, and others were actually seen and at some other point were auditorily imagined," (322). Henkel, Franklin, and Johnson conclude that source confusion was most likely when an event was visually imagined but actually heard (351); an interesting study given that most would have heard Hermas's visions being read aloud.

71. Boyer, "What are Memories For? Functions of Recall in Cognition and Culture," 14.

cognitive process used in 'mental time-travel'. This is also the process known as the future thinking, which happens when one pauses to imagine the various consequences for moral decision-making.[72] While we take the view that Hermas is a fictional character, Hermas encounters visionary interlocutors and exercises the naturally occurring cognitive processes that are involved in imagining future consequences of moral decision-making. The vivid engagement of the imagination can be preparatory for the moral formation of the readers and hearers of this text.

While we could never determine if Hermas was a historical figure or if his visions were *real*, we can, however, observe that his decentering practices and introspective musings precede visionary encounters. Hermas cues readers to engage the imaginative and cognitive processes known as 'future-thinking', which are at work in moral decision-making. Hermas's deeply introspective reports in the Visions and his frequent experiencing of visionary presence could be said to create propaedeutic experiences for one who will read the Mandates that follow.

Conclusion

The Book of Visions repeatedly paints an image of the seer ruminating over events and visionary experiences, thereby scripting a scenario that could be re-enacted by subsequent readers of these visions.[73] Michael Swartz does well to remind us that the performative aspects of reading is itself far more embodied than most text based scholars acknowledge:

> Indeed, the force of recitation needs to be taken quite seriously as a potent form of ritual behavior and as an example of the actualization of sacred space in time. Memorization, recitation and performance, we must remember, are physical acts, requiring intensive preparation, stamina, and physical prowess.[74]

---

72. Boyer, "What are Memories For? Functions of Recall in Cognition and Culture," 16.

73. While we speak here about the experience of reading the visions of Daniel, it is worthwhile to consider the general effect of reading the book in its entirety, from beginning to end, as it would have been experienced with a scroll apparatus that would not allow for random access of passages. What kind of effect is achieved from sequencing the court tales before the amazing visions in chapters 7 to 12? Perhaps one, not unimportant effect from reading the court tales is the heightening of a reader's attentiveness to the visions that are described.

74. Michael D. Swartz, "Ritual about Myth about Ritual: Towards an Understanding of the Avodah in the Rabbinic Period," *The Journal of Jewish Thought and Philosophy* 6 (1997): 135–55 at 153. See too, Ophir Münz-Manor, "Narrating Salvation: Verbal Sacrifices in Late Antique Liturgical Poetry," in *Jews, Christians, and the Roman Empire: The*

The lasting power of apocalypses lies in their ability to generate immersive experiences of otherworldly experiences for readers. The visions of otherworldly narrative realms that are shown only to the seer are reported to subsequent readers with a first-hand vividness. Visions are described with counterintuitive elements and the strategic deployment of emotions through the element of surprise or suspense; these elements slow down the pace of reading and effectively enscript the emotional responses that can increase rumination on the events that are described. Features found in these apocalypses impact the reader by creating a deeper and more empathic bond with the seer.

Since individuals seldom had private copies of texts in the early Christian period, the hearing of texts would have allowed for greater movement of the eyes, a scenario in which the physical space could serve to intensify the process of mental imaging, thus strengthening an individual's emotional response.[75] The naturally associative aspects of emotion can also allow a hearer to actualize a text by allowing him/her the opportunity to reinvigorate memories of similar emotional experiences.[76] This complicated embodied process helps us imagine how actualization allows for the affective re-experiencing of a narrative with first-hand intensity and the generative process of updating that narrative in light of changing circumstances. A narrative that includes disorienting and counterintuitive elements slows down the cognitive process of reading and allows readers to engage the text more deeply. It encourages the reader to go back and re-read and ruminate over the visions. Counterintuitive elements and the role of suspense slow down and invite deeper thinking about a passage.

While writings like the Book of Visions in the first part of the Shepherd are thoroughly worked over and highly stylized fiction, they nevertheless offer interesting insights into visionary experiences. Practices in which the protagonist, Hermas, regularly engages prior to his visionary experiences—namely confession of sins, kneeling, and weeping—can be understood as decentering practices that lead to actual experiences of grief. The cultivation of rumination allows the mind to make presence from absence. Visions resemble dreams insofar as they happen to individuals, 'acting upon' them in ways that are unpredictable.[77] The visions that Hermas experiences can be understood as descriptions of otherworldly beings 'acting upon' him by

---

Poetics of Power in Late Antiquity, ed. Annette Y. Reed and N. Dohrmann (Philadelphia: University of Pennsylvania Press, 2013), 154–66; notes at 315–9.

75. Kuzmičová, "Does it Matter Where you Read? Situating Narrative in Physical Environment," 290–308.

76. Harkins, *Reading with an "I" to the Heavens*.

77. Amira Mittermaier, "Dreams from Elsewhere: Muslim Subjectivities Beyond

challenging him and morally constraining his thinking. These visionary encounters produce effects within Hermas that are similar to those produced by encounters with 'thisworldly' beings and highlight how individuals in antiquity understood themselves to be in complex intersubjective relationships with beings who were not of this world.

It is notable that the figure of Hermas appears only in the first section known as the Visions. The literary structure presumes, however, that the section known as the Mandates is a continuation of the fifth and final vision. Based on this information, we can hardly know anything about Hermas as a person. Even so, referential details to Hermas's life, his past experiences as a slave, the use of first-person reporting about his bodily and emotional state, and his highly emotive state throughout the Visions succeed in giving this figure significant depth and emotional complexity. All these features help readers to imagine this literary figure with the vividness of someone whom they might meet in real life. Rather than asking the usual historical questions (Who was Hermas?) the enactment of the bodily practices and emotional displays are described with verisimilitude. These could be understood as decentering practices that are also well-attested in Second Temple texts like Daniel 9 and *4 Ezra*, which describe seers engaging in similar behaviors of anguished weeping and fasting while uttering desolating prayers.[78] The bodily practices and penitential prayers generate physical states that have strong emotional and cognitive effects of longing that can be compared to recurring intrusive thoughts associated with rumination.

What are the experiential effects of this kind of behavior and of these prayers that Hermas reports in the Visions? This chapter has used the findings of integrative and interdisciplinary approaches based in cognitive psychology and evolutionary understandings of human thought and behavior as heuristic models for identifying larger patterns that sequence decentering behaviors and religious experiences. It is thought that these decentering practices serve a strategic role by generating the necessary preconditions for the visionary experiences that take place. By using a more comprehensive and integrated understanding of the embodied mind, this study hopes to expand how scholars imagine visionary literature as reflecting some naturally occurring patterns of emotional states and cognitive experiences. In so doing, this study seeks to break the problematic assumptions of mind/

---

the Trope of Self-Cultivation," *Journal of the Royal Anthropological Institute* (n.s.) 18 (2012): 247–65, here 254.

78. See for example the comments by Snyder, *The Shepherd of Hermas,* 8–9 which note the similarities between the Shepherd and *4 Ezra*; also Joly, *Hermas. Le Pasteur,* 47.

body dualism and offers a way of conceptualizing visionary experiences as embodied cognitive processes.

Hermas engages in several practices that are associated with mourning and are used in the Second Temple penitential prayer tradition. Hermas kneels, prays and confesses his sins, and weeps (Vis. 1.1.3 [1.3]) before his first vision. He fasts (Vis. 3.1.2 [9.2]) before the vision of the tower and in the third vision of Lady Church (Vis. 3.1.6–7 [9.6–7]). Hermas also weeps prior to his vision of the beast (Vis. 4.1.7 [22.7]). These scenes are also replete with his own anguished introspective musings. His encounters with his visionary interlocutors lead to further thoughts of self-doubt. What is striking is how much these accounts of Hermas resemble early Jewish prayer practices. In addition to his verbalization of shortcomings and sins, Hermas's practices of fasting, weeping, and collapsing on his knees could all be said to effect liminality and decentering. These effects are quite similar to the ones produced by ritual forms of penitential prayer, which in the Second Temple period had diverse social aims, including the making of transcendence perceptibly near.

Most of the autobiographical details about Hermas found in these four visions provide the gateway to the larger work. These referential details to Hermas's past, his first-person perspective, and his emotive responses help to give him the depth of a lived person, someone with whom readers can empathize. These visions could be understood as arresting the attention of readers and hearers, drawing them into the narrative world of the text, as anyone who has found themselves engrossed in a novel and desolate when it ends can attest. Whether or not any or all the details found there are historical does not alter the emotional impact of the language and the rhetorical effect of that narrative on the reader. It is through Hermas's emotional and embodied experiences that readers and hearers gain entry into the world of the text.

Chapter Four

Experiencing the Journey

Spatial images readily come to mind when we speak about the immersive quality of narrative. A good story 'pulls you in', or we speak of a plot's 'twists and turns' and how we 'got lost in a book'. This chapter explores how language about the environs of Hermas's visions can be understood to create experientially vivid ways for readers and hearers to access the passing of time and space in the narrative, thereby playing a strategic role in cultivating states of anticipation and watchfulness that heighten receptivity to instruction. Details about the landscape and the objects in the speaker's environment are described with painstaking precision in the scenes that stage the visionary experiences. On the surface, these details are tedious and slow down the pace of the narrative, yet they contribute significantly to the text's quality of vividness. Rather than understanding the spaces and the environment as a static literary backdrop for the events that take place in the Shepherd of Hermas, this chapter considers alternative ways the environs can be understood and the possible effects of these descriptions of space on how a flesh-and-blood reader experiences a text like the Book of Visions. We present certain spatial details in the Book of Visions within the context of the mind's natural proclivities for making mental maps and for enactively extending and completing the fragmentary spatial details provided by the narrative. We argue that applying cognitive approaches to the way the environs are described in the third and fourth visions can help us to appreciate how the visions contributed to the moral formation of its readers and hearers. In the case of Hermas's fourth vision of the beast, these cognitive approaches enable us to understand why ancient readers found the book to be appealing.

Hermas is presented to the reader in ways that appeal to our lived experiences of our own environments. Configuring Hermas's visions within a narrative of a journey by foot appeals to our own flesh-and-blood experiences of traveling by foot through new terrain.[1] It is important to note that

---

1. For study of critical spatiality and the Shepherd of Hermas, see Harry O. Maier, "From Material Place to Imagined Space: Emergent Christian Community as Thirdspace in the *Shepherd of Hermas*," 143–60. Maier borrows the language of firstspace, secondspace, and thirdspace from Edward W. Soja, *Thirdspace: Journeys to Los Angeles and*

Hermas's actual location and destination are not crucial for these narrative effects on readers and hearers, and the journey segments in the Book of Visions are not contiguous. All four of Hermas's Visions are situated in largely uncultivated areas. This makes the visualization of Hermas's narrative easily transferable to many Mediterranean regions in the Roman Empire, allowing readers in any locale to visualize the rural terrain based on their own local geography and the mind's proclivities for mapmaking.

When we imagine ourselves within specific spaces, we not only think of the spaces themselves, but we also remember the events that took place there and our emotional responses to those events. Nancy Easterlin offers the example of how we remember the specific spaces in which we learned as young children not just in terms of the physical space of the classroom or of the accoutrements found therein, but according to our experiences and emotional responses to what took place there. Key here is whether the experiences were joyful because of the relationships remembered there or traumatic because of the negative experiences that took place.[2] These aspects of how we experience being in environments can be extended to how we as readers might experience descriptions of literarily constructed imaginary spaces. Such narratives reflect aspects of lived experiences within spaces, such as how a character might be said to navigate phenomenally within a specific space and how he or she interacts with the environment, both emotionally and kinesthetically.

The cognitive literary approach known as ecocriticism investigates how readers pay attention to changes in the narrative environment: when and where landmarks appear, how literary references to the changes in the sun or the passing of time might mark how much progress has been made on a journey. These aspects of the text are useful for thinking about Hermas's experiences in the Book of Visions because they remind us of the embodied cognitive processes involved in how the mind constructs spatial imagery and how texts might have been experienced phenomenally by flesh-and-blood readers. Ecocriticism is an example of a biocultural approach to the study of literature that emerged from environmental activism in the late-twentieth century.[3] As a subdiscipline of cognitive literary criticism, it offers a

---

Other Real-and-Imagined Places (Malden: Blackwell, 1996). See too Harkins, *Reading with an "I" to the Heavens*, 114–205.

2. Nancy Easterlin gives the specific example of being bitten by another child in "'Loving Ourselves Best of All': Ecocriticism and the Adapted Mind," *Mosaic: An Interdisciplinary Critical Journal* 37 (2004): 1–18, here 8–9.

3. Stephen Kaplan, "Environmental Preference in a Knowledge-Seeking, Knowledge-Using Organism," *The Adapted Mind: Evolutionary Psychology and the Generation of Culture*, ed. Jerome Barkow, Leda Cosmides, and John Tooby (New York:

way of theorizing descriptions of non-human environmental elements that appear in the Book of Visions in ways that take into account evolutionary and adaptive models of the human mind. Biocultural approaches can offer insights into how flesh-and-blood readers conceptualize the otherworldly spaces and places that feature prominently in visionary literature.[4] According to the theory of mind, the fundamental structures of the human brain operate in adaptive ways by forming mental representations that appeal to descriptions of space that are then culturally expressed in myths and narratives.[5] Studies of the biological background of human thinking about spaces identify certain areas of the brain that govern spatial movement or cognitive processes necessary for navigation.[6] These neurological studies of the brain and its cognitive processes of spatial reasoning and experiencing suggest that people generally have some capacity for mapmaking, even though the actual contours of the map reflect culturally specific understandings of space and place.[7] These studies remind scholars who are interested in the spaces described in visionary texts that descriptions of spaces do more than just offer a literary setting for staging the main action of the narrative. In other words, the Book of Visions describes not only the landscape and environment of the visions, but also the crucial details about Hermas's emotional

---

Oxford University Press, 1992), 581–98; Glen A. Love, "Ecocriticism and Science: Toward Consilience?" *Ecocriticism* (ed. Ralph Cohen, *New Literary History* 30 (1999): 661–76; Nancy Easterlin, "'Loving Ourselves Best of All,'" 1–18; Nancy Easterlin, *A Biocultural Approach to Literary Theory and Interpretation* (Baltimore: Johns Hopkins University Press, 2012); also Lisa Zunshine (ed.), *Introduction to Cognitive Cultural Studies*.

4. Helpful here is the work of Armin Geertz, "Brain, Body and Culture: A Biocultural Theory of Religion," 304–21, which argues for an integrated understanding of religious experience. Luther Martin's investigation of cognition and experience offers a useful framework for how to think about the cognitive experience of space. Luther H. Martin, "Do Rituals Do? And How Do They Do It? Cognition and the Study of Ritual," in *Introducing Religion: Essays in Honor of Jonathan Z. Smith*, ed. W. Bruan and R. T. McCutcheon (London: Equinox, 2008), 311–25, esp. 312–3. Martin is referencing Jonathan Z. Smith's well noted comment that "ritual is, first and foremost, a mode of paying attention" and that *place* is what "directs the attention," Jonathan Z. Smith, *To Take Place* (Chicago: University of Chicago Press, 1987), 103.

5. Martin, "Do Rituals Do?" 313.

6. Pyramidal cells in the hippocampus are activated when the subject moves from place to place. Specific regions in the brain, like the hippocampus or the related area known as the postsubiculum, may be responsible for governing various spatial processes and experiences like navigation and cognitive mapping; Joseph LeDoux, *Synaptic Self: How Our Brains Become Who We Are* (New York: Penguin, 2002), 113; Eric R. Kandel, *In Search of Memory: The Emergence of a New Science of Mind* (New York: Norton, 2006).

7. Martin, "Do Rituals Do?" 313.

responses to the things that take place in those environments, thereby simulating how a person might experience such an environment for themselves.

Each vision in the Book of Visions includes detailed references to Hermas's environment and records specific physical interactions with these spaces and the things therein. The landscapes where the visionary experiences take place are generally ordinary non-urban spaces, not unlike those that a traveler might expect to find in the region around Rome. Specific place names are sprinkled throughout the Book of Visions: the Tiber River (Vis. 1.1.2 [1.2]), the countryside, also appearing as Cumae in later manuscripts (Vis. 1.1.3 [1.3], 2.1.1 [5.1]) and Via Campana (Vis. 4.1.2 [22.2]). We also find descriptions of the terrain. For example, the first vision is located in a harsh landscape, "the place was steep and split up by the courses of water" (ὁ τόπος κρημνώδης καὶ ἀπερρηγὼς ἀπὸ τῶν ὑδάτων, Vis. 1.1.3 [1.3]). All these references situate Hermas's visions in vaguely familiar environs, lending a quality of realism to the narrative. The journey segments in the Book of Visions do not converge into a single comprehensive journey, and they are only occasionally linked to one another by temporal references. For example, the second vision is said to take place approximately one year after the first vision (Vis. 2.1.1 [5.1]). Many times the visions begin with Hermas setting out by foot into diverse terrain. The seer encounters numerous strange figures along the way, as we might expect during any journey, and he engages in enigmatic conversations, like the exchange with the woman in Vision 1 who leaves him with the bizarre and wry parting exhortation: "Act like a man, Hermas!" (Ἀνδρίζου Ἑρμα, Vis. 1.4.3 [4.3]).[8] Hermas also has mind-boggling visions, such as that of a massive tower (Vis. 3.2.2–9 [10.2–9]). In the case of the fourth vision, we are given a number of measurements: the length of the beast whom he encounters on the way is about a hundred feet in length (Vis. 4.1.6 [22.6]), and the young Lady in white is met approximately thirty feet after the beast (Vis. 4.2.1 [23.1]).[9] These approximate measurements also lend a quality of realism to Hermas's foot journey.

Writing that is intended to communicate propositional content is generally more direct but writing that is intended to evoke an emotional response in the reader is slowed down by literary devices so that mental faculties of visualization can take place. When texts are written in a circuitous or

---

8. Young, "Being a Man: The Pursuit of Manliness in *The Shepherd of Hermas*," 237–55.

9. Readers are directed to the discussion of these scenes by Aldo Tagliabue as instances of verisimilitude and immersive narrative in "Experiencing the Church in the *Book of Visions* of the *Shepherd of Hermas*," 104–24; Aldo Tagliabue, "Experience through Narrative in the Shepherd of Hermas," in *Experiencing the Shepherd of Hermas*, ed. Angela Kim Harkins and Harry O. Maier, 137–51, here 145.

painstaking way, the pace of reading is significantly slowed down, creating the effect that David Miall and Don Kuiken refer to as *defamiliarization*.[10] The painstaking pace of the narrative just as visions are about to take place allow for the intensification of readerly attention, allowing the mind to emotionally engage the text and generate a more vivid mental image.

Readers are regularly given access to Hermas's interior emotional state when he is in a new environment and are told of his anguished responses to the visions experienced in those spaces. Before the arrival of the Lady in Vision 3, Hermas says the following upon seeing the ivory couch in the field: "When I saw these things sitting there and no one in the area, I was astonished and a fit of trembling seized me and my hair stood on end and I shuddered in panic, as it were, because I was alone" (Vis. 3.1.5 [9.5]). These interoceptive details resonate with the naturally occurring ways in which we think about and remember the environments that we have lived in, spaces that are oftentimes significant because of the events that have taken place in them. Using this approach, we will consider all the details that constitute the scene—references to the terrain, the landscape, geography, the sun, and the bizarre visions themselves. Readers are given details about how Hermas phenomenally navigates his environment and responds emotionally to the things that he sees or experiences.

As we try to imagine the effect of such environmental cues on flesh-and-blood readers, we will consider how the embodied mind is naturally predisposed to pay attention to how a body relates to its environment kinesthetically—that is, with respect to movement, and haptically, as it relates to touch. The first-person narrations of events in the Book of Visions could be said to allow a reader's visualization of the landscape to take on an egocentric vividness, thus contributing to how a reader might imagine the events as Hermas journeys. Just as a sojourner sets out in unfamiliar terrain with a special attentiveness to the lay of the land and to the landmarks seen on the way, so too a reader takes careful note of how Hermas sees the environment, moves phenomenally in the spaces, and responds emotionally to what he sees. This evolutionary adaptation in favor of mental map-making is what allows a traveler to retrace his or her steps so that he or she can eventually find the way back home, a cognitive process known as navigation or wayfinding.

---

10. David S. Miall and Don Kuiken, "Foregrounding, Defamiliarization, and Affect: Response to Literary Stories," *Poetics* 22 (1994): 389–407.

Cultivating Watchfulness

The Book of Visions, like other ancient apocalypses, strategically cultivates a state of watchfulness and suspense in the reader, signaling that something significant will happen. In this section, we will examine how changes in the environment in another ancient apocalypse, the book of Daniel, effect emotional responses of fear, wonder, and confusion, all of which help the reader to anticipate what will come next, the heavenly throne scene in Dan. 7.9–14. Emotional responses to the night visions help to heighten receptivity to what will soon take place.

Daniel's nighttime dream vision of the four beasts begins with a churning sea in chapter 7.[11] The vast sea takes on a quality of solidity when we visualize the effects of the invisible winds battering its surface, swirling the waters into towering waves. Imagining the effects of the winds on the surface of the waters transforms it from a still two-dimensional background into a watery space with depth and solidity.[12] In other words, the depth and density of the waters are realized when we imagine the *effects* of the blustery wind as it churns the sea into thick white foamy waves. The four monstrous beasts that make their appearance from the waters are not unlike the shapes that are formed spontaneously while watching the towering and crashing waves. The first three beasts resemble fierce predators from the natural world: the lion, the bear, and the four-headed leopard. These creatures are presented with multiple features in a monstrous composite, with the first and third having wings and the third one having four heads. Such incongruous details remind the reader that these beasts are 'otherworldly'. Daniel's vision of the four

---

11. Reinhard Kratz, "The Visions of Daniel," in *The Book of Daniel: Composition and Reception. Volume 1*, ed. John J. Collins and Peter W. Flint (Leiden: Brill, 2001), 91–113. Daniel was highly regarded shortly after its publication and generated many interpretations and re-writings in the form of Danielic legenda and other apocryphal traditions. At Qumran, a significant number of copies of the book of Daniel or scrolls mentioning Daniel have been identified from Caves 1, 4, and 6 (1Q71, 1Q72; 4Q112–116; 6Q7), which correspond to the text found in all but one (12) of the chapters of the MT edition of the book; and there are as many as nine additional scrolls that contain texts that can be associated with Danielic traditions (4Q242–246; 4Q489, 4Q551–553); see Peter W. Flint, "The Daniel Tradition at Qumran," in *The Book of Daniel: Composition and Reception. Volume 2*, ed. John J. Collins and P. W. Flint (Leiden: Brill, 2001), 329–67, here 330–2. For an excellent discussion of the writings that have been generated by Daniel, see Lorenzo DiTommaso, *The Book of Daniel and the Apocryphal Daniel Literature* (Leiden: Brill, 2005).

12. Elaine Scarry illustrates this quality of narrative description in her example of light passing over a two-dimensional wall, "On Vivacity: The Difference between Daydreaming and Imagining-Under-Authorial-Instruction," *Representations* 52 (1995): 1–26 at 6.

beasts capitalizes on what is already known about these large predatory animals from our own lived experience—they are unpredictable, violent, and dangerous. The first three beasts call to mind the three animals in Hos. 13.7–8, which signify the foreign powers that enact YHWH's larger cosmic plan. The fourth beast, however, is not described in the same way; instead, the reader must somehow imagine its "ten horns" with "another one growing; and still other horns being taken away"—a challenge to visualize, although artists have tried. The description goes on to say that one of these horns had eyes and a mouth that spoke arrogantly. The fourth beast results in a monstrosity whose features epitomize the dangers of a fierce predator: menacing horns that eviscerate, sinister eyes that watch closely, and a large mouth that emits terrifying sounds; however, nothing is said about what kind of animalian shape it is—that is left to the imagination. The four-fold pattern of beasts in the nighttime vision calls to mind the four-fold composite statue from Nebuchadnezzar's dream in Dan. 2 and transfers the natural terror of the predatory animals onto the scenario of being subjugated by these four fierce foreign empires. The four beasts that emerge from the sea in Dan. 7 also correspond to the later vision of the single terrifying beast in Rev. 13.

The monsters that appear here in Daniel 7 and the enormous beast in Hermas's fourth vision suggest the usefulness of cognitive literary theory's study of fantasy literature, which highlights the way narratives generate responses within a reader, often seeking to disturb and unsettle.[13] Laura Feldt notes the way that bizarre details in religious narratives destabilize readers by generating a confusion that ultimately leads to greater cognitive engagement.[14] Texts that include fantastic elements effectively seize a reader's attention and slow down the pace of reading as the mind struggles to visualize and make sense of these bewildering, counterintuitive elements. Theoretical approaches to fantasy literature are especially relevant for the study of apocalypses since both literary genres rely on the use of bizarre and counterintuitive elements, but apocalypses strategically use these elements to cultivate watchfulness within the reader and hearer. Apocalypses create the conditions that stimulate the cognitive processes of rumination as readers struggle to understand what is happening. This response is also modeled by the seer who endeavors to understand the bizarre events that are taking place.

---

13. See Renata Lachmann, *Erzählte Phantastik. Zu Phantasiegeschichte und Semantik phantastischer Texte* (Frankfurt am Main: Suhrkamp, 2002), which Laura Feldt has successfully applied to descriptions of the fantastic in the book of Exodus; see Laura Feldt, "Religious Narrative and the Literary Fantastic: Ambiguity and Uncertainty in Ex. 1–18," *Religion* 41 (2011): 251–83.

14. Feldt, "Religious Narrative and the Literary Fantastic," 272–3.

A heightened watchfulness is cultivated in the reader of Daniel's nighttime vision of the monsters that emerge from the dark water, one by one. The narrative seizes the reader's attention and slows down the narrative pace, thus assisting in the generation of an emotional response from him or her. The cultivation of the reader's natural watchfulness concerning what will happen next effectively prepares the reader for the heavenly throne room experience that follows. In the case of Daniel 7, the vision shifts to that of the Ancient of Days who is ministered to by a myriad of heavenly beings (7.9–10) then returns quickly to a grisly scene in which the terrifying fourth beast is destroyed and burned in fire (7.11). After a brief mention of the fate of the three other beasts (v. 12), Daniel gives his report of his vision of the "one like a son of Man" (7.13–14). Readers are brought to the heavenly scenes of the Ancient of Days and the "one like the Son of Man" through the vision of the beasts who emerge one after the other.

The dream world of Daniel becomes more solid in our imaginations when we imagine the beasts emerging from the stormy sea, one after the other, as they move in their environment and change shape. For example, the solidity of space is achieved by the narrative details of the first beast, a lion with eagle's wings:

קַדְמָיְתָא כְאַרְיֵה וְגַפִּין דִּי־נְשַׁר לַהּ חָזֵה הֲוֵית עַד דִּי־מְּרִיטוּ גַפַּיהּ וּנְטִילַת מִן־אַרְעָא וְעַל־רַגְלַיִן
כֶּאֱנָשׁ הֳקִימַת וּלְבַב אֱנָשׁ יְהִיב לַהּ:

> The first was like a lion and had eagle's wings. Then, as I watched, its wings were plucked off, and it was lifted up from the ground and made to stand on two feet like a human being; and a human mind was given to it. (Dan. 7.4)

The beast undergoes a change as its wings are "plucked off," its body is made to stand upright, and it is given the "heart of a human being" within it (7.4). During this redirection of the reader's attention, the environment suddenly shifts from a marine view to firm land. A reader may imagine here the back paws of the beast pressing down on the soft earth. It is notable that these nighttime visions have a dynamic quality, with the beasts changing before the seer's eyes. The beasts emerge, each one more terrifying than the one before it. The fourth beast also undergoes a series of bizarre transformations before the seer's eyes: "While I was observing these horns—Behold! Another little horn came up among them. The three earlier horns were uprooted before it. And Behold! There were eyes like a human eye in this one horn and a mouth speaking arrogantly" (7.8). After the beasts, Daniel's vision report then shifts quickly to the heavenly throne room with little advance warning.

Daniel's nighttime vision of the beasts functions strategically to cultivate a keen watchfulness in a reader who has read with fascination how the monsters emerge from the stormy waters, one by one, and change shape before the seer's own eyes. The fourth and final beast is infinitely more terrifying and more peculiar than the previous ones. It is described solely in terms of its menacing traits—horns for gouging, eye for stalking, and a mouth for ferocious roars and, of course, mauling victims. The description resembles the experience of being stalked by an animal under the cover of night in which the terrifying jaws or horns of a predator in pursuit become disproportionately magnified in the imagination. The building of narrative expectation is also a key structural feature of the book of Revelation, whose series of seven seals (6.1–8.5), seven trumpets (8.6–9.21), and seven bowls (15.1–16.21) similarly cultivates the reader's attention and watchful eye. The descriptions in Daniel 7 effectively slows down the pace of the narrative and creates a dramatic tension that is artfully built up from the first to the fourth beast, dissipated, and then built up again. The changing shape of the beasts also contributes to the overall effect of training the reader's watchfulness as the visions progress, thus preparing the reader for the events that immediately follow in the heavenly throne room.

Achieving the Solidity of Space

The figure of Hermas and the stories of his visions have a quality of realism because of the way the author has chosen to depict Hermas in relation to his environment. His kinesthetic experiences and his embodiment within the scenes are compelling aspects of the story. Spaces have the capacity to take on qualities of solidity through the scaffolding of descriptions about them and through detailed accounts of a character's navigation through and interaction with the objects found in those spaces.[15] Some kind of journey by foot in a vast non-urban space provides the backdrop for Visions 1 to 4 of the Book of Visions.[16] In the case of the first and second visions, Hermas journeys by foot into the countryside, but notably we are not told if he ever reaches his final destination. In the third vision, Hermas is instructed to go to an undetermined spot in a field and to wait there for the Lady for five hours. The fourth vision takes place during Hermas's journey into the countryside on the Via Campana. In that vision, we are given the coordinates for the Via Campana, which is about a mile into the countryside. Just prior to his encounter with the bizarre beast on the road, one reads about the perceptible

---

15. Elaine Scarry, *Dreaming by the Book*, 10–30.
16. There are other details that set Vision 5 apart from the other visions in the Book of Visions. The perspective of the text changes, and the reader assumes the persona of Hermas.

changes in the environment: an extraordinary dust cloud that reaches into the heavens and the increased intensity of the sun (4.1.5-6 [22.5-6]). These details about the distance traveled on the road and the changes in the environment can cultivate readerly dispositions of being attentive and watchful for what might happen next. The activity of journeying in an uncultivated space remains a notable feature of the Book of Visions, even though Hermas is never said to have reached any specific destination.

Not long after the opening scene of Hermas seeing the bathing Rhoda, readers are provided with an account of Hermas's first visionary experience that takes place on his journey into the countryside. According to the first vision, Hermas is praising God and contemplating the grandeur of the created world when he falls into a deep sleep while walking, at which point he experiences a rapture. According to the first vision, and presumably the second one as well, Hermas simply falls asleep during his journey through the countryside. This might strike us as a bizarre narrative detail, yet contemplative prayer or meditation can lead to a response by the parasympathetic nervous system that resembles a sleep state that includes muscle relaxation. This trophotrophic state is one that might be a response to extreme stress or activity and is correlated with spiritual experiences.[17] Notable for our discussion is the way in which the spatial details are concretely described in the lines leading up to the encounter with the woman. Hermas is carried away by the spirit to an untrodden place that is rocky and impassable. Once he arrives at the plain on the other side of the river, he kneels (τὰ γόνατα), prays, and confesses his sins:

> 1.3 μετὰ χρόνον τινὰ πορευομένου μου εἰς κώμας καὶ δοξάζοντος τὰς κτίσεις τοῦ θεοῦ ὡς μεγάλαι καὶ ἐκπρεπεῖς καὶ δύναταί εἰσιν περιπατῶν ἀφύπνωσα καὶ πνεῦμά με ἔλαβεν καὶ ἀπήνεγκέν με δι' ἀνοδίας τινός δι' ἧς ἄνθρωπος οὐκ ἐδύνατο ὁδεῦσαι ἦν δὲ ὁ τόπος κρημνώδης καὶ ἀπερρηγὼς ἀπὸ τῶν ὑδάτων διαβὰς οὖν τὸν ποταμὸν ἐκεῖνον ἦλθον εἰς τὰ ὁμαλά καὶ τιθῶ τὰ γόνατα καὶ ἠρξάμην προσεύχεσθαι τῷ κυρίῳ καὶ ἐξομολογεῖσθαί μου τὰς ἁμαρτίας.

> 1.3 When some time had passed, I was traveling to the countryside, glorifying the creations of God and thinking how great, remarkable, and powerful they are. On the way, I fell asleep and a spirit took me and carried me through a certain deserted place that was impassable, for the place was steep and split

---

17. Andrew B. Newberg and Eugene G. D'Aquili, "The Neuropsychology of Spiritual Experience," in *Handbook of Religion and Mental Health*, ed. Harold G. Koenig (San Diego: Academic Press, 1998), 75-94, esp. 85-8. The resemblance between slumbering states and the highest level of spiritual contemplation is acknowledged widely in the medieval period; e.g., Bonaventure, in his Commentary on Luke, interprets Luke's account of the disciples' failure to keep awake during Jesus' prayer as a sign of their having achieved the highest spiritual contemplative state—interestingly, Bonaventure does not read their slumber negatively.

up by the courses of water. When I crossed the river I came to level ground and bowed my knees; and I began praying to the Lord and confessing my sins.

Here, the location of Hermas's journey lacks specificity. As Carolyn Osiek notes in her commentary, later manuscripts read εἰς Κούμας ("to Cumae"), but it is preferable to follow the Greek manuscripts, which reads "to the countryside."[18] It is at this point that Hermas encounters the Lady whom he had desired in a vision. Not long afterward, Hermas encounters a second vision of a Lady, but this time, she is elderly (Vis. 1.2.1–1.4.3 [2.1–4.3]). Her words to Hermas offer clear instruction that he should teach his family in the ways of repentance and righteousness. The reader is told that his second vision occurs in much the same way as the first, at the same time of the year and on a foot journey into the countryside:

5.1 ("Ορασις β) Πορευομένου μου εἰς κώμας κατὰ τὸν καιρὸν ὃν καὶ πέρυσι, περιπατῶν ἀνεμνήσθην τῆς περυσινῆς ὁράσεως, καὶ πάλιν με αἴρει πνεῦμα καὶ ἀποφέρει εἰς τὸν αὐτὸν τόπον ὅπου καὶ πέρυσι. 2 ἐλθὼν οὖν εἰς τὸν τόπον τιθῶ τὰ γόνατα καὶ ἠρξάμην προσεύχεσθαι τῷ κυρίῳ καὶ δοξάζειν αὐτοῦ τὸ ὄνομα, ὅτι με ἄξιον ἡγήσατο καὶ ἐγνώρισέν μοι τὰς ἁμαρτίας μου τὰς πρότερον. 3 μετὰ δὲ τὸ ἐγερθῆναί με ἀπὸ τῆς προσευχῆς βλέπω ἀπέναντί μου τὴν πρεσβυτέραν ἣν καὶ πέρυσιν ἑωράκειν, περιπατοῦσαν καὶ ἀναγινώσκουσαν βιβλαρίδιον. καὶ λέγει μοι· Δύνῃ ταῦτα τοῖς ἐκλεκτοῖς τοῦ θεοῦ ἀναγγεῖλαι; λέγω αὐτῇ· Κυρία, τοσαῦτα μνημονεῦσαι οὐ δύναμαι· δὸς δέ μοι τὸ βιβλίδιον, ἵνα μεταγράψωμαι αὐτό. ⸀Λάβε, φησίν, καὶ ἀποδώσεις μοι⸃.

5.1 I was traveling to the countryside at the same time as the previous year, and on the way I remembered the vision from the year before. And again a spirit took me and bore me to the same place I had been then. 2 And so, when I came to the place I bowed my knees and began praying to the Lord and glorifying his name, because he considered me worthy and showed me my former sins. 3 When I arose from prayer I saw across from me the elderly woman I had seen the year before, walking and reading a little book. And she said to me, "Can you announce these things to the ones chosen by God?" I said to her, "Lady, I cannot remember so many things. Give me the book to make a copy." "Take it," she said, "and then return it to me."

The seer replicates his journey from the previous year, and at the same location he experiences another rapture in which he has a second vision of the elderly lady whom he had met previously.

Enactive reading generates perceptions of phenomenal presence and relies on literary cues of first-person voice, spatial descriptions, and bodily movement.[19] It also depends upon the character's emotional responses to various events. As we discussed in the previous chapter, features such as the

---

18. Osiek, *The Shepherd of Hermas*, 43.
19. Kuzmicova, "Literary Narrative and Mental Imagery," 280.

pious, self-diminishing practices that Hermas regularly takes part in prior to his visionary experiences are well-known visionary practices described in other late Second Temple apocalyptic texts (e.g., Daniel and *4 Ezra*).[20] After a distressing exchange with the lady in his first vision, Hermas begins to anguish about the sin of excessive desire (ἐπιθυμία) that has been revealed to him (Vis. 1.2.1–2 [2.1–2]). Then, while distressed and in a weeping state of grief, he encounters a second woman, seated in a white chair. In this second vision, the Lady instructs him to copy a book. Readers would remember that prior to his first visionary encounter, Hermas was engaged in similar behaviors: walking alone, thinking about the previous year's vision, kneeling, praying, and contemplating God's greatness and his own sinful state (Vis. 2.1.1–2 [5.1–2]; cf. 3.1.4–5 [9.4–5]). In the second vision, Hermas copies the book, which he cannot read. Then we are told that he ruminates over the contents of the writing while fasting and praying for fifteen days and gains understanding of the contents (Vis. 2.2.1 [6.1]). In the case of the third vision, Hermas is said to have fasted and prayed for a considerable amount of time (3.1.2 [9.2]). His encounters with the Lady happen at night, which could suggest either that he was sleep deprived or that the vision resembled a dream experience.[21]

There is no doubt that the reader is given a significant amount of information about Hermas's emotional state and has access to the seer's emotional responses to what is happening as it unfolds. While Hermas's excessive weeping and overwrought emotional state may strike us as implausible, his introspective musings express self-doubt and worry that speak to a compelling vulnerability. It is also the case that the repetitive behaviors of fasting, weeping, praying, and confessing sins are themselves highly performative and routinely imitable, and they would have been understood as such by ancient readers. Hermas's first-person narration of his emotions and his phenomenal experiences in his environment allow readers the possibility of accessing the text immersively with the quality of presence.

Hermas's Third Vision

The Book of Visions does not typically offer the kinds of lengthy detailed examples of *ekphrasis* that appear in the heavenly visions found in the book

---

20. Daniel Merkur, "Visionary Practices of Jewish Apocalypticists."
21. The Second Vision begins as a revelation that comes to Hermas in his sleep. He is asked who is the old Lady who has appeared to him, and he identifies her (incorrectly) as the Sybil. Both female figures are said to be of old age, sitting, holding a book, and identified as revealing knowledge. The Sibyl was probably well known in Rome during this time; Osiek, *The Shepherd of Hermas*, 58 nn. 2, 3.

of Revelation or the scenes of hell in the Apocalypse of Peter, both of which have been the subject of recent books.[22] An exception to this is the Tower of Stones in Vision 3—which is an exceptional passage in the Book of Visions. Rather, as we have seen, readers and hearers are given much smaller, discrete details that provide partial glimpses of Hermas's narrative world and are then used to construct a coherent image in the reader's or hearer's imagination. The Book of Visions does create the conditions for readers and hearers to generate palpable mental images that are awash with strong emotions.

The centerpiece of the Book of Visions is arguably the third vision of the Tower, which is both the longest of the visions and the image that returns for lengthy discussion in Similitude 9.2–16 (79–93) and 30–33 (107–110).

In our following treatment, we will discuss two major scenes from the third vision. The first is the narration of the journey into the field, and the second is the Tower of Stones. These offer an opportunity to consider the ways in which the reader's enactive perception is cultivated by the text's painstaking details about Hermas's bodily experiences. These tedious details about Hermas's journey through the field and the mundane things that he both encounters and interacts with in Vision 3 serve to slow down the pace of the narrative and prime the reader for an even greater attentiveness to what will be seen next—namely the Tower (Vis. 3.2.4 [10.4]). In this instance of enactive perception, the reader is able, through the bodily experiences of the protagonist, to achieve some degree of familiarity with the environment, which further heightens the anticipation about what will come next. Hermas's bodily experiences of locomotion and of the physical space serves to prepare the reader for the vision of the Tower which becomes part of the landscape in the field.

Experiencing the Journey into the Field

The climactic vision of the Tower is strategically staged by the preceding vision of Hermas's nighttime journey into the field. While the Tower in Vision 3 and its significance have been discussed at length by previous scholars, the tedious details that are given about Hermas prior to the Tower vision are rarely examined in any detail. Using the framework developed by classicist Rutger J. Allan for the analysis of ancient immersive narratives, Aldo Tagliabue describes how changes in temporal perception take place in descriptions of the revelatory experiences in the Book of Visions.[23]

---

22. Whitaker, *Ekphrasis, Vision, and Persuasion in the Book of Revelation*; Meghan Henning, *Educating Early Christians through the Rhetoric of Hell*, WUNT 382 (Tübingen: Mohr Siebeck, 2014).

23. Tagliabue, "Experience through Narrative in the Shepherd of Hermas," 137–51,

Tagliabue's work applies enactive reading to the literary elements that Allan denotes as verisimilitude, the concrete details that give the appearance of lived experience.[24] Harry O. Maier has also noted how the use of the historical present contributes to a temporal verisimilitude of the scenes in the Shepherd.[25] Temporality in the Book of Visions challenges the culturally specific modern conception of time—and history—as the regular successive ordering of one event to another.[26] Maier does well to note how the events in the Book of Visions are depicted in a way that "interrupts the flow of time and recategorizes the time and place of its recipients."[27]

The elaborate report of Hermas in the field with the ivory couch strikes many commentators as a needlessly protracted passage that serves the purpose of illustrating Hermas's timidity. Instead, we propose that the scene is well-crafted to create an immersive experience that heightens a reader's experience of anticipation, allowing the reader to respond emotionally to the nighttime events that take place in the field. We propose that Hermas's experiences in the field can be re-read as strategically cultivating a heightened sense of watchfulness in the reader by effectively slowing down the pace of the narrative and priming the reader for an even greater attentiveness to what will happen next. This is not unlike the way that Daniel's nighttime vision of the beasts functions in chapter 7 of that book, in which the steady succession of bizarre beasts that emerge one by one serves to cultivate anticipation, thereby preparing readers and hearers for the heavenly vision of the Ancient of Days and the Son of Man. So too Hermas's long nighttime wait in the field prepares the reader for the third vision of the Tower, an important image that will be the setting for further events in the third section of the Shepherd, known as the Similitudes (Sim. 9.2–16

---

esp. 140–42; Rutger J. Allan, "Herodotus and Thucydides: Distance and Immersion," in *Textual Strategies in Ancient War Narrative: Thermopylae, Cannae and Beyond*, ed. Lidewij van Gils, Irene J. F. de Jong, and Caroline Kroon (Leiden: Brill, 2018), 131–54. See also Tagliabue's earlier discussion, "Experiencing the Church in the *Book of Visions* of the *Shepherd of Hermas*," 107.

24. Allan, "Herodotus and Thucydides," 133–5; Tagliabue, "Experience through Narrative in the Shepherd of Hermas, 140–3.

25. Harry O. Maier, "Making History with the Shepherd of Hermas," *Early Christianity* 10 (2019): 501–20.

26. Harry O. Maier, "Making History with the Shepherd of Hermas," 504–5. Maier relies on Walter Benjamin's distinction between modern ideas of temporality that see time as "naturalistic" and non-modern conceptualizations of temporality that have competing and contradictory understandings of time; Walter Benjamin, "Theses on the Philosophy of History," in *Illuminations*, ed. H. Arendt, trans. H. Zohn (New York: Harcourt, Brace & World, 1968), 253–64, 261.

27. Maier, "Making History with the Shepherd of Hermas," 503.

4. *Experiencing the Journey* 145

[79–93]; 30–33 [107–110]). In this instance of enactive perception, the reader is able, through the descriptions of the bodily experiences of the protagonist, to achieve some degree of familiarity with the environment, which further heightens the anticipation about what will come next. Hermas's bodily experiences of locomotion and of the physical space serve to prepare the reader for the vision of the Tower that is built before his eyes as he watches from the field (Vis. 3.2.4–13.4 [10.4–21.4]).

The vision of the Tower begins with a protracted nighttime scene of Hermas in the field in which there are many details provided to the reader of Hermas's kinesthetic movements and emotions. The scene begins with the report that Hermas has already spent a long time fasting and in prayer while asking for an explanation of the promised revelation (Vis. 3.1.2 [9.2]). The Lady promises to meet Hermas in the field and instructs him to walk out into the field at a certain nighttime hour, although the precise location is left undetermined by the lady.[28] As we imagine Hermas walking to some unspecified area, we can also imagine the disorienting experience of stumbling through a field at night. The circumstances lead us to pay careful attention to the terrain so that we retrace our steps afterward. In the following scene that details the encounter, the author has provided several details of Hermas's proprioception and interoception, which have been underlined below:

9.2 νηστεύσας <u>πολλάκις</u> καὶ δεηθεὶς τοῦ Κυρίου ἵνα μοι φανερώσῃ τὴν ἀποκάλυψιν ἣν μοι ἐπηγγείλατο δεῖξαι διὰ τῆς πρεσβυτέρας, αὐτῇ τῇ νυκτὶ ὦπταί μοι ἡ πρεσβυτέρα καὶ εἶπέν μοι· Επεὶ οὕτως ἐνδεὴς εἶ καὶ σπουδαῖος εἰς τὸ γνῶναι πάντα, ἐλθὲ εἰς τὸν ἀγρὸν ὅπου ⌜χονδρίζεις, καὶ περὶ ὥραν πέμπτην ἐμφανισθήσομαί σοι καὶ δείξω σοι ἃ δεῖ σε ἰδεῖν. 3 ἠρώτησα αὐτὴν λέγων· Κυρία, εἰς ποῖον τόπον τοῦ ἀγροῦ; Ὅπου, φησίν, θέλεις. ἐξελεξάμην τόπον καλὸν ἀνακεχωρηκότα. πρὶν δὲ λαλῆσαι αὐτῇ καὶ εἰπεῖν τὸν τόπον, λέγει μοι· Ἥξω ἐκεῖ ὅπου θέλεις. 4 ἐγενόμην οὖν, ἀδελφοί, <u>εἰς τὸν ἀγρόν, καὶ συνεψήφισα τὰς ὥρας, καὶ ἦλθον εἰς τὸν τόπον ὅπου διεταξάμην αὐτῇ ἐλθεῖν</u>, καὶ βλέπω συμψέλιον κείμενον ἐλεφάντινον, καὶ ἐπὶ τοῦ συμψελίου ἔκειτο κερβικάριον λινοῦν, καὶ ἐπάνω λέντιον ἐξηπλωμένον λινοῦν καρπάσινον. 5 <u>ἰδὼν ταῦτα κείμενα καὶ μηδένα ὄντα ἐν τῷ τόπῳ ἔκθαμβος ἐγενόμην, καὶ ὡσεὶ τρόμος με ἔλαβεν, καὶ αἱ τρίχες μου ὀρθαί· καὶ ὡσεὶ φρίκη μοι προσῆλθεν, μόνου μου ὄντος</u>. ἐν ἐμαυτῷ οὖν γενόμενος καὶ μνησθεὶς τῆς δόξης τοῦ Θεοῦ καὶ λαβὼν θάρσος, θεὶς τὰ γόνατα ἐξωμολογούμην τῷ Κυρίῳ πάλιν τὰς ἁμαρτίας μου ὡς καὶ πρότερον.

9.2 <u>After I fasted a great deal</u> and asked the Lord to show me the revelation that he promised to reveal through the elderly woman, that same night the elderly woman appeared and said to me, "Since you are so needy and eager to know everything, come to the field where you farm, and around eleven in

---

28. This scene bears some general resemblance to the apocalypse known as *4 Ezra*, which visions are also staged by instructions that the seer retreat into a field (cf. *4 Ezra* 9.26; 10.53).

the morning I will be revealed to you and show you what you must see." 3 I asked her, "Lady, in what part of the field?" "Wherever you wish," she said. I chose a beautiful spot that was secluded. But before I could speak with her to tell her the place, she said to me, "I will come there, wherever you wish." 4 And so, brothers, (sic) <u>I went into the field and counted the hours. I arrived at the place that I had directed her to come</u>, and I saw an ivory couch set up. On the couch was placed a linen pillow, with a piece of fine linen cloth on top. 5 <u>When I saw these things laid out with no one there, I was astounded and seized with trembling, and my hair stood on end—terrified, because I was alone</u>. Then when I came to myself, <u>I remembered the glory of God and took courage. I bowed my knees and confessed my sins again to the Lord, as I had done before</u>.

The narrative world of the Tower gains three-dimensionality through the proprioceptive report of Hermas, who walks tentatively through the field and counts the hours that pass in darkness (Vis. 3.1.4 [9.4]).

Several descriptions of Hermas's embodied movements in this nighttime encounter are colored by his interior emotional states of fear, confusion, and grief. All these details preceding the vision of the Tower contribute to the hearer's perception of Hermas's nervousness. The events leading up to the vision of the Tower are slow-moving and especially rich in proprioceptive details and spatial imagery. The narrative pace allows the reader and hearer to engage the emotional experiences that Hermas undergoes. Like Hermas, we may find these references to the meeting place to be frustratingly vague, yet they nevertheless provide the necessary details that allow a reader to enact the scene in the imagination, perhaps adding their own experiences of confusion and apprehension to the events as they visualize them in their mind.

In the field, the reader is told about the things in the environment that Hermas sees as he happens upon them. Hermas also freely discloses his emotional responses to these things. After fasting intensely, Hermas becomes agitated in the field upon seeing an ivory couch: "I saw an ivory couch set up, on the couch a linen pillow, and a piece of good linen covering it. When I saw all this set out, but no one there, I was seized with terror and began trembling and my hair stood on end. I was panic-stricken because I was alone" (Vis. 3.1.4–5 [9.4–5]). In addition to his emotional state upon being in the field and seeing the peculiar couch, Hermas engages in a perturbing conversation with the lady about the couch, an interlude that recounts in painstaking detail where Hermas should sit.

The Lady invites Hermas to sit down, and he initially approaches to sit on her right. We gain a strong sense of Hermas's chagrin as she then tells him he cannot sit on her right (Vis. 3.1.8–9 [9.8–9]).

> 9.8 καὶ μετὰ τὸ ἀναχωρῆσαι τοὺς νεανίσκους καὶ μόνων ἡμῶν γεγονότων λέγει μοι· Κάθισον ὧδε. λέγω αὐτῇ· Κυρία, ἄφες τοὺς πρεσβυτέρους πρῶτον καθίσαι.

4. *Experiencing the Journey* 147

Ὅ σοι λέγω, φησίν, κάθισον. 9 θέλοντος οὖν μου καθίσαι εἰς τὰ δεξιὰ μέρη οὐκ εἴασέν με, ἀλλ᾿ ἐννεύει μοι τῇ χειρὶ ἵνα εἰς τὰ ἀριστερὰ μέρη καθίσω. διαλογιζομένου μου οὖν καὶ λυπουμένου ὅτι οὐκ εἴασέν με εἰς τὰ δεξιὰ μέρη καθίσαι, λέγει μοι· Λυπῇ, Ἑρμᾶ; ὁ εἰς τὰ δεξιὰ μέρη τόπος ἄλλων ἐστίν, τῶν ἤδη εὐαρεστηκότων τῷ θεῷ καὶ παθόντων εἵνεκα τοῦ ὀνόματος· σοὶ δὲ πολλὰ λείπει ἵνα μετ᾿ αὐτῶν καθίσῃς· ἀλλὰ ὡς ἐμμένεις τῇ ἁπλότητί σου, μεῖνον, καὶ καθιῇ μετ᾿ αὐτῶν, καὶ ὅσοι ἐὰν ἐργάσωνται τὰ ἐκείνων ἔργα καὶ ὑπενέγκωσιν ἃ καὶ ἐκεῖνοι ὑπήνεγκαν.

9.8 After the young men left and we were alone, she said to me: "Sit here." I said to her, "Lady, let the elders sit first." Do what I tell you," she said. "Sit." 9 But then, when I wanted to sit on the right side, she did not let me, but signaled with her hand for me to sit on the left. As I was mulling this over and becoming upset that she did not allow me to sit on the right, she said to me, "Are you upset, Hermas? The place on the right is for others, who have already pleased God and suffered on behalf of the name. Many things must happen to you before you can sit with them. But continue in your simplicity, as you are doing, and you will sit with them, as will everyone who does what they have done and endures what they have endured."

Later, Hermas throws himself at the Lady's feet and implores her to reveal the vision that she had promised (Vis. 3.2.3 [10.2]). The protracted scene of Hermas in the field affords the reader the time to become aware of Hermas's interoceptive experiences and to cultivate a state of watchfulness that resembles Hermas's heightened apprehension. With an eye to the work's catechetical aim, the scene, more importantly, encourages the reader to pay careful attention to the long-awaited words of the Lady, which includes the following exhortation in Vis. 3.2.1–2 (10.1–2):

10.1 (Ὅρασις γ) Τί, φημί, ὑπήνεγκαν; Ἄκουε, φησίν· μάστιγας, φυλακάς, θλίψεις μεγάλας, σταυρούς, θηρία εἵνεκεν τοῦ ὀνόματος· διὰ τοῦτο ἐκείνων ἐστὶν τὰ δεξιὰ μέρη τοῦ ἁγιάσματος, καὶ ὃς ἐὰν πάθῃ διὰ τὸ ὄνομα· τῶν δὲ λοιπῶν τὰ ἀριστερὰ μέρη ἐστίν. ἀλλὰ ἀμφοτέρων, καὶ τῶν ἐκ δεξιῶν καὶ τῶν ἐξ ἀριστερῶν καθημένων, τὰ αὐτὰ δῶρα καὶ αἱ αὐταὶ ἐπαγγελίαι· μόνον ἐκεῖνοι ἐκ δεξιῶν κάθηνται καὶ ἔχουσιν δόξαν τινά. 2 σὺ δὲ κατεπιθυμεῖς καθίσαι ἐκ δεξιῶν μετ᾿ αὐτῶν, ἀλλὰ τὰ ὑστερήματά σου πολλά· καθαρισθήσῃ δὲ ἀπὸ τῶν ὑστερημάτων σου· καὶ πάντες δὲ οἱ μὴ διψυχοῦντες καθαρισθήσονται ἀπὸ πάντων τῶν ἁμαρτημάτων εἰς ταύτην τὴν ἡμέραν.

10.1 "What have they endured?" I asked. "Listen," she said: "floggings, imprisonments, great afflictions crucifixions, and wild beasts—for the sake of the name. For this reason, the right side of holiness belongs to them, and to anyone who suffers on account of the name. And the left side is for the others. The same gifts and promises belong to both—those seated on the right and those on the left. But they alone sit on the right and have a certain glory. 2 You wanted to sit on the right side with them, but you have many shortcomings. But you will be cleansed of your shortcomings. And all those who are not of two minds will be cleansed from all the sins they have committed up to this day."

It is noteworthy that the details about Hermas's locomotion and the report of his interaction with the various objects that he encounters in the field are instrumental in assisting the reader in perceiving the narrative space as a virtual reality to enter. Similar to being in a new environment, Hermas notices things gradually—things do not appear to him all at once. The discussion of seating continues through the third vision of the Tower (Vis. 3.2.1–4 [10.1–4]), culminating with Hermas being unable to see anything at first. It is only later that he is able to gradually perceive the Tower being built (Vis. 3.2.5 [10.5]).

Modern scholars frequently describe these details leading up to the Tower vision and Hermas's kinesthetic and emotional responses to the various things that he sees as tedious and boring. Yet these details and responses are better understood as instrumental in creating an immersive experience of the text. The slow narrative pace allows the reader and hearer to visualize the space and imagine the events that are described, first, in the instructions given by the lady, and then in Hermas's execution of those instructions. We also gain important information about Hermas in Vision 3, that he falls "far short" of sitting on the right with the martyrs. This detail conveys that Hermas was an ordinary figure, thus suggesting something about the ordinary circumstances of the implied reader of these visions. The discussion of seating continues through Vis. 3.2.1–4 (10.1–4) and culminates with the Tower. Hermas is not able to see the Tower at first—he is only gradually able to apprehend it, but once he does, the Tower is dynamically described, allowing it to gain density and solidity.

The lengthy prelude to the Vision of the Tower describes Hermas engaged in locomotion and changing postures, viz., walking, sitting, and standing. Hermas's nighttime walk into the field not only slows down the narrative, but it also effectively builds momentum toward the Tower vision. We are told what Hermas sees as things gradually come into focus, and how he feels as things happen—all of which express the acquisition of knowledge gained by investigation. Hermas sees the couch and he moves closer to inspect it, allowing the scene to resemble how individuals might also experience being in a new place by moving closer to investigate something that is unexpectedly encountered. Such images could be experienced in the mind as egocentric episodes in which the first-person perspective of Hermas become the reader's guide of the landscape, which he or she is expected to visualize in detail.

According to Yael Avrahami, there is a correlation in the Hebrew Bible between kinaesthetic and visual apprehension, two sensory experiences that are associated with the acquisition of personal knowledge.[29] In the bibli-

---

29. Yael Avrahami, *The Senses of Scripture*, 75–84.

cal imagination, the joining of the two expresses the idea of understanding gained by investigation.[30] This feature of imagined locomotion and visual apprehension ('navigation' or sometimes referred to as 'wayfinding') is described by Alan Richardson as the cognitive capacity to perceive the self as it journeys with vividness, "especially in relation to foot travel through unpredictable environments, calculating times (such as sunrise and sunset) along with routes" taken.[31] Some have suggested that the human mind is predisposed to visualizing paths and journeys.[32] The opening of the third vision painstakingly provides a narrativized travel itinerary, Hermas's steps taken in the field, the things seen along on the journey, and the individuals encountered along the way. The ivory couch, the linen pillow, and the fine linen covering, as well as the Tower, all become landmarks of a journey by foot that the reader is expected to follow and remember.

What have been described as tedious and insignificant details about Hermas's walking itinerary are better understood, we propose, as preparation for the vision of the Tower. Hermas's walk through the field slows down the pace of the crucial vision of the Tower, thus affording the reader the time to visualize the space and imagine the events being recounted. We also gain important information about Hermas in Vis. 3, that he falls "far short" of sitting on the right with the martyrs. The scene allows a reader to imagine Hermas's emotions as he is told to move to a different seat and access empathically the feeling of one who is deeply uncertain of one's own moral state.

On the Solidity of Stones (Vis. 3)

The Tower, the crucial component of the third vision, is not revealed until well after Hermas has situated himself and has fully taken in his new surroundings. The slowing down of the pace of events gives the reader the opportunity to engage the details of the narrative and to re-enact them in the mind's imagination.[33] The Tower itself is given a special kinesthetic quality in the vision, which describes it as "being built in a square by the six young

---

30. Several examples are provided by Avrahami in *The Senses of Scripture*: 'Your word is a lamp to my feet and a light to my path' (Ps 119:105); 'you have kept my feet from falling so that I may walk before God in the light of life' (Ps 56:14); 'come and see what God has done' (Ps 66:5; see Avrahami, *The Senses of Scripture*, 76-7).

31. Alan Richardson, "Imagination: Literary and Cognitive Intersections," in *The Oxford Handbook of Cognitive Literary Studies*, ed. Lisa Zunshine (Oxford: Oxford University Press, 2015), 225–45, here 236.

32. Easterlin, "Cognitive Ecocriticism: Human Wayfinding, Sociality, and Literary Interpretation," 257–74; Mithen, "The Evolution of Imagination: An Archaeological Perspective," 28–54.

33. Kuzmičová, "Literary Narrative and Mental Imagery."

men" (Vis. 3.2.5 [10.5]). The movement and activity of building lends a three-dimensional vividness to the vision. Elaine Scarry speaks about the way writing is able to express perceptual qualities of solidity, or what she calls "perceptual mimesis."[34] Scarry writes: "[W]riters known for their sensory vivacity explicitly build objects within their pages, with the result that we are shown a discrete path along which to build them in our own minds".[35] This scaffolding of perceptual experiences takes place through the careful attention given to the constituent elements of the spatial details. The Tower is not inert; rather, it is animated as the mind carefully contemplates handling, rotating, inspecting each stone for cracks and flaws. Feeling the dust and hearing the noise of the construction become additional aspects of the enactive perception that can be supplied by the readers' and hearers' imaginations. One might imagine the smooth and cool feel of the stones that click together and fit tightly into the Tower. So too the sounds of the stones being smashed, the color, shape, and roughness of the stones are described for the reader.

> 10.5 ἐν τετραγώνῳ δὲ ᾠκοδομεῖτο ὁ πύργος ὑπὸ τῶν ἓξ νεανίσκων τῶν ἐληλυθότων μετ᾿ αὐτῆς· ἄλλαι δὲ μυριάδες ἀνδρῶν παρέφερον λίθους, οἱ μὲν ἐκ τοῦ βυθοῦ, οἱ δὲ ἐκ τῆς γῆς, καὶ ἐπεδίδουν τοῖς ἓξ νεανίσκοις. ἐκεῖνοι δὲ ἐλάμβανον καὶ ᾠκοδόμουν· 6 τοὺς μὲν ἐκ τοῦ βυθοῦ λίθους ἑλκομένους πάντας οὕτως ἐτίθεσαν εἰς τὴν οἰκοδομήν· ἡρμοσμένοι γὰρ ἦσαν καὶ συνεφώνουν τῇ ἁρμογῇ μετὰ τῶν ἑτέρων λίθων· καὶ οὕτως ἐκολλῶντο ἀλλήλοις, ὥστε τὴν ἁρμογὴν αὐτῶν μὴ φαίνεσθαι· ἐφαίνετο δὲ ἡ οἰκοδομὴ τοῦ πύργου ὡς ἐξ ἑνὸς λίθου ᾠκοδομημένη. 7 τοὺς δὲ ἑτέρους λίθους τοὺς φερομένους ἀπὸ τῆς ξηρᾶς τοὺς μὲν ἀπέβαλλον, τοὺς δὲ ἐτίθουν εἰς τὴν οἰκοδομήν· ἄλλους δὲ κατέκοπτον καὶ ἔρριπτον μακρὰν ἀπὸ τοῦ πύργου. 8 ἄλλοι δὲ λίθοι πολλοὶ κύκλῳ τοῦ πύργου ἔκειντο, καὶ οὐκ ἐχρῶντο αὐτοῖς εἰς τὴν οἰκοδομήν· ἦσαν γάρ τινες ἐξ αὐτῶν ἐψωριακότες, ἕτεροι δὲ σχισμὰς ἔχοντες, ἄλλοι δὲ κεκολοβωμένοι, ἄλλοι δὲ λευκοὶ καὶ στρογγύλοι, μὴ ἁρμόζοντες εἰς τὴν οἰκοδομήν. 9 ἔβλεπον δὲ ἑτέρους λίθους ῥιπτομένους μακρὰν ἀπὸ τοῦ πύργου καὶ ἐρχομένους εἰς τὴν ὁδὸν καὶ μὴ μένοντας ἐν τῇ ὁδῷ, ἀλλὰ ⌜κυλιομένους ἐκ τῆς ὁδοῦ εἰς τὴν ἀνοδίαν· ἑτέρους δὲ ἐπὶ πῦρ ἐμπίπτοντας καὶ καιομένους· ἑτέρους δὲ πίπτοντας ἐγγὺς ὑδάτων καὶ μὴ δυναμένους κυλισθῆναι εἰς τὸ ὕδωρ, καίπερ θελόντων κυλισθῆναι καὶ ἐλθεῖν εἰς τὸ ὕδωρ.

> 10.5 The tower was being built in a square by the six young men who had come with her. And thousands of other men were brining stones, some of them from the depths of the sea and some from the land, and they were handing them over to the six young men, who were taking them and building. 6 Thus they placed all the stones drawn from the depths in the building; for they fit together and were straight at their joints with the other stones. And they were placed together so that their joints were invisible. The tower building

---

34. Scarry, *Dreaming by the Book*, 11.
35. Scarry, *Dreaming by the Book*, 20.

seemed to have been made out of a single stone. 7 But they tossed aside some of the other stones that were brought from the dry land, while others they placed in the building. Others they broke up and cast far from the tower. 8 Many other stones were lying around the tower, and they did not use them in the building. For some of them had a rough surface, others had cracks, others were broken off, and others were white and round, and did not fit in the building. 9 I saw other stones cast far away from the tower; these came onto the path, but did not remain there, but rolled from the path onto the rough terrain. Others fell into the fire and were burned. And others fell near the water, but could not be rolled into it, even though they wanted to be. (Vis. 3.2.5–9 [10.5–9])

In this detailed passage that reports how the stones were chosen and rejected, the scene achieves a vivid state of solidity by the interactive quality of the description—the image of the Tower is neither inert nor static. Each type of stone is accounted for in excruciating detail and described at length in the interpretation of the vision that follows (Vis. 3.3.1–3.7.6 [11.1–15.6]). The description of the Tower uses *enargeia* to draw the reader into a deeper state of contemplation about the experiences that Hermas is having in the vision itself. *Enargeia* uses language to create a vivid perception of the things described. Jane Heath describes *enargeia* as an rhetorical strategy that "represented what was actually not there in a way that made it seem so vivid, so clear, so animated or immediate that it appeared to be practically perceptible to the senses."[36] The details that some stones are rolling, a few falling into the fire, and others are coming perilously close to the edge of the water draw the mind's eye into a dynamic experience of the objects, one that has the perceptual qualities of first-hand experience. Such sensory complexities are true to the experience of sight in life as lived.

We can imagine that the hearers of Hermas's third vision were also stimulated by their own eyes moving in their environment, their own sight path crossing common objects that resemble the stones that are described in the vision. When we imagine such a scenario, it becomes possible to recognize how the activity of listening to a visionary text could generate mental imagery that is also highly individualized according to the hearer's own memory of the objects described, and the hearer's own experience of the environment at the moment of reading. According to Anežka Kuzmičová, listening to a text can potentially be more stimulating and more generative of mental imagery than reading a text in solitude, since in the latter one's eyes are tethered to the written page and thus subject to less stimulation

---

36. Heath, "Absent Presences of Paul and Christ: *Enargeia* in 1 Thessalonians 1–3," 4–5.

from the environment.[37] Whereas a hearer does not have control over the speed at which a text is read to him or her, a reader has the ability to slow down, amplify, to intone key descriptions, and to use his or her posture to mark those scenes that are important to experience with enactive perception, all of which can further stimulate the listener's imagination. The vision of the Tower can have an elastic quality in that the details of its perception become shaped by the hearer's own lived experience: the unique environment of the hearer or his or her own personal memories of being in a quarry or on a building site, for example. In this way, the sight path of his or her eyes becomes incorporated into the individual's mental image of the Tower and its stones.

Hermas's Fourth Vision

Hermas's visions takes place in ordinary settings, like those routinely experienced day to day, but they exemplify the kinds of encounter scenes that generate what James Kugel calls 'moments of confusion'.[38] In this sense, they do not differ from the lived experience of religious phenomena in which the lines between 'thisworld' and the 'otherworld' are blurred—a topic we will explore more in the next chapter. James Kugel helpfully describes this back and forth movement between 'thisworld' and the 'otherworld' as a 'moment of confusion':

> In the light of all of this, the moment of confusion begins to come into somewhat clearer focus. It seems to straddle two realms: what we might call regular reality and the supernatural. The fact that people are confused for a while appears to be a necessary element, a way of indicating how these two realms overlap, or can overlap, without people noticing anything at first. Indeed, the moment of confusion always leads to that sudden click whereby an ordinary encounter turns out to be something else entirely. It is all about perception, something that suddenly opens in the human mind. The biblical figure's confusion announces this fact, indeed celebrates it, which is apparently why these biblical narratives seem to make so much of it.[39]

While journeying to otherworldly spaces is not clearly present in Hermas's reports in the Book of Visions, there is a strong and consistent presentation of his visions within a journey narrative and reminders that Hermas is encountering extraordinary beings on way (although it is important to remember that these journeys are not contiguous). Instead of highlighting

---

37. Kuzmičová, "Does it Matter Where You Read?" 221–22.
38. James L. Kugel, *The God of Old: Inside the Lost World of the Bible* (New York: The Free Press, 2003), 24.
39. Kugel, *The God of Old*, 24.

the distinction between 'thisworld' and the 'otherworld'—a maneuver that consigns extraordinary phenomena to the inert spaces beyond our ordinary reach and tacitly privileges human exploration of otherworldly realms—our rereading of the Shepherd reintegrates these disconnected binaries and analyzes them as they might have been experienced through a reader's enactment of Hermas's embodied perceptions of his environs.

According to Alva Noë, sighted individuals do not visually apprehend the world in a single and unified panoramic view, what is sometimes referred to as a *snapshot conception* of the experience of seeing—even though this is often how we imagine our visual apprehension of the world around us.[40] Noë argues that visual perception of spaces is not something passively received, but rather something that is actively constructed through an exploratory process, more like the activity of touch.[41] We might think here of the fictional and unusually shaped vessel known as the Starship Enterprise in the long-running show *Star Trek*.[42] Viewers are never given a complete and comprehensive look at the interior of the ship or a blueprint of what it is like to walk from one point to another. Yet, the vessel's integrity and completeness can be said to be constructed by the viewer who enactively imagines how he or she might maneuver in the interior space.

The events in the Book of Visions are described as happening with surprising or counterintuitive details, either about the landscape itself or the bizarre beings encountered therein. Hermas's first-person reports provide rich details about the seer's environs, including the geography, architectural structures, and non-human beings that are encountered during the vision. Changes in the environment signal to the reader that something special is happening. For the most part, Hermas's visions occur in porous spaces that are generally recognizable by the ordinary reader as mundane spaces.

Notably, upon entering a visionary experience, Hermas comments on the specific changes that take place in his environment as they occur and his emotional responses to them. In the fourth vision, we come across Hermas's

---

40. Alva Noë (*Action in Perception*, Cambridge: MIT Press, 2004, 50) discusses what is called "inattentional blindness" to argue that the lived experience of seeing is not like viewing a panoramic photograph in full detail. See also, O'Regan and Noë, "A Sensorimotor Account of Vision and Visual Consciousness," 939–1031; This point about 'blindspots' is also discussed in Caracciolo, "Ungrounding Fictional Worlds," and Polvinen, "Enactive Perception and Fictional Worlds," 27.

41. Alva Noë, *Varieties of Presence* (Cambridge: Harvard University Press, 2012), 70.

42. Rebecca Raphael, "Sacred Schematics, or Ships and Sanctuaries," *Journal for Interdisciplinary Biblical Studies* 3 (2021): 41–62.

154 *An Embodied Reading of the Shepherd of Hermas*

description of the dust cloud and the thoughts that occurred to him as he saw it:

> 22.5 καὶ προσέβην μικρόν, ἀδελφοί, καὶ ἰδοὺ βλέπω κονιορτὸν ὡς εἰς τὸν οὐρανόν, καὶ ἠρξάμην λέγειν ἐν ἑαυτῷ· Μήποτε κτήνη ἔρχονται καὶ κονιορτὸν ἐγείρουσιν; οὕτω γὰρ ἦν ἀπ᾽ ἐμοῦ ὡς ἀπὸ σταδίου. 6 γινομένου μείζονος καὶ μείζονος κονιορτοῦ ὑπενόησα εἶναί τι θεῖον·.

> 22.5 I passed on a bit, brothers, and suddenly saw a cloud of dust, reaching up to the sky. And I began to say to myself, "Is that a herd of cattle coming raising the dust?" But it was still about two hundred yards away from me. 6 And as the dust cloud grew larger and larger, I realized that it something supernatural.

Descriptions of narrative worlds in apocalypses optimize features that are fitting to the cultural and historical periods of the seer, while introducing specific details about the landscape or its inhabitants to remind the reader that this is a narrative world. For example, comparative studies of other possible worlds, like paradise, note the similarity between the general features of the landscape and those of our everyday world as well as how the landscape differs from everyday spaces in specific counterintuitive ways, such as the presence of divine inhabitants and talking animals, and the lack of conflict, disease, or perishability, all of which remind readers that this is a narrative world.[43] In the case of the Book of Visions, Hermas's visions are often staged by details about the environment that signal that things are not quite as they should be. The encounters described in the fourth vision of a huge beast with flaming locusts pouring out of its mouth and the young bride are both incongruous events. These visionary encounters are framed by Hermas noting subtle changes in his environment. There is nothing particularly spectacular about the cloud on a rural road, but its enormity suggests to Hermas that it is not an ordinary cloud. Hermas notices that the brightness of the sun has also changed (Vis. 4.1.5–6 [22.5–6]). The environment, namely the cloud and the sun, are both familiar, but curious details about them signal to Hermas and to the reader that something is out of the ordinary—the cloud is too thick and the sun's intensity feels different. The beast with flaming locusts, of course, is the incongruous element in this scene. While the enormous beast is certainly

---

43. On the counterintuitiveness of religious concepts, see Pascal Boyer, *The Naturalness of Religious Ideas: A Cognitive Theory of Religion* (Berkeley: University of California Press, 1994); Pascal Boyer, *Religion Explained: The Evolutionary Origins of Religious Thought* (New York: Basic Books, 2001); Pascal Boyer and Charles Ramble, "Cognitive Templates for Religious Concepts: Cross-Cultural Evidence for Recall of Counter-intuitive Representations," *Cognitive Science* 25 (2001): 535–64; and Ilkka Pyysiäinen et al., "Counterintuitiveness as the Hallmark of Religiosity," *Religion* 33 (2003): 341–55; Jani Närhi, "Beautiful Reflections: The Cognitive and Evolutionary Foundations of Paradise Representations," *MTSR* 20 (2008): 339–65.

bizarre, the young woman is equally out of place in the remote countryside in her white garments.

Incongruities like the monstrous beast and the woman in a wedding gown on an open rural road are elements that provoke our curiosity. The beast, like most monsters in apocalypses, is a pastiche of familiar animals and elements that have been brought together in a bizarre, nightmarish way. The reader realizes gradually, along with Hermas, that something unusual is taking place. Hermas's tears are an interoceptive response to the situation. His fear becomes palpable to the reader, as he ponders what to do:

> 22.6b μικρὸν ἐξέλαμψεν ὁ ἥλιος, καὶ ἰδοὺ βλέπω θηρίον μέγιστον ὡσεὶ κῆτός τι, καὶ ἐκ τοῦ στόματος αὐτοῦ ἀκρίδες πύριναι ἐξεπορεύοντο. ἦν δὲ τὸ θηρίον τῷ μήκει ὡσεὶ ποδῶν ρ τὴν δὲ κεφαλὴν εἶχεν ὡσεὶ κεράμου. 7 καὶ ἠρξάμην κλαίειν καὶ ἐρωτᾶν τὸν κύριον ἵνα με λυτρώσηται ἐξ αὐτοῦ. καὶ ἐπανεμνήσθην τοῦ ῥήματος οὗ ἀκηκόειν· μὴ διψυχήσεις, Ἑρμᾶ. 8 ἐνδυσάμενος οὖν, ἀδελφοί, τὴν πίστιν τοῦ ⌜κυρίου καὶ μνησθεὶς ὧν ἐδίδαξέν με μεγαλείων, θαρσήσας εἰς τὸ θηρίον ἐμαυτὸν ἔδωκα. οὕτω δὲ ἤρχετο τὸ θηρίον ῥοίζῳ, ὥστε δύνασθαι αὐτὸ πόλιν λυμᾶναι. 9 ἔρχομαι ἐγγὺς αὐτοῦ, καὶ τὸ τηλικοῦτο κῆτος ἐκτείνει ἑαυτὸ χαμαὶ καὶ οὐδὲν εἰ μὴ τὴν γλῶσσαν προέβαλλεν, καὶ ὅλως οὐκ ἐκινήθη μέχρις ὅτε παρῆλθον αὐτό· 10 εἶχεν δὲ τὸ θηρίον ἐπὶ τῆς κεφαλῆς χρώματα τέσσερα· μέλαν, εἶτα πυροειδὲς καὶ αἱματῶδες, εἶτα χρυσοῦν, εἶτα λευκόν.

> 22.6b The sun began to shine a bit and suddenly I saw an enormous wild beast, something like a sea monster, with fiery locusts spewing from its mouth. The beast was nearly a hundred feet long, and its head looked like a ceramic jar. 7 And I began to weep and ask the Lord to save me from it. Then I remembered the word that I had heard: "Do not be of two minds, Hermas." 8 And so, putting on the faith of the Lord, brothers, and remembering the great things he had taught me, I courageously gave myself over to the beast. And so it came on with a roar, enough to lay waste a city. 9 But when I approached it, the huge sea monster stretched itself out on the ground and did nothing but stick out its tongue; otherwise it did not move at all until I had passed it by. 10 And the beast had on its head four colors: black, fire-and-blood red, gold, and white.

The description of the beast gives an impression of its great size, approximately one hundred feet long (Vis. 4.2.6 [23.6]). The beast is likened to a sea monster (κῆτός), the same word used in the LXX to describe Jonah's whale (cf. Matt. 12.40) and Job's Rahab.[44] The reader receives fragmentary details about the beast, which he or she must then construct in the imagination to make a coherent image. Striking details include Hermas's report of its enormous maw, which is attached to a head shaped like a ceramic jar. The description of the beast's head, resembling a ceramic jar, is puzzling. It suggests a wide-mouthed jar, whose opening resembles the round-rimmed

---

44. Osiek, *The Shepherd of Hermas*, 92n17.

mouth of a fish, like a bass, as it is yawning. A swarm of fiery locusts pours forth from its open mouth, and its head is curiously rainbow colored, most notably with black, red, gold, and white markings.

Unlike the bride, the incongruous beast in the fourth vision is part of Hermas's porous narrative world—a topic that will receive further discussion in the next chapter. The creature does not fit easily into our framework of known animals, and so readers cannot readily draw upon a prior experience to identify it. Even so, it is possible to draw on what Merja Polvinen describes as 'experiential traces' and associate related lived experiences with what is being described. In the following example, Polvinen applies enactive reading to the equally bizarre image found in the science fiction novella by Catherynne M. Valente, "Silently and Very Fast":

> As to the special case of metaphor, Marco Caracciolo notes how 'literary texts can convey a sense of what it is like to have a given experience by metaphorically associating another experience with it" (2014: 106). Thus, even an impossible experience, such as that of Cassian, in Valente's story, holding in her lap a crying little boy who suddenly turns into a cauldron spilling over with apples, can be enacted by readers' imaginations when it is conveyed to them through language that connects the unprecedented experience to the familiar, such as the simple shifting of a weight in your lap (Valente 2014: 355). As Caracciolo (2014: 108) notes, metaphorical language can combine 'experiential traces' into expressions that may have an immense influence on the experience of reading, and a physical change, like that of weight, becomes a reinforcing echo of a conceptual change, like that between being something and being someone.[45]

The beast in the fourth vision has a gaping maw and sticks out its tongue. This detail can be enacted by the reader, as one imagines one's own tongue sticking out of his or her mouth. Having done so, it may become clear that the beast's protruding tongue means that its grisly jaws will not snap shut anytime soon. Hermas also encounters the sea monster (κῆτός) on dry land, allowing a reader to infer that, like a fish out of water, the beast would be similarly incapacitated. The partial description of the beast invites readers to draw upon other lived experiences of creatures with protruding tongues and flying insects swarming out of their gaping maws–all sure signs that the animal has died and so is not able to inflict harm. At the conclusion of the fourth vision, readers are told that Hermas is startled by a noise, and "turned

---

45. Merja Polvinen, "Sense-Making and Wonder: An Enactive Approach to Narrative Form in Speculative Fiction," in *The Edinburgh Companion to Contemporary Narrative Theories*, ed. Zara Dinnen and Robyn Warhol (Edinburgh: Edinburgh University Press, 2018), 67–80, here 74–5. Caracciolo, *The Experientiality of Narrative*; and Catherynne M. Valente, "Silently and Very Fast," in *Clarkesworld: Year Six*, ed. Neil Clarke and Sean Wallace (Stirling, NJ: Wyrm, 2014), 331–73.

around out of fear, thinking that the beast was coming" (Vis. 4.3.7 [24.7]). Here, ancient readers who have enacted Hermas's encounter with the sea monster in their minds, may well have been amused by Hermas's excessive timidity in the face of what appears to be a dead animal.

After Hermas walked thirty feet past the sea monster (Vis. 4.2.1 [23.1]), readers are told that he encounters a curious young woman (Vis. 4.2.4 [23.4]) whom some have seen to be pregnant with Jewish apocalyptic allusions. She is dressed in white, with white hair, white sandals, and a band around her veiled head (Vis. 4.2.1[23.1]). The maiden is clothed in what resembles Roman bridal attire.[46] Readers are told that Hermas's mood here is "cheerful" (ἱλαρώτερος, Vis. 4.2.2 [23.2]). Upon seeing him, the young Lady asks Hermas in a playful way if he happened to see anything on the road (Vis. 4.2.3 [23.3]). Hermas responds by gasping out an account of the terrifying beast: "an enormous wild beast, Lady, able to destroy entire peoples" (Κυρία, τηλικοῦτο θηρίον, δυνάμενον λαοὺς διαφθεῖραι, Vis. 4.2.3 [23.3]). The overall scene is light-hearted. Ancient readers and hearers who would have already sensed that the sea monster is no danger might have been amused by the exaggerated report that Hermas gives here, again an inescapable mark of his endearing servile character. The overall light-hearted tenor of this exchange suggests that the fourth vision intends to entertain readers.

The unnamed young woman whom Hermas meets in the fourth vision is not identified as an angelic figure, but functions in a manner that resembles the *angelus interpres* frequently encountered in apocalypses. She gives Hermas an explanation of what has just taken place:

> 23.4 Καλῶς ἐξέφυγες, φησίν, ὅτι τὴν μέριμνάν σου ἐπὶ τὸν Θεὸν ἐπέριψας καὶ τὴν καρδίαν σου ἤνοιξας πρὸς τὸν Κύριον, πιστεύσας ὅτι δι᾿ οὐδενὸς δύνῃ σωθῆναι εἰ μὴ διὰ τοῦ μεγάλου καὶ ἐνδόξου ὀνόματος. διὰ τοῦτο ὁ Κύριος ἀπέστειλεν τὸν ἄγγελον αὐτοῦ τὸν ἐπὶ τῶν θηρίων ὄντα, οὗ τὸ ὄνομά ἐστιν Θεγρί, καὶ ἐνέφραξεν τὸ στόμα αὐτοῦ, ἵνα μή σε λυμάνῃ. μεγάλην θλῖψιν ἐκπέφευγας διὰ τὴν πίστιν σου, καὶ ὅτι τηλικοῦτο θηρίον ἰδὼν οὐκ ἐδιψύχησας·

> 23.4 "You escaped well," she said, "because you cast your anxiety upon God and opened your heart to the Lord, believing that you could not be saved except through his great and glorious name. For this reason the Lord sent his angel, named Thegri, who is in charge of the wild beasts; and he shut the beast's mouth, so that it could not harm you. You have escaped a great affliction because of your faith, and because you were not of two minds even though you saw such an enormous wild beast.

---

46. For example, Leutzsch, *Die Wahrnehmung sozialer Wirklichkeit im "Hirten des Hermas"*, 175; Unlike other commentators, Carolyn Osiek does not identify the vision of the young woman as a bride; Osiek, *The Shepherd of Hermas*, 93, n. 29.

The young maiden's explanation, "and he shut the beast's mouth, so that it could not harm you," is understood as an allusion to the scene in Dan. 6.22, in which the seer explains to the king that God's angel preserved him while he was in the lions' den. She alludes to the reading found in the Aramaic and corresponding Latin of Dan. 6.22, which is not attested to in the LXX.[47] Both this passage in the Shepherd and the passage from Daniel affirm that the preservation of the seer in the face of danger testifies to an act of God, which reflects the seer's faith and virtue.

The young Lady goes on to state that there is a coming tribulation, and she urges those who are 'doubleminded' to repent.

> 23.5 ὕπαγε οὖν καὶ ἐξήγησαι τοῖς ἐκλεκτοῖς τοῦ κυρίου τὰ μεγαλεῖα αὐτοῦ, καὶ εἰπὲ αὐτοῖς ὅτι τὸ θηρίον τοῦτο τύπος ἐστὶν θλίψεως τῆς μελλούσης τῆς μεγάλης· ἐὰν οὖν προετοιμάσησθε καὶ μετανοήσητε ἐξ ὅλης καρδίας ὑμῶν πρὸς τὸν κύριον, δυνήσεσθε ἐκφυγεῖν αὐτήν, ἐὰν ἡ καρδία ὑμῶν γένηται καθαρὰ καὶ ἄμωμος, καὶ τὰς λοιπὰς τῆς ζωῆς ἡμέρας ὑμῶν δουλεύσητε τῷ κυρίῳ ἀμέμπτως. ἐπιρίψατε τὰς ⌜μερίμνας⌝ ὑμῶν ἐπὶ τὸν κύριον, καὶ αὐτὸς κατορθώσει αὐτάς. 6 πιστεύσατε τῷ κυρίῳ, οἱ δίψυχοι, ὅτι πάντα δύναται καὶ ἀποστρέφει τὴν ὀργὴν αὐτοῦ ἀφ᾿ ὑμῶν καὶ ἐξαποστέλλει μάστιγας ὑμῖν τοῖς διψύχοις. οὐαὶ τοῖς ἀκούσασιν τὰ ῥήματα ταῦτα καὶ παρακούσασιν· αἱρετώτερον ἦν αὐτοῖς τὸ μὴ γεννηθῆναι.

> 23.5 And so, go and explain the great acts of the Lord to his chosen ones, and tell them that this wild beast is a foreshadowing of the great affliction that is coming. If then all of you prepare and repent before the Lord from your whole heart, you will be able to escape it—if your heart becomes clean and blameless and you serve the Lord blamelessly the rest of your days. Cast your anxieties upon the Lord and he will take care of them. 6 Trust in the Lord, you who are of two minds, because he can do all things; he both diverts his anger from you and sends punishments to you who are doubleminded. Woe to those who hear these words and disobey. It would be better for them not to have been born.

The Lady exhorts Hermas to go and urge the chosen ones to repent. Like the previous visions in the Book of Visions, the revelation has a strong moralizing tone that urges preparation and repentance in light of the tribulation that is not clearly identified.

At this point, we might imagine how this vision of the beast and the young Lady in white was entertaining to the readers at Oxyrhynchus, who

---

47. The MT of Dan. 6.23 reads: "my God sent his angel and he shut the mouth of the lions so that they would not harm me;"

אֱלָהִי שְׁלַח מַלְאֲכֵהּ וּסֲגַר פֻּם אַרְיָוָתָא וְלָא חַבְּלוּנִי

The Latin reads, "my God sent his angel and he shut the mouths of the lions," (*Deus meus misit angelum suum, et conclusit ora leonum*); cf. the LXX reads, "And God saved me from the lions," (καὶ σέσωκέ με ὁ θεὸς ἀπὸ τῶν λεόντων).

may have read and heard this narrative with a wry smile and a chuckle. The scene deploys an unflattering but endearing image of Hermas as an overly cautious figure who is seized by fear in the face of a grotesque but motionless beast. The beast is massive, but there is only the slightest hint of danger. The light-hearted affect that can be detected in Hermas's opening exchange with the Lady in white suggests that the vision up to this point is engaging and entertaining, especially if we imagine it being read aloud with exaggerated vocal inflections and bodily gestures. When we consider the role of the Book of Visions within the overall aim of the Shepherd to form its readers and hearers ethically, the humorous overtones of the fourth vision can be said to contribute to the greater memorability of the moral instruction imparted by the young Lady.

Like other modern commentators, Richard Bauckham reads Hermas's fourth vision out of sequence. He begins with the strong moral exhortation, which he interprets through the lens of biblical and Qumranic imagery. This imagery of suffering and tribulation is then read back into the beast.[48] Bauckham is intent on demonstrating that the fourth vision is best understood as evidence of the text's eschatological horizon, a scholarly point that others have not affirmed.[49] In his analysis, he evokes texts that speak in an extended way of torment and cosmic warfare, like the Qumran War Scroll (16.9–17.9) and the Community Rule (e.g., 8.4, cf. 1.17).[50] Bauckham's discussion, however, does not account for the amusing way the beast and Hermas's exaggerated slavish cowering might have been understood by ancient readers and hearers, who would have experienced the fourth vision in a linear way, as a bookroll demands. Having read and heard the peculiar vision of the beast and the exchange with the young Lady, readers and hearers would have been even more primed to hear the Lady's explanation with piqued curiosity. Instead, Bauckham reads the scene out of sequence. He begins with the Lady's moral exhortation and situates it within the biblical and late Second Temple apocalyptic worldview. Then he works backward to present the beast solely through the eschatological lens of terror and suffering. Our point here is not to minimize the seriousness of the Lady's moral exhortation, but rather to consider the range and type of emotions that the ancient reader and hearer might have as they moved first from the beast, and then to the young Lady's exhortation to Hermas. Anticipation and curiosity likely would have been a strong response to the engaging and entertaining

---

48. Richard J. Bauckham, "The Great Tribulation in the Shepherd of Hermas," *JTS* (n.s.) 25 (1974): 27–40.
49. Bauckham, "The Great Tribulation in the Shepherd of Hermas," 30–31.
50. Bauckham, "The Great Tribulation in the Shepherd of Hermas," 39.

story of the beast. This too would have been the experience guided by the bookroll format, which would constrain readers from moving back and forth in the story by imposing a linear order on the text.

Modern scholars often carry certain expectations about religious writings that then influence how such narrative details are appreciated. When modern scholars read ancient apocalypses and catechetical literature as serious genres, they overlook the way in which ancient authors sought above all to make their writing appealing to ancient readers. Humor and exaggeration were essential components for memorable story-telling. Furthermore, these elements can create conditions in which what is seen and heard is more easily retained and remembered, which is an important effect for a catechetical work like the Shepherd.[51] Humor's ability to facilitate the remembering of that which has been taught on the naturally associative properties of emotions. We should also acknowledge how humor may produce other appropriate effects like consolation during distressing experiences, like "the great affliction that is coming" (θλίψεως τῆς μελλούσης τῆς μεγάλης) referenced in the Lady's exhortation of repentance (Vis. 4.2.5 [23.5]).[52] Our view is that specialized scholars bring their own expectations to the Book of Visions, which often requires that they read against the grain of the narrative. We have argued that Hermas's fourth vision could be read as an amusing tale to ancient readers and hearers, achieving the desired effect—that they would remember the Lady's strong moral exhortation to repent.

Conclusion

Journeying by foot over a new terrain invites the reader to be especially watchful as new sights and landmarks are passed along the way. The Book of Visions uses various strategies to generate a response in a reader by slowing down the pace of reading so that s/he can engage emotionally with what is being described. In this chapter, we have discussed how the motif of journeying by foot can be understood to offer readers and hearers an experiential way of enacting Hermas's nighttime fear and anticipation in the field prior to the vision of the Tower in Vision 3. The Book of Visions also

---

51. Heidi L. Lujan and Stephen E. DiCarlo, "Humor Promotes Learning!" *Advances in Physiology Education* 40 (2016): 433–34; Mark A. McDaniel and Gilles O. Einstein, "Bizarre Imagery as an Effective Memory Aid: The Importance of Distinctiveness," *Journal of Experimental Psychology: Learning, Memory, and Cognition* 12 (1986): 54–65.

52. Madelijn Strick, Rob W. Holland, Rick B. van Baaren, Ad. van Knippenberg, "Finding Comfort in a Joke: Consolatory Effects of Humor through Cognitive Distraction," *Emotion* 9 (2009): 574–78.

exploits the commonplace experience of encountering new and surprising animals and creatures while walking along a path. Vision 4 draws out a humorous response in those who enactively read and hear about Hermas's adventures with the beast and the young Lady, both of whom he meets on the road. These two examples highlight how stories that narrate journey experiences offer readers an experiential way of accessing a sense of the passing of time and space enactively, heightening the sense of watchfulness and increasing receptivity to what is taking place in the story.

The discussion of the effects that journey narratives have on readers and hearers has also highlighted how different the range of readerly responses are to Hermas's third and fourth visions. Modern scholars who are trained to look for exegetical, historical, and theological meaning in ancient texts overlook the immersive qualities of the third vision, preferring to bypass Hermas's nighttime walk in the field and rushing to examine the Tower of Stones and unpack its significance. Modern scholars also move quickly to relate Hermas's curious vision of the beast to other known Jewish and Christian apocalypses that are intended to produce a very different set of emotional responses, namely fear and terror. In doing so, scholars today fail to appreciate the entertaining quality of Hermas's fourth vision, which likely contributed to its popular success in the ancient world among ancient readers and hearers.

Hermas's visions take place in a porous narrative world that has familiar environmental features that can be recognized today but that also contains divine figures and strange non-human beings. As narratives, apocalypses seek to generate a response in their readers that is not unlike the experience of the seer: confusion and a deep desire to understand what is happening. The events that take place in apocalypses seek to engage readers by cultivating a heightened watchfulness within the reader. Narratives may use counterintuitive elements to surprise the reader and stimulate curiosity or confusion, thus resulting in a deeper engagement with the events being described. This is the case with the events that take place in the fourth vision, in which Hermas encounters an incongruous beast and a young Lady in white. The emotional response to these two figures met on the way has been presented here as amusement, which ultimately facilitates the remembering of the ethical exhortation to repent.

The Book of Visions has been underappreciated in the modern elite culture of the academy. Enactive reading can help us appreciate how Hermas's narrative world can achieve a quality of density, thus allowing readers and hearers to become immersed in the encounters and experiences he has on his journey by foot. In enactive reading, the reader gropes through a narrative world based solely on the fragmentary details that the author chooses to impart. Readers and hearers must then construct these partial fragments into a single coherent image by extending the everyday experiences and awareness of the lived world to Hermas's narrative world where the unexpected may happen.

Modern scholars read the bizarre and puzzling scenes in the third and fourth visions through the standard lens of their own academic training, according to which they investigate exegetical, historical, or theological questions by reading against the grain of the text. In the case of the vision of the beast, this has meant reading the scenes out of sequence. These modern disciplinary approaches to ancient apocalypses fail to appreciate how the Shepherd of Hermas was entertaining and popular among ancient readers and hearers—and non-specialist readers—who are willing to suspend their disbelief in order to be moved or entertained by a narrative. Applying enactive reading to Hermas's third and fourth visions helps us to understand how this part of the Shepherd participates in the work's larger program of moral formation by cultivating watchfulness and attentiveness and by creating amusing and memorable scenarios that increase the retention of teachings about repentance. Appreciating these effects of enactive reading also helps us to reintegrate the Book of Visions with the Mandates and the Similitudes by highlighting how the narrative creates the emotional conditions for moral instruction within the reader, a goal that we hold as common to all three sections of the Shepherd.

This chapter has argued that the narrative world of the Book of Visions is one in which Hermas encounters divine beings, fantastic beasts, and a Tower that materializes from nowhere. All of these could be said to possess the quality of vividness and offer the possibility of 'realness' to ancient readers and hearers who willingly suspended their disbelief as they journey along a narrative's 'twists and turns'. Cognitive literary theorists describe this as a reader's ability to take on the 'fictional consciousness' of a character like Hermas, thereby immersing themselves in the 'possible world' of the visions.[53] The compelling quality of Hermas's narrative world can be compared to the experience enjoyed by modern-day readers of fantasy novels or by participants in role-playing video games. Hermas's proprioception and his wide-ranging emotional and sensory experiences of his environment bear the marks that readers associate strongly with our own experience of consciousness, thereby attributing to Hermas the 'realness' of one who has an inner-life. These details continue to be applied enactively to Hermas and updated as we read more and more about his experiences. In the next chapter, we examine the limitations of the modern category of

---

53. Marco Caracciolo, "Fictional Consciousnesses," 43–9.

'apocalypse' for a text like the Book of Visions. The modern disciplinary framework for understanding 'apocalypse' assumes essentializing categories that are peculiar to the modern world. They not only constrain how we understand the Book of Visions but also other ancient apocalypses.

Chapter Five

Immersion in the Narrative World of Apocalyptic Visions

The manuscript evidence for the Shepherd points to its widespread popularity in the ancient world. This appeal among ancient readers, however, has neither been appreciated nor replicated in the modern academy. Integrative approaches, like enactive reading, consider the role of the embodied mind in the immersive reading and hearing of narrative. Academic training in reading against the grain of a narrative, with specific exegetical, historical, or theological questions in mind, prevents modern scholars from appreciating the experiential way the Book of Visions invites readers to suspend disbelief and experience what Hermas is experiencing. As we saw in the previous chapter, a reader who reads enactively is invited to experience Hermas's anticipation during his nighttime walk in the field. Doing so can be understood to be preparatory for the Tower scene which follows because it increases the anticipation and watchfulness of the ancient readers and hearers. Also, the humor of Hermas's exaggerated timidity and fear of the beast and the somewhat jocular beginning to the conversation he has with the beautiful young Lady draw out emotional responses of amusement which can heighten the remembering of the moral teaching of repentance. In these two examples from the previous chapter, readers and hearers can be guided to strategic immersive states that are preparatory for heightening receptivity to ethical instruction. Such insights into how the Book of Visions contributes to the overall program of moral formation of readers and hearers of the popular catechetical work known as the Shepherd have been overlooked by modern scholars.

This chapter investigates further reasons for why the scholarly study of this work has neglected to understand the role of apocalyptic visions in moral formation, by investigating the modern analytical framework for understanding 'apocalypse'. We argue that this genre presumes a sharp distinction between 'thisworld' and the 'otherworld' that is peculiar to the modern scholars and the modern western academy. In its place, we will propose that ancient apocalypses sought to give readers and hearers access to narrative worlds, what critical literary theorists refer to as 'possible' and 'fictional worlds'.[1] Such worlds are experientially fluid spaces that are

---

1. Caracciolo, "Ungrounding Fictional Worlds," 113–31. This approach to spaces

generated in part by the text and in part by the imaginations of the readers who enact the narrative. Previously, we have described enactive reading as a groping through an unknown environment. The most important literary details for enactive reading are the first-person accounts of a character's extended body in movement as it sensorially explores the hitherto unknown world of the apocalypse, relying solely on the fragmentary details the author chooses to provide. In addition to these proprioceptive details, the seer's interoception, that is the body's awareness of being in that new environment, are key for gathering glimpses of this newly revealed apocalyptic world, which readers and hearers then construct and explore in their own imaginations. We have argued that modern scholars tend to overlook the importance of Hermas's proprioceptive and interoceptive experiences in their studies of the Book of Visions which oftentimes focus on understanding the meaning of the revelations. These overlooked details are, however, crucial for making the narrative world of the visions possible because they give the spaces in that narrative density and solidity.

Modern scholarly approaches to understanding 'apocalypse' have not been able to adequately account for Hermas's visions, because they prefer to preserve essentializing features of the analytical category rather than expand it to allow for the diversity of expressions of this type of writing. We propose that broadening out the traditional scholarly understanding of apocalypse to account for the actual diversity of first-person narrations of visionary experiences like the Shepherd of Hermas can offer a more capacious understanding of 'apocalypse' generally and give insight into the enduring and compelling power of this type of writing. Our study begins with a presentation of the modern framework for understanding apocalypses which presumes a strict distinction between 'thisworld' and the 'otherworld'—one that prioritizes the seer's agency in journeying out into the 'otherworld'. We argue that this categorical distinction between 'thisworld' and the 'otherworld' imposes a peculiarly modern perspective on ancient texts, and that ancient narratives like apocalypses can be better and more efficiently understood as porous realms, what cognitive literary theorists refer to as 'possible worlds'. The second part of the chapter applies the enactive reading approach to descriptions of seers found in a wide range of apocalypses, those that speak of otherworldly journeys and those that do not. We argue that the enactive reading of these apocalypses makes the experiences of the seer experientially accessible to readers

---

also informs the discussion found in Angela Kim Harkins, "Experiencing the Solidity of Spaces in the Qumran Hodayot," in *The Dead Sea Scrolls, Revise and Repeat: New Methods and Perspectives on the Dead Sea Scrolls*, ed. Andrew Krause, Carmen Palmer, Eileen M. Schuller, and John Screnock (Atlanta: SBL Press, 2020), 353–71.

and hearers. These responses in turn cultivate commitment and belief among the readers and hearers of apocalypses and help us to see how these compelling narratives contributed to the religious lives of ancient people. In the case of modern non-specialist readers of apocalypses, readers who are not trained to read against the grain of the narrative or to ask discipline-specific questions about the text, it also helps us to understand how apocalypses offer the possibility of the 'realness' of these narrative worlds to people today.

The Modern Scholarly Understanding of 'Apocalypse'

Modern historical-critical scholars have labored long and hard to understand the strange visions of otherworldly realia found in ancient apocalypses, oftentimes with the aim of identifying how these visions can be correlated with specific historical moments and political regimes. More recent studies have rightly challenged the long-standing assumption that apocalypses were writings generated by communities experiencing social and political crises, thereby raising important questions about how these writings came to be.[2] We cannot say definitively that apocalypses originate from a specific milieu—to do so would be to overdetermine a genre that clearly defies specific historical parameters. Our rereading of the Shepherd has moved beyond the traditional approaches that seek to excavate ancient apocalypses for historical information or to analyze them from a strictly literary approach that engages academic genre debates. Instead, we have highlighted the ways in which the Book of

---

2. While the sociological context of social and political crisis may indeed be a characteristic feature of some apocalypses, it is not a necessary one. The recent work of Paul Kosmin (*Time and its Adversaries in the Seleucid Empire* [Cambridge: Belknap Press, 2018], 139) has shown well that the common assumption that apocalypses are resistance literature has overdetermined these writings. The oldest apocalypse, the Book of the Watchers, is dated to the third century BCE, a period when traditional genres of Jewish writings persisted and when new literary forms emerged, without signs of resistance to Hellenistic culture. George W. E. Nickelsburg, *1 Enoch 1*. Hermeneia (Minneapolis: Fortress, 2001); Angela Kim Harkins, Kelley Coblentz Bautch, and John C. Endres, S.J. (ed.), *The Watchers in Jewish and Christian Traditions* (Minneapolis: Fortress Press, 2014); Harkins, Coblentz Bautch, and Endres (ed.), *The Fallen Angels Traditions: Second Temple Developments and Reception History*, Catholic Biblical Quarterly Monograph Series 53 (Washington, D.C.: Catholic Biblical Association, 2014).

While the third century was a time of new writings, there was no tell-tale stamp of Hellenization in these works and no sharp rupture with previous genres. Seth Schwartz notes that "life in Hellenistic Judaea was significantly continuous with life in Persian Yehud," *The Ancient Jews from Alexander to Muhammad* (Cambridge: Cambridge University Press, 2014), 32; Seth Schwartz, *Imperialism and Jewish Society: 200 B.C.E. to 640 C.E.* (Princeton: Princeton University Press, 2001), 29–32.

Visions cultivates the emotions and necessary predispositions that heighten receptivity to moral formation: attentiveness, curiosity, and watchfulness.

Hermas's repeated engagement in familiar practices and scenarios associated with visionary experience (viz., prayer, fasting, weeping and rumination) is reminiscent of a larger cross-cultural performance of cultivating visionary experiences. It is notable that Hermas's visions in the Book of Visions departs significantly from the standard patterns that we see in Jewish and Christian apocalyptic visions; the angelic beings in Hermas's reports are sent to dialogue with Hermas, instead of guides who lead the seer through otherworldly terrain. Even so, Hermas shares features known from other apocalypses like the 'open heaven' (ἠνοίγη ὁ οὐρανός, Vis. 1.1.4 [1.4]) and the experience of being carried away by the Spirit.[3]

The classification of the Shepherd as an apocalypse has been debated by scholars, with many qualifying the identification in one way or another.[4] For example, in his comments on the literary character of the work, Martin Dibelius acknowledged the apocalyptic features in the Shepherd, but doubted that it possessed a truly prophetic core ("einen echt prophetischen Kern").[5] This may be contrasted with the comment by Burnett H. Streeter, who faulted Hermas for being too proud of his "prophetic gift."[6] Philipp Veilhauer referred to the Shepherd as a "pseudo-Apocalypse" because it lacked an eschatological horizon.[7] According to Dan Batovici, others have denied that the Shepherd is an apocalypse not only because it lacks eschatological material but also

---

3. "A short time after this, as I was walking on my road to the villages, and magnifying the creatures of God, and thinking how magnificent, and beautiful, and powerful they are, I fell asleep. And the Spirit carried me away, and took me through a pathless place, through which a man could not travel, for it was situated in the midst of rocks; it was rugged and impassable on account of water. Having passed over this river, I came to a plain. I then bent down on my knees, and began to pray to the Lord and to confess my sins." (Vis. 1.1.3 [1.3]).

4. For an excellent up-to-date discussion of the genre debates, see Batovici, "Apocalyptic and Metanoia in the *Shepherd of Hermas*," 151–70.

5. Dibelius, *Der Hirt des Hermas*, 419.

6. Streeter, *The Primitive Church*, 203.

7. Philipp Vielhauer, "Apocalyptic in Early Christianity: Introduction," in Edgar Hennecke, *New Testament Apocrypha, Volume 2: Writings Relating to the Apostles, Apocalypses and Related Subjects,* trans. R. M. Wilson (London: SCM Press, 1974), 2:608–42, here 630. Idem, *Geschichte der urchristlichen Literatur: Einleitung in das Neue Testament, die Apokryphen und die Apostolischen Väter* (Berlin: De Gruyter, 1975), 522. Hellholm, *Das Visionenbuch des Hermas als* Apokalypse, 13–4.

future-oriented teachings.[8] One scholar, J. Christian Wilson, has even referred to the Shepherd as a "failed apocalypse."[9]

The oft-cited definition of apocalypse by John Collins is as follows:

> Apocalypse is a genre of revelatory literature with a narrative framework, in which a revelation is mediated by an otherworldly being to a human recipient, disclosing a transcendent reality which is both temporal, insofar as it envisages eschatological salvation, and spatial insofar as it involves another, supernatural world.[10]

According to Collins's definition, the Shepherd could be understood as a kind of qualified apocalypse, that has "neither historical review nor otherworldly journey."[11] Under such a schema, the Shepherd would be grouped along with other early Jewish apocalypses like *4 Ezra* and *2 Baruch*, which report fantastic visions but no narration of journeying to heavenly realms. In his 2015 return to the Semeia definition of apocalypse, Collins engages the criticisms of his 1979 Semeia definition by noting that it was an etic description that sought to make scholarly use of the term 'apocalypse' more systematic and consistent.[12] Here Collins helpfully reviews the various objections to the classification of apocalypse, including objections that dispense with the very premise of genre classification systems.[13] The Semeia definition has been critiqued many times for overemphasizing form and content with insufficient attention to the function of these ancient texts. Even with these critiques, it must be emphasized that much of the ground breaking work on apocalypses during the past fifty years would not have

---

8. Batovici ("Apocalyptic and Metanoia in the *Shepherd of Hermas*," 151–60) writes, "Is the Shepherd of Hermas an apocalypse? Given that, despite many similarities, the apocalyptic outlook of the book is still quite different from other works of apocalyptic literature, the response to this question has varied considerably in past scholarship. The fact that it seems to lack eschatological material and of the teachings related to the future, common in other apocalypses, has led to a negative answer to this question" (153).

9. J. Christian Wilson, *Five Problems in the Interpretation of the Shepherd of Hermas: Authorship, Genre, Canonicity, Apocalyptic, and the Absence of the Name "Jesus Christ"*, Mellen Biblical Press Series 34 (Lewinston: Mellen Biblical Press, 1995), 41; cited by Batovici in "Apocalyptic and Metanoia in the *Shepherd of Hermas*," 153.

10. John J. Collins, "Apocalypse: The Morphology of a Genre," *Semeia* 14 (1979): 1–59, especially p. 9.

11. John J. Collins, "Apocalypse," 22–3.

12. John J. Collins, "Introduction: The Genre Apocalypse Reconsidered," in *Apocalypse, Prophecy, and Pseudepigraphy: On Jewish Apocalyptic Literature* (Grand Rapids: Eerdmans, 2015), 1–5.

13. John J. Collins, "Introduction: The Genre Apocalypse Reconsidered," 5–13. Similarly, Adela Yarbro Collins, "Apocalypse Now: The State of Apocalyptic Studies Near the End of the First Decade of the Twenty-First Century," *HTR* 104 (2011): 447–57.

been possible without the clarity and precision of the systematic formulation provided by John Collins in this Semeia volume.

Collins is right to emphasize that the Semeia definition of apocalypse is a modern construction in service to scholars of the academy. Its presumption of a sharp distinction between 'thisworld' and the 'otherworld' speaks of the modern epistemic bifurcations that have become thoroughly embedded in the analytical framework used by modern biblical scholars—distinctions that persist in our classification systems.[14] The reference point of 'thisworld' highlights the world that we inhabit and know empirically, and simultaneously distinguishes this world from the 'otherworld', a term that consolidates all other speculative spaces. Implicit in the Semeia definition's reference to journeying is the notion that the human seer has been transported into another realm, like an explorer who has left the familiar behind and is led by an indigenous guide through a faraway land.

While modern classification systems can be useful etic frameworks for analysis, we should still interrogate them, if only to review how our own assumptions might overdetermine our understanding of the past. According to Greek historian Greg Anderson, dualistic distinctions, like the categories 'thisworld' and the 'otherworld' that are often used in discussions of apocalypses, say more about how modern scholars understand the world than the lived experiences of ancient people. Norbert Brox had compared the Shepherd to "trivial fiction" and "a series of banalities" ("als triviale Fiktion... . wie eine Abfolge von Banalitäten"), but this text may have been regarded by ancient people as having the significance of what Anderson calls 'realness'.[15] He writes:

> First, our discipline's standard analytical models, categories, and other devices do not just occlude or suppress the experiences of non-western and previously colonized peoples. They require us to flatten and homogenize all non-modern lifeworlds, those of the pre-modern 'West' included. The problem with conventional historicism is not its Eurocentrism as such, but its essential, indelible modernism. Second, this modernism is problematic because it shapes the very ontological premises of our practice. The tools of our historicism predispose us to impose post-Enlightenment standards of truth and realness upon all non-modern experiences, western and non-western alike, thereby denying extinct past peoples the power to determine what was and what could be really there at the time. Third, to produce histories that are more ethically defensible, more philosophically robust, and more historically meaningful, we need to analyze each non-modern life world on its own ontological terms, in its own metaphysical environment.[16]

14. Anderson, *The Realness of Things Past*, 2.
15. Brox, *Der Hirt des Hermas*, 5.
16. Anderson, *The Realness of Things Past*, 10.

Greg Anderson's critique of modern historical accounts of ancient Greece highlights how these analytical templates make the ancient world more palatable to scholars by constraining complex aspects of ancient life that the modern academy finds unpleasant. These universalist models extend post-Enlightenment systems that are familiar to the modern western world into the past and systematize the complexity of an ancient world by using frameworks that are foreign to it. Anderson writes:

> This universalist model begins by imposing a primordial dichotomy on all the contents of experience, separating once and for all what seem to be objectively real, material phenomena, like practices and institutions, from subjective, cultural phenomena, like beliefs, values, and ideologies. It would then assign each of these phenomena to its designated place in 'the world,' which the model objectifies in abstract, spatial terms as a kind of disenchanted, functionally divisible arena or terrain. Among the various possible divides in this terrain, the most fundamental would be that which separates a human, societal order from a non-human order of nature. And within the broad confines of the human order, experience can then be further subdivided into various realms, spheres, and fields, like the sacred and the secular, the public and the private, and the political, the social, and the economic. As for the human inhabitants of this abstract societal terrain, the model presumes them all to be natural, self-actualizing, psycho-physical individuals, albeit individuals whose thoughts and actions are influenced by whatever cultural phenomena happen to prevail at any given time.[17]

Anderson's critiques apply well to the analytical descriptions that biblical scholars have given to ancient Jewish and early Christian apocalypses that make too stark a distinction between the experiences that happen in the mundane places of this world and the extraordinary things that occur in otherworldly spaces.[18]

Ancient people—actually, one could say, most people throughout history and even today—experience and understand the world in a dramatically different way from modern academics. We might point to the many readers today, even those from the modern West, who find ancient apocalyptic worlds incredibly alluring. These non-academic readers use multiple interpretive systems to actualize and reconcile the 'enchanted' world described in biblical texts with the mundane reality of the modern scientific West.[19] Adela Yarbro Collins acknowledges that the complex world of dreams and visions found in apocalypses are not unfamiliar realities to non-academic readers from

---

17. Anderson, *The Realness of Things Past*, 10.
18. We might use the language of 'enchanted' spaces to describe how the ordinary and the supernatural were experienced by the people of the past. Charles Taylor, *A Secular Age* (Cambridge: Harvard University Press, 2007).
19. Luhrmann, *Persuasions of the Witch's Craft*.

the modern West today, "for whom the canonical apocalypses are historical fact."[20] Psychological studies of reading—the empirical basis for much of cognitive literary theory—can be incredibly useful for thinking about this divide because the empirical sciences are interested in understanding patterns in reading that cut across a wide spectrum of human diversity. Cognitive literary theorist Andrew Elfenbein explains the usefulness of psychological studies that examine the mental imaging activity that takes place during reading among non-specialist readers who read texts for enjoyment, in contrast to academic readers who are highly trained to read texts against the grain, in counterintuitive ways, to search for information.[21] Elfenbein describes how integrative approaches from the cognitive sciences have helped him to realize the extent to which his training as a reader is highly specialized and, in a way, removed from the everyday processes of mental imagining used by ordinary readers who read for pleasure. Elfenbein writes about the scholarly task of reading, which he calls 'literary reading' in the following excerpt:

> Despite the stumbling blocks I encountered in redisciplining myself as a psychologist, the interdisciplinary work had a payoff: the ability to write this book about reading from a new perspective. The two chief modes of discussing reading in literary scholarship, reader-response criticism and archival work on real readers, felt inadequate to me. Reader-response criticism did not progress beyond the recognition that meaning arises from an interaction between reader and text, whereas work on real readers amassed archival evidence with few principles about how to make sense of it. Psychology let me see what reading looks like when approached with a different set of assumptions. I realized that my starting point had to be reading per se rather than literary reading, as assumed by previous reader-response critics. This starting point separates my approach from that of most other scholars working in cognitive literary studies. They start with books and literature, or at least narrative, and look for findings in psychology to help understand them. In contrast, rather than assuming that literary reading needs to be cordoned off from other reading, I argue that literary reading involves a specialized subset of skills used both in reading more generally and in cognition as a whole.[22]

It should be noted that empirical studies like those conducted in cognitive psychology and other forms of empirically tested psychology have been criticized for the lack of diversity among the subjects who are studied, since oftentimes college students are used for testing.[23] Even so, these subjects

---

20. A. Yarbro Collins, "Apocalypse Now," 457.
21. Elfenbein, *The Gist of Reading*, 4.
22. Elfenbein, *The Gist of Reading*, 8–9.
23. Joseph Henrich, *The WEIRDest People in the World: How the West Became Psychologically Peculiar and Particularly Prosperous* (New York: Farrar, Straus and Giroux, 2020). The title refers to an earlier published study in which the author critiques the lack of diversity of the standard subject pool for psychological studies. Western college students

are still able to yield useful data about how non-specialist readers today engage with texts.

According to the philosopher Bruno Latour, it is not just premodern people who reject the stark division between 'thisworld' and the 'otherworld'. Many ordinary people outside the academy today also reject this divide and find ancient apocalypses—as bizarre as they are—to be incredibly compelling.[24] Hermas's world, likely understood as a possible narrative world to ancient readers, had the compelling quality of 'realness' that is strikingly implausible for modern scholars. In large part, this is because modern western scholars rely on illusory analytical categories that Latour describes as dividing different critical stances and establishing what he calls systems of 'purification'.[25] Latour writes, "Our intellectual life is out of kilter. Epistemology, the social sciences, the sciences of texts—all have their privileged vantage point, *provided that they remain separate*" (italics mine).[26]

Implicit in the standard scholarly division between 'thisworld' and the 'otherworld' are assumptions about who inhabits these spaces. 'Thisworld' is the space ordered by humans and within which they alone enjoy agency, whereas the 'otherworld' serves as a consolidated space for all other supernatural beings: angels, demons, and deities. The consolidation of appropriate beings in either 'thisworld' or the 'otherworld'—standard categories applied to apocalypse—is not unlike the essentializing way complex human experiences are overdetermined into neat and tidy categories, a move that has been rightly rejected as erasing the signs of diversity that are routinely experienced among actual peoples.[27] According to Julian Go, classical sociologists (e.g., Marx, Weber, and Durkheim) "far from simply providing neutral observations on society—effectually portrayed non-Western societies in their theories as homogeneous essences, blanketing over 'intergroup complexity and differences' and transforming the non-West into a

---

are oftentimes overrepresented among the findings of psychological research. WEIRD is an acronym for these students: Western, Educated, Industrialized, Rich, and Democratic. See his earlier study, Joseph Henrich, Steven J. Heine, Ara Norenzayan, "The Weirdest People in the World?" *Behavioral and Brain Sciences* (2010): 1–75.

24. Bruno Latour, *We Have Never Been Modern*, translated by Catherine Porter (Cambridge: Harvard University Press, 1993), 76.

25. Latour, *We Have Never Been Modern*, 5.

26. Latour, *We Have Never Been Modern*, 5.

27. See for example, Jonathan Z. Smith, "Fences and Neighbors: Some Contours of Early Judaism," in *Imagining Religion: From Babylon to Jonestown* (Chicago: University of Chicago Press, 1982), 1–18; and similarly the point against homogenizing and essentializing groups is made by Stowers, "The Concept of 'Community' and the History of Early Christianity," 238–56.

generalized 'other'."[28] This routinization of an analytic bifurcation or "law of division" contrasts an 'us' with a 'them', and presupposes that each is internally consistent and distinct.[29] Julian Go writes:

> The law of division, or analytic bifurcation, is unmistakable in many classical works. Durkheim postulated transitions from various types of solidarity (that he neatly mapped onto binaries like 'primitive' or 'modern,' 'preindustrial' or 'industrial,' etc.) but never considered that one may have been dependent upon the imperial consolidation of the other.[30]

This colonializing way of segregating empires from colonies effectively restricts power, making the inhabitants of colonies inert and powerless. This analytical framework was made even more efficient by the disembodied understandings of the other, which essentialized groups by flattening distinct and particular experiences.[31]

In the case of apocalypses, this analytical law of separation assumes a hard division between 'thisworld' and the 'otherworld'—and consigns the inhabitants associated with each to their respective realms. The beings that one might imagine in the 'otherworld' are rendered as exceptions, guides who bridge the divide to bring the seer into the 'otherworld'. Such a scenario privileges and prioritizes how the human seer journeys out and explores new frontiers. The Semeia definition resonates strongly with the modern desire to highlight how we as a species have the agency and capability to move out of our realm into a space far beyond. Culturally speaking such framing of the apocalyptic seer's journey mirrors the specific modern western experience of our movement into outer space, perhaps fueled by post-WWII dystopia.

While biblical scholars often look to history and the social sciences to provide a theoretical framing, they rarely think critically about the implicit biases that are deeply embedded in those disciplines and their methodological perspectives; but doing so is a worthy task. Greg Anderson, Julian Go, and Bruno Latour critique the analytical classifications used in their respective disciplines—history, sociology, and philosophy—to speak to the conceptual limitations of the modern western academy. In part, their insights are profoundly illuminated by postcolonialism, which has critiqued how their respective disciplines have perpetuated ways of seeing people and

---

28. Julian Go, "For a Postcolonial Sociology," in *Theory and Society* 42 (2013): 25–55, here 32; Julian Go, *Postcolonial Thought and Social Theory* (Oxford University Press, 2016).

29. Edward Said, *Culture and Imperialism* (New York: Knopf: Distributed by Random House, 1993), xxviii.

30. Go, *Postcolonial Thought and Social Theory*, 89.

31. Go, *Postcolonial Thought and Social Theory*, 30.

spaces that are peculiar to the modern West—not timeless and objective. These insights have proven instructive for our inquiry into the Shepherd, which seeks to move beyond the usual categorical distinction between 'thisworld' and the 'otherworld'. While these spaces are imagined as dramatically different realms, their boundaries are more fluid than our usual analytical frameworks allow.[32] Natural boundaries like mountain ranges or rivers, often used as markers between countries and regions, differ from brick and mortar walls erected by politicians, insofar as natural geography is porous and allows for movement between spaces.[33] The transition from one realm into another is either more gradual, in the case of a mountain range like the Alps or Pyrenees, or fluid, as in the case of a river like the great Mississippi, which serves as some part of the border for ten states. This permeability between 'thisworld' and the 'otherworld' is more compatible with the way individuals experience religion, highlighting the artificial nature of the division insisted upon by scholars in the modern academy who strongly resist hybrid or mixed systems.

Ethnographic studies by anthropologist Tanya Luhrmann examine the mental imaging and experiences of presence among ordinary modern individuals in the post-industrial western world.[34] Her work often highlights the way religious practices cultivate and train how individuals can perceive voices or visions within ritual or prayer experiences, although such experiences are not predetermined to happen. Luhrmann's findings indicate that practitioners of religion often do not carry the skepticism that scholars of religion hold. The human imagination is capacious and able to hold what

---

32. Taylor uses the expression, "enchanted world," an intentional contrast to Max Weber's "disenchanted world" to describe this worldview; *A Secular Age*, 446.

33. James McGrath uses the imagery of natural boundaries to conceptualize how distinctions between God and creation can be imagined: "it may well have been more like a river than a wall ... like a river that marks a country's border, the existence of a border, indeed its general location, may be clear, and nevertheless the edges of that border may be quite literally 'fluid'," James F. McGrath, *The Only True God: Early Christian Monotheism in its Jewish Context* (Chicago: University of Illinois Press, 2009), 13.

34. Tanya M. Luhrmann's first book, *Persuasions of the Witch's Craft*, is an ethnographic study of how magic and witchcraft are incorporated into the worldviews of individuals in modern England who are otherwise fully immersed in their modern urban context. Luhrmann has also conducted ethnographic studies of American Evangelicals whose prayer practices have allowed them to achieve a sense of auditory or visionary experiences. This work is entitled, *When God Talks Back: Understanding the American Evangelical Relationship with God*. While the title emphasizes contemporary Evangelical prayer practices, Luhrmann includes studies of visualization in other Christian traditions, like those used in Ignatian Spirituality which meditate and visualize specific scenes from the Gospels; see Luhrmann, *When God Talks Back*, 157–78.

might be contradictory understandings of 'thisworld' in tension with 'otherworldly' experiences of voices or visions, experiences of the sort found in apocalypses.[35] In her study of witchcraft in modern-day England, Tanya Luhrmann writes the following:

> I became interested in modern magic because these particular people seemed to pose difficulties for the standard interpretations of magic. Modern magicians are sophisticated, educated people. They know a way of explaining nature—science—which has been remarkably successful in its explanation and remarkably antagonistic towards ritualistic magic. They do not come from a background which accepts magic easily and their rites are novel creations; their magic cannot be explained as some burden of the past. They are clearly equipped with the mental equipment to think non-magically.[36]

Her research has shown how ordinary people, who have an active and vibrant life in modern post-industrial western society, are also actively engaged in various witch cults in modern-day England. These individuals negotiate multiple worldviews, namely that of modern science and the "powerful emotional and imaginative" experiences associated with modern magic. These are realities that are typically thought to be incompatible because they presume different and competing epistemological systems.

Epistemic categories like 'thisworld' and the 'otherworld' are used regularly in the study of apocalypses. While these categories are important for scholarly discourse about ancient texts, they constrain how we conceptualize the lived experience of religion because they artificially segregate these realms and falsely assume them to be pure and distinct systems. Anthropological studies and cognitive literary theories about religion indicate that non-specialist practitioners of religion, like non-specialist readers, do not maintain the same strict adherence to these distinctions as modern scholars are trained to do. The malleability of the mind allows it to hold two contrary realities in tension with one another.[37] Sarah Iles Johnston illustrates well how Greek myths are able to create narrative worlds in which an ancient reader could imagine him- or herself within the possibilities of actual encounter with 'otherworldly' beings.[38] This is not unlike the activity of immersive reading, which allows Hermas's world in the Book of Visions to achieve the quality of 'realness' in the reader or achieve what we call the 'possible world of the apocalypse'.

---

35. Luhrmann, *When God Talks Back*; also Luhrmann, *How God Becomes Real*.
36. Luhrmann, *Persuasions of the Witch's Craft*, 10.
37. Luhrmann, *How God Becomes Real*, 27.
38. Sarah Iles Johnston, "Narrating Myths," *Arethusa* 48 (2015): 173–218, here 201; Johnston, "How Myths and Other Stories Help to Create and Sustain Beliefs," 141–56; Johnston, *The Story of Myth*.

Breaking down the hard and fast scholarly distinction between 'thisworld' and 'otherworld' can be difficult for academic discourse, but recent years have introduced alternative ways of conceptualizing the past that complicate the distinct categories that scholars regularly use. For example, based on studies of the material culture, archaeologists have argued that there was no hard and fast distinction between ancient 'Israelites' and 'Canaanites', raising serious questions about a massive migration or infiltration into the Levant.[39] In fact, the material evidence suggests that there may have been few physical or ethnic differences between these groups. So too, early Christ followers may be equally identifiable as members of one or another of the many Jewish groups during the late Second Temple period, challenging the long-held division between 'Jews' and 'Christians' that neatly consolidated individuals into two major monolithic groups.[40] The hard and fast distinction between 'thisworld' and the 'otherworld' is yet another categorical divide that should be hybridized conceptually. Laura Feldt describes this hybridized way of thinking about such experiences as a movement between worlds. She writes, "[R]eligious narrative does not encourage a resolution of tensions in the gap it opens between two worlds, a mundane, everyday world, and an extraordinary, divine world. Instead, it encourages a fascination with the movement between the worlds."[41]

---

39. Readers are referred to William G. Dever, *Who Were the Early Israelites and Where Did They Come From?* (Grand Rapids: Eerdmans, 2003); Elizabeth Bloch-Smith, "Israelite Ethnicity in Iron I: Archaeology Preserves What Is Remembered and What Is Forgotten in Israel's History," *JBL* 122 (2003): 401–25; Israel Finkelstein and Neil Asher Silberman, *The Bible Unearthed: Archaeology's New Vision of Ancient Israel and the Origin of Its Sacred Texts* (New York: Simon and Schuster, 2002); Avraham Faust and Susan Niditch, "The Emergence of Israel and Theories of Ethnogenesis," in *The Wiley Blackwell Companion to Ancient Israel*, ed. Susan Niditch (Malden: John Wiley & Sons, Ltd., 2016), 152–73; J. P. Dessel, "Looking for the Israelites: The Archaeology of Iron Age I," in *The Old Testament in Archaeology and History*, ed. Jennie Ebeling, J. Edward Wright, Mark Elliott, and Paul V. M. Flesher (Waco: Baylor University Press, 2017), 275–98.

40. Adam H. Becker and Annette Yoshiko Reed (ed.), *The Ways That Never Parted: Jews and Christians in Late Antiquity and the Early Middle Ages* (Minneapolis: Fortress Press, 2007). Also relevant is the reconceptualization of ancient Israel's God as both immaterial and material by Benjamin D. Sommer, *The Bodies of God and the World of Ancient Israel* (New York: Cambridge University Press, 2009) and the excellent discussion inspired by that book by Brittany E. Wilson, "God's Multiple Forms: Divine Fluidity in the Shepherd of Hermas," in *Experiencing the Shepherd of Hermas*, ed. Angela Kim Harkins and Harry O. Maier, 171–92.

41. Feldt, "Religious Narrative and the Literary Fantastic," 272.

Porous Worlds and Porous Bodies

Using ethnographic approaches that focus on a thick description of individual experience, anthropologists have studied 'otherworldly' experiences, such as spirit possession, visions, and voices, as they are said to occur in a wide range of cultures and societies today, including post-industrial and post-enlightenment western societies. We have already discussed the work of anthropologist Tanya Luhrmann who has conducted multiple ethnographic studies of how competing thought systems are negotiated by individuals who live in the modern post-industrial world.[42] Scholars of antiquity have applied interdisciplinary approaches to the study of religious phenomena with original and creative findings.[43] The most recent example of this is Giovanni Bazzana's stimulating discussion of spirit possession in early Christ groups.[44] Using the work of anthropologists who study spirit possession in cross-cultural contexts today, in particular that of Michael Lambek, Bazzana draws out the implications of how modern western understandings of the self constrain how we examine the ancient material concerning spirit phenomena. His study offers a methodological reframing of how academics read and conceptualize the religious phenomena described in early Christian texts.[45] Bazzana begins with a modern-day account of spirit possession and exorcism of an unidentified woman in Milan,[46] thus illustrating how even modern western contexts can yield data about porosity for spirit experiences. The modern possession event illustrates well how 'thisworld' and the 'supernatural' world are permeable and overlapping realms—not just in antiquity, but also for many peoples and cultures today.[47]

---

42. Luhrmann, *Persuasions of the Witch's Craft*, 337. Her subsequent work (*When God Talks Back*) compares kataphatic and apophatic forms of prayer practices used by different religious groups in contemporary America and investigates how prayer is cultivated through a range of visualization and non-visualization practices. Her research seeks to explain to non-believers how modern people can "experience God as real" (xv).

43. For example, Colleen Shantz (*Paul in Ecstasy*) applies cognitive science of religion questions to the first century figure, Paul.

44. Bazzana, *Having the Spirit of Christ*.

45. See too the excellent discussion of possession and the Mandates by Giovanni B. Bazzana, "Negotiating the Experience of Possession in Hermas's Shepherd," in *Experiencing the Shepherd of Hermas*, edited by Angela Kim Harkins and Harry O. Maier, 9–29. In that same volume, Jung Choi also discusses the idea of the porous self, "A True Prophet as a Mouthpiece of the Spirit? Cultivating Virtue and Control," 31–56.

46. Bazzana, *Having the Spirit of Christ*, 1–3.

47. Anthropologists and religious studies scholars have conducted ethnographic studies of spiritual or ecstatic experiences in the modern West: Luhrmann, *When God Talks Back*, Luhrmann, *Persuasions of the Witch's Craft*; Robert A. Orsi has also written about spirit experiences between 'thisworld' and the 'otherworld'. The opening scene

Bazzana highlights the inadequacy of the idea of the agentic self and proposes that other models of the self are better able to understand the phenomenon of the possessed self that we see in these ancient texts.[48] Especially valuable is his point that the self, particularly in the case of spirit possession, is best understood as a continual and ongoing negotiation. Identity flexes from the state of being possessed by a spirit to the state of hosting a spirit in the state of possession. Bazzana presents the Pauline language, 'in Christ' (ἐν χριστῷ), within the broader framework of spirit possession.[49] Bazzana writes,

> Though it may appear so at first, that Christ lives within the believers is not really at odd with their being 'in him.' This is particularly clear when the articulation of these ideas in Paul's writing is looked at from the vantage point of spirit possession... . Paul treats Christ as a 'spirit' conceived in the sense that has been sketched elsewhere in the book: 'spirit' as a person and not at all immaterial but not a 'person' in the modern sense of the self-contained and autonomous individual self either.[50]

In other words, Paul understands the relationship between Christ and believers as intersubjective, one that is continually 'in flux' and always (re)negotiated; thus Christ's presence and absence are felt at different times among believers.[51] The idea of the self that is in flux, negotiating and renegotiating

---

in his work, *Between Heaven and Earth: The Religious Worlds People Make and the Scholars Who Study Them* (Princeton: Princeton University Press, 2005) paints a parallel between his mother with her fat stack of memorial cards of her deceased Jesuit friends, and Mama Lola, a medium whom Orsi will interview later that evening. Orsi describes his mother laying out her memorial cards like a kind of 'celestial solitaire'. Orsi's mother is disturbed by Orsi's plans to go out to a voodoo celebration in honor of Papa Gede, a spirit who will come to possess Mama Lola later that night, and who in fact delivers a special message to Orsi. Of course the contrast is intended to be highly ironic since both women, Orsi's mother and Mama Lola, attest to similar phenomena embedded in different cultural contexts in NYC—one which uses the language of spirit possession and the other we might describe as continuing bonds, yet both underscore the diverse ways in which, even in the modern West, individuals experience intersubjectivity with beings who are not of this world.

48. Other important studies that critique the agentic self are Saba Mahmood, "Feminist Theory, Embodiment, and the Docile Agent: Some Reflections on the Egyptian Islamic Revival," *Cultural Anthropology* 16 (2001): 202–36; Saba Mahmood, *The Politics of Piety: The Islamic Revival and the Feminist Subject* (Princeton: Princeton University Press, 2005, 2011).

49. Bazzana, *Having the Spirit of Christ*, 106–11.

50. Bazzana, *Having the Spirit of Christ*, 110.

51. Bazzana, *Having the Spirit of Christ*, 110. Later, Bazzana writes that Jesus, because of his death and resurrection, has "become a 'spirit' who can now be experienced by all Christ believers through possession" (115).

its identity within the larger framework of spirit possession, offers a capacious model for also thinking about other types of experiences in which the self is not agentic, but acted upon, like that of a visionary encounter.

Bazzana's work constructs a worldview in which 'thisworld' and the 'otherworld' are intertwined in a way that allows the self to be acted upon from the outside. He understands that the ability to be an agent/actant is not consolidated in human persons. Instead, agency is something that can be possessed by supernatural beings, who can produce a real effect on an individual. In her study of dreams and dreaming in modern-day Egypt, anthropologist Amira Mittermaier indicates that for the Muslims whom she studied, dreams and visions are ways to imagine realities that are assumed to always be there, even though they may not be perceptible:

> For Shaykh Qusi, visions and visionary dreams are real imagined experiences. The Prophet and his companions are already around us, yet it is through the imagination that we can perceive them. They are already present, and they are made present through the imagination. Imagining here is not a creative act performed by an autonomous individual subject; it is more akin to a tuning-in.[52]

Mittermaier's discussion of dreams relates well to visions because her description allows us to conceptualize a different view of the world in which materiality is not the sole measure of what is real. Paul Christopher Johnson describes such worlds as 'spirit-infused':

> [P]resences 'pour' into things, and 'saturate' my walk. Such formulations grant spirits a liquid form that is moving and fluid but at least provisionally able to be contained or blended. The aqueous fusibility endows the spirits of the dead with different characteristics than were they fitted with cosmic, electrical, or telluric terms, to name a few of the obvious alternatives.[53]

Johnson's description of a 'spirit-infused' world is perhaps more like the kind of worldview the ancient readers of the Shepherd presumed.

While our study of the Book of Visions proceeds with the idea that Hermas is a fictional character, his experiences model understandings of the world and the self that would be recognizable to ancient readers. Descriptions of Hermas's subjectivity highlight the limitations of extending our modern conceptualization of an autonomous 'buffered' self into the narrative world of the past. The detail that Hermas was a former slave in Vis. 1.1.1 (1.1) evokes a kind of subjectivity often presumed in spirit possession phenomena, namely of a porous self that has been enslaved. As a

---

52. Mittermaier, *Dreams that Matter: Egyptian Landscapes of the Imagination*, 19.
53. Johnson, "Introduction: Spirits and Things in the Making of the Afro-Atlantic World," 3.

manumitted slave, Hermas negotiates and renegotiates his understanding of the self through his various exchanges with his visionary interlocutors. These resemble actual conversations had with flesh-and-blood interlocutors because they challenge and surprise him, by revealing information that was previously unknown. As a result, even though Hermas is manumitted, he continues to model what it is like to be enslaved. This slave-subjectivity is well suited for the spirit-related encounters that Hermas experiences in the Book of Visions.

Immersion in Imagined Worlds

Visions of otherworldly spaces and encounters with the strange beings who inhabit them produce what anthropologist Tanya M. Luhrmann calls a 'paracosm': "a private-but-shared imagined world sufficiently rich in detail that people become engaged in the stories and can return to them again and again, exploring them from different angles, reliving different moments, recasting the scenes as if they were there, even adding new chapters to the story."[54] Here, this participation in the activities of the virtual world is described elsewhere as a 'fandom'—a term that recognizes the illusory nature of these virtual spaces and the deep personal investment in such spaces.[55] Empirical studies of these non-specialist readers show that they readily suspend their disbelief when reading narratives that describe fantastic experiences, thereby achieving an immersive experience of otherworldly realia.

Immersive experiences of non-specialist readers have been analyzed by empirical studies that point to the compelling and 'real' perceptions of the imagined worlds constructed by popular culture—those of fantasy novels like *Harry Potter* or *Lord of the Rings* or of the virtual worlds of apocalyptic online role-playing games like *World of Warcraft*, *Ground Zero*, and *After the End*.[56] In her insightful analysis of apocalyptic themes in role-playing games, Rachel Wagner writes:

> Both immersion and extractability are forms of media materialization in which things pass from the virtual to the physical, cultivating a sense of presence for the world beyond. Props—whether religious or secular—become a bridge between this world and another beyond. Props, relics, and sacred objects promise presence—a tangible link to a desirable world beyond. It is easy to see how fandom and religion similarly truck in both immersion

---

54. Luhrmann, *How God Becomes Real*, 27.
55. Rachel Wagner, "A Sense of Presence: Mediating an American Apocalypse," *Religions* 12, 1 (2021): 1–11, here 2.
56. The live-action role playing games, *Ground Zero* and *After the End* are discussed in Wagner, "A Sense of Presence," 6–7.

and extractability, with special spaces that wrap around participants and hierophanic material objects that make otherworldly places feel immediately present. It is not much of a stretch to see how Orsi's observations about contemporary religious presence can then successfully be applied—in ways he did not anticipate—to the dark apocalyptic fandoms of American gun culture.[57]

The narrative worlds accessed through games or fantasy novels feel compelling and real "through the use of various objects and abilities." In the case of narratives about fantasy worlds or otherworldly realms, certain literary details are used that contribute to intensifying a reader's or gamer's experience of the narrative world. Such experiences can be immersive and feel 'real', even for modern, post-industrial people who willingly suspend their disbelief and allow themselves to become absorbed into a fantasy world.

We can use this observation to consider the following question: Do discipline-specific ways of reading ancient visions impede the ability of modern biblical scholars to understand them as compelling narratives that generated further experiences and writings among the people who read and heard them in antiquity? Does our scholarly training form us to overlook the very details that non-specialist readers see and to which they readily respond? What can we as scholars learn from the proliferation of apocalyptic groups in the modern period about how ancient readers read and responded to first-person reports of visionary experiences?

We know that ancient apocalypses could and did lead to the production of further writings on similar themes. An excellent example is the broad variety of 'para-Danielic' traditions and writings associated with the visions of Daniel.[58] Visions of the otherworld, like the further scene of paradise that appears in the Greek—but not the Syriac—text of *Odes of Solomon* 11 may also be thought of as examples of texts that can be said to preserve some additional glimpse of the narrated world.[59] While apocalypses are

57. Wagner, "A Sense of Presence," 3.
58. See Lorenzo DiTommaso, *The Book of Daniel and the Apocryphal Daniel Literature*. While the Greek additions to Daniel, viz., Prayer of Azariah and the Song of the Three Youths, Susanna and the Elders, and Bel and the Dragon, are well known, there is a sizeable body of apocalypses that extend the characters and scenes known from the biblical book of Daniel to new settings. Some of these apocryphal Daniel apocalypses locate the seer in new lands, Cyprus, Persia, Elam, a 'seven-hilled city', Crete, etc. and describe his encounters with different personalities, and his new visions; DiTommaso describes these in 87–224, with a bibliography in 316–508.
59. Angela Kim Harkins, "The Garden Space in Odes of Solomon 11 and the Reinvigoration of Memories about Paradise," *Biblical & Qur'ānic Traditions in the Middle East*. Edited by Cornelia Horn and Sidney Griffith, Eastern Mediterranean Texts and Contexts Series 2 (Warwick: Abelian Academic Press, 2016), 1–33; revised and

relatively rare as a genre, interdisciplinary approaches associated with cognitive literary theory that describe how narratives about otherworldly experiences were compelling can help us to think about the generative process of immersive reading. Perhaps the immersive qualities of visionary narratives play some role in the further generation of visions by ancient Jewish and Christian readers. During immersive reading, a reader enters the narrative world by constructing and extending the fragmentary details found in visionary reports with his/her own knowledge and lived experience of the world.

Immersion in Hermas's World

The protracted details about Hermas moving through his landscape and the information that is provided about his interior experiences along the way contribute to the immersive quality of the narrative. These details found throughout the Book of Visions function in a preparatory way to heighten receptivity to the ethical teachings in the Mandates by cultivating states of curiosity, anticipation, and watchfulness.

The character of Hermas is crucial for the immersive reading of the Book of Visions. Descriptions of the movements of his extended body and first-person reports of his interior state allow a reader to construct Hermas in their imagination. In the Mandates, the figure of Hermas no longer appears as a named character. While the last mention of Hermas's name occurs in Vis 4.1.7 (22.7), his persona persists through the fifth Vision. Here, the moment of encounter with the Shepherd, a visionary interlocutor, is accompanied by the usual first-person reporting of Hermas's interior state. We read in Vis. 5.4 (25.4):

> ἔτι λαλοῦντος αὐτοῦ ἠλλοιώθη ἡ ἰδέα αὐτοῦ, καὶ ἐπέγνων αὐτόν, ὅτι ἐκεῖνος ἦν ᾧ παρεδόθην, καὶ εὐθὺς συνεχύθην, <u>καὶ φόβος με ἔλαβεν, καὶ ὅλος συνεκόπην ἀπὸ τῆς λύπης</u>, ὅτι οὕτως αὐτῷ ἀπεκρίθην πονηρῶς καὶ ἀφρόνως.

> While he was still speaking, his appearance was changed, and I recognized him as the one to whom I was entrusted; <u>and immediately I was confused, and fear seized me, and I was completely afflicted with grief</u>, because I had answered him so wickedly and foolishly.

The fifth Vision serves as a transition from the Book of Visions to the second section known as the Mandates. In that section, the character of Hermas disappears while the Shepherd addresses the reader/hearer directly. This shift in style allows the reader/hearer to assume the role of Hermas

---

reprinted in *Experiencing Presence in the Second Temple Period: Revised and Updated Essays*, 219–44.

through the second-person address, making the reader a participant in the giving of instruction. The intensification of the shift to second-person address in the Mandates resembles that which takes place in the giving of the Law at Sinai as it is told in the Book of Deuteronomy. There Moses retells the story of the wilderness trek in first-person voice (chs. 1–5), but from chapter 5 onward, he addresses the reader/hearer directly in second-person, as he speaks on behalf of God at Sinai in the teaching of the Law at Sinai. This rhetorical move assists the reader/ hearer to imagine themselves personally as one who receives the instruction at Sinai. Thus, while Hermas is never again named in the entirety of the work after Vis. 4.1.7 (22.7), the persona of Hermas that is created in the Book of Visions persists in the Mandates but with greater involvement on the part of the reader/hearer who is addressed directly by the Shepherd.[60]

The Re-actualization of Visionary Texts

The immersive reading that takes place in the Book of Visions sets the stage for the intensification of teachings in the Mandates in which the reader/hearer receives instruction directly. This deeper engagement can allow for the possibility of other experiences in which the reader/hearer may become a participant in the visionary experience of receiving even further instruction from the Shepherd. This intensification can be seen in apocalypses like the Book of Revelation in which the seer (John) is no longer just reporting new visions that he has been granted, but he becomes a participant in prior visionary experiences. In contrast to Rev. 1, wherein John the seer reports his own visionary experience, the seer is granted his own glimpse of the heavenly throne room described by Daniel and the four living creatures described by the exilic prophet Ezekiel (Rev. 4).[61] In the case of John the seer, the immersive narratives of the written prophetic traditions are told in such a way that they allow him to enact and experientially see more of what had been partially disclosed in former times.

Luca Arcari discusses a curious instance of an addition found in a fragment of Mand. 11.9–10 (43.9–10).[62] This is a papyrus scrap that is 12×11.4 cm

---

60. Harkins, *Reading with an "I" to the Heavens*, 189–90; Christopher Rowland with Patricia Gibbons and Vicente Dobroruka, "Visionary Experience in Ancient Judaism and Christianity," in *Paradise Now*, ed. April D. DeConick (Atlanta: Scholars, 2006), 41–56.

61. Rowland, with Gibbons and Dobroruka, "Visionary Experience in Ancient Judaism and Christianity," 41–56.

62. Luca Arcari, "P.Oxy. 1.5 and the Codex Sangermanensis as 'Visionary Living Texts': Visionary *habitus* and Processes of 'Textualization' and/or 'Scripturalization' in Late Antiquity," in *Lived Religion in the Ancient Mediterranean World: Approaching*

in size and written in an informal uncial hand dated to approximately the III/IV centuries. Known as P.Oxy. 1.5, 2.8–16, the scrap contains an addition that appears to comment on the scene in a way that transforms the episode. In his discussion of Mand. 11, Arcari uses the term 'visionary *habitus*' to describe a process in which a received visionary text like the Shepherd of Hermas can possibly generate further visionary experiences in a process of 're-actualization'.[63]

In this overlap with Mand. 11.9–11 (43.9–11), there is additional material in P.Oxy. 1.5 immediately after Mand. 11.9–10 (43.9–10). The larger literary context of this mandate is the passage on the process of inspiration, specifically the task of distinguishing between a true prophet and a false prophet. The relevant passage from the mandate is given below in brackets as context for the addition:[64]

> P.Oxy. 1.5 (Mand. 11.9 [43.9]) [ὅταν οὖν ἔλθῃ ὁ ἄνθρωπος ὁ ἔχων τὸ πνεῦμα τὸ θεῖον εἰς συναγωγὴν ἀνδρῶν δικαίων τῶν ἐχόντων πίστιν θείου πνεύματος, καὶ ἔντευξις γένηται πρὸς τὸν Θεὸν τῆς συναγωγῆς τῶν ἀνδρῶν ἐκείνων, τότε ὁ ἄγγε-]
> λος τοῦ πνεύματος τοῦ προφητ[ι]
> κοῦ ὁ κείμενος ἐπ' αὐτῷ[65]
> π[ληροῖ τὸν ἄνθρωπο]ν, καὶ
> (5) πληρωθεὶς ὁ ἄνθρωπος ἐκεῖ-
> νος τῷ πν(εύματ)ι τῷ ἁγίῳ λα
> λεῖ καθὼς ὁ κ(ύριο)ς βούλεται.

Religious Transformations from Archaeology, History and Classics, ed. Valentino Gasparini et al. (Berlin: De Gruyter, 2020), 469–91. See also the discussion by Angela Kim Harkins, "Entering the Narrative World of Hermas's Visions," 129–36.

63. Arcari uses the interdisciplinary theoretical model of Relevance Theory (RT), a branch of cognitive linguistics associated with the work of Dan Sperber and Deirdre Wilson, Arcari, "P.Oxy. 1.5 and the Codex Sangermanensis as 'Visionary Living Texts'," 471–73; Dan Sperber and Deirdre Wilson, *Relevance: Communication and Cognition* (Oxford: Oxford University Press, 1995); Sperber and Wilson, "The Mapping Between the Mental and the Public Lexicon," in *Thought and Language. Interdisciplinary Themes*, ed. Peter Carruthers and Jill Boucher (Cambridge: Cambridge University Press, 1998), 184–200; Sperber and Wilson, *Meaning and Relevance* (Cambridge: Cambridge University Press, 2012).

64. Only the extant portion of the Greek fragment is presented here in a way that shows the line breaks of the fragment. Cf., Manlio Simonetti's textus receptus ("Il Pastore di Erma," in *Seguendo Gesù. Testi cristiani delle origini, vol. 2*, edited by Emanuela Prinzivalli and Manlio Simonetti. Scrittori Greci e Latini. Fondazione Lorenzo Valla [Milan: Mondadori, 2015], 328) which reads: τότε ὁ ἄγγελος τοῦ πνεύματος τοῦ προφητικοῦ ὁ κείμενος ἐπ' αὐτῷ. πληροῖ τὸν ἄνθρωπον, καὶ πληρωθεὶς ὁ ἄνθρωπος τῷ πνεύματι τῷ ἁγίῳ λαλεῖ εἰς τὸ πλῆθος, καθὼς ὁ Κύριος βούλεται. 10 οὕτως οὖν φανερὸν ἔσται τὸ πνεῦμα τῆς θεότητος. ὅση οὖν περὶ τοῦ πνεύματος τῆς θεότητος ...

65. Cf. πρὸς αὐτόν.

5. *Immersion in the Narrative World of Apocalyptic Visions* 185

οὕτως [οὖν] φανερὸν ἔστε τὸ
πν(εῦμ)α τῆς θεότητος. τὸ γὰρ
(10) προφητικὸν πν(εῦμ)α τὸ σω-
μάτειόν ἐστιν τῆς προ-
φητικῆς τάξεως, ὅ ἐστιν
τὸ σῶμα τῆς σαρκὸς Ἰ(ησο)ῦ Χ(ριστο)ῦ
τὸ μιγὲν τῇ ἀνθρωπότη
τι διὰ Μαρίας. ὅτι δὲ
δοξῇ δεκτικόν ἐστιν

P.Oxy.1.5 (Mand. 11.9 [43.9]) [When, then the person who has the divine spirit comes into an assembly of righteous people who have the faith of a divine spirit, and a petition is made to God by the assembly of those people, then the ang]el of the prophetic spirit who lays upon him, f[ills the man]; and (5) being filled with the holy sp(iri)t the man speaks as the Lord wishes. Thus the spirit of the deity will become manifest. <u>For the (10) prophetic spirit is the corporate body of the prophetic order, which is the body of the flesh of J(esu)s Ch(ris)t which was mingled with human nature (15) through Mary</u>…

The P.Oxy.1.5 fragment contains a significant addition (underlined above) that consists of a mention of Jesus Christ and Mary by name, neither of whom ever appears in the Shepherd as it has been received. This passage falls within the literary context depicting the process of inspiration—an experience of the prophetic spirit who 'covers over' (ὁ κείμενος ἐπ' αὐτῷ) and 'fills the person' (π[ληροῖ τὸν ἄνθρωπο]ν) during the moment of prophetic inspiration. It is from this condition that the spirit of the deity becomes present. The passage reflects how an ancient reader appears to have incorporated new information about Jesus Christ and Mary, based on his/her understanding of the Spirit based revelation and specific knowledge of Christianity into the reading of Mand. 11.9–10 (43.9–10), thereby transforming the text. The papyrus fragment P.Oxy.1.5 can be said to illustrate the further revelation that is generated when one experiences prophetic inspiration.

Luca Arcari's discussion of P.Oxy.1.5 offers a model for conceptualizing the growth of texts over time. His study highlights the inadequacies of models for textual transmission that presume that changes in the text arise *strictly* from the usual scribal errors of parablepsis or homoioteleuton. Arcari's model of a 're-actualization' process helpfully draws attention to the phenomenon of the growth of apocalyptic texts over time. While some variant readings may be traced, of course, to mundane mechanical errors or confusions from the scribal processes, Arcari describes a process by which new texts are generated over time through various reading practices.

The production of new texts may possibly be one of the effects of immersive reading when considered in light of the phenomenon that Tanya Luhrmann describes as a paracosm:

> [A] paracosm in this sense is a private-but-shared imagined world sufficiently rich in detail that people become engaged in the stories and can return to them again and again, exploring them from different angles, reliving different moments, recasting the scenes as if they were there, even adding new chapters to the story. Many paracosms are created by fiction, and it is the text that people share.[66]

While it is not the case that all individuals will have such experiences, enactive reading and deep imaginative engagement with the narrative world can contribute to the phenomenon of a 'living text', one in which the readers and hearers can interact with and transform. In other words, immersive entry into a narrative world can be thought to play some role in the generation of texts, especially in writings that describe alternative realities like the visionary experiences and revelatory events that are described in the Shepherd of Hermas and other ancient apocalypses.

Conclusion

The resurgence of interest in the Shepherd is partly an aftereffect of the explosion of research in early Jewish apocalypses and of the emerging field of Second Temple Studies, which is the larger historical context of ancient Jewish and Christian apocalypses. Ancient Jewish apocalypses had an enduring hold on readers' imaginations that reached far beyond the historical period in which they were composed.[67] Enoch reports emphatically, "No one has seen what I have seen" (*1 En.* 19.3). Hermas, like other apocalyptic seers, goes to great lengths to describe his travels, what he sees, and his emotional responses to the events that take place. The ancient imagination understood seeing holistically, with the entire body in mind. So too, the cognitive science of visual perception has introduced new ideas of how seeing is an embodied and holistic experience, with a special emphasis on how our experiential knowledge plays a key role in how we see. The spaces and creatures, like the Tower in Vision 3 or the beast in Vision 4, are knowable only through the details narrated by the seers. In this case, apocalypses, like fantasy literature and other forms of virtual realities, resemble the experience of groping blindly through a space that has never been visited previously.[68]

---

66. Luhrmann, *How God Becomes Real*, 27.

67. For an excellent discussion of the texts generated by ancient apocalypses of Daniel and the Book of the Watchers, see DiTommaso, *The Book of Daniel and the Apocryphal Daniel Literature* and Annette Yoshiko Reed, *Fallen Angels and the History of Judaism and Christianity: The Reception of Enochic Literature* (Cambridge: Cambridge University Press, 2005).

68. Caracciolo, *The Experientiality of Narrative*, 96.

5. *Immersion in the Narrative World of Apocalyptic Visions* 187

The reader/hearer enters the apocalypse through the first-person report of the seer and listens attentively to the first-person report of proprioceptive and interoceptive details, using them to construct a fuller understanding of the narrative world. The seer in ancient apocalypses often emphasizes the genuine reliability of the first-person report and seeks to share with readers and hearers what was experienced. For example, Enoch's proprioceptive experiences in the new environment are provided as he moves further into the house and loses his balance as he collapses on his face. A little later, we are given details about how exactly his body is configured when one of the angels lifts him up onto his feet, with Enoch's head downward the entire time (*1 En.* 14.24–25). In this scene, Enoch also gives us interoceptive details when he describes the temperature of the heavenly space as "hot as fire, and cold as snow" (14.13). Rather than studying whether ancient seers were historical figures or whether their visions were real, the enactive reading offered here focuses on what these texts might do to the ancient reader/hearer. Apocalypses include proprioceptive descriptions of the seer as he enters a new environment, oftentimes reporting these figures as they collapse and fall to the ground at the moment of encounter with a divine being.[69]

Hermas's reports of his foot-journeys replicate our own lived experiences of entering a new environment. In the case of the Fourth Vision of the beast, Hermas reports the changes in the intensity of the sun and the appearance of the dust cloud (Vis. 4.1.5–6 [22.5–6]). We read too that Hermas is startled and turns in fear to see if the beast is pursuing him, stopping to take a final look (Vis. 4.3.7 [24.7]). Today television and other media artificially give us access to views from a disembodied vantage point as the camera zooms quickly in to see the expression on someone's face, and then zooms out to a panoramic view of an entire city skyline in a moment's time. This differs significantly from our actual physical experience of entering a new environment where the activity of looking around integrates and involves the entire body. The experience is gradual and unfolding. We crane our necks and move around the space, or we position our bodies closer to the item we wish to examine, taking note of our emotional responses during the exploration. Enactive perception is a way of depicting embodied experiences that include both proprioceptive and interoceptive phenomena.

The seer's interoception is a significant way in which a narrative world described in ancient apocalypses can be experienced by a reader. These

---

69. This literary form of collapsing at the moment of encounter is discussed by Loren T. Stuckenbruck in the context of what he calls the 'refusal tradition' in which the veneration of angels was corrected, *Angel Veneration and Christology: A Study in Early Judaism and in the Christology of the Apocalypse of John* (Tübingen: Mohr Siebeck, 1995).

emotional responses, which express the seer's evaluation of the space as terrifying or soothing, can be far more compelling than a detailed, static description of the features of an apocalyptic landscape and the things found within it. Even though narrative worlds are described in piecemeal, the reader relies on these emotional responses when constructing the space and literary characters in the imagination. Seers disclose a great deal of information about their emotional experiences of fear or worry, their physical awareness of their bodily responses (trembling, shaking), and their introspective thinking within new spaces, thereby giving us access to evaluative assessments and their emotional responses to being in a new environment.[70]

The Shepherd of Hermas was a popular catechetical work that presents Hermas as a seer who was compelling and engaging to ancient readers. Unlike modern scholars who are trained to read for discipline-specific information, ancient readers read with the aim of immersing themselves in the possible world of the narrative. This included the possibility of having a transformative experience of the text, like that preserved in P.Oxy. 1.5, which describes what has happened during the re-actualization of the text.

Enactive reading assists a reader in accessing and constructing an experience of the apocalypse, a possible narrative world. This space is experientially fluid insofar as it is generated by cues in the text and by the imagination of the reader who enacts the narrative. By drawing attention to the complex ways the embodied mind and memories are engaged during immersive reading, this enactive reading of ancient apocalypses helps to overcome the deeply entrenched patterns of thinking that are influenced by distinctly western worldviews that make a sharp distinction between 'thisworld' and the 'otherworld', along with other inadequate patterns of thinking like the mind/body dualism that is deeply rooted in the humanities. Our rereading of ancient apocalyptic seers offers a preliminary look at how the integration of biocultural elements of lived experiences can be brought to bear on how scholars imagine the activity of reading as an embodied experience.

---

70. We might think about these immersive narrative worlds as being marked by a high level of absorption—like a reader losing oneself in a book. Literary theorists who study the experiential effects of reading emotionally arousing fantasy literature note that language about the emotional experiences of the protagonists assist in deepening a reader's immersive experiences. In such studies, "immersion ratings were significantly higher for fear-inducing than for neutral passages," see Chun-Ting Hsu et al., "Fiction Feelings in Harry Potter: Haemodynamic Response in the Mid-Cingulate Cortex Correlates with Immersive Reading Experience," *Neuroreport* 25 (2014): 1356–61 at 1356.

Conclusion

The early Christian work known as the Shepherd of Hermas was popular among ancient readers and widely known as a useful catechetical text. This study has proposed that the traditional scholarly approach to this work has asked specific disciplinary questions concerning genre and historicity without asking how this text was effective as a catechetical work in antiquity. What did ancient readers find engaging about the Shepherd? Our study has considered the Book of Visions from the perspective of Hermas's embodied experiences, his awareness of his emotions, and other sensory experiences. Using the enactive reading approach associated with cognitive literary theory, we have described how immersive readings of the visions create effects that are experientially vivid and draw readers and hearers into Hermas's narrative world. Immersive reading gives insight to the character of Hermas, who is easily imagined as a figure with an inner-life and consciousness. This analysis of the Book of Visions brings to light the embodied responses of readers *and hearers*, including the introspective examination of their own private desires, a longing to understand what is taking place, and amusement, all of which can assist in the retention of what is being revealed. Such effects of reading can be described as cultivating preparatory predispositions for moral formation, thereby illustrating how the Book of Visions contributes to the overall catechetical aim of the Shepherd, a role that is seldom appreciated in previous scholarship on the work.

The various approaches associated with cognitive literary theory have been employed to draw attention to how reading is an embodied practice in which the life experiences of the reader are brought to bear on the narrative that is being read. Cognitive literary approaches highlight how reading practices and mental imagining from literary descriptions are culturally specific. Scholars who are trained to read with discipline-specific questions in mind often read against the grain of the narrative and overlook the very literary details that invite a reader into an immersive experience of Hermas's visions. The enactive reading process used in this study helps us to appreciate the way the Book of Visions offers a lively and vivid narrative of Hermas's experiences. Enactive reading relies on the kind of concrete language that is also important for classical rhetorical strategies like *ekphrasis, enargeia,* and *phantasmia*, all of which seek to make compelling mental images by making what is absent present. The distinctive contribution of cognitive literary theory is that it highlights how peculiar the reading habits of modern academics are. By identifying larger patterns in reading among non-specialists, cognitive literary studies draw attention to the disparity between specialist readers, who read against the grain of a narrative, and non-specialist readers, who are willing to suspend disbelief and immerse themselves in a possible narrative world.

The Book of Visions gives readers access to various introspective experiences of Hermas, a figure who narrates his various journeys and visionary experiences in first-person voice. In contrast to traditional historical-critical methods, which rely on disembodied understandings of texts and readers, this study uses a biocultural understanding of the body and the embodied mind. We have analyzed Hermas's experiences with the specific approaches known as enactive reading, ecocriticism, and with attention to other ways the text invites cognitive processes like rumination, which creates experiences of presence from absence. Our rereading of the popular early Christian work offers a way of understanding the compelling way the text immerses readers and hearers into the possible world of Hermas's visions, thereby accounting for its popularity and success in the ancient world as a catechetical work. Approaches associated with cognitive literary theory conceptualize reading as complex and embodied. First-person narrations of emotion and other bodily perceptions such as the strangeness of the visions and Hermas's own reported experiences of space and the environment in the Book of Visions are re-read strategically as inculcating a heightened sense of watchfulness, which cultivates the necessary predisposition for and receptivity to the ethical material that follows in the Mandates and Similitudes.

Especially important for this project has been the focus on embodied experiences and how they are imagined by a reader. While modern readers think of sensory perception through the sensorium of the five senses (see, hear, smell, taste, touch), these are often imagined as functions segregated from one another. In contrast, enactive reading highlights how the senses are perceived holistically by an embodied person, with special attention to the interrelation of the senses in kinesthetic experiences, both proprioception and interoception. This critical framework is grounded in cognitive psychology, which shows how the sensorimotor areas of the brain are actively engaged in imaginative reading. Enactive reading is a way of conceptualizing how a reader might experience the textualized narrative of the Book of Visions with first-hand intensity. Certain rhetorical features in these first-person texts—such as Hermas's strong emotional responses, explicit references to the body, and his kinesthetic experiences in his environs—serve to intensify enactive processes and allow us to theorize the effects of imaginative reading in flesh-and-blood readers.

Various details often overlooked by historical-critical scholars are crucial for bringing vividness and realism to the figure of Hermas, allowing him to be imagined as one with an inner-life and consciousness. Cognitive literary approaches help us to reintegrate the embodied experiences of readers and hearers as they move in a linear way through the Book of Visions and come to access the narrative world through Hermas's proprioception and his awareness of interoceptive experiences. For example, Hermas's interior physiological or emotional state is manifest or mediated through the skin or the viscera, and includes a range of experiences like embarrassment, temperature, pain, itch, tickle, sensual touch, sexual arousal, vasomotor flush, hunger, and thirst. Hermas's interior state is expressed in his physical trembling after his encounters with the woman (Vis. 1.2.2. [2.2]; 3.1.5 [9.5]). Proprioception refers to the body's sensations of moving through space, such as its active movement through a landscape or the passive sensation of a body as it falls or loses balance. While we are unwilling to affirm that Hermas was an actual historical figure, we can observe that his interoceptive and proprioceptive experiences scaffold elements of realism and allow a reader to infer an inner-life and consciousness, thus making his presence more vivid and compelling in the reader's imagination.

In addition to rereading Hermas, this monograph has also reread the landscape, objects, and visionary encounters in the Book of Visions. The multi-disciplinary approach known as literary ecocriticism offers a way of describing how the embodied mind perceives the environment and the advantage this cognitive capacity for spatial mapping and wayfinding might offer within the context of the Book of Visions. The Book of Visions opens with Hermas recounting an encounter at a riverbank. Other spaces are referenced in subsequent episodes, like the countryside and the Via Campagna. Hermas frequently ruminates as he walks (Vis. 2.1.1–2 [5.1–2]), and lengthy passages lay out the landscapes for the visions and supply odd mundane details about what is seen along the way. For example, the famous vision of the Tower in the third vision is preceded by a protracted account of Hermas walking in a field and a painstaking account of the otherwise ordinary (but out of place) things that he sees there, viz., an ivory couch and a linen covered pillow. In the fourth vision, the sun's intensity and an ominous cloud (Vis. 4.1.5–6 [22.5–6]) set the stage for other odd encounters with the beast and the Lady in white.

We have argued that Hermas's journeying and his physical movement through his environment contribute to the larger process of moral formation insofar as the inexplicable and bizarre events that happen to him inculcate certain dispositions that are useful for remembering and learning. A heightened sense of watchfulness and a piqued curiosity are examples of the effects that these journey experiences have on the reader. Such experiences prepare the reader for paranetic passages in the Book of Visions, the Mandates, and the Similitudes. Along the way Hermas encounters strange figures who speak enigmatically to him (for example the woman from the first vision who exhorts him to, "Act like a man, Hermas!") and experiences mind-boggling visions like that of a massive tower and a terrifying beast. These bizarre and fantastic elements generate ambiguity and draw out a cognitive response from the reader, effectively moving him or her to ponder deeper meaning from Hermas's encounters.

Details about the environment not only stimulate a reader's spatial reasoning, but also provide the opportunity for analysis. The journey structure of the narrative allows for vivid descriptions of the landscape and the objects encountered along the way. Our rereading of the Book of Visions has paid close attention to the ways the environment, objects, and other non-humans are described with vividness and with language that suggests they are agents in the narrative. This research into the role of the environment in the Book of Visions is also informed by postcolonial critiques of the modern discipline of history. These critiques make the point well that the scholarly conceptualization of the landscape and the environment as static and inert is peculiar to the post-Enlightenment West.

The geographical details that surround Hermas's visions appeal to the phenomenon of 'wayfinding', a heightened attention to one's surroundings that engages cognitive mapping processes. Ecocriticism has provided part of the theoretical framework for understanding Hermas's body and how its placement and locomotion within a literary environment can be perceived in a reader's mind. Although the geography in the Book of Visions is culturally specific, attentiveness to one's surroundings during the cognitive process of wayfinding is a process that can be stimulated by the reading of the visions. What previous scholars have described as the tedious and protracted style of Hermas's journey reports can be understood as having a strategic purpose. In these instances, spatial details do more than simply provide the coordinates for the events that take place; they effectively slow down the reading pace and heighten anticipation. The journey structure of the Book of Visions allows a reader to enter an immersive virtual landscape and engage various enactive processes that can prepare him or her for the paraenetic material that follows. Just as a sojourner becomes more aware of his or her environs when embarking on unfamiliar terrain, a careful reader of the Book of Visions takes note of landmarks and geography as the narrative moves along, effecting a heightened watchfulness regarding what will happen in the subsequent sections of the Shepherd. The sequencing of fantastic scenes that generate a strong emotional response of dismay or awe prior to hearing about ethical teachings is a pattern that is familiar to other works whose macroform resembles a compilation of mixed literary genres. We could compare this structure to the foundational narrative of the Exodus, which sequences a series of wonders and a theophany in the wilderness prior to the reception of the legal material. In Jewish apocalyptic writings, this literary sequencing can also be recognized in the work known as *2 Enoch*. This work opens with the protagonist, Enoch, journeying through the ten heavens (chs. 1–22) and experiencing a wondrous theophanic encounter with God in which Enoch is transformed (chs. 23–37); these events are then followed by various moral teachings and instructions (chs. 38–68). This pattern can also be seen in early Christian book of Revelation, which sequences a series of fantastic and disturbing visions of the seer prior to the ethical exhortation in ch. 22. Our rereading of the Shepherd proposes that the sequencing of the Book of Visions prior to the Mandates and Similitudes replicates a general pattern in which extraordinary events embedded in a journey narrative serve to heighten a reader's watchfulness and prepare him or her for the moral instruction that follows.

This book makes two significant contributions to the understanding of ancient religion. First, it integrates biocultural models of the human body and embodied mind with the study of ancient texts, overcoming the outdated Cartesian mind/body dualism that is reinforced by traditional historical-critical approaches, which regard ancient writings as purely disembodied discourse. Neuropsychological studies of cognitive processes during imaginative reading, which are now being produced by cognitive literary theorists, offer useful heuristic models for understanding how emotions intensify and heighten receptivity to other experiences. This monograph considers the complexity of the reading process and asks what the effects of reading an immersive narrative might have been on ancient flesh-and-blood readers and *hearers*.

Second, this monograph offers scholars of early Judaism and Christianity a different approach to understanding 'apocalypse'. Rather than the binary framework of 'thisworld' and 'otherworld', we have suggested a more capacious understanding of apocalypse as a narrative that seeks to offer readers and hearers with an embodied way of accessing the revelatory experience. A different approach to understanding apocalypse can better accommodate the diversity of texts that describe visionary experiences, like the Shepherd of Hermas. While traditional historical-critical studies isolate the Book of Visions from the following literary units of the Shepherd, we have sought to reintegrate it into its larger literary context by highlighting how the visions cultivate emotions and predispositions that heighten receptivity to the exhortations revealed to Hermas. In so doing, we hope to expand how visions and apocalypses in general are understood by scholars.

The Shepherd of Hermas was well-known in antiquity as an important catechetical work. While it enjoyed enormous success in the ancient world, modern commentators have not appreciated its popularity because they are trained to read against the grain of the narrative; in so doing, they overlook the way the narrative constructs vivid experiences for readers and hearers who read Hermas's first-person reports immersively. Our study has sought to account for why and how the Book of Visions was appealing and entertaining to ancient audiences. This rereading of the Book of Visions also firmly situates it within the larger catechetical program of the Shepherd by describing how the emotional effects of being surprised and engaged by Hermas's experiences work to heighten receptivity to instruction and moral formation.

Bibliography

Abrams, Meyer H. *The Mirror and the Lamp: Romantic Theory and the Critical Tradition*. Oxford: Oxford University Press, 1953.

Ahmed, Sara. "Happy Objects." 29–51 in *The Affect Theory Reader*. Edited by Melissa Gregg and Gregory J. Seigworth. Durham: Duke University Press, 2010.

—*The Cultural Politics of Emotion, 2d ed.* Edinburgh: Edinburgh University Press, 2014.

Allan, Rutger J. "Herodotus and Thucydides: Distance and Immersion." 131–54 in *Textual Strategies in Ancient War Narrative: Thermopylae, Cannae and Beyond*. Edited by Lidewij van Gils, Irene J. F. de Jong, and Caroline Kroon. Leiden: Brill, 2018.

Anderson, Gary. *A Time to Mourn, a Time to Dance: The Expression of Grief and Joy in Israelite Religion*. University Park, PA: Pennsylvania State University Press, 1991.

Anderson, Greg. *The Realness of Things Past: Ancient Greece and Ontological History*. Oxford: Oxford University Press, 2018.

Arcari, Luca. "P.Oxy. 1.5 and the Codex Sangermanensis as 'Visionary Living Texts': Visionary *habitus* and Processes of 'Textualization' and/or 'Scripturalization' in Late Antiquity." 469–91 in *Lived Religion in the Ancient Mediterranean World: Approaching Religious Transformations from Archaeology, History and Classics*. Edited by Valentino Gasparini, Maik Patzelt, Rubina Raja, Anna-Katharina Rieger, Jörg Rüpke, Emiliano Rubens Urciuoli, Elisabeth Begemann. Berlin: De Gruyter, 2020.

—*Vedere Dio: le apocalissi giudaiche e protocristiane (IV sec. a.C.-II sec. d.C.)*. Rome: Carocci editore, 2020.

Archer, John and Helen Fisher. "Bereavement and Reactions to Romantic Rejection: A Psychobiological Perspective." 349–72 in *Handbook of Bereavement Research and Practice: Advances in Theory and Intervention*. Edited by Margaret S. Stroebe, Robert O. Hansson, Henk Schut, and Wolfgang Stroebe. Washington, D.C.: American Psychological Association, 2008.

Auyoung, Elaine. *When Fiction Feels Real: Representation and the Reading Mind*. Oxford: Oxford University Press, 2018.

Avrahami, Yael. *The Senses of Scripture: Sensory Experience in the Hebrew Bible*. New York: T&T Clark, 2012.

Ayán Calvo, J. J. *Hermas: El Pastor*. Fuentes Patrísticas 6. Madrid: Ciudad Nueva, 1995.

Bagnani, Gilbert. "Hellenistic Sculpture from Cyrene." *The Journal of Hellenic Studies* 41 (1921): 232–46.

Barker, Don C. "Codex, Rolls, and Libraries in Oxyrhynchus." *Tyndale Bulletin* 57 (2006): 131–48.

Barnard, L.W. "The Shepherd of Hermas in Recent Study." *Heythrop Journal* 9 (1968): 29–36.

Barsalou, Lawrence et al. "Embodiment in Religious Knowledge." *Journal of Cognition and Culture* 5 (2005): 14–57.

Batovici, Dan. "Hermas in Clement of Alexandria." *StPatr* 66 (2013): 41–51.
—"Textual Revisions of the *Shepherd of Hermas* in Codex Sinaiticus." *ZAC* 18 (2014): 443–70.
—"Apocalyptic and Metanoia in the *Shepherd of Hermas*." *Apocrypha* 26 (2015): 151–70.
—"A New Hermas Papyrus Fragment in Paris." *Archiv für Papyrusforschung* 62 (2016): 20–36.
—"Two Notes on the Papyri of the *Shepherd of Hermas*." *Archiv für Papyrusforschung* 62 (2016): 384–95.
—"The *Shepherd of Hermas* in Recent Scholarship on the Canon: A Review Article." *ASE* 34 (2017): 89–105.
—*The Shepherd of Hermas in Late Antiquity*. Piscataway, NJ: Gorgias Press, forthcoming.
Bauckham, Richard J. "The Great Tribulation in the Shepherd of Hermas." *JTS* (n.s.) 25 (1974): 27–40.
Bazzana, Giovanni B. "'You Will Write Two Booklets and Send One to Clement and One to Grapte': Formal Features, Circulation, and Social Function of Ancient Apocalyptic Literature." 43–70 in *Scribal Practices and Social Structures among Jesus Adherents: Essays in Honour of John S. Kloppenborg*. Edited by William Arnal. BETL 285. Leuven: Peeters, 2016.
—*Having the Spirit of Christ: Spirit Possession and Exorcism in the Early Christ Groups*. New Haven: Yale University Press, 2020.
—"Negotiating the Experience of Possession in Hermas's Shepherd." 9–29 in *Experiencing the Shepherd of Hermas*. Edited by Angela Kim Harkins and Harry O. Maier.
Becker, Adam H. and Annette Yoshiko Reed (ed.). *The Ways That Never Parted: Jews and Christians in Late Antiquity and the Early Middle Ages*. Tübingen: Mohr Siebeck, 2003.
Benjamin, Walter. "Theses on the Philosophy of History." 253–64 in *Illuminations*. Edited by H. Arendt. Translated by H. Zohn. New York: Harcourt, Brace & World, 1968.
Bennett, Jane. *Vibrant Matter: A Political Ecology of Things*. Durham: Duke University Press, 2010.
Blidstein, Moshe. *Purity, Community, and Ritual in Early Christian Literature*. Oxford: Oxford University Press, 2017.
Bloch-Smith, Elizabeth. "Israelite Ethnicity in Iron I: Archaeology Preserves What Is Remembered and What Is Forgotten in Israel's History." *JBL* 122 (2003): 401–25.
Bonner, Campbell. "A New Fragment of the Shepherd of Hermas (Michigan Papyrus 44–H)." *HTR* 20 (1927): 105–16.
Bonner, Campbell. *A Papyrus Codex of the Shepherd of Hermas (Similitudes 2–9) with a Fragment of the Mandates*. University of Michigan Studies Humanistic Series 22. Ann Arbor: University of Michigan, 1934.
Borenstein, Elhanan and Eytan Ruppin. "The Evolution of Imitation and Mirror Neurons in Adaptive Agents." *Cognitive Systems Research* 6 (2005): 229–42.
Boyarin, Daniel. "Semantic Differences or 'Judaism'/ 'Christianity'." 65–85 in *The Ways that Never Parted: Jews and Christians in Late Antiquity and the Early Middle Ages*. Edited by Adam H. Becker and Annette Yoshiko Reed. Tübingen: Mohr Siebeck, 2003.
Boyarin, Daniel. *Border Lines: The Partition of Judaeo–Christianity*. Philadelphia: University of Pennsylvania Press, 2004.

—*Judaism: The Genealogy of a Modern Notion.* New Brunswick: Rutgers University Press, 2019.
Boyer, Pascal. *The Naturalness of Religious Ideas: A Cognitive Theory of Religion.* Berkeley: University of California Press, 1994.
—*Religion Explained: The Evolutionary Origins of Religious Thought.* New York: Basic Books, 2001.
—"What Are Memories For? Functions of Recall in Cognition and Culture." 3–28 in *Memory in Mind and Culture.* Edited by P. Boyer and J. V. Wertsch. Cambridge: Cambridge University Press, 2009.
Boyer, Pascal and Charles Ramble. "Cognitive Templates for Religious Concepts: Cross–Cultural Evidence for Recall of Counter–intuitive Representations." *Cognitive Science* 25 (2001): 535–64.
Bradley, Keith. *Slavery and Society at Rome.* Key Themes in Ancient History. Cambridge: Cambridge University Press, 1994.
Brooke, George. "The Qumran Scrolls and the Demise of the Distinction between Higher and Lower Criticism." 26–42 in *New Directions in Qumran Studies: Proceedings of the Bristol Colloquium on the Dead Sea Scrolls, 8–10 September 2003.* Edited by J. G. Campbell, W. J. Lyons, and L. K. Pietersen. London: T & T Clark International, 2005.
Brox, Norbert. *Der Hirt des Hermas.* Ergänzungsreihe zum Kritisch–exegetischen Kommentar über das Neue Testament Band 7. Göttingen: Vandenhoeck & Ruprecht, 1991.
Bucur, Bogdan G. "The Son of God and the Angelomorphic Holy Spirit: A Rereading of the Shepherd's Christology." *ZNW* 98 (2007): 120–42.
Burkitt, F. C. *Jewish and Christian Apocalypses.* London: Oxford University Press, 1914.
Burrus, Virginia. *"Begotten, not Made": Conceiving Manhood in Late Antiquity.* Stanford: Stanford University Press, 2000.
— *The Sex Lives of Saints: An Erotics of Ancient Hagiography.* Philadelphia: University of Pennsylvania Press, 2004.
Cairns, Douglas. "Mind, Body, and Metaphor in Ancient Greek Concepts of Emotion." *L'Atelier du Centre de recherches historiques* 16 (2016). https://journals.openedition.org/acrh/7416.
—"The Horror and the Pity: *Phrikê* as a Tragic Emotion." *Psychoanalytic Inquiry* 35 (2015): 75–94.
Caracciolo, Marco. "Fictional Consciousnesses: A Reader's Manual," *Style* 46 (2012): 42–65.
—"Narrative, Meaning, Interpretation: An Enactivist Approach." *Phenomenology and the Cognitive Sciences* 11 (2012): 367–84.
—*The Experientiality of Narrative: An Enactivist Approach.* Berlin: De Gruyter, 2014.
—"Ungrounding Fictional Worlds: An Enactivist Perspective on the 'Worldlikeness' of Fiction." 113–31 in *Possible Worlds Theory and Contemporary Narratology.* Edited by Alice Bell and Marie-Laure Ryan. Lincoln: University of Nebraska Press, 2019.
—*Slow Narrative and Nonhuman Materialities.* Lincoln: University of Nebraska Press, 2022.
Carlini, Antonio with the collaboration of Luigi Giacconi, *Papyrus Bodmer XXXVIII. Erma: Il Pastore (Ia–IIIa visione). Edito con introduzione e commentario critico. Appendice: Nouvelle description du Codex des Visions par Rodolphe Kasser, avec*

la collaboration de Guglielmo Cavallo et Joseph van Haelst. Fondation Martin Bodmer Cologny-Genève. Munich: Saur, 1991.
Carlini, Antonio, L. Giaccone, R. Kasser, G. Cavallo, and J. van Haelst, *Erma; edito con introduzione e commentario critic da Antonio Carlini*. Papyrus Bodmer 38. Cologny-Genève, 1991.
Carlini, Antonio. "I nuovi papyri di Ossirinco e il testo del Pastore di Erma." 207–16 in *Studi offerti ad Alessandro Perutelli*. Edited by P. Arduini. Rome: Aracne, 2008.
—"La tradizione testuale del Pastore di Erma e I nuovi papyri." 23–43 in *Le strade del testo*. Edited by. G. Cavallo. Lecce: Adriatica Editrice, 1987.
Castelli, Emanuele. "Gli esordi alternativi del *Pastore* di Erma." *Adamantius* 26 (2020): 551–75.
—"Dati storici e aspetti romanzeschi nelle prime due Visioni del *Pastore* di Erma. Una riconsiderazione del problema alla luce di nuove scoperte testuali." *Augustinianum* 60 (2020): 321–40.
—"Il I capitolo del *Pastore* di Erma alla luce delle recenti acquisizioni sul P. Bodmer XXXVIII e sulla *Vulgata*." *Vetera Christianorum* 57 (2020): 65–84.
Cecconi, Paolo. "The Codex Sinaiticus and Hermas: The Ways of a Crossed Textual Transmission." *ZAC* 22 (2018): 278–95.
—"1200 Years of Materialities and Editions of a Forbidden Text." 309–30 in *Antike Texte und ihre Materialität: Ancient Texts and Their Materiality: Presence, Media Semantics, and Literary Reflection in Daily Life. Alltägliche Präsenz mediale Semantik, literarische Reflexion*. Edited by Cornelia Ritter-Schmalz and Raphael Schwitter. Materiale Textkulturen 27. Berlin: De Gruyter, 2019.
Cerquiglini, Bernard. *Éloge de la variante: Histoire critique de la philologie*. Paris: Seuil, 1989.
Chaniotis, Angelos. "The Life of Statues: Emotion and Agency." 143–58 in *Emotions in the Classical World: Methods, Approaches, and Directions*. Edited by Douglas Cairns and Damien Nelis. Stuttgart: Franz Steiner Verlag, 2017.
Chechi, Alessandro. "The Return of Cultural Objects Removed in Times of Colonial Domination and International Law: The Case of the Venus of Cyrene." *Italian Yearbook of International Law* 18 (2008): 159–81.
Choat, Malcolm and Rachel Yuen-Collingridge. "The Egyptian *Hermas*: The *Shepherd* in Egypt before Constantine." 191–212 in *Early Christian Manuscripts: Examples of Applied Method and Approach*. Edited by Thomas J. Kraus and Tobias Nicklas. Texts and Editions for New Testament Study 5. Leiden: Brill, 2010.
Choi, Jung. "A True Prophet as a Mouthpiece of the Spirit? Cultivating Virtue and Control." 31–56 in *Experiencing the Shepherd of Hermas*. Edited by Angela Kim Harkins and Harry O. Maier. Ekstasis 10.
Clements, Niki Kasumi (ed.). *Religion: Mental Religion*. Macmillan Interdisciplinary Handbooks. Farmington Hills, MI: Macmillan Reference USA, 2016.
Coleborne, W. "The Shepherd of Hermas: A Case for Multiple Authorship and Some Implications." *StPatr* 10 (1970): 65–70.
Coleman III, Thomas J., James E. Bartlett, Jenny M. Holcombe, Andrew Atkinson, Sally B. Swanson, Christopher F. Silver, Ralph W. Hood. "Absorption, Mentalizing, and Mysticism: Sensing the Presence of the Divine." *Journal for the Cognitive Science of Religion* (2019): 63–84.
Coleridge, Samuel Taylor. *Biographia Literaria*. London: J. M. Dent, 1975.
Collins, John J. *The Apocalyptic Vision of the Book of Daniel*. Missoula: Scholars Press, 1977.

—"Apocalypse: The Morphology of a Genre." *Semeia* 14 (1979): 1–59.
—*Apocalypse, Prophecy, and Pseudepigraphy: On Jewish Apocalyptic Literature*. Grand Rapids: Eerdmans, 2015.
Corso, A. "Ancient Greek Sculptors as Magicians." *Quaderni Ticinesi. Numismatica e Antichità Classiche* 28 (1999): 97–111.
Cowley, A.E. "Notes on Hebrew Papyrus Fragments from Oxyrhynchus." *Journal of Egyptian Archaeology* 2 (1915): 209–13.
Craig, A. D. "How Do You Feel? Interoception: The Sense of the Physiological Condition of the Body." *Nature Reviews Neuroscience* 3 (2002): 655–66.
Crislip, Andrew. "*The Shepherd of Hermas* and Early Christian Emotional Formation." *StPatr* 83 (2017): 231–50.
Czachesz, István. *Cognitive Science & the New Testament: A New Approach to Early Christian Research*. Oxford: Oxford University Press, 2017.
D'Angelo, Mary Rose. " 'Knowing How to Preside over His Own Household': Imperial Masculinity and Christian Asceticism in the Pastorals, *Hermas*, and Luke-Acts." 265–95 in *New Testament Masculinities*. Edited by Stephen D. Moore and Janice Capel Anderson. Atlanta: SBL Press, 2003.
Davidsen, Markus Altena Davidsen. "Fiction-based Religion: Conceptualising a New Category against History-Based Religion and Fandom." *Culture and Religion: An Interdisciplinary Journal* 14 (2013): 378–95.
Davidsen, Markus Altena and Bastiaan van Rijn. "Studying Religions as Narrative Cultures: Angel Experience Narratives in the Netherlands and Some Ideas for a Narrative Research Program for the Study of Religion." 91–122 in *Narrative Cultures and the Aesthetics of Religion*. Edited by Dirk Johannsen, Anja Kirsch, and Jens Kreinath. Leiden: Brill, 2020.
Degelmann, Christopher. "Symbolic Mourning." 447–67 in *Lived Religion in the Ancient Mediterranean World: Approaching Religious Transformations from Archaeology, History and Classics*. Edited by Valentino Gasparini, Maik Patzelt, Rubina Raja, Anna-Katharina Rieger, Jörg Rüpke, Emiliano Urciuoli. Berlin: De Gruyter, 2020.
Dever, William G. *Who Were the Early Israelites and Where Did They Come From?* Grand Rapids: Eerdmans, 2003.
Dibelius, Martin. *Der Hirt des Hermas*. Die Apostolischen Väter 4. Tübingen: Mohr Siebeck, 1923.
DiBattista, Maria and Emily O. Wittman. "Introduction." 1–20 in *The Cambridge Companion to Autobiography*. Cambridge: Cambridge University Press, 2014.
Denzey Lewis, Nicola. "Review of Kathleen E. Corley, *Maranatha: Women's Funerary Rituals and Christian Origins*. Minneapolis: Fortress, 2010." *CBQ* 74 (2012): 594–96.
Depauw, M. and T. Gheldof. "Trismegistos. An Interdisciplinary Platform for Ancient World Texts and Related Information." 40–52 in *Theory and Practice of Digital Libraries—TPDL 2013 Selected Workshops*. Edited by L Bolikowski, V. Casarosa, P. Goodale, N. Houssos, P. Manghi, J. Schirrwagen. Communications in Computer and Information Science 416. Cham: Springer, 2014.
Desjarlais, Robert and C. Jason Throop. "Phenomenological Approaches in Anthropology." *Annual Review of Anthropology* 40 (2011): 87–102.
Dessel, J. P. "Looking for the Israelites: The Archaeology of Iron Age I." 275–98 in *The Old Testament in Archaeology and History*. Edited by Jennie Ebeling, J. Edward Wright, Mark Elliott, and Paul V. M. Flesher. Waco: Baylor University Press, 2017.

DiTommaso, Lorenzo. *The Book of Daniel and the Apocryphal Daniel Literature*. Leiden: Brill, 2005.
Doka, Kenneth J. "Disenfranchised Grief in Historical and Cultural Perspective." 223–40 in *Handbook of Bereavement Research and Practice: Advances in Theory and Intervention*. Edited by Margaret S. Stroebe et al. Washington DC: American Psychological Association, 2008.
Dunbabin, Katherine M. D. "Baiarum Grata Voluptas: Pleasures and Dangers of the Baths." *Papers of the British School at Rome* 57 (1989): 6–46.
Easterlin, Nancy. " 'Loving Ourselves Best of All': Ecocriticism and the Adapted Mind," *Mosaic: An Interdisciplinary Critical Journal* 37 (2004): 1–18.
—"Cognitive Ecocriticism: Human Wayfinding, Sociality, and Literary Interpretation." 257–74 in *Introduction to Cognitive Cultural Studies*. Edited by Lisa Zunshine. Baltimore: Johns Hopkins University Press, 2010.
—*A Biocultural Approach to Literary Theory and Interpretation*. Baltimore: Johns Hopkins University Press, 2012.
Ehrman, Bart D. *The Apostolic Fathers 2: Epistle of Barnabas, Papias and Quadratus, Epistle to Diognetus, The Shepherd of Hermas*. LCL 25. Cambridge: Harvard University Press, 2003.
Eidinow, Esther. "Networks and Narratives: A Model for Ancient Greek Religion." *Krenos* 24 (2011): 9–38.
—"Oracular Consultation, Fate, and the Concept of the Individual." 21–39 in *Divination in the Ancient World: Religious Options and the Individual*. Edited by Veit Rosenberger. Potsdamer altertumswissenschaftliche Beiträge 46. Stuttgart: Franz Steiner Verlag, 2013.
Elfenbein, Andrew. *The Gist of Reading*. Stanford: Stanford University Press, 2018.
Emmott, Catherine. *Narrative Comprehension: A Discourse Perspective*. Oxford: Clarendon Press, 1997.
Epp, Eldon Jay. "The Oxyrhynchus New Testament Papyri: 'Not Without Honor Except in their Hometown'?" *JBL* 123 (2004): 5–55.
—"The Jews and the Jewish Community in Oxyrhynchus: Socio-Religious Context for the New Testament Papyri." 13–52 in *New Testament Manuscripts: Their Texts and Their World*. Edited by T. J. Kraus and T. Nicklas. Leiden: Brill, 2006.
Esrock, Ellen J. *The Reader's Eye: Visual Imaging as Reader Response*. Baltimore: Johns Hopkins University, 1994.
Faust, Avraham and Susan Niditch. "The Emergence of Israel and Theories of Ethnogenesis." 152–73 in *The Wiley Blackwell Companion to Ancient Israel*. Edited by Susan Niditch. Malden: John Wiley & Sons, Ltd., 2016.
Feldt, Laura. "Religious Narrative and the Literary Fantastic: Ambiguity and Uncertainty in Ex. 1–18." *Religion* 41 (2011): 251–83.
Ferguson, Everett. "Canon Muratori: Date and Provenance." *StPatr* 17 (1982): 677–83.
Finkelstein, Israel and Neil Asher Silberman. *The Bible Unearthed: Archaeology's New Vision of Ancient Israel and the Origin of Its Sacred Texts*. New York: Simon and Schuster, 2002.
Flint, Peter W. "The Daniel Tradition at Qumran." 329–67 in *The Book of Daniel: Composition and Reception. Volume 2*. Edited by John J. Collins and Peter W. Flint. Leiden: Brill, 2001.
Francis, James A. "Metal Maidens, Achilles' Shield, and Pandora: The Beginnings of 'Ekphrasis'." *American Journal of Philology* 130 (2009): 1–23.

Freud, Sigmund. "Mourning and Melancholia." 237–59 in *The Standard Edition of the Complete Psychological Works of Sigmund Freud*. Vol. 14. Edited and translated by James Strachey. London: Hogarth Press, 1957, repr. 1917.

Fuchs, Thomas. "Presence in Absence. The Ambiguous Phenomenology of Grief." *Phenomenology and the Cognitive Sciences* 17 (2018): 43–63.

Gallagher, Edmon L. "Origen on the Shepherd of Hermas." *Early Christianity* 10 (2019): 201–15.

Gallese, Vittorio. "Mirroring, a Liberated Embodied Simulation and Aesthetic Experience." 27–37 in *Mirror Images: Reflections in Art and Medicine*. Edited by Helen Hirsch and Alessandra Pace. Vienna: Verlag für moderne Kunst, 2017.

Gamble, Harry Y. *Books and Readers in the Early Church: A History of Early Christian Texts*. New Haven: Yale University, 1995.

Gardner, Ernest A. "The Aphrodite from Cyrene." *The Journal of Hellenic Studies* 40 (1920): 203–205.

Garnsey, P. *Ideas of Slavery from Aristotle to Augustine*. Cambridge: Cambridge University Press, 1996.

Geertz, Armin. "Global Perspectives on Methodology in the Study of Religion." *MTSR* 12 (2000): 49–73.

—"Comparing Prayer: On Science, Universals, and the Human Condition." 113–39 in *Introducing Religion: Essays in Honor of Jonathan Z. Smith*. Edited by Willi Braun and Russell T. McCutcheon. London: Equinox, 2008.

—"Brain, Body and Culture: A Biocultural Theory of Religion." *MTSR* 22 (2010): 304–21.

—"Religious Bodies, Minds and Places. A Cognitive Science of Religion Perspective." 35–52 in *Spazi e Luoghi Sacri: Espressioni ed Esperienze di Vissuto Religioso*. Edited by Laura Carnevale. Santo Spirito [Bari]: Edipuglia, 2017.

Geertz, Armin, Leonardo Ambasciano, Esther Eidinow, Luther H. Martin, Kristoffer L. Nielbo, Nickolas P. Roubekas, Valerie van Mulukom, Dimitris Xygalatas (eds.). *Studying the Religious Mind: Methodology in the Cognitive Science of Religion*. Sheffield: Equinox Press, 2022.

Gerrig, Richard J. *Experiencing Narrative Worlds: On the Psychological Activities of Reading*. New Haven: Yale University Press, 1993.

Giet, Stanislas. *Hermas et les pasteurs. Les trois auteurs du Pasteur d'Hermas*. Paris: Presses universitaires de France, 1963.

Gillmayr-Bucher, Susanne. "Body Images in the Psalms." *JSOT* 28 (2004): 301–26.

Glancy, Jennifer. "Slaves and Slavery in the Matthean Parables." *JBL* 119 (2000): 67–90.

—"The Sexual Use of Slaves: A Response to Kyle Harper on Jewish and Christian *Porneia*." *JBL* 134 (2015): 215–29.

Gleason, Maud W. "The Semiotics of Gender: Physiognomy and Self–Fashioning in the Second Century CE." 389–415 in *Before Sexuality: The Construction of Erotic Experience in the Ancient Greek World*. Edited by David M. Halperin; John J. Winkler and Froma I. Zeitlin. Princeton: Princeton University Press, 1990.

Go, Julian. "For a Postcolonial Sociology." *Theory and Society* 42 (2013): 25–55.

—*Postcolonial Thought and Social Theory*. Oxford University Press, 2016.

Goodkin, K. et al. "Physiological Effects of Bereavement and Bereavement Support Group Interventions." 671–703 in *Handbook of Bereavement Research*. Edited by M. S. Stroebe et al. Washington, D.C.: American Psychological Association, 2001.

Gregg, Melissa and Gregory J. Seigworth (eds.). *The Affect Theory Reader*. Durham, NC: Duke University Press, 2010.

Gregory, A. "Disturbing Trajectories: *1 Clement*, the *Shepherd of Hermas* and the Development of Early Roman Christianity." 142–66 in *Rome in the Bible and the Early Church*. Edited by Peter Oakes. Grand Rapids: Baker Academic, 2002.

Grethlein, Jonas and Luuk Huitink. "Homer's Vividness: An Enactive Approach." *Journal of Hellenic Studies* 137 (2017): 67–91.

Grundeken, Mark R. C. "The Shepherd of Hermas and the Roman Empire." 187–204 in *People Under Power: Early Jewish and Christian Responses to the Roman Empire*. Edited by Michael Labahn and Outi Lehtipuu. Amsterdam: Amsterdam University Press, 2018.

Grundeken, Mark R. C. and Joseph Verheyden. "The Spirit Before the Letter: Dreams and Visions as the Legitimization of the *Shepherd of Hermas*: A Study of Vision 5." 23–56 in *Dreams as Divine Communication in Christianity: From Hermas to Aquinas*. Edited by Bart J. Koet. Studies in the History and Anthropology of Religion 3. Leuven: Peeters, 2012.

Gusdorf, Georges. "Conditions et limites de l'autobiographie." 105–24 in *Formen der Selbstdarstellung: Analekten zu einer Geschichte des literarischen Selbstportraits*. Edited by Gunther Reichenkron and Erich Hasse. Berlin: Duncker & Humblot, 1956.

—"Conditions and Limits of Autobiography." 28–48 in *Autobiography: Essays Theoretical and Critical*. Translated by James Olney. Princeton: Princeton University Press, 1980.

Hagman, George. "Beyond Decathexis: Toward a New Psychoanalytic Understanding and Treatment of Mourning." 13–31 in *Meaning Reconstruction & the Experience of Loss*. Edited by Robert A. Neimeyer. Washington, D.C.: American Psychological Association, 2000.

Hahneman, Godffrey M. *The Muratorian Fragment and the Development of the Canon*. New York: Oxford University Press, 1992.

Haines-Eitzen, Kim. *The Gendered Palimpsest: Women, Writing, and Representation in Early Christianity*. Oxford: Oxford University Press, 2012.

Haran, Menahem. "Book-Scrolls at the Beginning of the Second Temple Period: The Transition from Papyrus to Skins." *HUCA* 54 (1983): 111–22.

—"The Size of Books in the Bible and the Division of the Pentateuch and the Deuteronomistic Work." *Tarbiz* 53 (1984): 329–52.

Harkins, Angela Kim. *Reading with an "I" to the Heavens: Looking at the Qumran Hodayot through the Lens of Visionary Traditions*. Ekstasis 3. Berlin: De Gruyter, 2012.

—"Who is the Teacher of the Teacher Hymns? Re-examining the Teacher Hymns Hypothesis Fifty Years Later." 449–67 in *A Teacher for All Generations: Essays in Honor of James C. VanderKam,* Vol. 1. Edited by Eric F. Mason et al. Leiden: Brill, 2012.

—"The Emotional Re-Experiencing of the Hortatory Narratives Found in the Admonition of the Damascus Document." *DSD* 22 (2015): 285–307.

—"Ritual Mourning in Daniel's Interpretation of Jeremiah's Prophecy." *The Journal of Cognitive Historiography* 2.1 (2015): 14–33.

—"The Pro-Social Role of Grief in Ezra's Penitential Prayer." *BibInt* 24 (2016): 466–91.

—"The Garden Space in Odes of Solomon 11 and the Reinvigoration of Memories about Paradise." 1–33 in *Biblical & Qur'ānic Traditions in the Middle East*. Edited by Horn, Cornelia and Sidney Griffith. Eastern Mediterranean Texts and Contexts

Series 2. Warwick, R.I.: Abelian Academic Press, 2016, revised and reprinted as 219–44 in *Experiencing Presence in the Second Temple Period: Revised and Updated Essays*. CBET 111. Leuven: Peeters, 2022.

—"The Function of Prayers of Ritual Mourning in the Second Temple Period." 80–101 in *Functions of Psalms and Prayers in the Late Second Temple Period. Conference Proceedings for the Copenhagen Meeting*. Edited by Mika S. Pajunen and Jeremy Penner. BZAW 486. Berlin: De Gruyter, 2017.

—"Another Look at the Cave 1 Hodayot: Was CH I Materially Part of the Scroll 1QHodayot^a?" *DSD* 25 (2018): 185–216.

—"Experiencing the Solidity of Spaces in the Qumran Hodayot." 353–71 in *The Dead Sea Scrolls, Revise and Repeat: New Methods and Perspectives on the Dead Sea Scrolls*. Edited by Andrew Krause, Carmen Palmer, Eileen M. Schuller, and John Screnock. Atlanta: SBL Press, 2020.

—*Experiencing Presence in the Second Temple Period: Revised and Updated Essays*. CBET 111. Leuven: Peeters, 2022.

—"Entering the Narrative World of Hermas's Visions." 117–36 in *Experiencing the Shepherd of Hermas*. Edited by Angela Kim Harkins and Harry O. Maier. Berlin: De Gruyter, 2022.

—"Sticky Emotions from Second Temple Prayers: A Study of Paul's Grief in 2 Corinthians." 159–83 in *Experiencing Presence in the Second Temple Period: Revised and Updated Essays*.

Harkins, Angela Kim, Kelley Coblentz Bautch, and John C. Endres, S.J. (eds.). *The Watchers in Jewish and Christian Tradition*. Minneapolis: Fortress Press, 2014.

Harkins, Angela Kim, Kelley Coblentz Bautch, and John C. Endres, S.J. (eds). *The Fallen Angels Traditions: Second Temple Developments and Reception History*. Catholic Biblical Quarterly Monograph Series 53. Washington, DC: The Catholic Biblical Association, 2014.

Harkins, Angela Kim and Harry O. Maier (eds). *Experiencing the Shepherd of Hermas*. Ekstasis 10. Berlin: De Gruyter, 2022.

Harkins, Franklin T. "Nuancing Augustine's Hermeneutical Jew: Allegory and Actual Jews in the Bishop's Sermons." *JSJ* 36 (2005): 41–64.

Harper, K. *Slavery in the Late Roman World AD 275–425*. Cambridge: Cambridge University Press, 2011.

—"*Porneia*: The Making of a Christian Sexual Norm." *JBL* 131 (2012): 363–83.

—*From Shame to Sin: The Christian Transformation of Sexual Morality in Late Antiquity*. Cambridge: Harvard University Press, 2013.

Harrill, J. Albert. *Slaves in the New Testament: Literary, Social, and Moral Dimensions*. Minneapolis: Fortress Press, 2006.

Harris, J. Rendel. "On the Angelology of Hermas." 21–25 in *Hermas in Arcadia, and Other Essays*. Cambridge: The University Press, 1896.

Havelock, Christine Mitchell. *The Aphrodite of Knidos and Her Successors: A Historical Review of the Female Nude in Greek Art*. Ann Arbor: University of Michigan Press, 1995.

Heath, Jane M. F. "Ezekiel Tragicus and Hellenistic Visuality: The Phoenix at Elim." *JTS* (n.s.) 57 (2006): 23–41.

—"Absent Presences of Paul and Christ: *Enargeia* in 1 Thessalonians 1–3." *JSNT* 32 (2009): 3–38.

—*Paul's Visual Piety: The Metamorphosis of the Beholder*. Oxford: Oxford University Press, 2013.

Heaton, Robert D. *The Shepherd of Hermas as Scriptura Non Grata: From Popularity in early Christianity to Exclusion from the New Testament Canon.* Lanham: Lexington Books, 2023.

Hedstrom, Darlene L. Brooks. *The Monastic Landscape of Late Antique Egypt: An Archaeological Reconstruction.* Cambridge: Cambridge University Press, 2017.

Heffernan, Thomas J. *The Passion of Perpetua and Felicity.* Oxford: Oxford University Press, 2011.

Heide, Martin K. "Assessing the Stability of the Transmitted Texts of the New Testament and the *Shepherd of Hermas.*" 125–208 in *The Reliability of the New Testament: Bart D. Ehrman & Daniel B. Wallace in Dialogue.* Edited by R. B. Stewart. Minneapolis: Fortress Press, 2011.

Hellholm, David. *Das Visionenbuch des Hermas als Apokalypse: Formgeschichtliche und texttheoretische Studien zu einer literarischen Gattung. Vol. 1: Methodologische Vorüberlegungen und makrostruckturelle Textanalyse.* ConBNT 13.1. Lund: C.W.K. Gleerup, 1980.

Henkel, Linda A., N. Franklin, and M. K. Johnson. "Cross-modal Confusions between Perceived and Imagined Events." *Journal of Experimental Psychology: Learning, Memory, & Cognition* 26 (2000): 321–35.

Henning, Meghan. *Educating Early Christians through the Rhetoric of Hell.* WUNT 382. Tübingen: Mohr Siebeck, 2014.

Henne, Philippe, O.P. *L'unité du Pasteur d'Hermas.* Cahiers de la Revue Biblique. Paris: Gabalda, 1992.

Henrich, Joseph. *The WEIRDest People in the World: How the West Became Psychologically Peculiar and Particularly Prosperous.* New York: Farrar, Straus and Giroux, 2020.

Heine, Steven J. and Ara Norenzayan. "The Weirdest People in the World?" *Behavioral and Brain Sciences* (2010): 1–75.

Hersey, G. L. *Falling in Love with Statues: Artificial Humans from Pygmalion to the Present.* Chicago: University of Chicago Press, 2009.

Hezser, Catherine. *Jewish Slavery in Antiquity.* New York: Oxford University Press, 2005.

Hilhorst, Anton. "Hermas." *RAC* 14 (1988): 682–701.

Hilhorst, Antonius. "Erotic Elements in the Shepherd of Hermas." 193–204 in *Groningen Colloquia on the Novel IX.* Edited by H. Hofmann and M. Zimmerman. Groningen: Egbert Forsten, 1998.

Hogan, Patrick Colm. *What Literature Teaches Us about Emotion.* Cambridge: Cambridge University Press, 2011.

Holmes, Michael W. *The Apostolic Fathers: Greek Texts and English Translations,* 3rd ed. Grand Rapids: Baker Academic, 2007.

Hsu, Chun-Ting et al. "Fiction Feelings in Harry Potter: Haemodynamic Response in the Mid-Cingulate Cortex Correlates with Immersive Reading Experience." *Neuroreport* 25 (2014): 1356–61.

Hurst, André and Jean Rudhardt. *Papyri Bodmer XXX–XXXVII. "Codex des Visions" Poèmes divers. Edités avec une introduction générale des traductions et des notes.* Munich: Saur, 1999.

Hutto, Daniel D., Michael D. Kirchhoff, and Erik Myin, "Extensive Enactivism: Why keep it all in?" *Frontiers in Human Neuroscience* 8 (2014): 1–11.

Idel, Moshe. "Mystical Techniques." 438–94 in *Essential Papers on Kabbalah.* Edited by Lawrence Fine. New York: New York University Press, 1995.

Jeremias, Gert. *Der Lehrer der Gerechtigkeit*. SUNT 2. Göttingen: Vandenhoeck & Ruprecht, 1963.

Johnson, Paul Christopher. "An Atlantic Genealogy of 'Spirit Possession'." *Comparative Studies in Society and History* 53 (2011): 393–425.

—"Introduction: Spirits and Things in the Making of the Afro-Atlantic World." 1–20 in *Spirited Things: The Work of "Possession" in the Afro-Atlantic World*. Chicago: University of Chicago, 2014.

Johnston, Sarah Iles. "Narrating Myths: Story and Belief in Ancient Greece," *Arethusa* 48 (2015): 173-218.

—"How Myths and Other Stories Help to Create and Sustain Beliefs." 141–56 in *Narrating Religion*. Macmillan Interdisciplinary Handbooks. Farmington Hills, MI: Macmillan, Reference USA, 2017.

—*The Story of Myth*. Cambridge: Harvard University Press, 2018.

Johnson, William A. *Readers and Reading Culture in the High Roman Empire: A Study of Elite Communities*. Oxford: Oxford University Press, 2010.

Joly, R. *Hermas. Le Pasteur.* SC 53. Paris: Cerf, 1958, 1968, 2011.

Kandel, Eric R. *In Search of Memory: The Emergence of a New Science of Mind*. New York: Norton, 2006.

Kaplan, Stephen. "Environmental Preference in a Knowledge–Seeking, Knowledge-Using Organism." 581–98 in *The Adapted Mind: Evolutionary Psychology and the Generation of Culture*. Edited by Jerome Barkow, Leda Cosmides, and John Tooby. New York: Oxford University Press, 1992.

Kartzow, Marianne Bjelland. *The Slave Metaphor and Gendered Enslavement in Early Christian Discourse: Double Trouble Embodied*. Routledge Studies in the Early Christian World. New York: Routledge, 2018.

Kasher, Aryeh. "The Jewish Community of Oxyrhynchus in the Roman Period." *JJS* 32 (1981): 151–57.

Kaster, Robert A. *Emotion, Restraint, and Community in Ancient Rome*. Oxford: Oxford University Press, 2005.

Kee (trans.). "The Testament of Reuben." *OTP* 1: 783.

Kennedy, George A. (trans. and ed.). *Progymnasmata: Greek Textbooks of Prose Composition and Rhetoric*. Atlanta: SBL Press, 2003.

King, Daniel. "Galen and Grief: The Construction of Grief in Galen's Clinical Work." 251–72 in *Unveiling Emotions, Vol. II*. Edited by Angelos Chaniotis. Stuttgart: Franz Steiner Verlag, 2012.

Klass, Dennis and Edith Maria Steffen. "Introduction: Continuing Bonds—20 Years On." 1–14 in *Continuing Bonds in Bereavement: New Directions for Research and Practice*. Edited by D. Klass and E. M. Steffen. New York: Routledge, 2018.

Kleege, Georgina. *Sight Unseen*. New Haven: Yale University Press, 1999.

Konstan, David. *The Emotions of the Ancient Greeks: Studies in Aristotle and Classical Literature*. University of Toronto Press, 2001.

Körtner, Ulrich H. J. and Martin Leutzsch (eds.). *Papiasfragmente: Hirt des Hermas*. Schriften des Urchristentums 3. Darmstadt: Wissenschaftliche Buchgesellschaft, 1998.

Kosmin, Paul. *Time and its Adversaries in the Seleucid Empire*. Cambridge: Belknap Press, 2018.

Kratz, Reinhard. "The Visions of Daniel." 91–113 in *The Book of Daniel: Composition and Reception. Volume 1*. Edited by John J. Collins and Peter W. Flint. Leiden: Brill, 2001.

Kugel, James. "Reuben's Sin with Bilhah in the Testament of Reuben." 525–54 in *Pomegranates and Golden Bells: Studies in Biblical, Jewish, and Near Eastern Ritual Law, and Literature in Honor of Jacob Milgrom.* Edited by D. P. Wright et al. Winona Lake: Eisenbrauns, 1995.
—*The God of Old: Inside the Lost World of the Bible.* New York: The Free Press, 2003.
Kukkonen, Karin and Marco Caracciolo. "What is the 'Second Generation?'" *Style* 48 (2014): 261–74.
Kuzmičová, Anežka. "Presence in the Reading of Literary Narrative: A Case for Motor Enactment." *Semiotica* 189 (2012): 23–48.
—"Literary Narrative and Mental Imagery: A View from Embodied Cognition." *Style* 48 (2014): 275–93.
—"Mental Imagery: A View from Embodied Cognition." *Style* 48 (2014): 275–93.
—"Does It Matter Where You Read?" *Communication Theory* 26 (2016): 290–308.
Lachmann, Renata. *Erzählte Phantastik. Zu Phantasiegeschichte und Semantik phantastischer Texte.* Frankfurt am Main: Suhrkamp, 2002.
Lai, Barbara M. Leung. *Through the 'I'-Window: The Inner Life of Characters in the Hebrew Bible.* Sheffield: Phoenix Press, 2011.
Lake, Kirsopp. "The Shepherd of Hermas and Christian Life in Rome in the Second Century." *HTR* 4 (1911): 25–46.
Latour, Bruno. *We Have Never Been Modern.* Translated by Catherine Porter. Cambridge: Harvard University Press, 1993.
—*Reassembling the Social: An Introduction to Actor-Network-Theory.* Oxford: Oxford University Press, 2005.
Lawrence, Louise J. *Sense and Stigma in the Gospels: Depictions of Sensory-Disabled Characters.* Oxford: Oxford University Press, 2013.
LeDoux, Joseph. *Synaptic Self: How Our Brains Become Who We Are.* New York: Penguin, 2002.
Leinhardt, Godfrey. *Divinity and Experience: The Religion of the Dinka.* Oxford: Clarendon Press, 1961.
Lejeune, Philippe. "The Autobiographical Pact." 3–30 in *On Autobiography.* Translated by Katherine Leary. Minneapolis: University of Minnesota Press, 1989.
Leutzsch, Martin. *Die Wahrnehmung sozialer Wirklichkeit im "Hirten des Hermas".* Göttingen: Vandenhoeck & Ruprecht, 1989.
Lindemann, Erich. "Symptomatology and Management of Acute Grief." 59–77 in *Beyond Grief: Studies in Crisis Intervention.* Edited by Erich Lindemann and Elizabeth Lindemann. New York: Aronson, 1979.
Lipinski, E. *La liturgie penitentielle dans la bible.* Paris: Cerf, 1969.
Lipsett, B. Diane. *Desiring Conversion: Hermas, Thecla, Aseneth.* New York: Oxford University Press, 2011.
—"Gender, Volubility, and Transformation in the Shepherd of Hermas." 57–72 in *Experiencing the Shepherd of Hermas.* Edited by Angela Kim Harkins and Harry O. Maier.
Lookadoo, Jonathan. *The Shepherd of Hermas: A Literary, Historical, and Theological Handbook.* London: T & T Clark, 2021.
Love, Glen A. "Ecocriticism and Science: Toward Consilience?" *Ecocriticism.* Edited by Ralph Cohen. *New Literary History* 30 (1999): 661–76.
Lührmann, Dieter. *Die Apokryph gewordenen Evangelien: Studien zu neuen Texten und zu neuen Fragen.* NovTSup 112. Leiden: Brill, 2004.

Luhrmann, Tanya M. *Persuasions of the Witch's Craft*. Oxford: Basil Blackwell Ltd., 1989.
—*When God Talks Back: Understanding the American Evangelical Relationship with God*. New York: Knopf, 2012.
—*How God Becomes Real: Kindling the Presence of Invisible Others*. Princeton: Princeton University Press, 2020.
Luijendijk, AnneMarie. "Sacred Scriptures as Trash: Biblical Papyri from Oxyrhynchus." *Vigiliae Christianae* 64 (2010): 217–43.
Luijendijk, AnneMarie. "Reading the *Gospel of Thomas* in the Third Century: Three Oxyrhynchus Papyri and Origen's Homilies." 241–67 in *Reading New Testament Papyri in Context/ Lire les papyrus du Nouveau Testament dans leur context*. Edited by Claire Clivaz and Jean Zumstein, in collaboration with Jenny Read-Heimerdinger and Julie Paik. BETL 242. Leuven: Peeters, 2011.
Lujan, Heidi L. and Stephen E. DiCarlo. "Humor Promotes Learning!" *Advances in Physiology Education* 40 (2016): 433–34.
Mahmood, Saba. "Feminist Theory, Embodiment, and the Docile Agent: Some Reflections on the Egyptian Islamic Revival." *Cultural Anthropology* 16 (2001): 202–36.
—*The Politics of Piety: The Islamic Revival and the Feminist Subject*. Princeton: Princeton University Press, 2005, 2011.
Mahoney, Dennis F., ed. *The Literature of German Romanticism*. Rochester, NY: Camden House, 2004.
Maier, Harry O. *The Social Setting of the Ministry as Reflected in the Writings of Hermas, Clement and Ignatius*. Waterloo: Wilfrid Laurier University Press, 1991.
—*Apocalypse Recalled: The Book of Revelation after Christendom*. Minneapolis: Fortress Press, 2002.
—"From Material Place to Imagined Space: Emergent Christian Community as Thirdspace in the Shepherd of Hermas." 143–60 in *Early Christian Communities between Ideal and Reality*. Edited by Mark Grundeken and Joseph Verheyden. Tübingen: Mohr Siebeck, 2015.
—"Vision, Visualisation, and Politics in the Apostle Paul." *MTSR* 27 (2015): 312–32.
—"Making History with the Shepherd of Hermas." *Early Christianity* 10 (2019): 501–20.
—"The Affect and Happy Objects of the Shepherd of Hermas." 73–97 in *Experiencing the Shepherd of Hermas*. Edited by Angela Kim Harkins and Harry O. Maier.
Marchal, Joseph A. "The Usefulness of an Onesimus: The Sexual Use of Slaves and Paul's Letter." *JBL* (2011): 749–70.
Martin, Dale B. *Slavery as Salvation: The Metaphor of Slavery in Pauline Christianity*. New Haven: Yale University Press, 1990.
Martin, Dale B. *Inventing Superstition: From the Hippocratics to the Christians*. Cambridge: Harvard University Press, 2004.
Martin, Leonard L. and Abraham Tesser, "Some Ruminative Thoughts." 1–47 in *Advances in Social Cognition*. Edited by R. S. Wyer, Jr. Ruminative Thoughts 9. Mahwah: Lawrence Erlbaum Associates, Inc., 1996.
—"Clarifying Our Thoughts." 189–208 in *Advances in Social Cognition*. Edited by R. S. Wyer, Jr.
Martin, Luther H. "Do Rituals Do? And How Do They Do It? Cognition and the Study of Ritual." 311–25 in *Introducing Religion: Essays in Honor of Jonathan Z. Smith*. Edited by W. Bruan and R. T. McCutcheon. London: Equinox, 2008.

Martin, Michael Wade and Mikeal C. Parsons. *Ancient Rhetoric and the New Testament: The Influence of Elementary Greek Composition.* Baylor University Press, 2018.

Mason, Steve. "Jews, Judeans, Judaizing, Judaism. Problems of Categorization in Ancient History." *JSJ* 38 (2007): 457–512.

McDaniel, Mark A. and Gilles O. Einstein. "Bizarre Imagery as an Effective Memory Aid: The Importance of Distinctiveness." *Journal of Experimental Psychology: Learning, Memory, and Cognition* 12 (1986): 54–65.

McGrath, James. F. *The Only True God: Early Christian Monotheism in its Jewish Context.* Chicago: University of Illinois Press, 2009.

McNamara, Patrick. *The Neuroscience of Religious Experience.* Cambridge: Cambridge University Press, 2009.

Merkur, Daniel. "The Visionary Practices of Jewish Apocalyptists." *The Psychoanalytical Study of Society* 14 (1989): 119–48.

Mermelstein, Ari. "Constructing Fear and Pride in the Book of Daniel: The Profile of a Second Temple Emotional Community." *JSJ* 46 (2015): 449–83.

—*Power and Emotion in Ancient Judaism: Community and Identity in Formation.* Cambridge: Cambridge University Press, 2021.

Miall, David S. "Emotions and the Structuring of Narrative Responses." *Poetics Today* 32 (2011): 323–48.

Miall, David S. and Don Kuiken. "Foregrounding, Defamiliarization, and Affect: Response to Literary Stories." *Poetics* 22 (1994): 389–407.

Mitchell, Karen J. and Marcia K. Johnson. "Source Monitoring 15 Years Later: What Have We Learned from fMRI about the Neural Mechanisms of Source Memory." *Psychological Bulletin* 135 (2009): 638–77.

Mithen, Steven. "The Evolution of Imagination: An Archaeological Perspective." *SubStance* 30 (2001): 28–54.

Mittermaier, Amira. "Dreams from Elsewhere: Muslim Subjectivities Beyond the Trope of Self-Cultivation." *Journal of the Royal Anthropological Institute* (n.s.) 18 (2012): 247–65.

—*Dreams that Matter: Egyptian Landscapes of the Imagination.* Berkeley: University of California Press, 2011.

Mouritsen, Henrik. "The Families of Roman Slaves and Freedmen." 129–44 in *A Companion to Families in the Greek and Roman Worlds.* Edited by Beryl Rawson. Oxford: Blackwell, 2011.

Münz-Manor, Ophir. "Narrating Salvation: Verbal Sacrifices in Late Antique Liturgical Poetry." 154–66 in *Jews, Christians, and the Roman Empire: The Poetics of Power in Late Antiquity.* Edited by Annette Y. Reed and N. Dohrmann. Philadelphia: University of Pennsylvania Press, 2013.

Närhi, Jani. "Beautiful Reflections: The Cognitive and Evolutionary Foundations of Paradise Representations." *MTSR* 20 (2008): 339–65.

Newberg, Andrew B. and Eugene G. D'Aquili. "The Neuropsychology of Spiritual Experience." 75–94 in *Handbook of Religion and Mental Health.* Edited by Harold G. Koenig. San Diego: Academic Press, 1998.

Nickelsburg, George W. E. *1 Enoch 1.* Hermeneia. Minneapolis: Fortress, 2001.

Nichols, Stephen. "Introduction: Philology in a Manuscript Culture." *Speculum* 65 (1990): 1–10.

Noë, Alva. *Action in Perception.* Cambridge: MIT Press, 2004.

—*Varieties of Presence.* Cambridge: Harvard University Press, 2012.

Nongbri, Brent. "Losing a Curious Christian Scroll but Gaining a Curious Christian

Codex: An Oxyrhynchus Papyrus of Exodus and Revelation." *NovT* 55 (2013): 77–88.
—*God's Library: The Archaeology of the Earliest Christian Manuscripts.* New Haven: Yale University Press, 2018.
O'Connor, Mary Frances O'Connor. *The Grieving Brain: The Surprising Science of How We Learn from Love and Loss*. New York: HarperOne, 2022.
Odell, D. W. "The Argument of Young's 'Conjectures on Original Composition'." *Studies in Philology* 78 (1981): 87–106.
Olney, James. "Autobiography and the Cultural Moment." 3–27 in *Autobiography: Essays Theoretical and Critical*. Princeton: Princeton University Press, 1980.
Olyan, Saul. *Biblical Mourning: Ritual and Social Dimensions*. Oxford: Oxford University Press, 2004.
—*Disability in the Hebrew Bible: Interpreting Mental and Physical Differences* Cambridge: Cambridge University Press, 2008.
O'Regan, Kevin J. and Alva Noë. "A Sensorimotor Account of Vision and Visual Consciousness." *Behavioral and Brain Sciences* 24 (2001): 939–1031.
O'Regan, J. Kevin. "The Illusion of Seeing Everything." 50–61 in *Why Red Doesn't Sound Like a Bell: Understanding the Feel of Consciousness*. Edited by J. Kevin O'Regan. Oxford: Oxford University Press, 2011.
Orsi, Robert. *Between Heaven and Earth: The Religious Worlds People Make and the Scholars Who Study Them*. Princeton: Princeton University Press, 2005.
Osiek, Carolyn. *The Rich and the Poor in the Shepherd of Hermas: An Exegetical and Social Investigation*. Catholic Biblical Quarterly Monograph Series 15. Washington, D.C.: Catholic Biblical Association, 1983.
—"The Genre and Function of the *Shepherd of Hermas*." *Semeia* 36 (1986): 113–21.
—"The Social Function of Female Imagery in Second Century Prophecy." *Vetera Christianorum* 29 (1992): 55–74.
—"The Oral World of Early Christianity in Rome: The Case of Hermas." 151–72 in *Judaism and Christianity in First-Century Rome*. Edited by Karl P. Donfried and Peter Richardson. Grand Rapids: Wm. B. Eerdmans, 1998.
—*The Shepherd of Hermas*, Hermeneia. Minneapolis: Fortress, 1999.
Parker, David C. *Codex Sinaiticus: The Story of the World's Oldest Bible*. London: British Library, 2010.
Pollatos, Olga and Rainer Schandry. "Emotional Processing and Emotional Memory are Modulated by Interoceptive Awareness." *Cognition and Emotion* 22 (2008): 272–87.
Polvinen, Merja. "Enactive Perception and Fictional Worlds." 19–34 in *The Cognitive Humanities: Embodied Mind in Literature and Culture*. Edited by Jean Peter Garratt. London: Palgrave, 2016.
—"Sense-Making and Wonder: An Enactive Approach to Narrative Form in Speculative Fiction." 67–80 in *The Edinburgh Companion to Contemporary Narrative Theories*. Edited by Zara Dinnen and Robyn Warhol. Edinburgh: Edinburgh University Press, 2018.
Polvinen, Merja and Howard Sklar. "Mimetic and Synthetic Views of Characters: How Readers Process 'People' in Fiction." *Cogent Arts & Humanities* 6 (2019): 1–16.
Pyysiäinen, Ilkka et al. "Counterintuitiveness as the Hallmark of Religiosity." *Religion* 33 (2003): 341–55.
Quintillian. *The Orator's Education*. Translated by Donald A. Russell. 5 Vols. LCL. Cambridge: Harvard University Press, 2001.

Raphael, Rebecca. "Sacred Schematics, or Ships and Sanctuaries." *Journal for Interdisciplinary Biblical Studies* 3 (2021): 41–62.
Reed, Annette Yoshiko. *Fallen Angels and the History of Judaism and Christianity: The Reception of Enochic Literature*. Cambridge: Cambridge University Press, 2005.
Richardson, Alan. *British Romanticism and the Science of the Mind*. Cambridge: Cambridge University Press, 2001.
—"Imagination: Literary and Cognitive Intersections." 225–45 in *The Oxford Handbook of Cognitive Literary Studies*. Edited by Lisa Zunshine. Oxford: Oxford University Press, 2015.
Ridgway, Brunilde Sismondo. *Hellenistic Sculpture II: The Style of c. 200–100 BC*. Madison, WI: University of Wisconsin Press, 2008.
Rives, James B. "Venus Genetrix Outside Rome." *Phoenix* 48 (1994): 294–306.
—*Religion and Authority in Roman Carthage from Augustus to Constantine*. Oxford: Clarendon Press, 1995.
Robinson, J. Armitage. *Barnabas, Hermas and the Didache*. London: SPCK, 1920.
Robinson, Jenefer. *Deeper than Reason: Emotion and Its Role in Literature, Music, and Art*. Oxford: Clarendon Press, 2007.
Rosen-Zvi, Ishay. "Bilhah the Temptress: The Testament of Reuben and 'the Birth of Sexuality'." *JQR* 96 (2006): 65–94.
Rowland, Christopher. *The Open Heaven: A Study of Apocalyptic in Judaism and Early Christianity*. New York: Crossroad, 1982.
Rowland, Christopher with Patricia Gibbons and Vicente Dobroruka. "Visionary Experience in Ancient Judaism and Christianity." 41–56 in *Paradise Now*. Edited by April D. DeConick. Atlanta: Scholars, 2006.
Rüpke, Jörg. "Apokalyptische Salzberge: Zum sozialen Ort und zur literarischen Strategie des 'Hirten des Hermas'." *Archiv für Religionsgeschichte* 1 (1999): 148–60.
—"Two Cities and One Self: Transformations of Jerusalem and Reflexive Individuality in the Shepherd of Hermas." 49–65 in *Religious Dimensions of the Self in the Second Century CE*. Edited by Jörg Rüpke and Greg Woolf. Tübingen: Mohr Siebeck, 2013.
—"Lived Ancient Religions." 1–22 in *Oxford Research Encyclopedia of Religion*. Oxford: Oxford University Press, 2019.
Ryan, Marie-Laure. *Narrative as Virtual Reality 2: Revisiting Immersion and Interactivity in Literature and Electronic Media*. Baltimore: Johns Hopkins University Press, 2015.
—"Text as World: Theories of Immersion." 61–84 in *Narrative as Virtual Reality 2: Revisiting Immersion and Interactivity in Literature and Electronic Media*.
—"Varieties of Immersion: Spatial, Temporal, Emotional." 85–114 in *Narrative as Virtual Reality 2. Revisiting Immersion and Interactivity in Literature and Electronic Media*.
Said, Edward. *Culture and Imperialism*. New York: Knopf, 1993.
Salzman-Mitchell, Patricia. "A Whole Out of Pieces: Pygmalion's Statue in Ovid's *Metamorphoses*." *Arethusa* 41 (2008): 291–311.
Scarry, Elaine. "On Vivacity: The Difference between Daydreaming and Imagining-Under-Authorial-Instruction." *Representations* 52 (1995): 1–26.
—*Dreaming by the Book*. Princeton: Princeton University Press, 1999, 2001.
Scholl, R. " 'Freilassung unter Freunden' im römischen Ägypten." 159–69 in *Fünfzig Jahre Forschungen zur antiken Sklaverei an der Mainzer Akademie 1950–2000. Miscellanea zum Jubiläum*. Edited by. H. Bellen and H. Heinen. Forschungen zur

antiken Sklaverei 35. Mainz: Akademie der Wissenschaften und der Literatur, 2001.
Schwartz, Seth. *Imperialism and Jewish Society: 200 B.C.E. to 640 C.E.* Princeton: Princeton University Press, 2001.
—"How Many Judaisms Were There? A Critique of Neusner and Smith on Definition and Mason and Boyarin on Categorization." *JAJ* 2 (2011): 208–38.
— *The Ancient Jews from Alexander to Muhammad*. Cambridge: Cambridge University Press, 2014.
Segal, Alan F. "Religious Experience and the Construction of the Transcendent Self." 27–40 in *Paradise Now: Essays on Early Jewish and Christian Mysticism*. Edited by April D. DeConick. Atlanta: Scholars, 2006.
Seigworth, Gregory J. and Melissa Gregg. "An Inventory of Shimmers." 1–28 in *The Affect Theory Reader*. Edited by Melissa Gregg and Gregory J. Seigworth. Durham, NC: Duke University Press, 2010.
Seth, Anil K. "Interoceptive Inference, Emotion, and the Embodied Self." *Trends in Cognitive Sciences* 17 (2013): 565–73.
Shantz, Colleen. *Paul in Ecstasy: The Neurobiology of the Apostle's Life and Thought*. Cambridge: Cambridge University Press, 2009.
Shinan, Avigdor and Yair Zakovitch. *The Story of Reuben and Bilhah*. (Hebr.) Jerusalem: Magnes Press, 1983.
Simonetti, Manlio. "Il Pastore di Erma" in *Seguendo Gesù. Testi cristiani delle origini, vol. 2*. Edited by Emanuela Prinzivalli and Manlio Simonetti. Scrittori Greci e Latini. Fondazione Lorenzo Valla. Milan: Mondadori, 2015.
Slingerland, Edward. *What Science Offers the Humanities: Integrating Body and Culture*. Cambridge: Cambridge University Press, 2008.
Small, Jocelyn Penny. *Wax Tablets of the Mind: Cognitive Studies of Memory and Literacy in Classical Antiquity*. London: Routledge, 1997.
Smith, Geoffrey. "The Willoughby Papyrus: A New Fragment of John 1:49–2:1 (P134) and an Unidentified Christian Text." *JBL* 137 (2018): 935–58.
Smith, Jonathan Z. *Imagining Religion: From Babylon to Jonestown*. Chicago: University of Chicago Press, 1982.
—"Fences and Neighbors: Some Contours of Early Judaism." 1–18 in *Imagining Religion: From Babylon to Jonestown*.
—*To Take Place*. Chicago: University of Chicago Press, 1987.
Smith, Mark S. "The Heart and Innards in Israelite Emotional Expressions: Notes from Anthropology and Psychobiology." *JBL* 117 (1998): 427–36.
Snyder, Graydon F. *The Shepherd of Hermas*. The Apostolic Fathers 6. London: Thomas Nelson & Sons, 1968.
Soja, Edward W. *Thirdspace: Journeys to Los Angeles and Other Real-and-Imagined Places*. Malden: Blackwell, 1996.
Solin, Heikki. *Die griechischen Personennamen in Rom: Ein Namenbuch*. 3 vols. Berlin: De Gruyter 1982.
Sommer, Benjamin D. *The Bodies of God and the World of Ancient Israel*. New York: Cambridge University Press, 2009.
Soyars. Jonathan E. *The Shepherd of Hermas and the Pauline Legacy*. Leiden: Brill, 2019.
Speer, Nicole K., Jeremy R. Reynolds, Khena M. Swallow, and Jeffrey M. Zacks. "Reading Stories Activates Neural Representations of Visual and Motor Experiences." *Psychological Science* 20 (2009): 289–99.

Sperber, Dan and Deirdre Wilson. *Relevance: Communication and Cognition*. Oxford: Oxford University Press, 1995.
—"The Mapping Between the Mental and the Public Lexicon." 184–200 in *Thought and Language. Interdisciplinary Themes*. Edited by Peter Carruthers and Jill Boucher. Cambridge: Cambridge University Press, 1998.
—*Meaning and Relevance*. Cambridge: Cambridge University Press, 2012.
Squire, Michael. "Introductory Reflections: Making Sense of Ancient Sight." 1–35 in *Sight and the Ancient Senses*. Edited by Michael Squire. New York: Routledge, 2016.
Starr, Gabrielle G. "Multisensory Imagery." 279–91 in *Introduction to Cognitive Cultural Studies*. Edited by Lisa Zunshine. Baltimore: Johns Hopkins University Press, 2010.
—*Feeling Beauty: The Neuroscience of Aesthetic Experience*. Cambridge: MIT Press, 2015.
Steiner, D.T. *Images in the Mind: Statues in Archaic Greek Literature and Thought*. Princeton: Princeton University Press, 2001.
Steiner, Pierre. "Enacting Anti–representationalism. The Scope and the Limits of Enactive Critiques of Representationalism." *Avant* 5 (2014): 43–86.
Stewart, Andrew. "A Tale of Seven Nudes: The Capitoline and Medici Aphrodites, Four Nymphs at Elean Herakleia, and an Aphrodite at Megalopis." *Antichthon* 44 (2010): 12–32.
Stökl, Ben Ezra, Daniel. "De l'arbre à la forêt: Quelques pensées quantitatives sur les papyrus littéraires juifs et chrétiens de l'Égypte ancienne." 169–188 in *Reading New Testament Papyri in Context: Lire les Papyrus du Nouveau Testament dans leur context*. Edited by Claire Clivaz and Jean Zumstein, in collaboration with Jenny Read-Heimerdinger and Julie Paik. BETL 242. Leuven: Peeters, 2011.
Stone, Michael E. "Apocalyptic—Vision or Hallucination?" *Milla Wa Milla* 14 (1974): 47-56. Reprinted as pages 419–28 in *Selected Studies in Pseudepigrapha and Apocrypha with Special Reference to the Armenian Tradition*. Leiden: Brill, 1991.
—"Apocalyptic Literature." In *Jewish Writings of the Second Temple Period*. Edited by M.E. Stone. CRINT 2.2. Assen and Philadelphia: van Gorcum and Fortress Press, 1984.
—"A Reconsideration of Apocalyptic Visions." *HTR* 96 (2003): 167–80.
—*Ancient Judaism: New Visions and Views*. Grand Rapids: Eerdmans, 2011.
Stowers, Stanley. "The Concept of 'Community' and the History of Early Christianity." *MTSR* 23 (2011): 238–56.
Streeter, Burnett Hillman. *The Primitive Church: Studied with Special Reference to the Origins of the Christian Ministry*. London: MacMillan and Co., Ltd., 1929.
Strick, Madelijn, Rob W. Holland, Rick B. van Baaren, Ad. van Knippenberg. "Finding Comfort in a Joke: Consolatory Effects of Humor through Cognitive Distraction." *Emotion* 9 (2009): 574–78.
Stroebe, Margaret S., Robert O. Hansson, Henk Schut, and Wolfgang Stroebe. "Bereavement Research: Contemporary Perspectives." 3–25 in *Handbook of Bereavement Research and Practice: Advances in Theory and Intervention*. Edited by M. Stroebe, R.O. Hansson, H. Schut, and W. Stroebe. Washington, D.C.: American Psychological Association, 2008.
Ström, Åke von. *Der Hirt des Hermas. Allegorie oder Wirklichkeit?* Uppsala: Wretmans, 1936.
Stuckenbruck, Loren T. *Angel Veneration and Christology: A Study in Early Judaism and in the Christology of the Apocalypse of John*. Tübingen: Mohr Siebeck, 1995.

—"Pseudepigraphy and First Person Discourse in the Dead Sea Documents: From the Aramaic Texts to Writings of the Yaḥad." 295–326 in *The Dead Sea Scrolls and Contemporary Culture*. Edited by Adolfo D. Roitman et al. Leiden: Brill, 2011.

Sundberg, Albert C. "Canon Muratori: A Fourth-Century List." *HTR* 66 (1973): 1–41.

Swartz, Michael D. "Ritual about Myth about Ritual: Towards an Understanding of the Avodah in the Rabbinic Period." *The Journal of Jewish Thought and Philosophy* 6 (1997): 135–55.

Tagliabue, Aldo. "An Embodied Reading of Epiphanies in Aelius Aristides' *Sacred Tales*." *Ramus* 45 (2016): 213–30.

—"Learning from Allegorical Images in the *Book of Visions* of *The Shepherd of Hermas*." *Arethusa* 50 (2017): 221–55.

—"Experiencing the Church in the *Book of Visions* of the *Shepherd of Hermas*." 104–24 in *Experience, Narrative, and Criticism in Ancient Greece: Under the Spell of Stories*. Edited by Jonas Grethlein, Luuk Huitink, and Aldo Tagliabue. New York: Oxford University Press, 2020.

—"Experience through Narrative in the Shepherd of Hermas." 137–51 in *Experiencing the Shepherd of Hermas*. Edited by Angela Kim Harkins and Harry O. Maier.

Taylor, Charles. *A Secular Age*. Cambridge: Harvard University Press, 2007.

Todd, Cain. "Fictional Immersion: Attending Emotionally to Fiction." *Journal of Value Inquiry* (2012): 449–65.

Todorovska, Marina Ončevska. "The Statue of Venus Pudica from Skupi." *Folia archaeologica Balkanica* 11 (2011): 347–58.

Tornau, Christian and Paolo Cecconi, ed., *The Shepherd of Hermas in Latin: Critical Edition of the Oldest Translation Vulgata*. Berlin: De Gruyter, 2014.

Tervahauta, Ulla. "A Just Man or Just a Man: The Ideal Man in the Visions of Hermas." *Patristica Nordica Annuaria* 35 (2020): 69-97.

Uro, Risto. *Ritual and Christian Beginnings: A Socio-Cognitive Analysis*. Oxford: Oxford University Press, 2016.

Valente, Catherynne M. "Silently and Very Fast." 331–73 in *Clarkesworld: Year Six*. Edited by Neil Clarke and Sean Wallace. Stirling, NJ: Wyrm, 2014.

Varela, Francisco J., Evan Thompson, and Eleanor Rosch. *The Embodied Mind: Cognitive Science and Human Experience*. Revised Edition. Cambridge: MIT Press, 1991, 2016.

Vielhauer, Philipp. "Apocalyptic in Early Christianity: Introduction." 608-42 in E. Hennecke, W. Schneemelcher, and Rm. M. Wilson, (eds.). *New Testament Apocrypha, Volume 2: Writings Relating to the Apostles, Apocalypses and Related Subjects*. English translation of *Neutestamentliche Apokryphen* volume II. London: Lutterworth. Translated by R. M. Wilson. London: SCM Press, 1974.

—*Geschichte der urchristlichen Literatur: Einleitung in das Neue Testament, die Apokryphen und die Apostolischen Väter*. Berlin: De Gruyter, 1975.

Wagner, Rachel. *GodWired: Religion, Ritual and Virtual Reality*. New York: Routledge, 2012.

—"A Sense of Presence: Mediating an American Apocalypse." *Religions* 12 (2021): 1–11.

Walsh, Lora. "Ecclesia Reconsidered: Two Premodern Encounters with the Feminine Church." *Journal of Feminist Studies in Religion* 33 (2017): 73–91.

—"The Lady as Elder in the *Shepherd of Hermas*." *JECS* 27 (2019): 517–47.

—"Lost in Revision: Gender Symbolism in Vision 3 and Similitude 9 of the *Shepherd of Hermas*," *HTR* 112 (2019): 467–90.

Ward, Roy Bowen. "Women in Roman Baths." *HTR* 85 (1992): 125–47.
Wayment, Thomas A. *The Text of the New Testament Apocrypha (100–400 CE)*. London: Bloomsbury, 2013.
Webb, Ruth. *Ekphrasis, Imagination and Persuasion in Ancient Rhetorical Theory and Practice*. New York: Ashgate, 2009.
—"Sight and Insight: Theorizing Vision, Emotion and Imagination in Ancient Rhetoric." 205–19 in *Sight and the Ancient Senses*. Edited by M. Squire. London: Routledge, 2016.
Welborn, Lawrence L. "On the Date of First Clement." *Biblical Research* 29 (1984): 35–54.
Whitaker, Robyn J. *Ekphrasis, Vision, and Persuasion in the Book of Revelation*. Tübingen: Mohr Siebeck, 2015.
Whittaker, Molly. *Die Apostolischen Väter. 1 Der Hirt des Hermas*, 2d ed. Berlin: Akademie Verlag, 1967.
Wiedemann, Thomas E. J. *Greek and Roman Slavery*. Baltimore: Johns Hopkins University Press, 1981.
Williamson, G.A. trans. revised by A. Louth. Missing title information Harmondsworth: Penguin Books, 1989.
Wilson, Brittany E. *Unmanly Men: Refigurations of Masculinity in Luke–Acts*. New York: Oxford University Press, 2015.
—"God's Multiple Forms: Divine Fluidity in the Shepherd of Hermas." 171–92 in *Experiencing the Shepherd of Hermas*. Edited by Angela Kim Harkins and Harry O. Maier.
Wilson, J. Christian. *Five Problems in the Interpretation of the Shepherd of Hermas: Authorship, Genre, Canonicity, Apocalyptic, and the Absence of the Name "Jesus Christ"*. Lewinston: Mellen Biblical Press, 1995.
Wolfson, Elliot R. *Through a Speculum that Shines: Visions and Imagination in Medieval Jewish Mysticism*. Princeton: Princeton University Press, 1994.
—*A Dream Interpreted within a Dream: Oneiropoiesis and the Prism of Imagination*. New York: Zone Books, 2011.
Wright, David P. " 'She Shall Not Go Free as Male Slaves Do': Developing Views about Slavery and Gender in the Laws of the Hebrew Bible." 125–42 in *Beyond Slavery: Overcoming Its Religious and Sexual Legacies*. Edited by Bernadette J. Brooten with Jacqueline L. Hazelton. New York: Palgrave Macmillan, 2010.
Yarbro Collins, Adela. "Apocalypse Now: The State of Apocalyptic Studies Near the End of the First Decade of the Twenty-First Century." *HTR* 104 (2011): 447–57.
Young, Edward. *Conjectures on Original Composition*. London: A. Millar, 1759.
Young, Steve. "Being a Man: The Pursuit of Manliness in *The Shepherd of Hermas*." *JECS* 2.3 (1994): 237–55.
Zahn, Theodor. *Der Hirt des Hermas*. Gotha: Friedrich Andreas Perthes, 1868.
Zanker, Graham. *Modes of Viewing in Hellenistic Poetry and Art*. Wisconsin: University of Wisconsin Press, 2003.
Zunshine, Lisa (ed.). *Introduction to Cognitive Cultural Studies*. Baltimore: Johns Hopkins University Press, 2010.
—"Introduction to Cognitive Literary Studies." 1–9 in *The Oxford Handbook of Cognitive Literary Studies*. Edited by Lisa Zunshine. Oxford: Oxford University Press, 2015.
—"Why Reasonable Children Don't Think that Nutcracker is Alive or that the Mouse King is Real." 225–48 in *Romanticism and Consciousness*. Edited by Richard C. Sha and Joel Faflak. Edinburgh: Edinburgh University Press, 2021.

Zwaan, Rolf A. and Carol J. Madden. "Embodied Sentence Comprehension." 224–45 in *Grounding Cognition: The Role of Perception and Action in Memory, Language, and Thinking.* Edited by Diane Pecher and Rolf A. Zwaan. Cambridge: Cambridge University Press, 2005.

Index of Ancient Texts

Hebrew Bible   12, 78, 148

Gen.   50, 57
- 6.2   107
- 35.22   105
- 49.4   105

Exod.   47, 48, 57, 137, 193
- 1–18   137
- 14–17   59
- 19   159
- 20–24   59

Num.
- 11   50

Deut.   183
- 1–5   183
- 5   183
- 22.24   106
- 22.27   106

2 Sam.
- 11   82
- 11.2   105
- 13.12   106

Job   155

Ps.   12, 81
- 55.22a   60
- 56.14   149
- 119.105   149

Jer.   103, 115, 124

Lam.
- 2.11   15

Index of Ancient Texts   217

Ezek.	183
Hos.	
13.7–8	137
Dan.	99, 103, 115, 123, 127, 136, 138, 142, 181, 186
2	137
6.22	60, 158
6.23	56, 158
7–12	127
7	136, 138, 139, 144
7.4	138
7.8	138
7.9–10	138
7.9–14	136
7.11	138
7.12	138
7.13–14	138
7.15	15
7.16	51
7.28	15
9	118, 124, 129
9–10	120
Ezra	115
9	98
10	98
1 Chron.	
5.1	105

Septuagint   32, 155, 158

Ps. LXX	
54.23a	60
Dan. LXX	
6.23	60
Susanna and the Elders	82, 105, 181

Prayer of Azariah	181
Bel and the Dragon	181
Pseudepigrapha	50, 57, 67, 106, 108
Book of Eldad and Modat	50, 60
Book of Jubilees	57, 106, 107
33.2–9	106
33.4	106
33.15	105
Testament of Reuben	106, 107, 108, 109, 114
1.10	107
2.4	107
3.11–15	105, 106
3.15	106, 109
4.9	107
5.5–6	107, 108
5.6	108
6.4	107
1 Enoch	23
Book of the Watchers	186
14.13	187
14.24–25	187
19.3	186
Parables	23
2 Enoch	193
1–22	193
23–37	193
38–68	193
4 Ezra	57, 117, 120, 129, 142, 168
8.19–36	118
9.26	145
10.53	145
2 Bar.	117, 168

Index of Ancient Texts 219

Dead Sea Scrolls	*12, 13*
Damascus Document	115
War Scroll (1QM)	159
Community Rule (1QS)	
1.17	159
8.4	159
16.9–17.9	159
Hodayot (1QH^a)	8, 38, 165
CH I (Community Hymns–I)	38
TH (Teacher Hymns)	64
1Q71	136
1Q72	136
4Q112–116	136
4Q242–246	136
4Q428	38
4Q489	136
4Q551–553	136
6Q7	136
New Testament	11, 32, 39, 41
Gospels	20, 24, 61, 78
Matt.	31
12.40	155
Mark	31
Luke	31, 140
John	31
1.49–2.1	41
Acts	
3	58
4	58
4.13	58

Rom.	
16.14	3
2 Cor.	101
1 Thess.	
1–3	70, 152
Heb.	
6.4–6	32
Rev.	9, 11, 48, 143, 183, 187, 193
1	183
1.4–7	47
4	183
6.1–8.5	139
13	137
15.1–16.21	139
22	193

Apostolic Fathers

Epistle of Barnabas	32, 125
1 Clement	3, 44
Shepherd of Hermas	1, 5, 8, 9, 12, 17, 20, 21, 22, 23, 24, 27, 30, 32, 33, 37, 38, 39, 40, 41, 43, 44, 45, 46, 52, 60, 61, 63, 64, 65, 66, 67, 68, 71, 72, 90, 95, 96, 97, 98, 107, 110, 112, 114, 115, 119, 125, 128, 131, 134, 153, 159, 162, 164, 165, 167, 168, 174, 176, 184, 185, 186, 188, 189, 192, 193, 194
Book of Visions	1, 2, 4, 5, 6, 7, 10, 11, 12, 13, 16, 17, 18, 19, 21, 23, 24, 25, 26, 27, 28, 29, 30, 31, 32, 33, 35, 36, 39, 40, 41, 42, 43, 45, 47, 48, 50, 51, 53, 54, 56, 59, 60, 61, 63, 65, 66, 67, 68, 72, 73, 76, 77, 82, 83, 88, 89, 91, 92, 94, 95, 98, 99, 100, 101, 102, 103, 104, 105, 109, 110, 112, 113, 114, 119, 122, 127, 128, 129,

Index of Ancient Texts   221

	131, 132, 133, 134, 135, 136, 139, 140, 142, 143, 144, 152, 153, 154, 158, 159, 160, 162, 163, 164, 165, 167, 175, 179, 180, 182, 183, 189, 190, 191, 192, 193, 194
Visions 1–4	37, 38, 139
First Vision	6, 18, 28, 34, 36, 40, 91, 95, 134, 140
Second Vision	6, 18, 34, 36, 116, 141, 142
Third Vision	4, 18, 20, 26, 27, 34, 36, 53, 59, 82, 83, 116, 135, 142, 143, 148, 149, 151, 152, 160, 161, 162, 186, 191
Fourth Vision	18, 35, 34, 36, 44, 83, 131, 134, 137, 152, 153, 154, 156, 157, 159, 160, 161, 162, 186, 187, 191
Fifth Vision	2, 12, 18, 37, 38, 129, 139, 182
Vis. 1.1.1–Mand. 4.3.6 (1.1–31.6)	36
1.1.1–5.1.7 (1.1–25.7)	31
1.1.1 (1.1)	46, 54, 179
1.1.1–2 (1.1–2)	44, 82, 85, 113
1.1.1–2.2 (1.1–2.2)	100
1.1.2 (1.2)	91, 106, 110, 113, 134
1.1.2–3 (1.2–3)	100
1.1.3 (1.3)	20, 55, 91, 92, 109, 115, 130, 134, 140, 167
1.1.3–5a (1.3–5a)	91
1.1.4 (1.4)	55, 83, 84, 92, 94, 100, 106, 110, 167
1.1.4–9 (1.4–9)	103
1.1.5–7 (1.5–7)	84
1.1.7 (1.7)	83, 84, 92, 95, 113
1.1.8 (1.8)	84, 107, 124
1.1.8–9 (1.8–9)	35, 113
1.2.1 (2.1)	15, 94, 112, 122
1.2.1–2 (2.1–2)	92, 103, 115, 142
1.2.1–1.4.3 (2.1–4.3)	141
1.2.2 (2.2)	18, 93, 94, 112, 122, 191
1.4.1 (4.1)	18, 93

Book of Visions *(cont.)*

1.4.1–2 (4.1–2)	93
1.4.2 (4.2)	93
1.4.3 (4.3)	93, 122, 134
2.1.1 (5.1)	55, 134
2.1.1–2 (5.1–2)	116, 142, 191
2.1.1–3 (5.1–3)	141
2.1.2 (5.2)	20
2.1.3–4 (5.3–4)	18
2.2.1 (6.1)	116, 142
2.2.2–3 (6.2–3)	55
2.2.3 (6.3)	52
2.2.3–4 (6.3–4)	58
2.2.4 (6.4)	52
2.3.4 (7.4)	50, 60
2.4.1 (8.1)	1, 18
2.4.3 (8.3)	3, 96, 97
3.1.1 (9.1)	96
3.1.1–2.4 (9.1–10.4)	98
3.1.2 (9.2)	1, 19, 20, 130, 142, 145
3.1.2–5 (9.2–5)	145, 146
3.1.4 (9.4)	18, 19, 146
3.1.4–5 (9.4–5)	116, 142, 146
3.1.5 (9.5)	135, 191
3.1.6–7 (9.6–7)	130
3.1.8–9 (9.8–9)	20, 146, 147
3.1.9 (9.9)	53, 122
3.2.1–2 (10.1–2)	42, 147
3.2.1–4 (10.1–4)	148
3.2.2 (10.2)	116
3.2.2–9 (10.2–9)	134
3.2.3 (10.2)	147
3.2.4 (10.4)	18, 143
3.2.4–13.4 (10.4–21.4)	145
3.2.5 (10.5)	148, 150
3.2.5–9 (10.5–9)	51, 150, 151
3.3.1–2 (11.1–2)	51, 52
3.3.1–7.6 (11.1–15.6)	151
3.4.3 (12.3)	36
3.6.6 (14.6)	36
3.9.1–10 (17.1–10)	43
3.9.7 (17.7)	36
3.10.7–13.4 (18.7–21.4)	18
3.11.3 (19.3)	122
3.13.2 (21.2)	122

Index of Ancient Texts   223

3.13.4–4.1.1 (21.4–22.1)	36
4.1.1 (22.1)	45, 55, 96
4.1.2 (22.2)	20, 134
4.1.5–6 (22.5–6)	140, 154, 187, 191
4.1.6–10 (22.6–10)	18, 155
4.1.6 (22.6)	20, 134
4.1.7 (22.7)	130, 183
4.1.7–9 (22.7–9)	36
4.2.1 (23.1)	134, 157
4.2.2 (23.2)	157
4.2.3 (23.3)	157
4.2.4 (23.4)	56, 60, 157
4.2.5 (23.5)	52, 60, 160
4.2.5–6 (23.5–6)	158
4.2.6 (23.6)	155
4.1.7 (22.7)	182
4.3.4 (24.4)	122
4.3.7 (24.7)	56, 157, 187
5.1.1 (25.1)	1
5.1 (25.1)	18
5.1.4 (25.4)	122
5.1.6–7 (33.6–7)	36
5.1.7 (25.1–7)	18
5.4 (25.4)	182
5.5 (25.5)	2
Mandates	1, 2, 5, 9, 12, 18, 21, 22, 23, 24, 28, 31, 33, 35, 36, 37, 38, 39, 40, 41, 42, 43, 47, 51, 59, 66, 99, 103, 127, 129, 162, 177, 182, 183, 190, 192, 193
1–12 (26.1–49.5)	31
2	42, 43
3	42, 43
4.1.7–8 (29.7–8)	46
4.3–4 (31–32)	36
4.3.1 (31.1)	32
4.3.2 (31.2)	32
6.1.3–5 (35.3–5)	36
7.5 (37.5)	36
8.6 (38.6)	36
9–12	42
9.7–8 (39.7–8)	36
10.1.1 (40.1)	36
11 (43)	184
11.9 (43.9)	185

Mandates *(cont.)*
    11.9–11 (43.9–11)   184
    11.9–10 (43.9–10)   183, 184, 185
    12.1 (44.1)   100

Similitudes   1, 2, 5, 9, 12, 18, 21, 22, 23, 24, 28,
                                          31, 33, 35, 36, 38, 39, 41, 43, 99,
                                          162, 190, 192, 193

    2–9   37
    2   40
    2.1–10.4 (51.1–114.4)   31
    2.1–4 (51.1–4)   45
    2.5–10 (51.5–10)   45
    4 (53)   40
    6 (61–65)   33
    7 (66)   33
    8 (67–77)   38
    9 (78–110)   4, 33, 38
    9.2–3 (79–80)   45
    9.2–16 (79–93)   143, 144
    9.30–33 (107–110)   143, 144
    10 (111–114)   38

Manuscripts

Codex Sangermanensis   183, 184

Codex Sinaiticus   32, 33. 34, 35, 36, 40

Muratorian Fragment   3, 4, 32, 72

P.Berl. 5513/ BKT 6.2.1   34, 35, 40
P.Berl. 13272   34, 35

P.Bodmer 38   33, 34, 35, 36, 37, 48, 54, 55

P.Hamburg 24/ P.Iand. 45   34, 35

P.Iand 1 4   34

P.Mich. 2/2 129   34, 36, 37, 38, 39
P.Mich. 2/2 130   34, 41, 42, 43
P.Mich. 6427   33

P.Oxy. 1.5	28, 183, 184, 185, 188
2.8–16	184, 185
P.Oxy. 100=CPJud. III, 454	48
P.Oxy. 1467	57
P.Oxy. 3.404	34, 35
P.Oxy. 355	48
P.Oxy. 4365	57
P.Oxy. 7.1007	50
P.Oxy. 8.1075	47
P.Oxy. 8.1079	47
P.Oxy. 9.1172	34, 35
p.Oxy. 9.1205	49
P.Oxy. 13.1599	34, 35
P.Oxy. 15.1783	34
P.Oxy. 15.1828	34, 35
P.Oxy. 5	33
P.Oxy. 404	33
P.Oxy. 50.3526	34
P.Oxy. 50.3527	34, 35
P.Oxy. 50.3528	34, 35
P.Oxy. 69.4705	33, 34, 35, 40
P.Oxy. 69.4706	24, 34, 35, 36, 40, 41, 42, 59
P.Oxy. 69.4707	34, 35
P.Oxy. 2192	44, 45
Papyrus Pragensis 1 + Papyrus Weill I 96	32

Early Christian Writings

Apocalypse of Peter	143
Clement	92, 125
Paed. III.32–3	85
Protrepticus 4.57.3	87
Cyprian	
De habitu virginum 19	85
Didymus the Blind	30
Eusebius	30
Hist. eccl. 3.3.6	3, 30, 32
Gospel of Thomas	40, 41, 49

Jerome
    De vir. ill. 10   3

Martyrdom of Perpetua and Felicity
    IV   13
    XI.3   13

Odes of Solomon
    11   181

Origen
    Comm. in. Rom 10.31   3
    Homilies   40

Tertullian   74
    Apol. 42.2   85
    Or. 16   46
    Paen. 11.3   85
    Pud. 10   46
    20   46
    Spect. 8.9   85

Ancient Greek and Roman Works

Aelius Aristides
Sacred Tales   15

Anthologia Palatina, 5.209   82

Aristotle
    On the Soul 3.3, 429a   79
    Metaphysics, 980a   79
    Politics 1.2 (1254b25–35)   54

Callimachus
    Hymn. 5.107–66   82

Cicero
    De or. 3.202   70

Hesiod
    Theogony   69
    Theogony §173   44, 84

Homer	76
Illiad 18.468–608	69
Hypsicrates	
Men who Appear in Comedies	44
Juvenal	
Satire 6.419–25	85
Longus	
Daphn. 1.32	82
Ovid	92, 109, 114
Ars amatoria 3.639–40	85
Metam.	87, 112
3.138–252	82
Petronius	
Satyricon	53
Plato	
Republic, Book 10	79
Pliny	92
Nat. 36.5	86
Plutarch	
Moralia	82
Mor. 681e–f	79
Progymnasmata	20, 69, 70, 71
(Ps–)Plutarch	
Love Stories, 1.771 E	82
Quintilian	110
Inst. 9.2.30	70
Seneca	
Epistulae Morales, 99	121
Thersagorus	
Myths of Tragedy	44
Venus / Aphrodite	86, 87, 88, 89, 90, 95, 109

Studies in Ancient Religion and Culture

Series Editors:
Philip L. Tite, University of Virginia
Michael Ng, Seattle University
https://www.equinoxpub.com/home/studies-in-ancient-religion-and-culture/

Published:
An Embodied Reading of the Shepherd of Hermas: The Book of Visions and its Role in Moral Formation
Angela Kim Harkins

Critical Theory and Early Christianity
Edited by Matthew G. Whitlock

Death's Dominion: Power, Identity, and Memory at the Fourth-Century Martyr Shrine
Nathaniel J. Morehouse

John Cassian and the Creation of Monastic Subjectivity
Joshua Schachterle

Social and Cognitive Perspectives on the Sermon on the Mount
Edited by Rikard Roitto, Colleen Shantz, and Petri Luomanen

The Complexity of Conversion: Intersectional Perspectives on Religious Change in Antiquity and Beyond
Edited by Valérie Nicolet and Marianne Bjelland Kartzow

Theorizing "Religion" in Antiquity
Edited by Nickolas P. Roubekas

Worth More than Many Sparrows: Essays in Honour of Willi Braun
Edited by Sarah E. Rollens and Patrick Hart

www.ingramcontent.com/pod-product-compliance
Lightning Source LLC
Chambersburg PA
CBHW050847240426
43667CB00022B/2946